P9-BYW-609

VOLUME I *dup 351449*

RISKING THE FUTURE

Adolescent Sexuality, Pregnancy, and Childbearing

Cheryl D. Hayes, Editor

Panel on Adolescent Pregnancy
and Childbearing

Committee on Child Development
Research and Public Policy

Commission on Behavioral and
Social Sciences and Education

National Research Council

NATIONAL ACADEMY PRESS
Washington, D.C. 1987

National Academy of Sciences   2101 Constitution Avenue, NW   Washington, DC 20418

NOTICE: The project that is the subject of this report was approved by the Governing Board of the National Research Council, whose members are drawn from the councils of the National Academy of Sciences, the National Academy of Engineering, and the Institute of Medicine. The members of the committee responsible for the report were chosen for their special competences and with regard for appropriate balance.

This report has been reviewed by a group other than the authors according to procedures approved by a report review committee consisting of members of the National Academy of Sciences, the National Academy of Engineering, and the Institute of Medicine.

The National Research Council was established by the National Academy of Sciences in 1916 to associate the broad community of science and technology with the Academy's purposes of furthering knowledge and of advising the federal government. The Council operates in accordance with general policies determined by the Academy under the authority of its congressional charter of 1863, which established the Academy as a private, nonprofit, self-governing membership corporation. The Council has become the principal operating agency of both the National Academy of Sciences and the National Academy of Engineering in the conduct of their services to the government, the public, and the scientific and engineering communities. It is administered jointly by both Academies and the Institute of Medicine. The National Academy of Engineering and the Institute of Medicine were established in 1964 and 1970, respectively, under the charter of the National Academy of Sciences.

This project was sponsored by the Ford Foundation, the Rockefeller Foundation, the William and Flora Hewlett Foundation, the Robert Wood Johnson Foundation, and the Charles Stewart Mott Foundation. The interpretations and conclusions contained in this publication represent the views of the panel and not necessarily those of the sponsoring foundations, their trustees, or officers.

Library of Congress Cataloging-in-Publication Data

National Research Council (U.S.). Panel on Adolescent
    Pregnancy in Childbearing.
    Risking the future.

    Includes bibliographies and index.
    1. Adolescent mothers—United States.   2. Pregnancy,
Adolescent—United States.   3. Pregnancy, Adolescent—
United States—Prevention.   4. Youth—United States—
Sexual behavior.   I. Hayes, Cheryl D.   II. Title.
HQ759.4.N38   1986   306.7'088055   86-31181
ISBN 0-309-03698-4   (v. 1)

First Printing, December 1986
Second Printing, March 1987
Third Printing, May 1987

Printed in the United States of America

Panel on Adolescent Pregnancy and Childbearing

DANIEL D. FEDERMAN (Chair), Harvard Medical School
WENDY H. BALDWIN, Center for Population Research, National Institute of Child Health and Human Development
EZRA C. DAVIDSON, JR., Department of Obstetrics and Gynecology, Charles R. Drew Postgraduate Medical School
JOY G. DRYFOOS, Hastings-on-Hudson, New York
JACQUELINE D. FORREST, Alan Guttmacher Institute, New York
FRANK F. FURSTENBERG, JR., Department of Sociology, University of Pennsylvania
BEATRIX A. HAMBURG, Mt. Sinai School of Medicine, City University of New York
RICHARD JESSOR, Institute of Behavioral Science, University of Colorado
JUDITH E. JONES, Center for Population and Family Health, Columbia University
FRANK LEVY, School of Public Affairs, University of Maryland
ROBERT H. MNOOKIN, Stanford Law School
KRISTIN A. MOORE, Child Trends, Inc., Washington, D.C.
ROSS D. PARKE, Department of Psychology, University of Illinois
HAROLD A. RICHMAN, Chapin Hall Center for Children, National Opinion Research Center, University of Chicago
MARIS VINOVSKIS, Department of History, University of Michigan

CHERYL D. HAYES, Study Director
SANDRA L. HOFFERTH, Adviser
MARGARET E. ENSMINGER, Consultant
DEE ANN L. WENK, Statistical Consultant
CELIA SHAPIRO, Staff Assistant

Committee on Child Development Research and Public Policy

Contents

Volume II, Working Papers

Contents

Volume II is available for sale through the Publication-on-Demand Program
of the National Academy Press.

Foreword

Adolescent pregnancy and childbearing are matters of substantial national concern. Even the analysis and description of these phenomena, much less prescriptions for altering present trends, are highly controversial. And it is all too easy to avoid or to deal only obliquely with issues that arouse so many deep-seated emotions and convictions. There is, nonetheless, broad agreement that the personal and public costs resulting from unintended pregnancies and untimely birth are far too high to countenance an indifferent response. Discontinued educations, reduced employment opportunities, unstable marriages (if they occur at all), low incomes, and heightened health and developmental risks to the children of adolescent mothers are a few of the most obvious and immediate personal costs. Sustained poverty, frustration, and hopelessness are all too often the long-term outcomes. Furthermore, the welfare, Medicaid, and Food Stamp program costs in 1985 for families begun by a birth to a teenager reached $16.65 billion.

Programs and services to prevent pregnancy and improve the life chances of teenage parents and their children have appeared in increasing number since the mid-1970s, frequently stirring up powerful or vocal advocates and opponents. An ever more impassioned debate has drawn public, private, voluntary, and philanthropic organizations into a continuing pursuit for "solutions" to the perceived problems. Yet, after more than a decade of experience, there seemed to many observers an imbalance in emphasis between what people believed and what policy makers, professionals, and society in general knew about the impacts and cost-effectiveness of alternative prevention and amelioration strategies in light of better scientific knowledge about early sexual and fertility behavior. There seemed to be distressingly little discussion about how various interventions work, for whom, under what circumstances, and with what intended and unintended effects. And what were the most promising directions for future policy and program development?

In 1983, at the urging of several of its members, the Committee on Child Development Research and Public Policy within the National Research Council proposed the establishment of a study panel to conduct a broad and dispassionate review of relevant research and program experience and to recommend approaches for policy formulation, program design, research, and evaluation. In 1984, with generous support from five foundations—the Rockefeller Foundation, the Ford Foundation, the William and Flora Hewlett Foundation, the Robert Wood Johnson Foundation, and the Charles Stewart Mott Foundation—the Panel on Adolescent Pregnancy and Childbearing began its study. Over a two-year period, this broadly interdisciplinary 15-person panel and its staff and consultants undertook three major tasks: (1) to assemble, integrate, and assess data on trends in teenage sexual and fertility behavior; (2) to review and synthesize research on the antecedents and consequences of early pregnancy and childbearing; and (3) to review alternative preventive and ameliorative policies and programs.

In meeting its charge, the panel developed two volumes. Volume I presents the panel's findings, conclusions, and recommendations. Detailed background reviews of existing research on factors affecting the initiation of sexual intercourse, contraceptive use, pregnancy and pregnancy resolution, and the consequences of teenage pregnancy, childbearing, and parenting for young mothers, fathers, and their children, as well as the costs and effects of policies and programs, constitute Volume II. Also included in Volume II is a comprehensive statistical appendix presenting data from a variety of sources on trends in teenage sexual and fertility behavior. Throughout Volume I the panel refers to the papers and the statistical appendix in Volume II to support its deliberations. The panel based its study on both existing information and new analyses of existing data. These sources were supplemented by workshops and individual discussions with many federal, state, and local policy makers, program designers, service providers, and evaluators, as well as site visits to a variety of programs across the nation. In accordance with institutional policy, this report has been extensively and thoroughly reviewed by individuals other than members of the study panel.

In recent years, many other individuals and groups representing an array of moral, philosophical, and political perspectives have addressed the complex and controversial issues surrounding adolescent pregnancy. Many have developed recommendations and guidelines for policy makers, service providers, parents, and adolescents themselves. This report is one step in a continuing process of inquiry, review, and synthesis. As a scientific body, the Panel on Adolescent Pregnancy and Childbearing sought to clarify the issues, sharpen awareness of crucial decision points, and define the limits of existing knowledge. Although science cannot resolve issues that are inextricably bound to differences in human values, it can illuminate the trade-offs among different political and ideological positions, and we believe this report will inform the continuing public debate.

On behalf of the members of the parent Committee on Child Development Research and Public Policy, I would like to acknowledge the special contribution of Daniel D. Federman, who served as panel chair. His commitment of time, energy, and intellectual resources over the past two years has been extraordinary. In large part, the success of this study is due to his exquisite leadership. Acknowledgment is also due to the other members of the Panel on Adolescent Pregnancy and Childbearing. All gave generously of their time and knowledge throughout the study. As a diverse group of individuals, they are to be commended for producing a unanimous report on a topic that inevitably raises public controversy and stirs personal convictions.

The members of the panel join the committee in extending our great appreciation to the staff of the study. Cheryl D. Hayes, the study director for the panel as well as the parent committee, once again demonstrated the enormous energy, outstanding thoroughness, and great skill for which she is well known to many of us. Special thanks go also to Celia Shapiro, staff assistant to the committee and the panel, for her tireless attention to administrative detail throughout the study and for her patience and persistence in assembling the references for the two volumes. We gratefully acknowledge the significant contribution of Sandra L. Hofferth of the National Institute of Child Health and Human Development, who authored many of the research reviews that informed the panel's deliberations and coedited Volume II of the report. The efforts of Dee Ann Wenk of the University of Kentucky, who served as statistical consultant and worked with members of the panel and the staff in compiling the data and preparing the numerous tables and figures that appear in the report and the statistical appendix, are also gratefully acknowledged. Margaret A. Ensminger and Donna M. Strobino, both of Johns Hopkins University, served as consultants and authored thoughtful background papers that are included in Volume II. Finally, Christine L. McShane, editor for the Commission on Behavioral and Social Sciences and Education, edited the report with a critical eye and managed the final production of the volumes.

The panel has also benefited from the contributions of several individuals who prepared special tabulations of existing data to help it address a number of difficult issues that remain unresolved in the available research. Special thanks are due Frank Mott of the Center for Human Resource Research at Ohio State University, William Pratt, Marjorie Horn, Christine Bachrach, and Stephanie Ventura of the National Center for Health Statistics, and Stanley Henshaw of the Alan Guttmacher Institute. Many other individuals played an important role in the panel's deliberations by providing information, critical analysis, advice, and reviews of the draft report and the draft background papers. Their thoughtful comments and insights are reflected in the final manuscripts.

Finally, this study would not have been possible without the generous support of our foundation sponsors. On behalf of the Committee on Child Development Research and Public Policy, I would like to extend special thanks to Mary Kritz of the Rockefeller Foundation, Prudence Brown of the Ford Foundation, Anne Firth Murray of the William and Flora Hewlett Foundation, Paul Jellinek of the Robert Wood Johnson Foundation, and Marilyn Steele of the Charles Stewart Mott Foundation. Their encouragement and advice greatly enhanced the study at every stage.

WILLIAM A. MORRILL, Chair
Committee on Child Development
Research and Public Policy

Preface

No human experience is at once so transiently private and lastingly public as an unintended pregnancy. When the mother herself is a young adolescent, only partially educated and almost wholly economically dependent, the pregnancy is inevitably enmeshed in a ragged tapestry of personal, interpersonal, social, religious, ethical, and economic dimensions. The peculiarly human gap between reproductive maturation and social self-sufficiency sets the stage for the problem. Many factors beyond the control—even the ken—of the young people involved complicate the scene. At every point, external expectations batter on newly emerging drives, challenging young adolescents to balance immediate satisfaction and long-range consequences radically disproportionate from anything they have previously had to deal with. It is little wonder that in this very complicated arena research has been difficult and social consensus elusive.

Our panel was convened to collect, review, and evaluate the data on trends in adolescent pregnancy and childbearing and on the antecedents and consequences of this phenomenon and to initiate proposals for the evolution of potentially helpful programs. We had the generous support of five foundations: the Ford Foundation, the Rockefeller Foundation, the William and Flora Hewlett Foundation, the Robert Wood Johnson Foundation, and the Charles Stewart Mott Foundation, all of which have demonstrated a long-standing interest in issues associated with adolescent pregnancy and childbearing. Many have made substantial investments in a growing body of relevant research and a lengthening list of targeted programs. Their interest in this study—and indeed, as a panel of scholars and experts, our interest in undertaking it—is a concern about the problems of early unintended pregnancy and parenting in our society and what is known about how to effectively address them. Our sponsors were models of what scholars hope for—generous, supportive, and never intrusive. The project officers were consistently helpful, but at no time was any of our work constrained by the foundations nor beholden to them. The staff of the National Research Council was consistently supportive, and our study director, Cheryl Hayes, who also serves as executive officer of the parent Committee on Child Development Research and Public Policy, was at once a colleague, a paragon, and the principal drafter of the report.

Few people can approach the problem of teenage pregnancy dispassionately. Becoming sexually active, using contraception, considering abortion or adoption—every step is invested with a panoply of moral and religious questions, and these decisions are often undertaken alone by a frightened and immature young woman who would be considered a child in nearly any other context. A consciousness of this poignance pervades our report, and deliberately so. The panel believes that at each step—however much one may wish for a different outcome of a prior decision—the potentially or actually pregnant teenager should be treated kindly and warmly and should have a complete set of options available without the interposition of moral hounding or economic barriers.

In general, we believe preventive strategies should be given more public and private support than is now available. An international comparison study by the Alan Guttmacher Institute, of which the panel was beneficiary, provided valuable insight into the role of preventive services in countries of comparable levels of teenage sexual activity.

Many social circumstances are closely related to the problem of teenage pregnancy and childbearing. Youth unemployment, poverty, poor education, single-parent families, television content—all these and more are accompaniments and very likely determinants of the high rates of adolescent pregnancy in the United States. The hope for a solution to the problem of teenage pregnancy is illusory without simultaneous amelioration of some of these contributing factors. Pending such comprehensive change, the panel urges prevention rather than denial, kindness rather than exhortation, and research rather than doctrine.

DANIEL D. FEDERMAN, Chair
Panel on Adolescent
Pregnancy and Childbearing

Summary

Adolescent pregnancy is widely recognized in our society as a complex and serious problem. Regardless of one's political philosophy or moral perspective, the basic facts are disturbing: more than 1 million teenage girls in the United States become pregnant each year, just over 400,000 teenagers obtain abortions, and nearly 470,000 give birth. The majority of these births are to unmarried mothers, nearly half of whom have not yet reached their eighteenth birthday.

For teenage parents and their children, prospects for a healthy and independent life are significantly reduced. Young mothers, in the absence of adequate nutrition and appropriate prenatal care, are at a heightened risk of pregnancy complications and poor birth outcomes; they are also more likely to experience a subsequent pregnancy while still in their teens. The infants of teenage mothers also face greater health and developmental risks.

Despite declining birth rates since 1970, adolescent pregnancy, abortion, and childbearing have remained considerably higher in the United States than in the majority of other developed countries of the world, even though the age of initiation and rates of early sexual activity are comparable. The most striking contrast is among the youngest teenagers: U.S. girls under age 15 are at least five times more likely to give birth than young adolescents in any other developed country for which data are available.

Teenage families with children are disproportionately fatherless, and most are poor. Teenage marriages, when they occur, are characterized by a high degree of instability. In addition, teenage parents, both male and female, suffer the negative impact that untimely parenting has on their education and the related limitation of career opportunities. Teenage parents are more likely than those who delay childbearing to experience chronic unemployment and inadequate income. Because these young people often fare poorly in the workplace, they and their children are highly likely to become dependent on public assistance and to remain dependent longer than those who delay childbearing until their twenties. Society's economic burden in sustaining these families is substantial.

Why do young people who are hardly more than children themselves become parents? Is it primarily due to a lack of individual responsibility, maturity, knowledge, and values? Or does it result from the pervasive problems associated with poverty, including limited education and employment opportunities and the likelihood of growing up in a fatherless family, so common among high-risk youth? The answer to both of these questions seems to be yes. Yet there is widespread disagreement among political, educational, and religious leaders, as well as parents, about the problems of adolescent pregnancy and what to do about them. Indeed, many people feel that the primary emphasis of U.S. social policy should be on eliminating poverty, strengthening family ties, and enhancing young people's perceptions of their futures. The panel joins those who believe that the primary goal should be to ameliorate these conditions, and perhaps in doing so also solve the problems of adolescent pregnancy and childbearing in America. Unfortunately, however, scientists, policy makers, and concerned citizens have so far been unable to find easy and effective solutions to these greater social and economic problems. As a result, during the past two decades, there has been no coherent U.S. policy toward adolescent pregnancy and childbearing, despite explicit recognition on the part of many that government involvement is needed and appropriate.

In part we lack a coherent approach toward policy because adolescents are not a monolithic group, and adolescent pregnancy is not a unitary problem. For young people of different ages, living in different social, economic, and cultural circumstances, the meaning of early sexual activity, pregnancy, and childbearing is not the same. In addition, sexual relationships and family formation have traditionally been regarded as personal matters in our society. As increasing numbers of young people have become involved in these behaviors outside marriage, however, many people have expressed concern about the appropriate jurisdiction of parents, the state, and teenagers themselves in these matters. At what age should adolescents, rather than their parents, have the authority to make decisions? Under what circumstances should the state intervene? These issues have not been resolved.

The past decade and a half have witnessed a dramatic burgeoning of policies and programs to help delay teenage pregnancies and to reduce the adverse consequences of early childbearing. Some of these have been promoted and supported by the federal government; others have been initiated by states and local communities; and still others have developed from significant investments by private foundations and philanthropic groups. Many have been the result of productive public-private partnerships. Some have focused on individual teenagers as the unit of treatment; others have focused on families. Some have provided specialized services; others have been comprehensive in their approach. Programs have been organized in schools, churches, community centers, social service agencies, clinics, and hospitals. Some have been single-site programs, while others have been replicated at several sites within a city or across the nation. Despite the magnitude of human and monetary resources that have been directed at tackling the problems of adolescent pregnancy, however, there has been no systematic attempt to assess the effects and effectiveness of alternative approaches in light of growing scientific understanding of early pregnancy and parenting.

With support from a consortium of private foundations, the Panel on Adolescent Pregnancy and Childbearing undertook a comprehensive examination of issues associated with teenage sexual and fertility behavior and reviewed what is known about the costs and benefits of alternative policies and programs to address these issues.

On the basis of two years of review, analysis, and debate, the panel has reached six general conclusions:

1. Prevention of adolescent pregnancy should have the highest priority. In both human and monetary terms, it is less costly to prevent pregnancy than to cope with its consequences; and it is less expensive to prevent a repeat pregnancy than to treat the compounded problems.

2. Sexually active teenagers, both boys and girls, need the ability to avoid pregnancy and the motivation to do so. Early, regular, and effective contraceptive use results in fewer pregnancies. Delaying the initiation of sexual activity will also reduce the incidence of pregnancy, but we currently know very little about how to effectively discourage unmarried teenagers from initiating intercourse. Most young people do become sexually active during their teenage years. Therefore, making contraceptive methods available and accessible to those who are sexually active and

encouraging them to diligently use these methods is the surest strategy for pregnancy prevention.

3. Society must avoid treating adolescent sexuality as a problem peculiar to teenage girls. Our concept of the high-risk population must include boys. Their attitudes, motivations, and behavior are as central to the problems as those of their female partners, and they must also be central to the solutions.

4. There is no single approach or quick fix to solving all the problems of early unintended pregnancy and childbearing. We will continue to need a comprehensive array of policies and programs targeted to the special characteristics of communities and to the circumstances of teenagers from different social, cultural, and economic backgrounds and of different ages. Because adolescents are not a monolithic group, they do not all experience sexual activity, pregnancy, and childbearing in the same way. Our broad goal is the same for all young people: that they develop the necessary capabilities to make and carry out responsible decisions about their sexual and fertility behavior. The strategies for achieving these goals and the specific interventions to carry them out, however, should be sensitive to differences in values, attitudes, and experiences among individuals and groups.

5. If trade-offs are to be made in addressing the special needs of one group over another, priority should be given to those for whom the consequences of an early unintended pregnancy and birth are likely to be most severe: young adolescents and those from the most socially and economically disadvantaged backgrounds. In many ways those at highest risk are hardest to serve, yet they are also the groups that have been shown to benefit most.

6. Responsibility for addressing the problems of adolescent pregnancy and childbearing should be shared among individuals, families, voluntary organizations, communities, and governments. In the United States, we place a high priority on ensuring the rights of individuals to hold different values and the rights of families to raise their children according to their own beliefs. Therefore, public policies should affirm the role and responsibility of families to teach human values. Federal and state governments and community institutions should supplement rather than detract from that role.

These general conclusions underlie all of our specific conclusions and recommendations for policies, programs, and research.

The panel presents its conclusions and recommendations with an intense awareness of the limits of scientific knowledge in dealing with the problems of adolescent pregnancy and childbearing. The issues involved are not only scientific; they also reflect widely differing values. We also recognize the importance of families in establishing attitudes, behavior patterns, and traditional values in developing children, and we encourage efforts to involve families as an essential component in the solution of the problems associated with adolescent sexuality. As scientists, however, our role is to contribute to the base of knowledge about the problems involved, and our goal is to inform the policy debate by clarifying the scientific issues.

PRIORITIES FOR POLICIES AND PROGRAMS

The panel's specific conclusions and recommendations cover a range of activities that include research, planning, policy development, service delivery, and monitoring. When existing knowledge supports new or revised policies and programs or highlights the effectiveness of ongoing initiatives, we propose specific new or continued programs or specific research and development. When existing knowledge provides insights but is incomplete, we advise further demonstration and evaluation to enhance understanding of the relative costs, effects, and effectiveness of promising approaches. When innovative policies have been initiated but there are as yet no scientifically measurable outcomes, we urge careful observation and monitoring. Many of our recommendations build on policies, programs, and research that are already under way, and many reinforce the priorities of other individuals and groups that are addressing the complex and controversial issue of adolescent pregnancy.

The panel has identified three overarching policy goals, presented in order of priority, that provide a framework for our specific conclusions and recommendations:

1. Reduce the rate and incidence of unintended pregnancy among adolescents, especially among school-age teenagers.
2. Provide alternatives to adolescent childbearing and parenting.
3. Promote positive social, economic, health, and developmental outcomes for adolescent parents and their children.

For most young people in the United States, realizing fulfilling adult work and family roles depends on completing an education and entering the labor force before becoming a parent. Accordingly, our highest priority should be to help teenagers, regardless of the timing of sexual initiation, to develop the ability and the motivation to avoid becoming parents before they are socially, emotionally, and economically prepared. Despite the amount of energy and resources devoted to prevention strategies, however, some teenagers will experience unintended and untimely pregnancies. For those who choose to keep and raise their children, supports and services to promote healthy development, educational attainment, and economic self-sufficiency should be available. Given the potentially adverse consequences of early parenthood for the life chances of young people, however, there should be alternatives to childbearing and childrearing. Abortion is a legal option for all women, including adolescents. We acknowledge that voluntary termination of pregnancy is controversial, and for many in our society it is morally reprehensible. Although the panel strongly prefers prevention of pregnancy to avoid parenthood, abortion is an alternative for teenagers for whom prevention fails. Adoption should also be available to those teenagers who choose to continue their pregnancies yet are unable or unwilling to assume the responsibilities of parenting.

Goal 1: Reduce the Rate and Incidence of Unintended Pregnancy Among Adolescents, Especially Among School-Age Teenagers

The panel is unequivocal in its conviction that the primary goal of policy makers, professionals, parents, and teenagers themselves should be a reduction in the rate and incidence of unintended pregnancies among adolescents, especially school-age teenagers. Several strategies can assist in achieving this goal: enhance the life options of disadvantaged teenagers, delay the initiation of sexual activity, and encourage contraceptive use for teenagers who are sexually active. Unfortunately, very little scientific evidence is available on the effectiveness of programs associated with the first two strategies, and so we can only endorse the development, implementation, and evaluation of such programs. For the third strategy, the scientific base is much greater, and programs can be based on the demonstrated effectiveness of contraceptive use.

Enhance Life Options   Poverty and hopelessness, which exacerbate many social problems, play an especially important role in the problems associated with adolescent pregnancy. Sexual activity and pregnancy among teenagers are not confined by race and income, yet the correlation between poverty and adolescent fertility is well documented. For too many high-risk teenagers, there are too few disincentives to early child-bearing. Inadequate basic skills, poor employment prospects, and the lack of successful role models for overcoming the overwhelmingly negative odds of intergenerational poverty have stifled the motivation of many to delay immediate gratification and avoid pregnancy. Young people need a reason to believe that parenthood is inappropriate at this point in their lives and that their opportunities for personal and occupational success will be enhanced by postponement. Several possible interventions are aimed at indirectly reducing adolescent fertility by nurturing the motivation to prevent untimely and unplanned parenthood, including life planning courses, programs to improve school performance, employment programs, and programs to provide role models for high-risk youth. Program research clearly demonstrating the effectiveness of these interventions is not currently available. Nevertheless, the panel endorses the development, implementation, and evaluation of such programs as a basis for future policy and program development.

Delay Sexual Initiation   A second strategy for reducing the rate of teenage pregnancy is to help teenagers, both male and female, develop ways to postpone sexual initiation until they are capable of making wise and responsible decisions concerning their personal lives and family formation. Several interventions are aimed at helping young people delay sexual initiation, including sex and family life education, assertiveness and decision-making training, programs to provide role models to young adolescents, and efforts to influence the media treatment of sexuality. Although there is little available evidence to document their effectiveness, the panel endorses the development and evaluation of such programs as a basis for future policy and program decisions. In addition, interventions to enhance the life options of teenagers may also encourage young people to delay the initiation of sexual activity.

Encourage Contraception   Because there is so little evidence of the effectiveness of the other strategies for prevention, the panel believes that the major strategy for reducing early unintended pregnancy must be the encouragement of diligent contraceptive use by all sexually active teenagers. Male contraception, as well as male support for female contraception, is essential. In light of the demonstrated effectiveness of contraceptive use, especially use of the contraceptive pill and the condom, in achieving this goal—

The panel concludes that use of the contraceptive pill is the safest and most effective means of birth control for sexually active adolescents. Aggressive public education is needed to dispel myths about the health risks of pill use by girls in this age group, and contraceptive service programs should explore nonmedical models for distribution of the pill.

The panel concludes that, to make this strategy effective, there must be continued public support for contraceptive services to adolescents, such as has been supplied primarily through Title X of the Family Planning Services and Population Research Act, Medicaid, and other federal and state maternal and child health programs. Such programs should minimize the potential barriers of cost, convenience, and confidentiality.

The panel urges that sex education programs include information on methods of contraception, how to use them, and how to obtain them.

The panel urges continued support for a variety of contraceptive service models—including private physicians—to reach adolescents. Contraceptive services should be available to all teenagers at low or no cost. Clinic service providers, whether based in hospitals, public health departments, private clinics, or community service organizations, should make efforts to improve the effectiveness of their programs by (1) enhancing their outreach efforts to encourage earlier use of contraceptive methods; (2) exploring more effective counseling approaches to encourage compliance; and (3) enhancing their follow-up of clinic patients to track their contraceptive use.

The panel concludes that school systems, in cooperation with various health care and youth-serving agencies, should further develop and refine comprehensive school-based clinic models for implementation in schools with large, high-risk populations.

The panel recommends the development, implementation, and evaluation of condom distribution programs.

The panel concludes that efforts should be undertaken to develop and test the effects on contraceptive use and unintended pregnancy of paid promotional messages for contraceptives that are directed at sexually active adolescents.

Goal 2: Provide Alternatives to Adolescent Childbearing and Parenting

The panel believes that prevention of pregnancy through abstinence or contraception is far preferable to unintended pregnancy among teenagers. Regardless of one's personal convictions, decisions concerning pregnancy resolution—whether to become a parent, to terminate a pregnancy, or to relinquish a child for adoption—are difficult, often painful choices. Nevertheless, when prevention fails, early parenthood is not the only available course. For young people who are unwilling to give birth or unable or unwilling to assume the responsibilities of parenthood, two alternatives exist—abortion and adoption.

Abortion   In 1973 the Supreme Court made abortion a legal option for pregnancy resolution for all women, yet its use by teenagers, especially young teenagers, remains a special issue. There is no evidence concerning either the cognitive capacity of adolescents to make decisions about pregnancy termination or the psychological consequences of abortion that would support or refute the imposition of age restrictions governing access to abortion services. There is, however, growing evidence that parental consent statutes cause teenagers to delay their abortions, if for no other reason than that those teenagers unwilling or unable to consult their parents must undergo the de facto waiting period associated with finding a lawyer and gaining access to the courts in order to obtain a judicial bypass. Such delays may increase the health risks associated with abortion if they result in postponing it until the second trimester of pregnancy. In general, the health risks associated with an early, legal abortion are no greater for adolescents than for adult women, and in most cases they are lower. They are also lower than the risks associated with pregnancy and childbirth.

The panel urges that at each step along the path from sexual initiation to parenting—regardless of whether one might wish that that step had not been reached—the girl or woman should be treated with the same dignity, confidentiality, kindness, and excellence of health care that are due any patient.

The panel concludes that there is no scientific basis for restricting the availability of abortion to adolescents. Evidence shows that to require minor teenagers to seek parental consent often causes them to delay abortions, with attendant health risks. On this basis, the panel concludes that minor adolescents should be encour-

aged, but not required, to involve their parents and partners in the decision-making process.

The panel believes there should be no compromise in the medical and personal supportive care for the 400,000 adolescents who have an abortion each year. For those adolescents who choose to terminate their pregnancy, abortion services should include both decision counseling and contraceptive counseling.

Adoption For pregnant adolescents who choose to continue their pregnancies but are unable or unwilling to assume the role and responsibilities of parenthood, adoption should be a viable option.

The panel recommends that relevant public agencies, in cooperation with the private sector, explore ways of strengthening adoption services, including (1) improved decision counseling for pregnant teenagers and (2) development of effective models for providing comprehensive care to pregnant girls who choose adoption as an alternative to parenthood.

Goal 3: Promote Positive Social, Economic, Health, and Developmental Outcomes for Adolescent Parents and Their Children

Regardless of pregnancy prevention strategies or available alternatives to parenthood, some teenagers experience unplanned pregnancies and become parents. Many of those who do are at serious risk of health and nutritional deficiencies, dropping out of school, unemployment, single parenthood, poverty, and long-term welfare dependence. Their children have a higher probability of physical, social, and cognitive problems and deficiencies. Although unmarried teenage parents represent a small proportion of the overall adolescent population, their problems and needs entail high public costs. Accordingly, a third important goal is to promote positive outcomes for adolescent parents and their children. Several strategies can assist in achieving this goal.

Promote Healthy Birth Outcomes and Support the Physical Health of Young Mothers and Their Babies Young expectant mothers who receive early and regular prenatal care and nutrition are significantly more likely to have healthy birth outcomes than those who do not. Similarly, young children who receive regular health care as well as appropriate emergency care are likely to be in better physical health than those who do not.

The panel recommends continued support for the provision of appropriate health and nutrition services, including prenatal, labor, and delivery care for pregnant adolescents and regular and emergency pediatric care for the children of teenage mothers, through Medicaid; the Early and Periodic Screening, Diagnosis and Treatment Program; and other federal and state maternal and child health programs. Bureaucratic barriers that prevent teenagers from receiving early, regular, and appropriate care for themselves and their children should be minimized.

Prevent Subsequent Untimely and Unintended Births   A second untimely and unintended birth is likely to compound the already complex and overwhelming problems faced by many adolescent parents. Prevention of subsequent pregnancies and births is thus an important strategy for promoting positive outcomes for teenage parents and their children.

The panel concludes that contraceptive services should be available and accessible to adolescent parents at low or no cost. Because of the special needs of this high-risk population, service providers should strengthen their programs by (1) enhancing their outreach efforts to encourage early use of contraceptive methods; (2) developing intensive individualized counseling and care techniques to encourage compliance; and (3) enhancing their follow-up procedures to track contraceptive use.

Ensure the Economic Well-being of the Teenage Family   Parents, including fathers, are obligated to provide support until their children reach age 18. But many fathers, especially teenage fathers, who may not have completed school and who are unemployed or employed only part-time, are unlikely to be able to make a significant contribution to the support of their children. For this reason, young fathers have often not been pursued by child support enforcement authorities. There has been renewed interest, however, in enforcing child support by fathers of children born to teenage mothers, both to provide additional financial assistance to young mothers and their children and to increase young men's sense of parental responsibility. There is little existing research or program experience to guide new policies in this area. Nevertheless, the panel urges efforts to educate young men about their child support obligations and to enforce those obligations over time. Experimental efforts to link child support enforcement to work requirements, including part-time and summer jobs for fathers who are enrolled in school, should be initiated and tested.

The parents of adolescent parents should also be encouraged to assume responsibility for the support and obligations of their minor (under age 18) children and the children of these minors. Again, research and program experience in this area is limited. Recent state legislation establishing grandparent liability should be carefully monitored to determine its effects.

Enhance Life Options for Adolescent Parents   Teenage parents must be encouraged to invest in their own futures. Both the motivation and the means to overcome the likely adverse consequences of early childbearing are essential. Therefore, another important strategy for improving social, economic, and health outcomes is to enhance the life opportunities of adolescent parents.

The panel urges that a broad array of special education programs and services for pregnant and parenting teenagers be developed and implemented to assist these young people in completing their education.

The panel concludes that efforts should be continued to strengthen and expand age-appropriate employment programs for pregnant girls and teenage parents, both male and female.

The panel recommends that support be provided for the development, implementation, and evaluation of model child care programs that are targeted to the needs of teenage parents. Schools and other community organizations should place high priority on establishing and maintaining these services for the children of adolescents.

The panel urges that public and voluntary community agencies explore ways of developing and evaluating case management capabilities to help adolescent parents obtain the necessary supports and services.

Promote the Social, Emotional, and Intellectual Development of the Children of Adolescent Parents   The children of adolescent parents are especially vulnerable to health, social, and cognitive problems. Special supports and services are needed by many adolescent parents to prevent or overcome these difficulties and to promote their children's healthy development.

The panel urges that parenting education for teenage parents, especially those from severely disadvantaged backgrounds, receive special attention and emphasis.

Schools and other community organizations should place high priority on the development, implementation, and evaluation of these programs.

RECOMMENDATIONS FOR DATA COLLECTION AND RESEARCH

Over the past several years, researchers have made significant advances in knowledge of teenage sexuality, pregnancy, and parenting. Yet many questions remain unanswered, and they suggest priorities for future data collection and research.

Program Evaluation Research

Despite the enormous commitment of public and private monetary resources and human effort toward designing and implementing preventive and ameliorative interventions, evidence of program costs, effects, and effectiveness is frequently unavailable or of poor quality. Although there are significant methodological, ethical, and practical problems associated with evaluations of these programs, they *can* be evaluated. Evaluation research methods have become quite sophisticated, yet they are frequently not used in studying the effects of adolescent pregnancy programs. Reliable data are needed as a basis for policy and program development.

The panel recommends that evaluation to measure the costs, effects, and effectiveness of service programs be an essential component of intervention strategies. Federal and state-level funding agencies should be urged to set aside adequate support for evaluation research, and the research community should be urged to take a more active role in designing and implementing these studies.

Data Collection

Data on teenage sexual activity, contraceptive use, pregnancy, abortion, childbearing, and other fertility-related behaviors have been vital to the panel's deliberations and are equally essential for future research and analysis. Relevant information is available from several different sources, including large-scale surveys, federal and state administrative reporting systems, and service providers. Individual data systems vary in their underlying purposes and special emphases as well as their specific characteristics (e.g., definitions, sample size, data collection intervals). For these reasons, and because information on sensitive issues requires validation from more than one source, a multidimensional strategy for data collection is needed.

The panel recommends that data systems that monitor fertility and fertility-related behaviors should be maintained and strengthened. Such data are essential for understanding trends and correlates of adolescent sexual activity, contraceptive use, pregnancy, abortion, and childbearing and as a basis for policy and program development. Fiscal cutbacks that affect ongoing data collection programs could seriously damage the quality and availability of these data systems.

Research on Adolescent Sexual and Fertility Behavior

Research on adolescent sexuality and fertility has increased substantially over the past decade, and this knowledge has provided an essential basis for the panel's deliberations. Nevertheless, there are several significant gaps. In some cases, the gaps reflect issues that have not been adequately studied because of methodological problems; in others, new issues have emerged from the accumulation of past findings. Future research should reflect the domains of causes and consequences of teenage pregnancy and childbearing: individuals, families, communities, and society.

The panel recommends the continued support of a broad-based research program on adolescent sexuality and fertility to enhance understanding of the causes and consequences of these behaviors and to inform policy and program development.

Experimentation

Although promising program models require further monitoring and evaluation, existing program development efforts should be expanded to include experimentation with innovative models for and novel approaches to pregnancy prevention and for the support and care of pregnant and parenting teenagers and their children.

The panel recommends that federal funding agencies, private foundations, and researchers cooperate in designing, implementing, and evaluating experimental approaches for pregnancy prevention among high-risk adolescents and for improving the well-being of teenage parents and their children.

1

Introduction

Adolescent pregnancy is widely recognized as a complex and serious problem in America. Why it is a problem, however, and what can or ought to be done to solve it are matters of dispute among individuals and groups with conflicting values, viewpoints, and agendas.

Adolescent pregnancy and childbearing are not new phenomena in the United States. Nor are they characteristic of most teenagers, as some accounts in the mass media suggest. Nevertheless, the simultaneous emergence of several social and demographic changes have made these issues more visible over the past two decades.

Levels of sexual activity and pregnancy increased dramatically during the 1970s among an expanding population of unmarried teenagers. Although these rates have declined slightly since their peak in the late 1970s, a significantly greater proportion of adolescents is sexually active and experiencing unintended pregnancy in the mid-1980s than in 1971 (Zelnik and Kantner, 1980; Pratt and Hendershot, 1984). Today approximately 45 percent of girls ages 15–19 are sexually active before marriage, and an estimated 36 percent of them become pregnant within two years of initiation of sexual activity (Zelnik and Shah, 1983; Koenig and Zelnik, 1982).

Not every pregnancy, however, results in a birth. The growing rate of abortion since 1973 has caused a reduction in the rate of childbearing among women under age 20. Nearly 40 percent of all teenage pregnancies are voluntarily terminated. Nevertheless, nearly 470,000 infants are born each year to mothers who have not yet reached their twentieth birthday; more than a third of them are born to women under 18 (National Center for Health Statistics, 1984b; see also Vol. II). It is striking to note that despite declining fertility rates since 1970, rates of adolescent pregnancy, abortion, and childbearing have remained considerably higher in the United States than in the majority of other developed countries with comparable levels of early sexual activity. The contrast is especially dramatic for girls under 15. Among these young adolescents, the U.S. rate, at five births per 1,000 girls of comparable age, is four times greater than that of Canada, the only other country with as many as one birth per 1,000 girls (Alan Guttmacher Institute, in press). There are similar patterns for pregnancies and abortions.

Though proportionately fewer U.S. teenagers are having babies, a growing percentage of all teenage births over the past 15 years have occurred outside marriage (National Center for Health Statistics, 1984b; see also Vol. II). Half the adolescents who carry their pregnancies to term are unmarried at the time of birth, compared with approximately 15 percent who gave birth outside marriage in 1960 (Bureau of the Census, 1984b). Among those who are married at the birth of their child or shortly thereafter, many divorce or separate while the child is still very young. A majority of teenage families with children are single-parent families, and an overwhelming proportion of them are poor.

THE NATURE OF THE PROBLEM

The problem of adolescent pregnancy and childbearing involves issues that are intensely debated and that raise a number of fundamental political, moral, and policy concerns.

Some view the problem as early, nonmarital sexual activity: if teenagers were not engaging in sexual intercourse, they would not become pregnant. Adolescent sexual activity, many would argue, regardless of the extent to which it reflects broader social trends, represents a decline in traditional family values. In addition, it affords exposure to sexually transmitted diseases and may pose additional undocumented psychological risks. Hence, many regard early sexual intercourse as the primary problem whether or not it results in pregnancy. According to this view, policies and programs that acknowledge sexual activity outside marriage are believed to undermine parental authority, to legitimize fundamentally immoral behavior, and probably to encourage teenagers to engage in sexual intercourse at younger ages. Advocates of this view hold that parents should have authority and responsibility for their minor (under age 18) children's sexual involvement. Sex education and counseling, contraceptive decision making, and pregnancy resolution, they believe, should be managed within the family and should not be matters of public policy.

Others, however, argue that changing patterns of teenage sexual behavior are the inevitable consequence of broader social trends, including adult sexual liberalization, the widespread use of contraception, feminism, changing family forms and patterns of marriage, and changing education and work patterns. Once norms of adult sexual behavior change, many believe it is unrealistic to think these norms will not also be adopted by young people. Public policy and programs, they suggest, should be directed at minimizing the personal and societal risks associated with early sexual activity and at helping teenagers become responsible for their actions. Many adolescents have a difficult time discussing sex with their parents, and many parents find it difficult to help their adolescent children understand and avoid the risk of pregnancy. Accordingly, advocates of this view believe that public programs should help teenagers guard against unintended pregnancy and should protect their confidentiality in the process. Moreover, the costs of preventing pregnancy, they contend, are far less than the costs of ameliorating the likely negative social, economic, and health consequences of early childbearing.

Still others believe abortion is the problem. Voluntary termination of an unintended pregnancy is regarded by many as inhumane and immoral regardless of the mother's age. Despite the legalization of abortion, debate continues among scientists, philosophers, theologians, and lay people about when life begins and when the intentional interruption of a pregnancy constitutes the unethical destruction of life. As medical technology increases the prospects of a normal life for many preterm infants, the issue becomes more difficult.

Others, however, argue that the legalization of abortion ensures the fundamental right of all women, regardless of age, to autonomy in matters of procreation. Whether or not to continue a pregnancy, they maintain, is a decision for each woman to make in consultation with her physician. Law and public opinion differ on how much parental involvement should be required in abortion decisions by minors. Some states require either consent by parents or judicial determination. Nevertheless, many people believe that public policy should be aimed at making legal, safe, and professionally provided abortion services available to teenage girls without restriction. Appropriate counseling, they suggest, should be provided to help young women make responsible decisions concerning the resolution of an unintended pregnancy and to minimize the emotional strain. Counselors should encourage adolescents to involve their parents and their partners in the decision-making process. Yet in circumstances in which a young woman is judged by health professionals to be mature and is unable or unwilling to consult her parents, proponents of this view believe she should be able to decide whether to terminate her pregnancy without parental consent or knowledge.

Still others in our society view the most compelling problem as neither early sexual activity nor abortion, but as teenage childbearing. Adolescent mothers are significantly more likely to curtail their education, to be relegated to low-paying jobs, to be single parents, and to be on welfare than are women who delay childbearing until their twenties. Teenagers who become fathers and assume parenting roles are significantly more likely to drop out of school and to be unemployed. Teenage marriages are more likely than those of older couples to end in separation and divorce. And for many young women, marriage is not a viable option. Adolescent childbearing makes economic success more difficult and further diminishes the opportunities of poor and minority young people who can ill afford the compounded hardships. In addition, the children of teenage parents are especially vulnerable to health and cognitive problems, and they are at greater risk of experiencing an early pregnancy and birth themselves. Many believe that the costs of early childbearing, both to individuals and to society, are too high. This group maintains that prevention of adolescent pregnancy should be the highest priority. Nevertheless, in those situations in which contraception fails and abortion is not an acceptable course, some advocate adoption as an alternative to early parenthood. Others urge the provision of special supports and services to ensure healthy outcomes for young mothers and their children and to promote long-term economic autonomy for young families.

THE SEARCH FOR SOLUTIONS

The widespread moral and political disagreement about why adolescent pregnancy is a problem has created confusion and conflict over what to do about it. Political, educational, and religious leaders, as well as parents of teenagers, appear divided over what their primary goals should be: to discourage or delay sexual intercourse among young, unmarried individuals; to reduce teenage pregnancies through the promotion of education, counseling, and contraceptive services; to ensure the availability and accessibility of abortion; to facilitate adoption; or to diminish the negative social, economic, and health consequences associated with early childbearing by the provision of special income and in-kind supports to pregnant and parenting teenagers.

In the United States during the past two decades, there has been no coherent policy toward adolescent pregnancy and childbearing. American teenagers receive conflicting messages about sexuality, sexual behavior, and sexual responsibility. As a recent Alan Guttmacher Institute study (in press) suggests, teenagers' exposure to sex through the popular media tells them that sex is exciting and romantic. Premarital sex, cohabitation, and nonmarital relationships are common ways of life among the adults they see and hear about, often including their own parents or the parents of their peers. Yet they receive little open and informed advice about sexuality, contraception, or the harsh realities of early pregnancy and parenting. What they are told is that good girls say no (Alan Guttmacher Institute, in press). Such confused messages inevitably result from the striking ambivalence about sex in our society. In turn, these mixed messages may contribute to the communication problems of many adolescents and thereby enhance the risks of early pregnancy, births outside marriage, and abortion.

The fact that adolescents are not a monolithic group and that adolescent pregnancy is not a unitary problem adds to the complexity of the issue. For young people of different ages, living in different social, economic, and cultural circumstances, the significance of early sexual activity, pregnancy, and childbearing is not the same. The values, norms, and expectations influencing their attitudes and behavior vary sharply. Young people who are poor do not have the same opportunities and experiences as those from more advantaged backgrounds. Moreover, most 14-year-olds are not the same as most 18- or 19-year-olds. Their levels of social, emotional, and cognitive development are different. Their abilities to establish life goals, to appraise opportunities, and to assess risks are different. Their mobility and legal status are different. Perhaps we lack a coherent approach to solving the problems of adolescent pregnancy and childbearing in the United States in part because of the enormous difficulties involved in designing a policy that is sensitive to our diverse population of young people.

In addition, defining an appropriate role for public policy in an area that until recently has been regarded as a private family affair is both difficult and delicate. Traditionally, an individual's sexual behavior has been regarded as a personal domain in which intrusion by others—even family members—is inappropriate. However, recent debates over teenagers' exposure to sex education in public schools, their access to family planning services, and their right to obtain an abortion have called into question the jurisdiction of parents, the state, and teenagers themselves in matters of their sexual and fertility behavior. Courts are currently struggling with these issues and finding them difficult to resolve, largely because of the ambiguous relationship of adolescents to their parents and to society. At what age should teenagers have the authority to make their own decisions? Under what circumstances should the state intervene? Perhaps an additional reason for the confusion and inconsistency in policies toward adolescent pregnancy and childbearing is the failure of policy makers to take account of the nature of adolescence, its place in the life span, and the dynamics of family relationships involving adolescents.

The past decade and a half has witnessed a dramatic burgeoning of policies and programs to help prevent teenage pregnancies and to reduce the negative effects of early childbearing. Some have been promoted and supported by the federal government; others have been initiated by states and local communities; still others have developed from significant investments by private foundations and philanthropic groups. Many have been the result of productive public-private partnerships. Their range and variation defy description. Some have focused on individual teens as the unit of treatment; others have focused on the family. Some have provided specialized treatments and services; others have been comprehensive in their approach. Programs have been organized in schools and churches, community centers and social service agencies, and clinics and hospitals. Some have been single-site programs, while others have been replicated at several sites within a region or across the nation.

Despite the magnitude of human effort and monetary resources that have been directed at solving the problems of adolescent pregnancy and childbearing, we do not know as much as we need to about what works, for whom, under what circumstances, and with what intended and unintended effects. While our understanding of the antecedents and consequences of early sexual and fertility behavior has advanced significantly since 1970, our knowledge of effective and efficient intervention strategies has not kept pace. In part this is because many programs have been launched by creative and enthusiastic service providers who lack the necessary methodological and statistical skills, as well as the financial resources, to include evaluation in their program designs. In addition, the evaluation of human service programs poses numerous theoretical, methodological, and practical difficulties that inhibit researchers and render the quality of the results highly variable. Few have been continued over a period of time sufficient to reveal their long-term effects. Perhaps most important, there has been no systematic effort to assess what is known (and what is not known) about the relative costs, effects, and effectiveness of alternative approaches in light of growing scientific knowledge about early pregnancy and parenting. Indeed, skeptical observers would suggest there has been little incentive to do so; efforts to develop solutions have stemmed from differing and frequently conflicting concepts of the problem.

PUBLIC POLICIES TOWARD ADOLESCENT PREGNANCY AND CHILDBEARING

Addressing the problems associated with adolescent pregnancy has only recently become an explicit priority for national policy. The Adolescent Health Services and Pregnancy Prevention and Care Act of 1978 (Title VI of the Health Services and Centers Amendments Act) represents the first federal legislative initiative to focus solely on the problems of early sexuality and pregnancy. Drafted and sponsored by the Carter administration, it was described by Joseph Califano, then Secretary of the Department of Health, Education, and Welfare, as "the centerpiece of the President's strategy to deal with the urgent problem of teenage pregnancy across the nation" (April 13, 1978).

Throughout the 1960s and 1970s, the federal government assumed a more and more active role in providing and financing pregnancy-related programs. Under the Child Health Act of 1967, Title V of the historic Social Security Act of 1935, maternal and child health funds were targeted at reducing infant mortality. Special project grants, administered by the Bureau of Maternal and Child Health Services, were made directly available to local health departments to provide comprehensive care to children and teenagers in low-income families and to improve pregnancy outcomes through pre- and postnatal care services. Under the Family Planning Services and Population Research Act, Title X of the Public Health Services Act of 1970, federal funds were allocated for support of family planning projects, including expanded accessibility to contraceptive services for low-income women, the development of improved methods of family planning, personnel training, and the preparation and distribution of educational materials. All these initiatives benefited adolescents as a subgroup of the larger at-risk population. Yet it was not until passage of the Title VI legislation that Congress specifically acknowledged the problems of increasing sexuality and pregnancy among young unmarried teenagers.

In 1978 the Office of Adolescent Pregnancy Programs (OAPP) was established in the Public Health Service to administer the Adolescent Pregnancy Prevention and Care Program mandated by the 1978 legislation and to coordinate all programs in the U.S. Department of Health, Education, and Welfare concerned with aspects of adolescent pregnancy and childbearing. Despite its stated concern with pregnancy prevention among adolescents, however, the program initially concentrated almost exclusively on developing comprehensive services for pregnant and parenting teenagers. This categorical initiative was short-lived, however. After less than three years, during which 38 local projects received grants, the program was dismantled. Consistent with the Reagan administration's philosophy of returning control of health and human services to the states, the appropriation was folded into the Maternal and Child Health Block Grant in 1981.

Also in 1978, Congress amended the Family Planning Services and Population Research Act of 1970 (Title X) to specifically require that programs authorized under the act also provide services to adolescents. Contraceptive services were and are available to teenagers through several other federal programs, including the maternal and child health and social services programs that were made block grants in 1981, and through Medicaid. Yet Title X is currently the largest federal initiative addressing the problem of adolescent pregnancy. In fiscal 1983, the program served 4.5 million individuals, more than a third of whom were under the age of 20 (Alan Guttmacher Institute, in press). The legislation encourages, but does not require, parental notification for minor teenagers to receive contraceptive services. The Reagan administration tried unsuccessfully to place the Title X legislation into a block grant in 1981 and again in 1984. Formal authorization for Title X expired in 1985, and during the remainder of 1985 and 1986 the program operated under a continuing resolution.

In 1981 the Omnibus Budget Reconciliation Act repealed the Adolescent Health Services and Pregnancy Prevention and Care Act, replacing it with the Title XX Adolescent Family Life Act. Like its ill-fated predecessor, the Adolescent Family Life Act represents an explicit acknowledgment by Congress that the federal government should address the problems of increasing adolescent sexual activity, pregnancy, and childbearing. In contrast to the 1978 legislation, however, the Adolescent Family Life Act places more emphasis on prevention of early sexual activity and less emphasis on the provision of contraceptive services, while retaining the previous program's commitment to providing care for pregnant and parenting teenagers. The prevention focus is primarily on promoting abstinence from premarital sexual activity through the development of strong family values. Contraceptive services to adolescents are not a major component of the program, since originators of the legislation presumed that such services are adequately provided under Title X. Program funds may not be used for abortion or abortion counseling. Adoption is emphasized as an important alternative to adolescent parenting. The legislation authorizes support for research and demonstration projects rather than permanent programs, the intent being to stimulate the development of innovative approaches that state and local, public and private funding sources can sustain. The legislation also specifies that all demonstration programs include rigorous evaluation, but it does not provide adequate funding for this component. Legislative authority for the Adolescent Family Life Program was renewed for one year in 1984 and expired in 1985. In 1986 it operated under a continuing resolution.

Critics of the program argue that its approach to prevention is inappropriately moralistic. Moreover, a lawsuit brought by the American Civil Liberties Union on the grounds of entanglement of church and state in the administration of the program could adversely affect its chances of reauthorization. Although the Title X and Title XX programs are supposed to be independent of one another, they have become linked in recent legislative deliberations. The House of Representatives has demonstrated a stronger interest in the reauthorization of Title X, and the Senate appears to be more committed to continued support of Title XX.

Government involvement in addressing the problems of adolescent pregnancy has not been limited to federal policies and programs. By 1985, nearly half the states had taken steps to develop their own responses to growing public concern about these issues. These initiatives have ranged broadly from coordinated statewide policies, to agendas for action by governors' blue-ribbon task forces, to single-agency programs and local isolated efforts to address the special needs of teenagers at high risk of pregnancy or parenthood (Kimmich, 1985). Illinois, for example, initiated a major program to coordinate the efforts of state-level education, health, and welfare agencies and to supplement Aid to Families With Dependent Children (AFDC) with targeted services. New York and North Carolina have launched programs to stimulate and facilitate local initiatives. California is developing networks of services with strong case management components. The governor of Maryland, among others, has established a special task force to assess the extent of the problem in that state, to identify existing programs that can be mobilized, and to develop recommendations for action. Some states have coupled these types of initiatives with public information campaigns and technical assistance to local service providers; others are supporting evaluation studies to document the results of their programs. Most states that have identified adolescent pregnancy and childbearing as a priority have defined an important aspect of their role as linking and mobilizing private and voluntary groups, such as churches, parent organizations, and community youth organizations, to work with public agencies and to build a broad base of public concern and support.

As federal and state support for adolescent pregnancy programs increased during the 1970s, interest in understanding the causes and consequences of early pregnancy and childbearing also expanded. The Center for Population Research within the National Institute of Child Health and Human Development was created by presidential directive in 1968 and given an explicit research agenda by the Family Planning Services and Population Research Act of 1970. As with the service provisions of Title X, the initial research emphasis was not on adolescent pregnancy but on more general issues related to population and family planning. In the mid-1970s, faced with dramatic increases in sexual activity and pregnancy among teenagers, the Center for Population Research targeted adolescent pregnancy as a priority for research support. Over the past decade, the center has administered a broad program of research on the antecedents and consequences of early sexual and fertility behavior, including the collection of national survey data on adolescent sexuality, contraceptive use, and pregnancy resolution. When the legislation was reauthorized in 1981, authorization for research was transferred to the general authority provided by the Public Health Service Act for research by the National Institutes of Health, thus relieving the population research program from further dependence on the reauthorization of the service provisions.

The Title XX Adolescent Family Life Act also contains a strong research component in keeping with the view of Congress that more and better information on the causes and consequences of adolescent sexual and fertility behavior is needed, especially information on prevention, abortion, repeat pregnancy, and the short- and long-term implications of adolescent childbearing and parenting. Since 1982, the Office of Adolescent Pregnancy Programs has supported studies of familial, institutional, and societal influences on early sexual behavior and adoption, as well as the provision of services to pregnant and parenting teenagers. Studies of factors affecting contraceptive use by sexually active adolescents and ways to encourage more diligent use have not been OAPP priorities.

Foundations have also played an important role in increasing knowledge about early pregnancy and childbearing and about the effectiveness of various interventions. The knowledge gained from research over the past decade has played an important role in the continuing debate over policies and programs.

Throughout 1985, congressional hearings were held on the issues involved in adolescent pregnancy, and several new pieces of legislation were drafted, offering a variety of approaches for national policy. Some emphasized services to help young people complete their education and prepare for jobs, on the theory that having an education and career goal will motivate teenagers to avoid becoming pregnant or having a repeat pregnancy. One proposed the establishment of school-based health care, family planning, and prenatal care services. Another has proposed more comprehensive approaches, including family life education, contraceptive services, abortion services, and care for pregnant and parenting adolescents. Still another proposed the establishment of a block grant program to provide support for state health and welfare agencies to operate programs to prevent teenage pregnancy and to help pregnant and parenting teens. There will undoubtedly be further activity in Congress and many state legislatures in the coming year or two, although the direction of legislative action is still uncertain. Debate continues over whether public policy can best and most appropriately address the problems of early unplanned childbearing by taking a pragmatic approach to teenage sexuality and pregnancy, or whether it should foster sexual abstinence among young people and greater responsibility and authority among their parents.

THE CHARGE TO THE PANEL

Our study has three major components. The first is a review and assessment of data on trends in teenage sexual and fertility behavior. Many of the public data on incidence of sexual activity by age, sex, race, and cohort in the United States, as well as trend data on pregnancy, abortion, childbearing, marriage, and adoption, are scattered across federal and private data banks and national surveys. Some of these data have not been previously published. Therefore, our first task was to assemble available data on trends in teenage sexual and fertility behavior and to assess their quality.

The second component of the study is a review and synthesis of the research on the antecedents and consequences of adolescent pregnancy and childbearing. A growing body of research from several disciplines has examined individual and societal factors that affect early sexual activity, contraceptive use, pregnancy, abortion, and childbearing. Similarly, there is an extensive literature on the social, economic, and health consequences of early pregnancy and childbearing for young mothers and their children, and to a lesser extent for young fathers. Although compilations and critiques of relevant research have been done before, the disparate and in some cases uneven threads of current research have not been systematically reviewed and synthesized. Nor have their methodological and theoretical strengths and weaknesses been adequately assessed. Accordingly, our second task was to critique the existing literature to clarify the current state of knowledge and to provide a basis for identifying future directions for research and analysis.

The third component is a review of alternative preventive and ameliorative interventions. Given the enormous variety of existing programs and approaches, questions emerge concerning relative costs, effects, and effectiveness. Are some interventions more appropriate than others for adolescents of different ages and gender, living in different social, economic, and cultural circumstances? Are certain institutions more appropriate than others for the establishment of various types of programs or for reaching different target populations? Are some otherwise attractive approaches too expensive to implement on a large scale? To begin to answer these questions, the panel undertook a broad examination of existing interventions, both those focused specifically on adolescent pregnancy and those focused more generally on problem behaviors of young people. Information from several sources—including the available evaluation literature, discussions with knowledgeable researchers, service providers, and policy makers, and firsthand visits to many programs—was assessed as a basis for developing conclusions and recommendations concerning promising directions for future programs.

Policies and programs designed to affect adolescent sexual and fertility behavior touch on deeply felt values. No review of existing statistics will ultimately resolve disputes arising from different moral and political orientations. Nevertheless, a broad interdisciplinary synthesis of what is known about the antecedents and consequences of early pregnancy and childbearing and a dispassionate assessment of the social and behavioral effects of alternative programs will serve several important purposes. First, it will help to clarify the issues, sharpen awareness of crucial decision points, and focus attention on the trade-offs and complementarities among different positions. Second, it will bring together in one source the many types of pertinent data that researchers, policy makers, funding agencies, and service providers regularly need. Third, it will identify gaps in data collection and analysis. Finally, and perhaps most important, such a review of available evidence will provide a useful contribution to the continuing debate of this salient but often divisive issue, and it will suggest promising directions for future initiatives to address the problems of adolescent pregnancy.

A CONTEXTUAL FRAMEWORK

For every young person, the pathway from sexual initiation to parenthood involves a sequence of choices: whether to begin having intercourse; whether to continue sexual activity; whether to use contraception and, if so, what method to use; if a pregnancy occurs, whether to seek an abortion or carry the pregnancy to term and give birth; whether to marry, if that is an option; and, if a child is born outside marriage, whether to relinquish it for adoption or raise it as a single parent (see Figure 1-1). Whether consciously or unconsciously, actively or passively, all adolescents make choices about their sexual and fertility behavior. These have significant implications for their own development and life options, for their families, and for society (Moore and Burt, 1982).

Each choice is complex, and each is significantly influenced by circumstance and by the available options. The historical time and the ecological setting are central, as are the special psychosocial, physical, and perceptual characteristics of the young person and his or her age and life

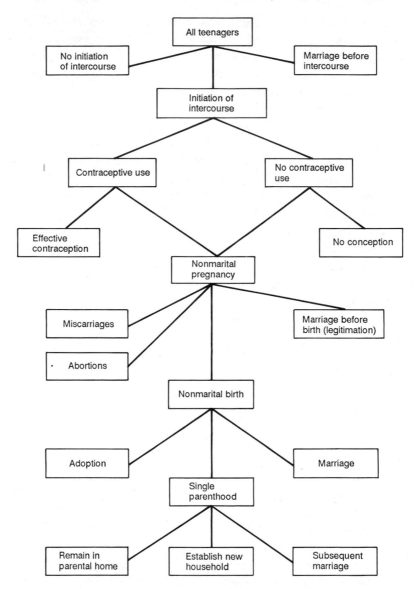

FIGURE 1-1 Sequence of decisions affecting adolescent sexual and fertility behavior.

experiences. At any given point in time, for adolescents living in different social, economic, and cultural contexts and having different personal characteristics and life histories, choices concerning sexual behavior will reflect different degrees of rational thinking and conscious decision making. Similarly, at different points in time, choices by the same individual will vary because his or her historical, social, or cultural milieu has changed.

Variations in the timing and sequence of events and choices during adolescence are significant because of their implications for coherent or discordant patterns of human development (Elder, 1980). Completion of education, leaving home, marriage, and economic independence are commonly regarded as baseline indications of the transition to adulthood, yet the timing of these events spans a wide range and may differ dramatically for individuals in different circumstances (Modell et al., 1976). The order and spacing of these events can also vary widely. Marriage may occur before the completion of schooling, and parenthood may precede marriage and economic independence. Such variations have important implications for an individual's social identity, personal integration, and life chances (Elder, 1968, 1975). For society, such variations often constitute problems when social institutions are unable to adapt. The problems of adolescent pregnancy and childbearing, therefore, are intimately related to the timing, sequence, and circumstances of choices concerning sexual and fertility behavior, as well as to an individual's and society's ability to adapt and promote a steady course toward adulthood (i.e., independence, responsible parenthood, and economic self-sufficiency).

Efforts to prevent pregnancy or ameliorate the consequences of early childbearing have given rise to a multiplicity of interventions targeted to the discrete choices in the sequence of sexual decision making. Most of these involve direct approaches, that is, interventions specifically intended to influence the decision-making process at the time of choice (e.g., family planning services to encourage the use of contraception, pregnancy and abortion counseling to affect decisions concerning pregnancy resolution). As Dryfoos (1984a) suggests, they are aimed at enhancing young people's "capacity to avoid early childbearing" by increasing their level of knowledge about reproduction and their access to appropriate services. Others involve indirect approaches, that is, interventions intended to alter the conditions of decision making—the ecological context of the individual and his or her personal characteristics (e.g., remedial education to improve academic performance and life-planning programs to help teenagers establish educational, occupational, and family formation goals). Such programs are aimed at enhancing young men's and women's "motivation to avoid parenthood" by making them cognizant of the consequences of early childbearing on their own lives (Dryfoos, 1984a). Some interventions are intended to affect more than one choice (e.g., comprehensive prevention approaches) and therefore have multiple goals.

Because choices at each successive point in the sequence depend on the outcomes of previous decisions, interventions aimed at later decisions are relevant to smaller numbers of teenagers. All young people must decide whether to become sexually active; only those who initiate intercourse must decide whether to use contraception; only those who become pregnant must decide whether to seek an abortion or to bear a child; only those who bear a child must decide whether to relinquish it for adoption or to raise it, either within or outside marriage. Yet as Moore and Burt (1982) point out, despite their smaller constituencies, interventions aimed at later decision points tend to entail greater public involvement and greater public costs.

Sexual activity, pregnancy, and parenting have different implications for teenagers of different ages. An unintended pregnancy or birth can have serious social, economic, and psychological consequences for adolescents, yet the personal problems and public issues are somewhat different for 18- and 19-year-olds than they are for those under age 18. Most 18- and 19-year-olds have completed high school; some live apart from their parents and are economically independent. In most states, they have reached the age of legal majority. In contrast, most teenagers under the age of 18 have not completed high school; most still live at home and depend on their parents' support. As minors they are under the legal jurisdiction of their parents. Throughout this report, the panel has been attentive to this difference. To the extent that available data permit, we have distinguished patterns of sexual and fertility behavior by age. In reviewing the research on the antecedents and consequences of early pregnancy and childbearing, we have given special attention to the effects of age on attitudes, behavior, and outcomes. In reviewing the evidence on program effects and effectiveness, we have considered issues of access to and availability of services as they influence patterns of use among teenagers of different ages.

The panel has questioned fundamentally whether interventions are needed and how they can be effective in helping teenagers to make better decisions about their sexual and fertility behavior. The sequence of choices constitutes a contextual framework for relating the personal and societal antecedents of adolescent pregnancy and parenting to the costs, effects, and effectiveness of alternative intervention strategies. It provides a basis for identifying gaps in existing knowledge, for considering new approaches to problem solving, and for mapping promising intervention strategies.

STRUCTURE OF THE REPORT

The findings, conclusions, and recommendations of the Panel on Adolescent Pregnancy and Childbearing are presented in the remaining chapters of this report. Chapter 2 summarizes the available data on trends in teenage sexual and fertility behavior and assesses their adequacy and reliability. Chapter 3 discusses the societal context of adolescent pregnancy. Chapter 4 focuses on the individual teenager, examining individual attributes that contribute to early sexual behavior and decision making. Chapter 5 summarizes the state of knowledge concerning the social, economic, and health consequences of early pregnancy and parenting. Chapters 6 and 7 examine what we know about the costs, effects, and effectiveness of alternative interventions. Chapter 8 presents the panel's conclusions and recommendations for future data collection and research. And finally, Chapter 9 presents the panel's views concerning priorities for future policy and program development.

2

Trends in Adolescent Sexuality and Fertility

The incidence of adolescent childbearing is the result of several social and demographic processes. The size of the teenage population, the proportion of teenagers who are married, the incidence of sexual activity among the unmarried, the consistency of contraceptive use, and the effectiveness of methods used are all factors that affect the probability of pregnancy. Among those who become pregnant, a number of resolutions are possible, including miscarriage, abortion, marriage, adoption, and motherhood without marriage. The frequency of these behaviors (except possibly miscarriage) has been changing over the past two decades, and in many cases the trends are moving in different directions. Moreover, some of these changes offset others, or one change affects the size of the population at risk of another behavior. Consequently, it is necessary to explore the entire range of behaviors in order to understand the phenomena of teenage pregnancy and childbearing.

Data from several sources are available. Vital statistics data report marriages, births, abortions, and deaths in the U.S. population. Census data provide information concerning the size and composition of the teenage population, the characteristics of their families, their living arrangements, their school enrollment, their employment status, and their economic well-being. Other national survey data provide information about sexual activity. They also provide information about pregnancy and abortion, although these behaviors appear to be less reliably reported. While census data and vital statistics data permit us to trace trends in teenage childbearing over several decades, survey data containing information about adolescent sexual behavior and pregnancy have been available

33

only since the early 1970s. Data concerning racial subgroups have been available from the census and the vital statistics system, as well as from surveys containing information on adolescent sexual and fertility behavior. Data describing ethnicity, however, began to be available only in the 1970s as some subgroups, especially Hispanics, became more prominent minorities in the United States. The census and other federal data sources based on census samples began to distinguish Hispanic origin in 1970; in 1978 selected states began to report information concerning ethnicity through the vital statistics system. Although data on Hispanics is included in recent surveys of sexual and fertility behavior, the samples are frequently too small to permit statistically meaningful national estimates according to the relevant variables (e.g., age, marital status). In addition, data concerning Hispanic origin are frequently not mutually exclusive of data concerning race. Hispanics may be of either race, and data concerning blacks and whites may also include Hispanics. Accordingly, information concerning trends in the sexual and fertility behavior of Hispanic teenagers is incomplete and not comparable to that for racial subgroups.

This chapter presents an overview of the social and demographic characteristics of the teenagers in the United States and trends in their sexual and fertility behavior. It also presents a critique of the strengths and weaknesses of the available data. More detailed information is presented in the statistical appendix to this report, which is part of Volume II.

ADOLESCENTS IN THE UNITED STATES

The post-World War II baby boom extended through the 1950s, peaking in 1957. As a result, the population of U.S. teenagers ages 15–19 grew until 1976, when it peaked at 21.4 million. Since then it has declined steadily to 18.4 million in 1985, consisting of approximately 9.0 million girls and 9.4 million boys. Recent population projections indicate that the number of teenagers will continue to decline to approximately 16.9 million in 1990; it will rise again to approximately 18.9 million by 2000 (Table 2-1). Despite the increase and subsequent decline in the adolescent population during the past three decades, the proportion of the total U.S. population 15–19 years of age has remained between 7 and 10 percent since 1940 (Bureau of the Census, 1980).

Over the past generation, the number and proportion of racial and ethnic minorities in the United States has increased. In 1984 blacks com-

TABLE 2-1 Total U.S. Population Ages 10–24 Years Old by Sex, 1960–2000 (in thousands)

	Males			Females		
	10–14	15–19	20–24	10–14	15–19	20–24
1960	8,524	6,634	5,272	8,249	6,586	5,528
1965	9,636	8,656	6,884	9,323	8,395	6,794
1970	10,622	9,714	8,034	10,230	9,517	8,544
1975	10,534	10,757	9,640	10,112	10,465	9,677
1976	10,251	10,896	9,893	9,837	10,582	9,901
1980	9,316	10,726	10,697	8,925	10,376	10,678
1981	9,374	10,419	10,813	8,964	10,074	10,779
1982	9,318	10,104	10,795	8,899	9,767	10,765
1985	8,590	9,398	10,820	8,207	9,019	10,481
1990	8,586	8,670	9,443	8,207	8,299	9,137
2000	9,986	9,681	8,723	9,532	9,262	8,422

SOURCES: Bureau of the Census, Detailed Population Characteristics, U.S. Summary, 1960, 1970, 1980; "Population Estimates and Projections," *Current Population Reports,* Series P-25, No. 965, 1985.

prised approximately 14 percent of the adolescent population, compared with 13 percent in 1970 and 11 percent in 1960. In 1984 Hispanics comprised approximately 7 percent, compared with 5 percent in 1970 (earlier data for Hispanics are not available). Overall the proportion of adolescents who are nonwhite has increased by 47 percent since 1960 (Bureau of the Census, 1980).

Marriage

Over this same period, early marriage has become less prevalent. Fewer young women and even fewer young men marry while still in their teens than did one or two decades ago. In 1984, both males and females ages 15–19 were less likely to have ever been married than their counterparts in the early 1970s. The proportion of all females under age 20 who remained single increased from 84 percent in 1960 to 91 percent in 1976 and to 93 percent in 1984. Among males the increase was from 96 percent in 1960 to 97 percent in 1976 to 98.5 percent in 1984. Although there was only a relatively small decline over the decade in the percentage of white teenagers who married, there was a much sharper decline among blacks, and it began a decade earlier. Between 1960 and 1984 the percentage of black women ages 15–19 who were ever married dropped from 16.2 percent to 1.6 percent. Similarly, the decline for black males was from 3.4 to 1.8 percent (Table 2-2). Hispanic teenagers, both male and female, were more likely to have married in 1984 than in 1970, and they were more likely to have married than either whites or blacks.

Older teenagers (18–19) have always been significantly more likely to be married than those who are under 18. In 1984, females 18–19 years old were four and a half times more likely to be married than those 15–17 years old, and older males were nearly seven times more likely to be married than those of school age. Because of the greater proportion of 18- and 19-year-olds who are married, it is the decline among these older teens that primarily accounts for the overall decline in teenage marriage. Among younger teenagers the percentage of males and females who are married has remained fairly stable at a very low level over the past two decades (see Table 2-2).

Schooling

Most teenagers under age 18 are enrolled in school, while fewer 18- and 19-year-olds are students. In 1984, 98 percent of 14- and 15-year-olds and 92 percent of 16- and 17-year-olds were in school, compared with approximately 50 percent of 18- and 19-year-olds. School enrollment has remained fairly constant among those under 18 over the past two decades and has increased slightly among those 18 and over. The proportion of males and females who are in school is virtually equivalent for all age groups (Bureau of the Census, 1985c).

Patterns of school enrollment vary by race and ethnic group. Approximately equal proportions of white and black teenagers ages 14–15 and 16–17 are enrolled in school, while fewer Hispanics ages 16–17 are students. Among teenagers 18–19 years old, whites are more likely to be enrolled than either blacks or Hispanics. Among older teenagers not in school, Hispanics are substantially more likely than whites or blacks to lack a high school diploma. Regardless of race or ethnic group, virtually all young people ages 14–15 and 16–17 who are not enrolled in school have dropped out before graduation. In 1984 approximately 615,000 teenagers ages 14–17 and 1.1 million teenagers ages 18–19 were out of school but had not graduated (Table 2-3).

TABLE 2-2 Percentage of Never-Married Boys and Girls Ages 15–19 by Race, 1960–1984

	Boys			Girls		
	15–17	18–19	15–19	15–17	18–19	15–19
1960						
Total	99.1	91.1	96.3	93.2	67.8	83.9
White	99.1	91.0	96.2	93.3	67.6	83.9
Nonwhite	99.2	91.9	96.6	92.3	69.3	83.8
1970						
Total	98.6	91.3	95.9	95.3	76.6	88.1
White	98.7	91.3	95.9	95.4	76.4	88.0
Black	98.0	91.0	95.5	95.0	77.7	88.6
Hispanic	97.7	87.4	94.0	93.1	70.6	84.7
1973						
Total	99.2	90.4	96.5[a]	96.2	75.8	89.6[a]
White	99.1	89.5	96.2[a]	96.2	74.4	89.1[a]
Nonwhite	99.5	95.6	98.4[a]	96.1	83.9	92.2[a]
Hispanic	N/A	N/A	N/A	N/A	N/A	N/A
1976						
Total	99.4	91.9	97.0[a]	97.0[a]	78.3	90.8[a]
White	99.3	91.2	96.7[a]	96.8[a]	77.2	90.2[a]
Black	99.6	95.9	98.5[a]	98.1[a]	85.0	93.8[a]
Hispanic	99.5	92.7	97.7[a]	94.6[a]	74.9	87.1[a]
1980						
Total	99.4	94.2	97.3	97.0	82.8	91.1
White	99.4	93.6	97.0	96.7	81.5	90.4
Black	99.4	97.7	98.8	98.3	90.9	95.4
Hispanic	98.5	92.2	95.8	94.6	79.2	88.2
1981						
Total	99.2	95.7	97.8	97.2	84.7	92.0
White	99.2	95.4	97.7	96.9	83.4	91.3
Black	99.6	97.0	98.6	98.8	92.7	96.4
Hispanic	99.2	91.8	96.3	95.3	74.0	86.7
1984						
Total	99.7	96.8	98.5	98.0	87.1	93.4
White	99.6	96.5	98.3	97.7	85.2	92.4
Black	100.0	98.2	99.3	99.3	97.2	98.4
Hispanic	99.0	93.5	96.8	95.7	79.1	88.8

NOTE: Hispanic persons may be of any race and black and white totals may include Hispanics.

[a]Includes boys and girls 14 years of age.

SOURCE: Bureau of the Census, "Marital Status and Living Arrangements," *Current Population Reports,* Series P-20, 1960, 1970, 1973, 1975, 1976, 1981, 1984, 1985.

TABLE 2-3   School Enrollment Status of Adolescents by Age and Race, 1984 (in thousands)

| | | Enrolled in School | | Not Enrolled in School | | | |
| | | | | Total | | Not High-School Graduate | |
	Population	Number	Percentage	Number	Percentage	Number	Percentage
All Races							
14–15	7,390	7,229	97.8	161	2.2	157	2.1
16–17	7,173	6,564	91.5	609	8.5	485	6.8
18–19	7,428	3,724	50.1	3,704	49.9	2,575	15.2
White							
14–15	6,057	5,924	97.8	133	2.2	129	2.1
16–17	5,909	5,391	91.2	518	8.8	421	7.1
18–19	6,139	3,135	51.1	3,004	48.9	913	14.9
Black							
14–15	1,077	1,055	97.9	22	2.1	22	2.1
16–17	1,061	981	92.4	80	7.6	55	5.2
18–19	1,092	483	44.3	609	55.7	186	17.0
Hispanic							
14–15	539	512	94.9	27	5.1	27	5.1
16–17	540	463	85.7	77	14.3	71	13.2
18–19	561	224	39.9	337	60.1	146	26.1

NOTE: Hispanic persons may be of any race, and black and white totals may include Hispanics.

SOURCE: Bureau of Census, "School Enrollment—Social and Economic Characteristics of Students: October 1984," *Current Population Reports*, Series P-20, No. 404, November 1985.

Employment

Approximately 7.8 million teenagers ages 16–19 reported that they were in the civilian labor force in July 1985. Approximately 6.3 million were employed either part or full time, despite the fact that many of them were also enrolled in school. Another 1.5 million were unemployed, because they either could not find a job or were not looking. Forty-eight percent of white teenagers ages 16–19 were employed compared with 25 percent of blacks. Unemployment (seasonally adjusted) was significantly greater among black teenagers than among white teenagers, 41 percent compared with 16 percent, and it was slightly higher for males of both races than for females (Table 2-4). Data on Hispanic employment and unemployment status are not published by age category.

TABLE 2-4   Employment Status by Race, Sex, and Age, 1984–1985 (seasonally adjusted, in thousands)

	1984	1985
Whites ages 16–19		
Civilian labor force	6,952	6,852
participation rate	57.5	57.7
Employed	5,893	5,733
Employment-population ratio	48.7	48.3
Unemployed	1,059	1,119
Unemployment rate	15.2	16.3
Men	15.2	17.5
Women	14.3	15.0
Blacks ages 16–19		
Civilian labor force	849	915
participation rate	39.4	42.4
Employed	490	537
Employment-population ratio	22.7	24.9
Unemployed	359	378
Unemployment rate	42.3	41.3
Men	42.3	43.3
Women	42.2	39.0

NOTE: Hispanic breakdowns not available for the years presented.

SOURCE: U.S. Department of Labor, "The Employment Situation: July 1985," *News,* U.S. Department of Labor 85-304, August 2, 1985.

THE POPULATION AT RISK OF PREGNANCY

Estimates of the adolescent population at risk of pregnancy depend on information concerning fecundity among adolescent females and sexual activity and contraceptive use among both males and females.

Fecundity

The Second National Health and Nutrition Examination Survey, 1976–1980, shows that more than 75 percent of adolescent females have started menstruation by age 13 and 96 percent have begun by age 15. The mean age of menarche differs slightly by race: for blacks the mean age is 12.5 years, for whites it is 12.7 years; the difference is not statistically significant (see Vol. II:appendix tables, section on changing contexts).

Sexual Activity

Less than half of all unmarried teenage girls in the United States are sexually active (i.e., have experienced coitus at least once); between 1971 and 1979, however, there was a dramatic increase in nonmarital sexual activity among 15- to 19-year-old females. As Figure 2-1 shows, during this period the proportion of unmarried girls in this age group who had ever had intercourse increased from 28 to 46 percent. Between 1979 and 1982 there was a slight decline, to 42 percent, in the proportion of those girls who were sexually active. (This may not represent a statistically significant reduction, and it is based on comparisons of data from different surveys.) Despite the decline (or leveling off), rates of sexual activity among unmarried teenage girls appear to be substantially higher than they were in 1971 (Table 2-5).

Throughout this period, blacks have had significantly higher levels of sexual intercourse outside marriage than whites. In 1982, nearly 53 percent of black girls ages 15–19 had had intercourse, compared with about 40 percent of whites. However, the proportion of sexually active white teenage girls increased steadily between 1971 and 1979 and then declined very slightly in the early 1980s. In contrast, levels of sexual activity among black girls rose sharply between 1971 and 1976, remained virtually unchanged between 1976 and 1979, and then declined substantially between 1979 and 1982. In 1982, the 13 percent difference between blacks and whites in levels of nonmarital sexual intercourse was

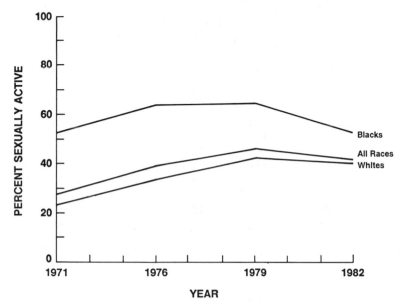

FIGURE 2-1 Sexual activity of adolescent girls ages 15–19, 1971–1982. Sources: M. Zelnik and J.F. Kantner (1980); W. F. Pratt (1984); unpublished tabulations, 1984.

the lowest it has ever been since such data were made available, and significantly less than the 31 percent difference reported in 1976. The apparent decline in sexual activity among blacks is primarily responsible for the overall decline during the early 1980s in the proportion of unmarried adolescent girls who had ever had intercourse (Table 2-6).

Data concerning trends in sexual activity among unmarried Hispanic adolescent girls are unavailable. Nevertheless, on the basis of estimates from the 1982 National Survey of Family Growth, it appears that levels of premarital sexual activity among Hispanic teenagers are closer to the level for whites than for blacks (see Vol. II:appendix tables, section on adolescent sexual activity).

By age 20, most unmarried young men and women are sexually active: over 80 percent of males and over 70 percent of females report that they have had intercourse at least once. With each successive year of age, a greater proportion of adolescents are sexually experienced. While only 5 percent of teenage girls and 17 percent of teenage boys report having had intercourse by their fifteenth birthday, 44 percent of girls and 64 percent of boys report that they were sexually active by their eigh-

TABLE 2-5   Percentage Never-Married Girls Ages 15–19 Living in
Metropolitan Areas Experiencing Sexual Intercourse, 1971–1982

Race and Age	1982	1979	1976	1971	Percent Change 1971–1982
All races[a]	42.2	46.0	39.2	27.6	52.9
15	17.8	22.5	18.6	14.4	23.6
16	28.1	37.8	28.9	20.9	34.4
17	41.0	48.5	42.9	26.1	57.0
18	52.7	56.9	51.4	39.7	32.7
19	61.7	69.0	59.5	46.4	33.0
White	40.3	42.3	33.6	23.2	73.7
15	17.3	18.3	13.8	11.3	53.1
16	26.9	35.4	23.7	17.0	58.0
17	39.5	44.1	36.1	20.2	95.5
18	48.6	52.6	46.0	35.6	36.5
19	59.3	64.9	53.6	40.7	45.7
Black	52.9	64.8	64.3	52.4	1.0
15	23.2	41.1	38.9	31.2	−15.6
16	36.3	50.4	55.1	44.4	−18.2
17	46.7	73.3	71.0	58.9	−20.7
18	75.7	76.3	76.2	60.2	25.7
19	78.0	88.5	83.9	78.3	−0.4

[a]Includes blacks, whites, and other races.

SOURCES: M. Zelnik and J.F. Kantner, 1980, "Sexual Activity, Contraceptive Use and Pregnancy Among Metropolitan-Area Teenagers: 1971–1979," *Family Planning Perspectives* 12(5), September/October: W. F. Pratt, 1984, NCHS National Survey of Family Growth, 1982, Cycle III; unpublished tabulations, 1984.

teenth birthday. Boys appear to initiate sexual activity earlier than girls but, by the later teenage years (18–19), the proportion of girls who report having had intercourse more closely approaches that of boys. Blacks (especially males) appear to initiate sexual activity earlier than whites, and at every age blacks are more likely than whites or Hispanics to be sexually active. Race differences in the proportion who are sexually active are especially pronounced among younger teenagers (Table 2-6).

Despite the increased proportion of teenagers who are sexually active, many have intercourse infrequently. Data from the National Survey of Young Women (Vol. II:appendix tables, section on adolescent sexual activity) indicate that in 1979 nearly a quarter of sexually active girls ages 15–19 had had intercourse only once or twice during the previous month. Over 40 percent reported that they had not had intercourse at all

TABLE 2-6   Cumulative Sexual Activity by Age of Initiation and Sex for the National Longitudinal Survey of Youth

Age	Cumulative Percentage Sexually Active	
	Boys	Girls
Total Sample (N = 4,657 boys, 4,648 girls)		
15	16.6	5.4
16	28.7	12.6
17	47.9	27.1
18	64.0	44.0
19	77.6	62.9
20	83.0	73.6
White (N = 2,828 boys, 2,788 girls)		
15	12.1	4.7
16	23.3	11.3
17	42.8	25.2
18	60.1	41.6
19	75.0	60.8
20	81.1	72.0
Black (N = 1,146 boys, 1,157 girls)		
15	42.4	9.7
16	59.6	20.1
17	77.3	39.5
18	85.6	59.4
19	92.2	77.0
20	93.9	84.7
Hispanic (N = 683 boys, 703 girls)		
15	19.3	4.3
16	32.0	11.2
17	49.7	23.7
18	67.1	40.2
19	78.5	58.6
20	84.2	69.5

NOTES: Sample is limited to respondents age 20 and over at 1983 survey date. Percentages reference birthday for specified ages, e.g., 15 means by fifteenth birthday or end of age 14.

Hispanics may be of any race, and black and white totals may include Hispanics.

SOURCE: Special tabulations from the National Longitudinal Survey of Youth, 1983, Center for Human Resource Research, Ohio State University.

during that period of time. Data from the 1982 National Survey of Family Growth show that 18 percent of unmarried, sexually active teenage girls had not had intercourse in the three months prior to the interview (Vol. II:appendix tables, section on adolescent sexual activity). Although the proportion of sexually experienced girls is higher at every age for blacks than for whites and the average age of initiation of sexual activity is younger for blacks, black girls appear to have intercourse somewhat less frequently than white girls (Zelnik, 1983).

Data from the 1982 National Longitudinal Survey of Youth show that adolescents from families of lower socioeconomic status tend to initiate sexual activity at earlier ages. One measure of family background that is available for nearly all teenagers and seems to be reliably reported by young people is their mother's level of schooling. When young people are differentiated by their mother's educational attainment, clear differences emerge among all sex and race groups. Teenagers with well-educated mothers are more likely to postpone initiation of sexual activity. Among boys, the percentage having had intercourse by age 18 increases from 56 to 62 to 72 as the mother's education declines from a level beyond high school, to the level of high school graduate, to a lower level. Among females, the comparable proportions are 34, 41, and 54 percent (Table 2-7). Nevertheless, the incidence of premarital sexual activity remains higher among blacks at all ages, even when mother's educational attainment is controlled. It is, of course, possible that the average education of the mothers of white teenagers is relatively high, even in a sample limited to those mothers who did not go beyond high school. However, when black teenagers whose mothers completed high school or more are compared with white teenagers whose mothers completed only high school and went no further, levels of sexual activity are still higher among blacks, both male and female, at all ages (Vol. II: appendix tables, section on adolescent sexual activity).

School dropout rates are another relevant indicator of social and economic disadvantage in which race differences are tested. In general, the proportion of sexually active teenagers is higher among those enrolled in schools with high dropout rates (more than 10 percent) than among those in schools with low dropout rates (less than 10 percent). The difference is greatest for black females under age 18: 62 percent of black girls in schools with high dropout rates were found to be sexually active compared with 49 percent of those in schools with low dropout rates. Among black males and among Hispanics of both sexes, school

TABLE 2-7 Cumulative Sexual Activity Estimates by Age, Race and Ethnicity, Mother's Educational Level, and High School Dropout Rate, 1982

	Percentage Sexually Active by Age 18				Percentage Sexually Active by Age 20			
	Total	White	Black	Hispanic	Total	White	Black	Hispanic
All teenagers								
Boys	64.0	60.1	85.6	67.1	83.0	81.1	93.9	84.2
Girls	44.0	41.6	59.4	40.2	73.6	72.0	84.7	69.5
Mother's educational level								
Boys								
Dropout	72.4	68.6	87.7	66.9	87.6	85.7	94.5	86.0
Graduate	61.8	58.8	85.1	65.5	82.8	91.5	94.0	79.9
Education beyond high school	55.6	52.9	—	—	76.5	74.9	—	—
Girls								
Dropout	53.7	53.5	63.2	39.0	81.3	82.0	87.2	68.0
Graduate	40.5	39.1	53.9	38.9	73.4	72.4	80.6	70.8
Education beyond high school	34.1	31.9	—	—	60.8	59.0	—	—
Dropout rate[a]								
Boys								
Low (<10%)	59.1	56.6	83.9	64.7	81.0	79.7	92.8	84.2
High (≥10%)	65.8	61.9	86.1	63.4	82.8	80.7	94.4	80.3
Girls								
Low (<10%)	36.5	35.4	48.8	34.3	68.3	67.5	78.5	63.5
High (≥10%)	45.1	41.9	62.3	36.4	75.4	73.8	86.3	66.3

NOTES: Sample is limited to respondents age 20 and over at 1983 survey date. Percentages reference birthday for specified ages, e.g., 18 means by birthday or by end of 17. Hispanics may be of any race, and whites and blacks may include Hispanics.

[a]The dropout rate is the number of students dropping out of high school per 100 students who began high school in 1979 for the school attended by the respondents.

SOURCE: Special tabulations from the National Longitudinal Survey of Youth, 1983, Center for Human Resource Research, Ohio State University.

dropout rate appears unrelated to sexual activity. Regardless of school dropout rate, however, black males and females were more likely to be sexually active than whites and Hispanics at all ages (Table 2-7).

Although underreporting is an issue when sensitive behaviors are addressed in an interview situation, several survey sources support the same conclusions: sexual activity among unmarried teenagers increased significantly during the 1970s and declined somewhat in the early 1980s. It remains higher among males, among blacks, among teenagers in schools with high dropout rates, and among economically disadvantaged teenagers.

Contraceptive Use

Contraceptive use among unmarried, sexually active, adolescent girls increased steadily during the 1970s and then leveled off in the early 1980s. In 1982, approximately 85 percent of sexually active teenagers ages 15–19 reported that they had ever used a contraceptive method, compared with approximately 66 percent in 1976, and nearly 73 percent in 1979. Moreover, the proportion who reported that they never used any method declined from more than 35 percent in 1976 to less than 15 percent in 1982. Blacks were more likely to report that they had never used birth control in all survey years. Despite the increased use of contraception by sexually active teenagers during the 1970s, adolescents still appear to be inconsistent users, with nearly 40 percent reporting that they use contraception only "sometimes" (Table 2-8).

Adolescents' use of the most effective medical methods, primarily contraceptive pills but also intrauterine devices (IUD), increased substantially during the early 1970s. Between 1976 and 1979, pill use declined, presumably in response to publicity about the dangers of oral contraceptives, and then increased again in the early 1980s. Use of the least effective method, withdrawal, declined slightly in the early 1970s but increased by 46 percent between 1976 and 1979. Use of other, less effective methods, including the diaphragm and foam, has increased steadily since the mid-1970s. Condom use, which decreased substantially in the early 1970s, increased somewhat during the late 1970s and subsequently leveled off. Among sexually active teenage girls who reported contraceptive use at last intercourse, approximately 62 percent took birth control pills, approximately 22 percent had partners who used condoms, and 6 percent used diaphragms (Bachrach and Mosher, 1984).

TABLE 2-8 Percentage Distribution of Sexually Active Girls Ages 15–19 by Contraceptive Use

Contraceptive Use	1982[a]			1979[b]			1976[b]		
	Total (N = 945)	White (N = 579)	Black (N = 342)	Total (N = 937)	White (N = 478)	Black (N = 459)	Total (N = 724)	White (N = 349)	Black (N = 375)
Always used	48.2	52.1	36.0	34.2	35.0	31.2	28.7	28.9	28.0
Used at first intercourse but not always				14.7	16.1	9.7	9.5	10.1	8.1
Did not use at first intercourse but used at some time	37.2	34.9	43.7	24.5	24.9	23.3	26.3	28.6	20.2
Never used	14.6	13.0	20.3	26.6	24.0	35.9	35.5	32.4	43.7
Total	100.0	100.0	100.0	100.0	100.0	100.0	100.0	100.0	100.0

[a]All women 15–19 sexually active, including married women.
[b]Premaritally sexually active women 15–19; contraceptive use refers to use prior to pregnancy, marriage, or time of survey, whichever event was earliest.

SOURCE: Unpublished tabulations from the 1982 National Survey of Family Growth; M. Zelnik and J.F. Kanter, 1980, "Sexual Activity, Contraceptive Use, and Pregnancy Among Metropolitan-Area Teenagers: 1971–1976," *Family Planning Perspectives* 12(5), September/October.

Although black adolescent girls were less likely to use contraception than whites, in 1979 they were more than twice as likely to use a medical method, primarily the pill, if they used anything at all. White teenagers were more than three times as likely as blacks to use withdrawal as a primary means of birth control.

According to data from the 1982 National Survey of Family Growth, teenagers who were older at first intercourse (18–19) were more likely to practice contraception than those under 18, and they were more likely to use a more reliable medical method. Teenagers under 18 were more likely to use withdrawal, douche, or rhythm at first intercourse (Figure 2-2).

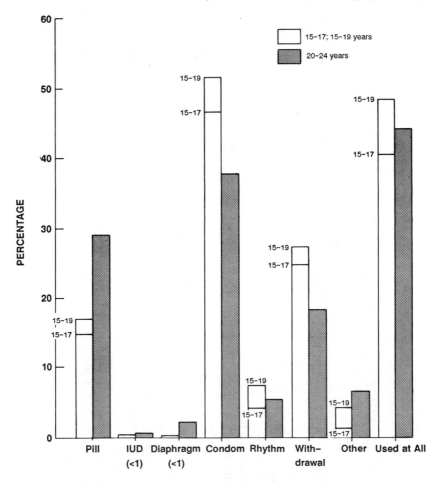

FIGURE 2-2 Contraceptive method used at first intercourse (users only), 1982. Source: W. F. Pratt et al. (1984).

According to data from the Kantner-Zelnik survey, the same appears to be true for males, with 59 percent of those over age 18 when they initiated sexual activity reporting the use of some method at first intercourse, compared with 49 percent of 15- to 17-year-olds and 34 percent of those under age 15 (Table 2-9).

In general, reported use of contraception at first intercourse increased during the 1970s, primarily because of the growing use of male methods (i.e., condom, withdrawal). Available data suggest that while many teenage girls who use contraception rely on male methods at the initiation of sexual intercourse, they later switch to more effective medical methods. Clearly, however, many teenagers fail to use any contraception at first intercourse, and the average delay between first intercourse and first use of a prescription method is about one year (Zelnik et al., 1984).

The probability of pregnancy is significantly affected by the use of contraception: within two years of initiating intercourse, nearly 50 percent of those who used no contraception became pregnant (Vol. II:appendix tables, section on premarital pregnancy). Within two years of initiating contraception, approximately 25 percent of those who used a nonmedical method and nearly 15 percent of those who used a medical method became pregnant (see Vol. II:appendix tables, section on premarital pregnancy).

TABLE 2-9 Use of Contraceptive at First Intercourse, 1979

Age at First Intercourse	Percentage Who Used Any Method			Percentage Who Used Prescription Method		
	Total	White	Black	Total	White	Black
Girls (15–19)	48.9	51.2	40.8	19.9	15.3	40.7
<15	31.0	33.2	26.9	10.2	4.7	22.9
15–17	52.1	52.9	48.8	18.8	12.1	48.0
≥18	62.3	63.7	47.7	29.4	28.9	*
Boys (17–21)	44.1	46.0	34.0	22.0	21.6	25.1
<17	34.0	36.4	27.8	16.8	15.6	20.8
18–20	48.5	48.9	44.7	20.5	19.2	34.1
≥21	59.1	59.4	*	38.3	40.0	*

NOTE: Prescription method includes the contraceptive pill, the IUD, and the diaphragm.

*Fewer than 20 cases; in all others, N > 30.

SOURCE: M. Zelnik and F. Shah, 1983, "First Intercourse Among Young Americans," *Family Planning Perspectives* 15(2). Reprinted by permission.

Estimating the Population at Risk of Pregnancy

A combination of several factors affects the probability of nonmarital pregnancy among adolescent girls: the proportion of the female adolescent population who are fertile, the increase in sexual activity among the unmarried, the use of contraception among those who are sexually active, and the effectiveness of the contraceptive methods employed. The base for this estimate is the size of the female adolescent population.

The result of an increased population of teenagers in the mid-1970s, fewer of whom were married and more of whom were sexually active, was a substantial increase in the number of adolescents likely to experience a nonmarital pregnancy. Since the late 1970s, the declining teenage population and the leveling off of sexual activity among this age group have produced a slight decrease in the number at risk. However, as shown in the appendix tables, section on adolescent sexual activity (Vol. II), comparing 1982 with 1971, the number of unmarried adolescent girls ages 18–19 who had had sexual intercourse rose from 1.4 million to 2.3 million, a 64 percent increase. Among younger teenagers 15–17, the increase was also great. In 1982, 1.5 million girls in this age group were sexually active compared with 1.0 million in 1971, a 50 percent increase. (These estimates are based on calculations using data from the 1971 Kantner-Zelnik survey and the 1982 National Survey of Family Growth.)

While there was some increase in contraceptive use during the 1970s and early 1980s, there was also an increase in the proportion of unmarried teenagers having intercourse. In particular, the proportion of those under 18 who are likely to become pregnant is significantly greater, largely because so many more young teenagers are sexually active, and young teenagers are less likely to use any contraceptive method, less likely to use the most reliable methods, and more likely to be inconsistent users.

Black teenagers are at greater risk of nonmarital pregnancy than whites at all ages because proportionately more blacks are sexually active, fewer are married, and they are less likely to practice contraception. Because black teenagers tend to become sexually active earlier than whites, and younger teenagers tend to be less diligent contraceptors than older teenagers, the probability of pregnancy is even higher among young black girls.

Using data from several sources (i.e., vital statistics, Current Population Surveys, the National Survey of Family Growth, and the Kantner-Zelnik surveys), Forrest (1986) estimates that 43 percent of all adolescent girls regardless of marital status will become pregnant at least once before their twentieth birthday, a slight increase in the probability of pregnancy since 1976. This figure includes 40 percent of white teenagers and 63 percent of black teenagers (Table 2-10).

PREGNANCY AND ITS RESOLUTION

Sexual activity does not always lead to pregnancy. Consistent use of contraception significantly reduces the probability of conception. However, many teenagers, especially blacks and very young teenagers, often do not use any form of birth control; if they do, they tend to be inconsistent or ineffective users. When a nonmarital pregnancy occurs, there are several alternatives for resolution, including abortion, marriage, adoption, and childbearing outside marriage.

Pregnancy

Although data for the early 1970s are incomplete and estimates vary, the number of adolescent pregnancies appears to have increased somewhat during the 1970s, from an estimated 950,000 in 1972 to 1,142,000 in 1978. On the whole, the rise in the pregnancy rate, from 94 per 1,000 women to 105 per 1,000, was modest compared with the rise in sexual activity during this period, largely because of increased use of contracep-

TABLE 2-10   Proportion of Girls Ever Pregnant Before Age 20, 1976 and 1981

	Percentage Experiencing First Pregnancy—	
	By Age 18	By Age 20
Total (1976)	23.7	41.1
Total (1981)	23.9	43.5
White	20.5	39.7
Black	40.7	63.1

SOURCE: Calculated by J.D. Forrest, July 1986. Derived from national surveys, Vital Statistics, and census data (see tables in the Statistical Appendix, section on premarital pregnancy, in Vol. II for a complete listing of sources).

tion. Since the late 1970s, the declining adolescent population has caused the estimated number of pregnancies to decline to 1,005,000 in 1984, although the pregnancy rate continued to climb to 109 per 1,000 women. Adjusting for sexual activity, however, the pregnancy rate has declined. In 1972, the pregnancy rate among sexually active teenagers was 272 per 1,000 women ages 15–19. It has declined to an estimated 233 per 1,000 women in 1984. This decline in the rate of pregnancy among sexually active teenagers at the same time that the rate was increasing among all adolescent girls is attributable to greater use of contraception (Table 2-11).

Data on male fertility provided by young men are scarce and tend to be less reliable than data on female fertility provided by young women. For this reason we are unable to present information on male fertility, but we do highlight the need for more and better data.

Very few pregnant teenage girls report that they intended to become pregnant, especially if they are unmarried. Data from the 1979 Kantner-Zelnik survey indicate that 82 percent of adolescent girls 15–19 who had a nonmarital pregnancy in 1978 did not intend to become pregnant, and nearly 31 percent of those who became pregnant but were not trying to conceive reported that they were using contraception. Black girls who reported becoming pregnant were only slightly less likely than white girls to say the pregnancy was unintended (to some extent because abortions are underreported): 79 percent compared with 84 percent among sexually active, metropolitan-area, 15- to 19-year-old girls (Table 2-12). Data concerning pregnancy intention are not available for Hispanics. The younger the teenager, the more likely that her pregnancy was unintended. Of the 30,000 pregnancies that occurred among girls under 15 in 1979, virtually none was intended, and 87 percent of the 429,000 pregnancies among girls 15–17 were unintended. Even among the 684,000 girls ages 18–19 who conceived in that year, 65 percent had not intended to become pregnant (Alan Guttmacher Institute, 1981). It is important to note, however, that these estimates probably understate the incidence of unintended pregnancy among adolescents because they are based on data from surveys in which abortions are underreported. On the basis of actual numbers of abortions and assuming that all abortions were terminations of unintended pregnancies, about 82 percent of abortions and births to adolescents are the result of unintended pregnancies (Alan Guttmacher Institute, in press).

Births

The increased number of adolescent pregnancies during the 1970s has not meant an increase in the number of births to teenagers. In fact, the number of births to teenagers of all ages declined between 1970 and 1984. Overall the decline was approximately 20 percent, but it was somewhat greater for the 18–19 age group (21 percent) than for the 15–17 age group (16 percent). Births to teenagers under 15 also declined, but the number of children born to mothers in this age group has always been relatively small: less than one-half of 1 percent of females ages 10–14 have given birth in any year since 1970 (Figure 2-3). Births to both white and black teenagers declined during this period, although the relative declines differed somewhat by age. Declines in births to teenagers ages 18–19 were greater among whites, 22 percent compared with 14 percent; declines in births to those under age 18 were greater among blacks, 20 percent compared with 16 percent (Vol. II:appendix tables, section on births). The decreasing size of the adolescent population since 1977 and the increased use of contraception have contributed to this decline in the number of births to teenagers. In addition, the difference is due to increased numbers of abortions in the late 1970s.

During the period 1975–1984, there was a steady reduction in the proportion of all births occurring to teenagers, just as childbearing by women age 30 and older became more prevalent. In 1984, 13 percent of all births were to women under age 20, the lowest proportion measured in the United States since 1957. Over the past decade, the birth rate for 15- to 19-year-olds dropped 8 percent to its lowest level since the 1940s, while the rate for women in their early thirties rose 27 percent and for women age 35–39 increased 17 percent (National Center for Health Statistics, 1986).

Information on births to Hispanic mothers was available for the first time in 1978, when 17 states included an item on the ethnic origin of mothers and fathers on birth certificates. In 1984, this information was available from 23 states and the District of Columbia. While these jurisdictions have the highest concentrations of Hispanic residents, estimates of Hispanic births available from the vital statistics system are still somewhat incomplete. In 1984, there were an estimated 59,000 births to Hispanic adolescents in the United States. Approximately 95 percent of these were to whites, less than 4 percent were to blacks, and other races

TABLE 2-11 Estimated Pregnancies and Pregnancy Outcomes, 1972–1984

	Pregnancies		Births		Abortions		Estimated Miscarriages	
	Number	Rate[a]	Number	Percentage of Pregnancies	Number	Percentage of Pregnancies	Number	Percentage of Pregnancies
1984								
<15	—		9,965		—		—	
15–17	420,713		166,744	39.6	200,564[c]	47.7	53,405	12.7
18–19	584,146		302,938	51.9	200,564[c]	34.3	80,644	13.8
Total <20	1,004,859	109 (233)[b]	469,682	46.7	401,128	40.0	134,049	13.3
1982								
<15	27,777		9,773	35.2	14,590	52.5	3,414	12.3
15–17	402,645		181,162	45.0	168,410	41.8	53,073	13.2
18–19	674,478		332,596	49.3	250,330	37.1	91,552	13.6
Total <20	1,104,900	110 (235)[b]	523,531	47.4	433,330	39.2	148,039	13.4
1978								
<15	29,547		10,772	36.5	15,110	51.1	3,665	12.4
15–17	429,370		202,661	47.2	169,270	39.4	57,459	13.4
18–19	683,367		340,746	49.9	249,520	36.5	93,101	13.6

Total <20	1,142,284	105 (245)[b]	554,179	49.7	433,900	38.9	154,225	13.8
1974								
<15	29,797		12,529	42.0	13,420	45.0	3,848	13.0
15–17	434,868		234,117	53.8	139,850[c]	32.2	60,824	14.0
18–19	587,361		361,272	61.5	139,850[c]	23.8	86,239	14.7
Total <20	1,052,026	99 (253)[b]	607,918	57.8	293,120	27.9	150,911	14.3
1972								
<15	—		12,082	—	—	—	—	—
15–17	389,019		236,641	60.8	95,500[c]	24.6	56,878	14.6
18–19	560,617		379,639	67.7	95,500[c]	17.0	85,478	15.3
Total <20	949,636	94 (272)[b]	628,362	66.2	191,000	20.1	142,356	15.0

[a]Pregnancy rates per 1,000 women ages 15–19 (derived by Sandra Hofferth).

[b]Pregnancy rates per 1,000 sexually active women ages 15–19 (derived by Sandra Hofferth).

[c]Estimated because data for women ages 15–17 and 18–19 were not available separately.

SOURCES: Births: National Center for Health Statistics, Vital Statistics of the United States, annual volumes; Advance Report of Final Natality Statistics 1982, *Monthly Vital Statistics Report* 33(6), 1984; pregnancies, abortions, miscarriages: J.D. Forrest, Alan Guttmacher Institute (published, unpublished, and derived data), 1984.

TABLE 2-12 Percentage Distributions of Women Ages 15–19 Who Ever Experienced a Premarital First Pregnancy and Were Unmarried at the Time of Resolution (metropolitan-area teenagers)

Pregnancy Intention and Contraceptive Use	1979			1976			1971		
	Total	White	Black	Total	White	Black	Total	White	Black
Pregnancy intention	(N = 312)	(N = 115)	(N = 197)	(N = 200)	(N = 59)	(N = 141)	(N = 249)	(N = 42)	(N = 207)
Wanted	18.0	16.4	20.9	24.6	21.9	28.0	24.2	23.6	24.6
Not wanted	82.0	83.6	79.1	75.4	78.1	72.0	75.8	76.4	75.4
Of those who did not want pregnancy—	(N = 246)	(N = 94)	(N = 152)	(N = 147)	(N = 46)	(N = 101)	(N = 183)	(N = 32)	(N = 151)
Used contraception	31.5	36.1	22.0	20.6	27.1	11.5	8.6	9.2	8.3
Did not use contraception	68.5	63.9	78.0	79.4	72.9	88.5	91.4	90.6	91.7
Total	100.0	100.0	100.0	100.0	100.0	100.0	100.0	100.0	100.0

NOTE: Includes respondents pregnant at time of interview.

SOURCE: M. Zelnik and J.F. Kantner, 1980, "Sexual Activity, Contraceptive Use and Pregnancy Among Metropolitan-Area Teenagers: 1971–1979," *Family Planning Perspectives* 12(5): Table 6, September/October. Reprinted by permission.

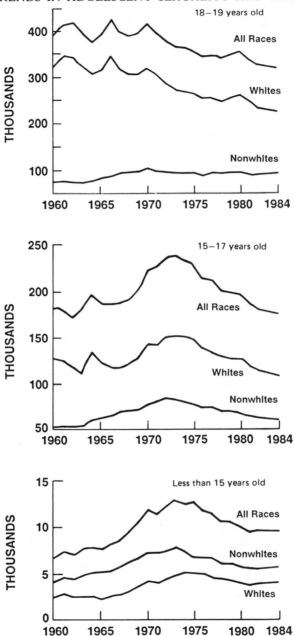

FIGURE 2-3 Total births to girls under age 20 by race, 1960–1984. Source: National Center for Health Statistics, Vital Statistics of the United States, annual volumes.

accounted for the remainder. The fertility of Hispanic adolescents is higher than that of non-Hispanic adolescents: approximately 17 percent of all Hispanic births were to women under age 20; 12.5 percent of non-Hispanic births are to women under age 20. Puerto Rican teenagers had proportionately more births in 1984 than other Hispanic or non-Hispanic teenagers (Table 2-13). Data concerning birth rates for Hispanic teenagers are not yet available for 1985.

Abortion

In 1971, teenagers ages 15–19 obtained just over 150,000 legal abortions. By 1973, the year the Supreme Court made abortion legal nationwide, the number had risen to 280,000. In 1982, the most recent year for which such data are available, an estimated 443,300 abortions were obtained by women under 20. About 30 percent of all abortions performed in the United States each year involve teenagers. Although the proportion of adolescent pregnancies terminated by induced abortion rose substantially after nationwide legalization in 1973, it appears to have stabilized during the late 1970s. An estimated 40 percent of all pregnancies of girls ages 15–19 end in abortion; among girls under 15, the number of abortions surpassed the number of births as early as 1974, and there are now 1.4 abortions for every live birth among girls in this age group (Table 2-11).

Black teenagers are slightly less likely to terminate an unintended pregnancy by abortion than are white teenagers. Yet because unintended pregnancies are far more prevalent among blacks, their abortion rates in 1981 were nearly twice as high as those of whites for girls ages 15–19: 68.9 per 1,000 women compared with 35.8 per 1,000. For girls under 15, the abortion rate for blacks was five times as high as that for whites: 26.6 per 1,000 compared with 4.5 per 1,000 (Table 2-14). Furthermore, as shown in the appendix tables, section on abortion, in Vol. II, the proportion of blacks obtaining abortions increased steadily throughout the 1970s, so that by 1978 black adolescent girls were three times as likely to obtain an abortion to resolve a nonmarital pregnancy as in 1971 (Ezzard et al., 1982). More recent data on abortions by age and race are unavailable; no data are available on abortions among Hispanic adolescents.

Since 1980 there appears to have been a slight decline in abortion (Vol. II:appendix tables, section on abortion). To some extent, it may reflect

TABLE 2-13 Number and Percentage of Live Births by Age and Hispanic Origin of Mother, 1984

| Age of Mother | All Origins | Mother of Hispanic Origin | | | | | | Non-Hispanic | Not Stated |
		Total	Mexican	Puerto Rican	Cuban	Central and South American	Other		
All ages	2,230,815	346,986	225,767	34,219	9,477	36,401	41,122	1,791,949	91,880
	(100.0)	(100.0)	(100.0)	(100.0)	(100.0)	(100.0)	(100.0)	(100.0)	(100.0)
Under 15	6,318	1,242	860	179	9	34	160	4,830	246
	(0.3)	(0.4)	(0.4)	(0.5)	(0.1)	(0.1)	(0.4)	(0.3)	(0.3)
15–19 years	288,346	57,717	39,712	7,112	766	2,930	7,197	218,930	11,699
	(12.9)	(16.6)	(17.6)	(20.8)	(8.1)	(8.0)	(17.5)	(12.2)	(12.7)
15–17 years	103,114	21,934	15,410	2,735	226	837	2,726	77,010	4,170
	(4.6)	(6.3)	(6.8)	(8.0)	(2.4)	(2.3)	(6.6)	(4.3)	(4.5)
18–19 years	185,232	35,783	24,302	4,377	540	2,093	4,471	141,920	7,529
	(8.3)	(10.3)	(9.8)	(12.8)	(5.7)	(5.7)	(10.9)	(7.9)	(8.2)

NOTE: Data are for births to all residents of the 23 states and the District of Columbia reporting ethnic of Hispanic origin, regardless of where the births occurred. Births occuring in nonreporting states to residents of the reporting states are included in the "not stated" category. Percentages do not total 100.0 because births to women ages 20 and over are not shown.

SOURCE: Unpublished tabulations from the National Center for Health Statistics, Division of Vital Statistics, January 27, 1986.

TABLE 2-14 Births and Estimated Abortions by Race, Age, and Percentage of Estimated Pregnancies, 1981

	Births		Estimated Abortions		Percentage of Estimated Total Pregnancies[b]	
	Number	Rate (per thousand)	Number	Rate (per thousand)	Births	Abortions
< 15[a]						
White	3,970	2.7	7,540	5.1	30.4	57.7
Black	5,425	20.2	7,240	27.0	37.5	50.0
15–19						
White	370,013	44.7	321,310	38.8	46.4	40.3
Black	143,278	96.9	97,930	66.3	51.2	35.0
15–17						
White	120,913	25.1	125,380	26.0	42.7	44.3
Black	61,850	70.4	45,280	51.5	49.9	36.5
18–19						
White	249,100	71.9	195,930	56.6	48.4	38.1
Black	81,428	135.9	52,650	87.9	52.3	33.8

[a]Numbers of births and abortions are for all girls younger than 15; the universe for the computation of rates and percentage of estimated total pregnancies is the number of 14-year-old girls.
[b]Percentages do not total 100 percent because of estimated miscarriages.

SOURCES: National Center for Health Statistics, 1983, Advance Report of Final Natality Statistics, 1981, *Monthly Vital Statistics Report* 32(9): Supplement; J.D. Forrest, personal communication.

the declining adolescent population and the decreasing number of teenage pregnancies; moreover, it mirrors a similar trend in abortions involving adult women.

Marriage Before Childbearing (Legitimation)

There have been important changes in the disposition of adolescent pregnancies that are carried to term: young women are significantly less likely to marry in order to legitimate their child's birth. In 1970, 30 percent of live births to women under age 20 occurred outside marriage. By 1984, the proportion had risen to 56 percent (Vol. II:appendix tables, section on births).

Among teenagers bearing children, there has been a decline in the proportion who marry between the conception and birth of their child, with a substantial difference between blacks and whites. During 1980–

1981, 28 percent of white and only 8 percent of black first births to adolescents were conceived outside marriage and born in marriage, compared with 37 percent and 15 percent, respectively, a decade earlier (Figure 2-4).

Older teenagers remained more likely than younger ones to marry to legitimate a birth. Between 1980 and 1984, on average, 26 percent of pregnant 15- to 17-year-olds married, compared with 35 percent of 18- to 19-year-olds. In contrast, 43 percent of pregnant 20- to 24-year-olds married to legitimate the birth of their child (personal communication with Martin O'Connell, Bureau of the Census; estimates based on data from the June 1985 Current Population Survey).

Adoption

Unfortunately, there is currently no national system for collecting information about women who carry their pregnancies to term and opt to relinquish their children for adoption. Therefore, precise estimates of the number and proportion of teenagers who choose this means of pregnancy resolution are impossible. Available agency data from selected states support survey evidence of a dramatic decline in adoption placements since the late 1960s; however, agency data do not take account of children placed through private adoption arrangements and therefore may underestimate to some extent the number of teens who relinquish their children. Despite the substantial proportion of teenage pregnancies and births that are unintended, in 1982 an estimated 93 percent of unmarried mothers ages 15–19—91 percent of whites and 95 percent of blacks—kept and raised their children (Bachrach, 1986). In some cases, especially among blacks, it appears that grandmothers, other relatives, or friends assumed responsibility for the child's care (Bachrach, 1986; Zelnik and Kantner, 1977). In contrast, available estimates for 1971 suggest that approximately 86 percent of mothers ages 15–19—72 percent of young white mothers and 92 percent of black mothers—kept and raised their children themselves (Table 2-15). Although substantial underreporting of adoption is likely, it appears that with the nationwide legalization of abortion, many adolescent girls experiencing an unintended nonmarital pregnancy elect to abort or to become single parents rather than carry to term and relinquish their children for adoption. Data concerning adoption of children born to Hispanic adolescent mothers are unavailable.

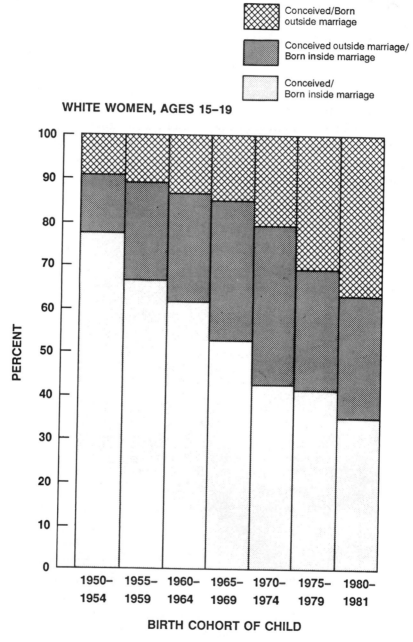

FIGURE 2-4   Firstborn children conceived either maritally or extramaritally to mothers ages 15–19. Source: From Table 6-1.

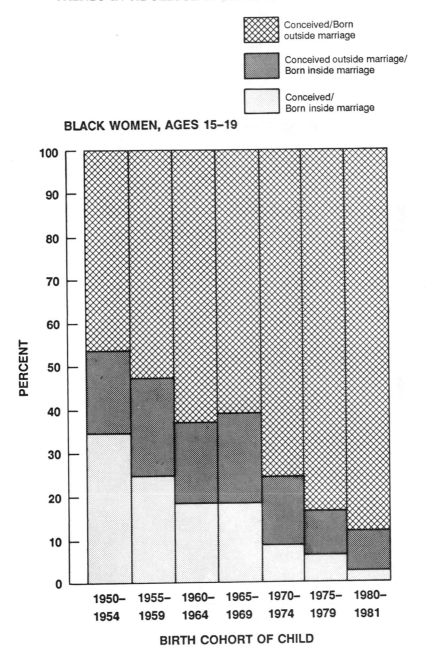

FIGURE 2-4 Continued.

TABLE 2-15 Disposition of First Births to Unmarried Mothers Ages 15–19 (percentage distribution)

Living Arrangements of Child	All Races			White and Other			Black		
	1982 (N = 133)	1976 (N = 148)	1971 (N = 259)	1982 (N = 50)	1976 (N = 25)	1971 (N = 39)	1982 (N = 83)	1976 (N = 123)	1971 (N = 220)
Total	100.0	100.0	100.0	100.0	100.0	100.0	100.0	100.0	100.0
In mother's household	92.6	93.3	85.6	91.1	87.2	72.2	94.7	96.8	92.4
With relatives or friends[a]	2.5	1.0	4.7	1.5	2.9	5.8	4.0	0.0	4.2
Adopted	4.6	2.6	7.6	7.4	7.0	18.4	0.7	0.0	2.0
No longer living	0.3	3.1	2.1	0.0	2.9	3.6	0.6	3.2	1.4

[a]"Friends" was a valid code in the 1971 and 1976 surveys but not in the 1982 survey.

SOURCE: C.A. Bachrach, 1986, "Adoption Plans, Adopted Children, and Adoptive Mothers," Journal of Marriage and the Family 48: 243–253, May. Reprinted by permission.

Nonmarital Childbearing

In the early 1980s, more than half of all births to adolescents occurred outside marriage, compared with only about one-third in 1970. In 1984, births to unmarried mothers under age 20 numbered more than 270,000; approximately 46 percent of them were to mothers under age 18 (Vol. II:appendix tables, section on births). Despite a decline in the number and rate of births to women in all adolescent age groups, rates of nonmarital childbearing increased steadily during the 1970s as rates of marital childbearing among teenagers decreased. However, nonmarital childbearing has also increased among adult women over the past decade and a half. As a result, births to unmarried teenagers now account for a smaller proportion of all nonmarital births, approximately one-third in 1984 compared with approximately one half in 1970 (Vol. II:appendix tables, section on births).

Trends in nonmarital childbearing among adolescents vary dramatically by race. Consistently, blacks have been significantly more likely to give birth outside marriage than whites. In 1984, the rate of nonmarital childbearing among blacks ages 15–19 was 4.5 times greater than the rate among whites—87.1 per 1,000 unmarried black women, compared with 19.0 per 1,000 unmarried white women. However, since 1970 there has been a sharp increase in the rate of unmarried parenthood among white teenagers and in the number of births to white girls: nonmarital birth rates for whites ages 15–19 rose by 74 percent between 1970 and 1984. It is this rise that explains the overall increase in births to unmarried teenagers, since the rate of black nonmarital childbearing among women under age 20 actually declined by 10 percent during this period (Table 2-16).

Hispanic teenagers are more likely than non-Hispanic whites but less likely than non-Hispanic blacks to give birth outside marriage. Approximately 45 percent of births to Hispanic women ages 15–19 were nonmarital births in 1984, compared with 34 percent of non-Hispanic white births and 87 percent of non-Hispanic black births (unpublished tabulations by the Division of Vital Statistics, National Center for Health Statistics, 1986).

Despite the substantial increase in unmarried parenthood among whites during the 1970s and the early 1980s, the proportion of all nonmarital births to teenage mothers (ages 15–19) remains significantly higher for blacks than for whites. In 1984, this proportion was more than twice as high for blacks as for whites—89 percent of live births to

TABLE 2-16 Birth Rates per 1,000 Unmarried Women, 1970–1984

Age Group and Race

Year	15–17			18–19			15–19			20–24		
	Total	White	Black	Total	White	Black	Total	White	Black	Total	White	Black
1984	21.9	13.5	66.8	43.0	27.6	116.2	30.2	19.0	87.1	43.2	27.8	110.7
1983	22.1	13.5	67.1	41.0	26.1	114.0	29.7	18.5	86.4	42.0	26.4	110.0
1982	21.5	12.9	67.6	40.2	25.1	115.8	28.9	17.7	87.0	41.4	25.7	110.2
1981	20.9	12.4	66.9	39.9	24.6	117.6	28.2	17.1	86.8	40.9	24.9	112.5
1980	20.6	11.8	69.6	39.0	23.6	120.2	27.6	16.2	89.2	40.9	24.4	115.1
1979	20.4	11.1	72.5	37.8	21.2	123.3	26.9	14.9	93.7	38.7	20.8	117.3
1978	19.5	10.5	70.3	35.7	19.5	124.3	25.4	13.8	90.3	36.1	18.5	114.2
1977	20.1	10.7	74.3	35.0	16.8	125.9	25.4	13.6	93.2	34.7	17.7	112.6
1976	19.3	9.9	74.6	32.5	17.0	121.6	24.0	12.4	91.6	32.2	16.0	109.3
1975	19.5	9.7	77.7	32.8	16.6	126.8	24.2	12.1	95.1	31.6	15.7	109.9
1974	19.0	8.9	79.4	31.4	15.4	124.9	23.2	11.1	95.1	30.9	15.2	111.2
1973	18.9	8.5	81.9	30.6	15.0	123.0	22.9	10.7	96.0	31.8	15.6	117.2
1972	18.6	8.1	82.9	31.0	15.1	129.8	22.9	10.5	98.8	33.4	16.7	122.0
1971	17.6	7.4	80.9	31.7	15.9	136.3	22.4	10.3	99.1	35.6	18.8	131.1
1970	17.1	7.5	77.9	32.9	17.6	136.4	22.4	10.9	96.9	38.4	22.5	131.5
Number change in rate 1970–1984	+4.8	+6.0	−11.1	+10.1	+10	−20.2	+7.8	+8.1	−9.8	+4.8	+5.3	−20.8
Percentage change in rate 1970–1984	+29.2	+80.0	−16.6	+23.5	+56.8	−14.8	+34.8	+74.3	−10.1	+12.5	+23.6	−15.8

NOTE: In 1980, a new estimation procedure was adopted; the table presents estimates for 1980 using the new procedure (see Source for explanation).

SOURCE: National Center for Health Statistics, 1986, Advance Report of Final Natality Statistics, 1984. Supplement to *Monthly Vital Statistics Report* 35(4) July:Table 19.

black women compared with 41.5 percent for white women (National Center for Health Statistics, 1986). Among Hispanic adolescents, the proportion of nonmarital births was 50.1 percent (unpublished tabulations by the Division of Vital Statistics, National Center for Health Statistics, 1986). In short, although white teenagers were more likely in 1984 to give birth outside marriage than they were in 1970, black teenagers were still at significantly greater risk than either whites or Hispanics of having a nonmarital birth.

Future Projections

What do these trends mean for the absolute numbers of children born to teenage mothers since 1970, and what do they suggest for adolescent childbearing into the 1990s? Over the past decade and a half, the annual number of children born to teenage mothers (regardless of marital status) dropped from 645,000 in 1970 to 479,600 in 1984. This reflects a decline both in the birth rate and, since 1976, in the size of the adolescent population. Congressional Budget Office analysts project that the total number of births to teenagers is likely to continue to decline somewhat for the next several years, as the number of adolescent girls continues to decline. Even if the adolescent birth rate remains at the 1984 level, the total number of births to teenage mothers would drop to 422,000 by 1992 (Levine and Adams, 1985). Future trends in nonmarital childbearing depend on individual decisions concerning marriage, which are more difficult to predict.

DATA ISSUES

Crucial to our understanding of adolescent pregnancy and childbearing is the availability of accurate data on the relevant issues. Without data, research cannot be conducted; with poor data, research conclusions may be misleading.

Data used in most studies of teenage childbearing come from one of three sources: surveys of individuals, government record systems, and information from service programs. Each type of data plays a different role and informs discussion from its particular perspective. When results obtained from several different types of data point toward the same conclusion, one can have particular confidence in that conclusion. Thus, though each type of data has a different contribution to make, all three types are important. Each is discussed in this section in turn.

The most complete data available on adolescent parenthood are on the total number of adolescents in the U.S. population and the number of births to adolescents. As indicated throughout this chapter, however, data on teenage sexuality, contraceptive use, pregnancy, abortion, and adoption are available though often incomplete, and the extent of misreporting and underreporting is often not accurately known.

These data come from several sources, each source providing information concerning specific aspects of adolescent sexuality and fertility and relevant associated factors. However, there are significant inconsistencies among these data sets—for example, in the use of age, race, and income categories, in the time frames for reporting, and in the definitions of core concepts, such as "at risk of pregnancy." Consequently, it is frequently difficult for researchers to integrate data from different sources in order to better understand causal relationships that may exist between the observed characteristics and the behaviors of teenagers. In addition, it is difficult to trace the relative importance of various factors at different points in the decision-making sequence leading to teenage childbearing.

Of special significance are the problems of explaining race differences in adolescent sexual activity, pregnancy, abortion, and nonmarital childbearing. Although available data contribute to understanding the associations between an individual's characteristics and behaviors—for example, living in a single-parent family, early sexual initiation, and early nonmarital childbearing—they do not lend themselves to forming conclusions concerning the chain of causality and how this may have changed over time.

A special data issue that has been highlighted throughout this chapter concerns the lack of complete and consistent information on ethnicity. In particular, we have pointed out the difficulties in presenting accurate estimates of the sexual and fertility behavior of Hispanic adolescents. The problems are even more pronounced for other ethnic groups, such as Native Americans. Problems of omission, small samples, and inconsistent and noncomparable categorization have hindered knowledge of the behavior of significant population subgroups.

Surveys

Much of the information on adolescent sexual activity and pregnancy discussed in this report is derived from household surveys in which individual teenagers are interviewed, typically in person in their homes.

Respondents are chosen for the interviews using carefully developed procedures designed to create a sample of individuals who accurately represent the larger population. Difficulties inevitably arise because some of the respondents selected refuse to be interviewed or the interviewer never manages to find them at home. When conducting a study among adolescents on a sensitive topic for which parental permission is required, there is an additional step in the process, and additional refusals may result. If such refusals occur randomly—that is, if the people who refuse or could not be located are just like the people who actually participate—then the substantive results would not be affected; however, this is rarely the case. Those persons who refuse differ in ways that cannot always be predicted but that may affect the conclusions of the research. If, for example, parents who hold very conservative and strict views about adolescent sexual activity are more likely to refuse permission for their child to be interviewed, then children reared in conservative homes will be underrepresented in the analyses conducted with the data.

Another source of difficulty arises when respondents do not accurately report their attitudes or experiences. This seems to be an acute problem for some respondents who have been pregnant and who have had an abortion or relinquished their children for adoption. Data on sexual activity appear to be more reliably reported by teenagers (although it is quite possible that some males overreport sexual activity). In addition, over time there have been changes in the public perception of particular behaviors, which may make them easier to discuss. For example, part of the increase in sexual activity during the 1970s may simply reflect a greater openness in reporting nonmarital sexual activity. It is very difficult to ascertain the accuracy of data coming from confidential interviews unless it can be verified by other sources. One such source is the rising incidence of reported sexually transmitted disease and abortion during the 1970s, which suggests that an increase in sexual activity has indeed occurred. In addition, data from several types of surveys concur in their estimated levels of sexual activity; thus data on sexual activity appear to be reliable in general. However, data from providers of abortion services indicate that there is considerable underreporting of abortion by respondents to surveys, particularly among unmarried black girls and boys and white girls. Thus estimates of pregnancy and of abortion derived from survey data must be viewed with caution. In the absence of nonsurvey data on adoption, it is impossible to validate the incidence of adoption reported in surveys except by comparing the number of women who report having adopted an American child to the number who report relinquishing a child.

There are other shortcomings of existing survey data. In particular, data from boys and from very young teenagers have been difficult to obtain. Teenage boys are less likely to agree to be interviewed about sexual activity and pregnancy, it appears, and they are less likely to provide accurate information. Hence, nonresponse and misreporting are more likely among boys. Parents frequently deny requests for interviews of very young adolescents. In addition, since sexual activity among teenagers 14 and younger is fairly uncommon, a very large sample is necessary in order to obtain enough cases to support statistical analysis. All of these problems—interview refusals, discrepancies in data from different sources, large samples that include few individuals with the relevant characteristics—increase the cost of data collection. Although there is good reason to have samples large enough so that blacks, whites, and Hispanics can be studied separately, the costs of data collection can be so large that periodic surveys may be infrequent or corners may be cut, and data quality suffers. And yet the substantive concerns are valid. It is important to have more and better data on young adolescents and on males, and it is very important to be able to study socioeconomic differences within as well as between racial and ethnic subgroups, as a basis for designing more sensitive policies and more effective interventions.

Record Systems

Although U.S. data are not as complete as data from the population registration systems of many European nations, several of the U.S. vital record systems are of high quality. In particular, most births are recorded on birth certificates and most deaths are similarly recorded on death certificates. Thus, the number of births to teenagers can be tracked accurately across time, and infant mortality can be measured with considerable certainty. By contrast, the reporting of miscarriages is far from complete. Similarly, in abortion data collected by the Centers for Disease Control (CDC) from state health departments, the number of abortions is significantly incomplete, primarily because some states do not have abortion reporting systems, and in many states that do have systems, not all service providers are covered. Estimates based on data obtained directly from providers of abortion services by the Alan Guttmacher Institute are consistently higher; however, these data do not provide information regarding the age, race, and marital status of women who obtain abortions. Information collected by both organizations must be integrated in order to obtain more accurate estimates of the incidence and rates of abortions among age, race, and marital subgroups.

Adoption is a potentially significant type of pregnancy resolution about which very little is known. Because the national adoption reporting system was discontinued in 1975, it is currently impossible to obtain a complete enumeration of adoptions nationwide and to assess trends in adoptions. Currently, the only system that gathers annual information is the Voluntary Cooperative Information System, managed by the American Public Welfare System. This system collects data only on children placed for adoption by public child welfare agencies and therefore does not count private placements. In addition, while it collects some information on the characteristics of adopted children and adoptive families, it contains little or no information on the characteristics of birth parents, the adoption process, and the subsequent fertility, marital status, and economic status of the birth mother.

Data From Service Programs

While household surveys are conducted for research purposes, and recordkeeping agencies are funded by the government to maintain basic public statistical data about the population, information collected by service programs is typically gathered for either fiscal or management purposes and thus is only occasionally suited for research purposes. For example, data may be collected on insurance or Medicaid coverage but not on family income or socioeconomic status. Clients may be given a different identification number every time they appear for service, making it impossible to track their use of the service across time. In addition, samples that are obtained from clinic populations tend to be small and are almost never representative. Thus, conclusions based on such samples cannot be extended to individuals who do not appear to receive the service. For example, contraceptive use among adolescents attending birth control clinics is likely to differ from use by those who see private physicians, or who use drugstore methods, or who use no method at all. Since control groups composed of similar individuals who do not receive the service are rarely obtained, it is usually difficult to isolate the effect of receiving the service from the selection process involved in requesting the service in the first place.

CONCLUSIONS

This chapter has described trends and differentials in adolescent sexual and fertility behavior, including the size and characteristics of the population at risk of early pregnancy and childbearing. The available data suggest a number of conclusions:

• Adolescent sexual activity increased sharply during the 1970s but appears to have declined slightly or leveled off since then.

• Among sexually active teenagers, contraceptive use has increased; however, many teenagers are inconsistent users, and many do not begin to use contraception for a year or more after they initiate intercourse.

• The number of pregnancies increased somewhat during the 1970s; subsequently the number of pregnancies has declined slightly.

• The pregnancy rate calculated for all adolescents has increased steadily since 1970. When calculated for those who are sexually active, however, the pregnancy rate has remained stable during the past decade as a result of increased contraceptive use.

• The rate of births to adolescent mothers declined in the 1970s, largely because of the rise in abortion and increased contraceptive use.

• Marriage among teenagers has declined since the early 1970s, and as a result, an increasing proportion—and an increasing absolute number— of births to adolescent mothers have occurred outside marriage.

The sequence of choices presented in Chapter 1 provides a context for understanding the social and demographic processes that lead to adolescent childbearing; choices at each step in the sequence affect the size of the population at risk of subsequent behaviors. Figure 2-5 adds to the contextual framework presented in Figure 1-1 our best estimates of the size of the population involved at each step in the sequence. Inconsistencies among the relevant data sets make it difficult to develop accurate estimates of the numbers of young women at each step in the sequence. Recognized inaccuracies (e.g., in reported pregnancies and abortions) and gaps in the data (e.g., on adoption placements) preclude precise estimates at any given point in time or for a particular cohort of adolescents.

Nevertheless, rough estimates based on calculations using data from several sources are interesting for two reasons. First, they help demonstrate the relative weight of these events by placing the number of individuals at each step of the sequence in the context of the total

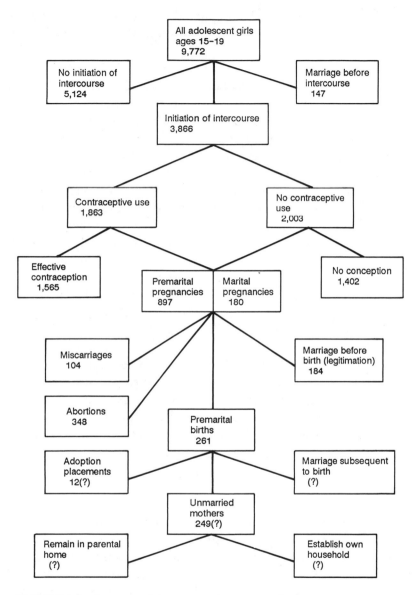

FIGURE 2-5 Sequence of decisions and estimates of population at each step, 1982 (in thousands).

population of adolescent girls. Second, they have significant implications for intervention strategies and for assessing the incremental effects of alternative approaches.

As Figure 2-5 shows, in 1982 among the total of 9.77 million adolescent girls ages 15–19, less than half initiated sexual intercourse. Of those who did, just less than half—1.86 million—were using some form of contraception. Of the estimated 2 million who were not using contraception, about 30 percent experienced a pregnancy in 1982; of the estimated 1.86 million contraceptive users, about 16 percent experienced contraceptive failure and became pregnant: of the estimated 897,000 premarital pregnancies that occurred, roughly one-third were to unsuccessful contraceptors and two-thirds were to nonusers. Among those who became pregnant, approximately 39 percent or about 348,000 obtained an abortion. Another estimated 12 percent or about 104,000 experienced a miscarriage. Approximately 445,000, just under half, carried their pregnancies to term: among this group, approximately 184,000 married to legitimate the birth, and roughly 261,000 gave birth without marriage. A very small proportion of these young women placed their children for adoption. The remainder, an estimated 249,000, became single parents.

These estimates have important implications for identifying target populations and designing strategies for intervention. A significant proportion of all teenagers initiate sexual activity each year, and a significant proportion of these experience an unintended pregnancy, either because they are not using contraception at all or are not using it effectively. A very small proportion of the total population of girls ages 15–19 become unmarried mothers in any given year, roughly 2.5 percent. Although they are a small target population, the cumulative proportion is much higher, and these young single mothers are at high risk of experiencing serious health, social, educational, and economic problems, and the public costs for their support are substantial. Increases in the number who delay sexual initiation and who effectively use contraception if they are sexually active could significantly reduce the number of adolescent girls at risk of unintended pregnancy, abortion, and childbearing outside marriage.

The next three chapters explore what is known about the changing societal context and relevant factors affecting adolescent sexual activity, contraception, abortion, and childbearing outside marriage.

3

The Societal Context

Adolescent sexuality is not a new phenomenon in the United States, but the issues are different today than they were in the 1960s. Enduring social changes during the past 20 years have had significant effects on many subgroups in our society. Adolescents, at a formative stage of development and striving to identify their niche in the world, are especially responsive to their societal context. The experience of growing up in the 1980s has changed since the 1960s and even the 1970s. Being the parent of an adolescent has also changed. Among different racial, ethnic, socioeconomic, regional, and religious subgroups there is substantial variation in the patterns of adolescent experience and the behavior of their parents.

The heterogeneity of the U.S. population makes it difficult to briefly describe the impact of society on its individual members. Yet to understand the changes in teenage sexual and fertility behavior described in the previous chapter and the specific determinants of individual sexual behavior and decision making discussed in the next chapter, it is useful to examine the changing societal context of adolescence. Of particular importance are several demographic changes, economic shifts, and legal changes. These include changes in patterns of family life, changes in the status of women and norms of adult sexual attitudes and behavior, changes in youth culture, changes in law and social policy, and technological changes that have altered employment patterns, household labor, and the use of leisure time, especially television. Evidence of these changes' is presented as background for examining the behavior of American adolescents in the 1980s, not as a delineation of the social causes of adolescent pregnancy and childbearing.

FAMILY CHANGES

Family Structure

Although a sizable proportion of teenagers still live in two-parent families in which the father is the primary earner and the mother is a homemaker, most do not. Since the mid-1960s, and especially since 1970, patterns of family structure and labor force participation in the United States have shifted dramatically. More teenagers than ever before live in single-parent families, usually female-headed. And more teenagers than ever before have either two parents or a sole parent who works outside the home.

Between 1959 and 1983 the number of female-headed families in the United States more than doubled. Both the rate of first marriage and the remarriage rate declined at the same time that the divorce rate doubled. Since the mid-1960s, separation and divorce have become the leading causes of single parenthood. For blacks, however, the rise in female-headed households and single parenthood began in the mid-1940s and increased more steeply after the mid-1960s. Despite the declining youth population following the post-World War II baby boom, the proportion of children under age 18 living in families headed by the mother also nearly doubled, from roughly 11 percent to nearly 20 percent (Bureau of the Census, 1984b). The impact of these trends has been felt differently by different subgroups of the population. While most white and Hispanic children and teenagers have continued to live with two parents, more than half of all blacks have not (Bureau of the Census, 1984b).

Since 1970, the rising rate of births outside marriage has been another factor contributing to the increasing number of teenagers in single-parent families. The relative prominence of these factors varies dramatically by race. Although marital disruption is still the leading cause of single parenthood for both races, childbearing outside marriage, particularly among adolescents, has become a significantly greater cause of single parenthood among blacks than among whites (U.S. Congress, House, 1985).

The dramatic rise in single-parent, female-headed families has been paralleled by an increase in absent fatherhood. Although proportionately more fathers in the United States live with rather than apart from their children, the number of absent fathers has increased in recent years, especially among younger men. Based on an analysis of data from the National Longitudinal Survey (NLS), it appears that among the cohort of men who were 14–21 in 1979, the number of absent fathers increased threefold between 1979 and 1983, from 320,000 to over 1 million. In 1983, one-third of all fathers ages 18–25 lived apart from at least one of their children (Lerman, 1985). However, there are dramatic racial and ethnic differences in the level and pattern of absent fatherhood among young men. More minority members than whites become fathers at young ages. By age 24–25, 48 percent of blacks and 43 percent of Hispanics had become fathers, compared with 28 percent of whites in 1983. Yet more young Hispanic fathers were living with their children in that year than either whites or blacks, about one-third compared with less than one-quarter and one-fifth, respectively. Across race groups, the proportion of fathers ages 24–25 who had their first child before age 19 was higher for absent fathers than for those living with their children (Lerman, 1985).

Patterns of Marriage

In part, the growth in childbearing outside marriage over the past 15 years reflects changing patterns of marriage. The average age of marriage has risen for the population as a whole. In 1960 the median age at first marriage was just over 20 for women and just under 23 for men; in 1983 it was just under 23 for women and over 25 for men (Bureau of the Census, 1984b). This pattern appears to be even more pronounced for blacks than for whites and Hispanics. At every age proportionately fewer black women were married in 1983 than in 1970, and at every age proportionately fewer black women were married than white and Hispanic women. The same appears to be true for men (Bureau of the Census, 1984b).

Changing patterns of marriage reflect changing values and attitudes about the importance of marriage in general, and in particular the importance of marriage to legitimate a birth. Many pregnant women, both adults and adolescents, seek abortion, delay marriage for months or even years after the birth of a child, or do not marry at all. Between 1960 and 1982 the percentage of premaritally conceived births that were legitimated by marriage declined substantially. Although the downward trend was significantly sharper for blacks, increasing numbers of white women also rejected marriage as a response to nonmarital pregnancy (O'Connell and Rogers, 1984; U.S. Congress, House, 1985).

Research on the relationship between marriage and fatherhood is scarce. Nevertheless, analyses based on NLS data suggest that the marital status of young fathers, both those who are living with and those who are living apart from their children, differs sharply by race and ethnic origin. Young black fathers, regardless of whether they are living with their children, are significantly less likely than whites and Hispanics to marry the mothers. Although most white and Hispanic fathers marry either before or after the birth of a child, most young black fathers do not. However, the marital and residential status of fathers, especially young black fathers, appears to shift over time (Lerman, 1985).

Patterns of Women's Employment and Unemployment

Since the mid-1960s and especially since 1970, the number and percentage of U.S. children and teenagers with working mothers has risen steadily, from approximately 45 percent in 1960 to approximately 62 percent in 1985. Among children under 18 in female-headed families, the proportion is even higher, with about 66 percent having mothers in the paid labor force (personal communication with staff of the Bureau of Labor Statistics). White single-parent mothers are more likely than either blacks or Hispanics to be working or looking for work outside the home, and divorced single-parent mothers are more likely than never-married mothers to be in the labor force. Although school-age children have always been more likely than very young children to have working mothers, the late 1960s and the 1970s saw a dramatic increase in the number and proportion of young people of all ages with mothers in the labor force.

As more and more mothers have joined the labor force, more have also become unemployed. In 1985 the annual unemployment rate for mothers of school-age children (6–17) was 7.1 percent compared with 5 percent in 1970 and 5.3 percent in 1960 (personal communication with staff at the Bureau of Labor Statistics). Unemployment is significantly higher among blacks and somewhat higher among Hispanics than among whites. It is also higher for single-parent mothers than for married mothers. This does not suggest that mothers with a husband present are better able to get and hold a job; instead, it probably reflects racial, age, and education differences among the different groups (Kamerman and Hayes, 1982).

Kamerman and Hayes (1982) highlight the shifting pattern of U.S. labor force participation during the past decade. Most notably, the dramatic increase in the number of mothers who are working outside the home represents a fundamental change in the activities and orientations of American women. It is attributable in part to the population growth over the three decades following World War II and in part to the dramatic increase during the 1960s and the 1970s in the proportion of women who chose (or were obliged) to seek paid employment. Changing patterns of maternal employment are undoubtedly linked to broader changes in social, cultural, ideological, and economic conditions in this nation. The economic growth of the 1960s increased the number of available jobs. There were growing social and legal pressures to ensure women equal access to the workplace. The spread of the feminist movement gave a focus and rhetoric to women's aspirations. Rising rates of inflation significantly increased the cost of living, and additional income was needed to maintain many households. Factors such as the declining income and rising unemployment of young men, especially blacks and Hispanics, have also undoubtedly contributed (O'Neill, 1980). Many young men without skills joined the ranks of the hard-core unemployed in the shift to a postindustrial economy, with its emphasis on jobs that require specialized skills and education. In sum, these factors provided major incentives for women to enter the job market and to stay in it. Regardless of the motivation for women to go to work, however, their employment has been accompanied by changes in the patterns of marriage, family structure, and family size, and their earnings have brought about changes in the patterns of family income (Kamerman and Hayes, 1982).

It seems likely that these changes have significant implications for adolescent development. First, adolescent girls increasingly have working women as role models. The attitudes of young women, as well as those of many young men, about work and housework, gender roles, and women's status relative to that of men may be influenced by the women they see in the workplace. Second, adolescent girls are increasingly aware of adult women who are living independently of men, whether as a result of divorce, a decision not to marry, or because marriage was not an option. Depending on a young woman's social reference group, her attitudes about the desirability and manageability of a woman's living independently as a single parent may be more or less positive.

Family Income

For nearly three decades following World War II, the United States enjoyed a period of steady economic growth. However, beginning in 1973, the economy entered a decade of stagnation due in part to the worldwide oil price increases of 1973–1974 and 1979–1980 and a sudden (and still unexplained) slowdown in the growth of worker productivity (Levy and Michel, 1985). The effects of the slowdown are evident in the patterns of family income. Between 1947 and 1973, median family income (in 1984 dollars) increased steadily, from $14,000 to $28,000. Even during the 1960s, a decade that saw a dramatic and rapid growth in female-headed families, median family income never went more than three years without reaching a new high. Since 1973, however, median family income has remained below $28,000, and in 1984, the most recent year for which such data are available, the figure stood at $26,400 (Bureau of the Census, 1985b; Levy and Michel, 1985). The net result of this stagnation has been that the average American family was little better off in 1984 than it was in 1970. Some families, especially black and Hispanic families headed by women, were more likely to be in poverty.

Regardless of race and family type, children with mothers in the labor force were in families with higher median incomes than children of nonworking mothers. For all two-parent families with children in 1983, the median income was $34,670 if the mother was in the labor force, and $23,580 if she was not (Bureau of the Census, 1985b). The median income of married-couple families rose more than that of any other family type from 1960 to 1983. Although the earnings of wives in black and Hispanic families are not substantially lower than those of their white counterparts, white children in two-parent families benefit from higher median family incomes. This is largely because the average earnings of white husbands are higher.

Children in single-parent families maintained by women are materially better off if their mothers are in the paid labor force than if they are not. However, on average they are not as economically advantaged as those living with both parents, regardless of the mothers' work status. This is because, on average, men tend to earn more than women at all job levels. In 1984, among children in single-parent families in which the mother worked, the median family income was $12,800, significantly less than half the median income of all married-couple families (Bureau of the Census, 1985b). It was higher for the families of white children (including teenagers) than it was for the families of blacks and Hispanics. In general, the earnings of single mothers are the most important source of income to their families, providing on average between 60 and 70 percent of all family monetary resources (Masnick and Bane, 1980). The median income in single-parent families in which the mother did not work was only $5,880 in 1983 (Bureau of the Census, 1984b).

SOCIETAL CHANGES

Poverty Status

In 1984, just under 5.5 million young people between the ages of 14 and 21, approximately 18 percent of all those in this age group, lived in families below the poverty level. The proportion of children in poverty, although significantly lower than in 1960, has risen since 1980. Not surprisingly, those in families headed by single mothers are far more likely than those in two-parent families to be poor—54 percent compared with about 12.5 percent (Bureau of the Census, 1985b). Black and Hispanic youth are far more likely to live in poverty than their white counterparts. Among minority children in single-parent families, the proportion in poverty is even greater. Approximately two-thirds of all blacks and Hispanics under age 18 living in female-headed families were below the poverty level in 1984 (Bureau of the Census, 1985b).

A major source of support for the nation's poor families with children is federal cash assistance programs, such as Aid to Families With Dependent Children (AFDC) and, to a lesser extent, Supplemental Security Income (SSI), and such noncash programs as food stamps, Medicaid, public or subsidized housing, energy assistance, and free or reduced-price school meals. Approximately 62 percent of all female-headed families with children received means-tested benefits in the first quarter of 1984: 35 percent received cash assistance and 61 percent participated in noncash programs. The proportion of black female-headed families receiving these benefits was even higher: nearly 80 percent, with more than 45 percent receiving cash benefits and nearly 80 percent participating in noncash programs (Bureau of the Census, 1985b).

The social and economic conditions of some minority children, especially middle-class blacks, improved throughout the decade of the 1960s, undoubtedly as a result of the civil rights movement and the war on poverty (Wilson, 1981). During the 1970s, however, the general circumstances of most minority young people did not continue to improve. The stagnant economy was accompanied by a dwindling federal commitment to social reform. The marital, employment, and income differences between white and minority parents became more pronounced; these differences affected their adolescent children as well. White teenagers, particularly those in two-parent, middle-class families, became materially better off; their educational and occupational opportunities increased, and they had reasonable prospects for a secure future.

Many minority young people, however, became less advantaged. Poverty and unemployment grew, not only among their parents, but also among young people themselves (Freeman and Holzer, 1985). Between 1964 and 1978 there was a widening gap between the employment-to-population ratios of white and black teenagers. While employment rates for whites were rising, those for black females were not rising as fast, and those for black males were falling (Betsey et al., 1985). Job opportunities increased for individuals with advanced education and specialized skills and experience, while the number of places in the job market for those with little education and employment training decreased. More minority families with teenagers became single-parent families during the 1970s, and more became dependent on public assistance. Young people from homes that depended on welfare benefits fared worse in the job market than those from homes that did not (Freeman and Holzer, 1985).

The declining position of young black males in the job market has increasingly been cited as an explanation for the growth in black, female-headed families. Over 20 years ago the Moynihan report (1965) presented data showing that black family instability was sensitive to unemployment rates between 1951 and 1963. More recently, black researchers have argued that dramatic drops during the 1980s in the number of employed young black men per 100 black women are associated with higher rates of single parenthood and absent fatherhood (Wilson and Neckerman, 1985). Regardless of race, absent fathers generally come from more economically disadvantaged homes than do other young men. In addition, their early school and employment experience is typically below average. Overall, however, young black absent fathers are not substantially different from their peers in terms of performance or standardized tests, early poverty status, presence of their fathers in the home, and success in school. In contrast, white absent fathers look very different from other young white men. They are much more likely to come from poor families, and their abilities, school performance, and work experience are generally much below average (Lerman, 1985).

The declining position of many disadvantaged youth during the 1970s significantly affected their self-perceptions and their attitudes. Young blacks, in particular, tended to become more pessimistic about their immediate and future prospects, more disillusioned about the value of education and employment skills, more doubtful about the viability of marriage, and more dissatisfied with society in general (Chilman, 1980a;

Auletta, 1982; Anderson, 1978). This pessimism similarly affected blue-collar white youth (Rubin, 1976). Moreover, these changing social and economic patterns appear to be related in fundamental ways to changing patterns of family formation and changing attitudes about sexual behavior, marriage, and childbearing.

Women's Roles and Norms of Sexual Behavior

During the 1960s and 1970s, many traditional American values and behavioral norms were called into question, among them the roles of women and the nature of male-female relationships. Modern efforts for equal rights for women began in the mid-1960s, as other dimensions of social change were developing, such as the civil rights movement, the antiwar movement, student revolts, and the hippie counterculture. When the women's movement began, the U.S. birth rate was already beginning to fall. The expanding economy offered more jobs, and women, especially those with special skills, were needed in the work force. Improved household technologies and conveniences, from the dishwasher to disposable diapers and TV dinners, reduced the amount of time many women spent doing housework. Although the women's movement per se did not command broad national support, it was influential as part of a constellation of factors that, taken together, caused many women to view their roles and status differently.

In addition, the introduction of biomedical contraceptive technologies during the 1960s (i.e., the pill and the intrauterine device) enabled women to control their own fertility without the knowledge or cooperation of their male partners. The new forms of contraception made it possible for sexual intercourse to be largely independent of pregnancy. The use of sterilization as a form of fertility control also grew in popularity during the 1970s, partly from concern about the side effects of the pill and partly because of the development and increased availability of simple, safe, and less expensive methods of female sterilization. Between 1969 and 1978, approval of surgical methods of contraception for both men and women more than doubled among married women, with vasectomy regarded somewhat more favorably than female sterilization. Since then, approval of both male and female methods of sterilization has remained fairly steady at around 70 percent. Among married women 30 and older, sterilization is the most common method of contraception, regardless of family size. Among those under 30, only women with two or more children prefer sterilization to the pill. By 1982, however, 21 percent of all U.S. women of reproductive age relied on sterilization (12 percent on female and 9 percent on male sterilization) to regulate their fertility (Forrest and Henshaw, 1983).

An evolving focus of the women's movement in the 1970s became equality of sexual expression. The findings of Masters and Johnson spurred many women to reject the traditional double standard concerning male-female sexual relations and to advocate the "right" to expect sexual fulfillment from their partners. Women, it was argued, could and should enjoy sex as much as men. Sexual attitudes and behavior increasingly became the focus of egalitarianism in gender roles (Reiss, 1973). As the popular author Reuben (1970) wrote, "an active and rewarding sexual life, at a mature level, is indispensable if one is to achieve his [or her] full potential as a member of the human race." At the close of the 1960s, Yankelovich found in his Youth Attitude Survey that a growing majority of college women thought that women should be free to initiate sexual relations and that concern with women's sexual satisfaction was the most important quality in a man (Yankelovich, 1974). By 1973 that attitude had spread to working-class youth as well. Premarital intercourse, abortion, and homosexual relations were viewed as morally acceptable by a majority of both college and noncollege youth (Yankelovich, 1974). For a minority of young people, favorable attitudes about sexual freedom extended to "open marriage," "group sex," and "group marriage," although there is no evidence that these practices were widespread (Chilman, 1980a).

The incidence of premarital sexual activity increased rapidly in the 1960s and into the mid-1970s. Cohabitation also became more prevalent (Glick, 1975). Among never-married women ages 18–19, for example, the percentage living with a man rose from 0.2 percent in 1970 to 2.5 percent in 1980 (Sweet and Bumpass, 1984; Alan Guttmacher Institute, in press). As in the case of attitudes toward premarital intercourse, studies of attitudes toward cohabitation show that by the mid-1970s most college students had come to accept such arrangements in the context of a strong, affectionate, and preferably monogamous relationship (Jessor and Jessor, 1975). Cohabitation did not replace marriage among older teenagers, however, nor did it compensate for the decline in the proportion of this age group who married. The total percentage of 18- to 19-year-old women who were currently married or cohabiting in 1980 was lower than the percentage who were currently married in 1970

(Alan Guttmacher Institute, in press). Moreover, Macklin (1981, cited in Chilman, 1980a) concluded that there is no single typical cohabitation relationship; they range broadly from those that are rather casual to those that are highly committed and directed toward marriage.

Throughout the 1960s and 1970s, as premarital intercourse and co-habitation became more accepted, separation and divorce increased. Whether growing sexual freedom among women actually caused or contributed to marital dissolution has not been documented. Nevertheless, divorce rose among all age groups during this period, not just among young, childless couples. As a result, many more adolescents than ever before were experiencing the breakup of their parents' marriages and living for some period during their formative years in single-parent families. Simultaneously, the rate of first marriages declined and childbearing outside marriage increased, particularly among adolescent women. For many women, especially poor and black ones, marriage came to be regarded as neither a social necessity nor an economic possibility (Ladner, 1972): high unemployment rates among young black men posed a barrier to establishing economically viable and stable marriages. In addition, as one scholar suggests, black women have had a strong orientation toward employment for several generations, and this, combined with declining employment among black men, may have made them less disposed toward marriage (Kenkel, 1986).

In 1973, the legalization of abortion added another dimension to women's growing sexual freedom. With the legal right to decide whether to give birth once pregnant, women gained even greater control over their social and economic destinies. Surveys in the early 1970s showed that people who were most likely to support the legality and availability of abortion were white, Protestant, and with higher income and education levels (reported by Chilman, 1980a). Nevertheless, federal funds to help cover the costs of abortions for eligible poor women receiving Medicaid benefits (many of whom were black) were also made available in 1973, thus extending this freedom of choice to those who were unable to purchase it on their own. By 1977 the abortion rate for black women was more than double that of white women, and it has remained disproportionately high into the 1980s, despite cuts in Medicaid funding for this procedure (Henshaw and O'Reilly, 1983).

The women's movement added yet another dimension to the growth of sexual freedom. Led primarily by white, middle-class women in the 1960s and 1970s, its message reached white women more readily than black women; as a result, whites were more significantly affected by it than blacks. As Ladner (1972) discusses, blacks and whites did not approach the women's movement with the same sociocultural realities and attitudes. Most black women had always needed to work outside the home and to assume responsibility for the economic support of their families. They had traditionally played a major, often dominant role in family decision making. Nonmarital sexuality for both men and women had long been accepted in the black community (Ladner, 1972; Moore et al., 1986). Although adolescent pregnancy has never been viewed as desirable, there is a tradition of acceptance when it occurs and a strong value placed on keeping the child. Black teenage mothers have typically found support and assistance from their families and kin network (Williams, 1977, cited in Moore et al., 1986; Stack, 1974; Hofferth, 1981). Therefore, although rates of nonmarital sexual activity, abortion, and childbearing outside marriage increased among blacks during this period, the most dramatic increases were among whites.

The women's movement has been aimed at changing the circumstances of adult women. Nevertheless, its influence has been strongly felt among adolescent women as well over the past two decades. It has helped to raise educational and occupational aspirations for many, and it has demonstrated that being a homemaker, wife, and mother is not the only available role for women. The women's movement encouraged many young women to recognize that they need not be passive and dependent in their relationships with men and urged them to pursue every opportunity to use their talents and energies as active, intelligent individuals, equal to their male counterparts. Moreover, it challenged many traditional moral values and indirectly encouraged young women to seek enjoyment and fulfillment in sexual expression. Changing attitudes about premarital intercourse, contraception, abortion, childbearing, and marriage became manifest in the actions of teenagers as well as adult women, and they reached a peak in the mid–1970s.

The early 1980s have seen the emergence of a new conservatism, both economic and social. In the wake of the sexual liberalism of the 1970s, the "new morality" has become a source of growing and vocal controversy. Many people sharply disapprove of adolescents' involvement in behaviors that had become accepted norms for adults. They attribute the rise in adolescent pregnancy to a disintegration of moral values. Efforts to limit adolescents' access to family planning services and to abortion services by requiring parental consent reflect the belief held by many that programs and policies that appear to legitimate premarital sexual activity among young people exacerbate and perpetuate the problem. The data bearing on these assumptions are examined in Chapter 6.

Youth Culture

The teenagers of the early 1960s were the first wave of the postwar baby boom. Their childhood years during the 1950s were largely characterized by peace, prosperity, convention, and rising levels of material comfort. In contrast, their teenage years were fraught with social unrest, revolt, and disillusionment about a society whose technological developments and prosperity failed to solve the problems of hunger, poverty, and social injustice and created many new problems, including urban decay and a shrinking market for unskilled labor. The unrest was exacerbated by a controversial war in Southeast Asia.

The youth movement and student revolts of the 1960s were actually a series of interrelated movements for social change. Opposition to the Vietnam War gave rise to protests against the military draft. Concerns about growing racial inequities stirred protests against segregation in schools, neighborhoods, churches, and places of employment. Disillusionment with a society that seemed not to hear the concerns of some of its young people fueled protests against academic censorship and in favor of student free speech on campuses across the country. And growing alienation in a society that apparently valued materialism, standardization, and conformity led to the emergence of the hippie counterculture, which fostered free self-expression and the cultivation of alternative lifestyles, including drug use and sexual freedom. Although many older people who were deeply concerned about the condition of society were also attracted to these movements, they were largely dominated by the young.

As scholars have observed, the effect of these movements on some young people was a rejection of traditional values (such as the merits of self-discipline, achievement, deferred gratification, and long-term commitment to goals) and confusion about what values should replace them (Chilman, 1980a; Panel on Youth of the President's Science Advisory Committee, 1974; Coleman, 1961; Douvan and Adelson, 1966; Keniston, 1968, 1971; Flacks, 1970, 1971). Alienation and conflict between generations as well as between socioeconomic and ethnic groups, ever present in our society, became even more pronounced. Disillusionment with the value and relevance of education led to an increasing tendency for young people to drop out of school (Bachman et al., 1971; Panel on Youth of the President's Science Advisory Committee, 1974). And impatience with an old moral order that appeared to lack sincerity, authenticity, individualism, and free self-expression became increasingly widespread.

Adolescents in the 1960s seemed to reject the world of growing public and private bureaucracy, standardization, materialism, and consumerism that their parents had helped create in the aftermath of World War II. They sought to replace it with a more natural, humanistic, individualistic, and classless society (Mahler, 1977; Westby and Braungart, 1970). In fact, however, the college-age activists of the 1960s were a small minority of the total university student population—perhaps as small as 5 percent (Flacks, 1971). Their vocal protests and demonstrations drew the attention of university administrators, scientists, journalists, politicians, and the public, many of whom behaved as though they were a more representative group (Hill and Monks, 1977). Indeed, some observers argue that the rebelliousness of 1960s activists is less significant for the attention it drew to the gap between themselves and their upper-middle-class parents than it was for the attention it drew to the gap between the values of socially and economically advantaged young people and those of less affluent, more conservative subgroups of the population, regardless of generation (Hill and Monks, 1977).

In contrast, the teenagers of the 1970s were young children during the turbulent decade of the 1960s. By the time they became teenagers, the Vietnam War was over, and the nation was rocked with revelations of corruption at the highest levels of government and the corporate world. The counterculture that flourished in the affluence of the 1960s faltered under the pressures of the inflation, recession, and unemployment of the early 1970s. And the campus rebellions died out as the fervor to change society faded (Eisenstadt, 1977). Among many young people a renewed interest in educational achievement, career, and family replaced political activism. As Chilman (1980a) reports, by 1973 the majority of young people (primarily middle-class and upper-middle-class) expressed satisfaction with their personal lives and future prospects. Most accepted the conventional life-styles of their parents and felt that society was essentially healthy and its problems manageable (Chilman, 1980a), although among some teens attitudes about drug use and sexual freedom continued to reflect the liberalism of the 1960s. There was, however, little faith among many young people in the political system as a way of promoting social well-being (perhaps influenced by the Watergate revelations), and few were motivated to become politically involved. The proportion of eligible young voters (18–20 years old) who went to the polls declined between 1972 and 1976 (Bureau of the Census, 1985d).

As the decade of the 1970s progressed, the economic conditions of the country worsened dramatically. Inflation soared, unemployment reached new heights, and for many young people the prospects of assured prosperity faded. Minority young people in particular were adversely affected by the economic decline of the mid- and late 1970s, as unemployment among those 16–19 reached a 20-year high in 1975 (Bureau of the Census, 1985d). Rates of poverty, which had declined in the late 1960s, increased with rising unemployment. The growing number of female-headed families were especially at risk of being poor, particularly if they were young and black. Approximately half of all black teenagers growing up in the 1970s lived in single-parent families, many became single parents themselves at young ages (Bureau of the Census, 1984b), and virtually all were poor. Apathy, alienation, and hopelessness became prevalent attitudes among many young blacks in the mid- and late 1970s. Similarly, among white, blue-collar youth, perceptions of inescapable deprivation and dwindling prospects of rewarding jobs, happy marriages, and adequate income became prevalent (Rubin, 1976).

The economic decline of the late 1970s and its associated social problems opened the door to the new conservatism of the early 1980s. Although the seeds had been sown in the previous three decades, economic conservatism, as well as moral and religious conservatism, began to flourish and found new expression in the political arena (Nisbett, 1985; Glazer, 1985). Excesses of personal indulgence and governmental waste were blamed for the declining position of the United States in the world market, in the arms race, and in technological development. They were similarly blamed for social problems ranging from criminal violence to adolescent pregnancy. As a result, the traditional Protestant work ethic began to gain new popularity. In education there was renewed interest in basic skills and enhanced math and science programs; in social welfare there was a push to cut programs in order to reduce public costs and to discourage long-term dependence; and in public policy generally, there was a movement to transfer authority and responsibility from government back to individuals, families, and communities. Religious fundamentalism began to gain new popularity, calling for a more traditional code of personal morality to curb the sexual liberalism that became widespread during the 1960s and 1970s. It reaffirmed the importance of the nuclear family as the primary social, economic, and cultural institution in society.

Ironically, as one observer has noted, although neoconservatives campaigned for less federal government involvement in family life, private business, and local communities, the sweeping thrust of the Reagan administration has been interpreted by many to be more government involvement, through proposed laws and constitutional amendments that cover sexual behavior among consenting adults, abortion, Baby Doe cases, school prayers, and contraception (Nisbett, 1985).

We have yet to realize the full effect of the conservatism of the early 1980s—whether it will create a stronger goal orientation among young people, whether it will actually result in reduced levels of premarital sexual activity, abortion, and childbearing outside marriage, whether it will foster high rates of early marriage reminiscent of the 1950s—or whether it will have no effects at all in these areas. It also remains to be seen whether the values and approaches of the 1980s will draw together or further differentiate young people of different racial, ethnic, and socioeconomic groups in our society.

Technological Change: Television

Beginning in the 1950s, U.S. society has experienced dramatic technological changes that affect virtually every aspect of daily life. Communications, travel, and household tasks, as well as commerce, industry, and defense, have all been revolutionized by new technologies. Perhaps none has been more influential, however, than the television. By 1960, 87 percent of American households had a television; by 1970, 95 percent had at least one television, and a majority had more than one (Bureau of the Census, 1985d).

Since the 1960s, television has been a significant vehicle for transmitting information, communicating ideas, and influencing culture. Programming for education, news, and entertainment has greatly expanded, and the Neilsen Company estimates that the average American-owned television set is on for seven hours each day (Bureau of the Census, 1985d). For adolescents growing up in the 1960s, the 1970s, and now in the 1980s, television is a predominant aspect of their lives. Analysts at the Center for Population Options estimate that by the time most young people reach 17 or 18, they will have spent 15,000 hours in front of a television set, compared with 11,000 hours in school (unpublished CPO memorandum, 1985).

Television viewing undoubtedly affects adolescents' knowledge and attitudes in many areas, including sexuality. Studies show that both explicit and implicit sexual behavior in television programming increased dramatically during the 1970s (Orr, 1984a). Sexual references are present in virtually all types of programs, including situation comedies, mystery and adventure shows, and family dramas. The incidence of implied or explicit sexual acts are most frequent, however, on soap opera series, which are aired in the afternoon and increasingly during prime time in the evening. In these programs, sex is made to seem romantic and desirable, especially when it is illicit. More often than not, sexual references are to intercourse (either discussion of or the act of) between unmarried partners (Greenberg et al., 1981). In addition, sex is commonly linked with prostitution and violence, and sexual relationships are rarely portrayed as "warm, loving, or stable" either inside or outside marriage (National Institute of Mental Health, 1982). Homosexual relationships are not the frequent subject of television programming, but references to homosexuality are increasingly common (Lowry et al., 1981). Contraception is almost never mentioned or referred to, and the negative consequences of an unintended pregnancy are rarely portrayed. Abortion and childbearing outside marriage are generally presented without reference to their negative dimensions and consequences.

Television advertising of all kinds of products, from cars to milk, also contains sexual innuendos and overtones. Advertisers commonly use physically attractive and seductive young women (and, increasingly, young men) to display their products, with the implication that buying them will make the purchaser more sexually desirable (Alan Guttmacher Institute, in press). Their message is aimed primarily at adolescents and young adults. Yet television advertising may be as influential for what it does not do as for what it does. While a variety of personal care products are advertised, including douches, sanitary napkins, and tampons, advertising of nonprescription contraceptives is essentially banned by broadcasters (advertising of prescription methods is prohibited by the federal government) (Alan Guttmacher Institute, in press). Television programming and advertising in general provide young people with lots of clues about how to be sexy, but they provide little information about how to be sexually responsible.

We know little about how and how much teenagers learn about sex from the unrealistic picture of it that is presented by television. However, it is difficult to believe that it does not influence their attitudes (if not their behavior) to some extent, in light of the amount of time young people spend watching and the frequency of their exposure to sexual references and innuendos. The literature on the effects of television violence suggests that the child's environment has a great deal to do with how he or she interprets the messages that are transmitted and how he or she acts on them (National Institute of Mental Health, 1982). Undoubtedly the same is true of sex on television.

Since 1980 television technology has taken a new turn with the introduction of the video cassette recorder. Although there is no existing research on the impact of this new technology on young people, it seems likely that historians a decade from now will find that it has been a predominant influence on them. With the development of the VCR has come the introduction of rock video productions—prerecorded cassettes that combine rock music by popular performers with dramatic interpretations of the lyrics. Lyrics are frequently sexually suggestive, and often the dramatic portrayals include explicit and implied sexual references, violent sexual acts, homosexuality, and aggressive male domination of women. Rock video cassettes are aggressively marketed to teenagers, and they have been extremely lucrative for the manufacturers. The prospect of their increasing popularity and influence throughout the decade is high.

Many observers believe that television has affected the course of American life during the twentieth century more than any other single development. Indeed, it has enormous potential to influence values and norms across racial, ethnic, and socioeconomic groups—in effect to alter the course of events and to change culture. Yet it remains for researchers to discover the long-term effects on human development and behavior for a generation of young people who have never lived without a TV.

CONCLUSION

The process of adolescent development, while constant and predictable in many aspects, is significantly influenced by the historical and social context in which it takes place. As Elder (1980) suggests, adolescent experience is shaped directly by historical events—for example, the Vietnam War, the women's movement, advances in contraceptive technology, and the legalization of abortion—and it is shaped indirectly by the life histories that young people bring to this stage of development—for example, their race, socioeconomic status, family circumstances, cultural niche, and personal experiences.

Sociocultural factors have important effects on individual development. Social status as it is mediated by race, ethnicity, income, religion, and geographic residence shapes cultural values, which in turn affect the way individuals view themselves and are viewed by others. Culture evolves from the life history and experiences of a group and the group's attempt, over time, to adapt to its environment (Chilman, 1980a). The developing individual is imbued with the values, norms, beliefs, and expectations of his or her social reference group (Elder, 1980).

In this way, societal attitudes about sexuality influence teenagers' developing attitudes, behaviors, and sexual identities. The 1960s and the 1970s gave rise to changing attitudes and norms of adult sexual behavior. While controversy continues about the extent to which adult norms should apply to adolescents, the prevalence of nonmarital sexual activity and cohabitation, the availability of biomedical contraceptives and abortion, and the growing acceptance of childbearing outside marriage have undeniably influenced adolescents.

Changing attitudes and behavior related to sexuality have been paralleled by pervasive changes in other areas of adolescent behavior as well, particularly licit and illicit drug use and normative transgressions in general. A wide variety of research indicates quite compellingly the covariation that is found among sexual activity, alcohol use, drug use, and delinquency during adolescence (Ensminger, Vol. II). In addition, it suggests that for many young people, sexual permissiveness is not an isolated phenomenon but instead one component of a complex pattern of interrelated behaviors. Such findings have important implications for understanding sexual behavior within the context of the adolescent's life as a whole, as well as for understanding the nature of the culture in which that behavior is embedded.

Culture fundamentally affects sexuality and fertility by creating values, norms, and expectations about sexual relationships, sex roles, sexual behavior, marriage, and parenting. The historical events of the 1960s and 1970s dramatically altered the social, economic, and cultural context of adolescence. Different subgroups in American society were differently affected. This social context of adolescent development has directly and indirectly influenced national trends in sexuality and fertility as well as individual sexual behavior and decision making among teenagers in the 1980s.

4

Determinants of Adolescent Sexual Behavior and Decision Making

The research on adolescent pregnancy in the United States over the past 15 years has made enormous strides in enhancing the understanding of teenage sexual behavior and decision making. For teenagers of different ages, at different stages of cognitive and socioemotional development, and living under different social, economic, and cultural circumstances, choices concerning sexual behavior reflect very different degrees of rational thinking and conscious decision making. For many, choices to initiate intercourse, to continue sexual activity, to use contraception, or to marry versus bearing a child and raising it as a single parent may in fact be nonchoices. A substantial body of research exists on the variety of individual, family, and social factors associated with adolescent sexual activity; Chapter 2 presented the trends of the past decade and a half in this activity. This chapter discusses the determinants of six components of adolescent sexual behavior: initiation of sexual activity, contraceptive use, abortion, marriage before childbearing (legitimation), adoption, and childbearing and rearing outside marriage.

DETERMINANTS OF ADOLESCENT SEXUAL ACTIVITY

Research suggests that a number of factors are strongly associated with the initiation of sexual activity before marriage. Among the most important of these are individual characteristics such as puberty and other developmental characteristics, age, race, and socioeconomic status, religiousness, intelligence and academic achievement, and dating behavior; family characteristics, such as family background and parental support and controls; and the influence of peer groups.

Individual Characteristics

Pubertal Development   There is almost universal agreement among the studies that have addressed the issue that early pubertal development (e.g., age of menarche for girls, body development and hormonal levels for boys) is strongly associated with the early initiation of sexual activity (Billy and Udry, 1983; Udry, 1979; Morris et al., 1982; Westney et al., 1983; Zelnik et al., 1981). However, the importance of physical maturity varies by sex and race. Recent studies of pubertal development, sexual motivation, and sexual behavior among white adolescent boys and girls provide strong evidence for the hormonal basis of motivation and behavior in boys. Among girls, hormonal levels were shown to have strong effects on levels of sexual interest but only weak effects on sexual behavior (Udry et al., 1985a, 1985b). These researchers conclude that girls' actual behavior is influenced to a greater extent by their social environment than by physical maturation. There are no comparable data for black boys and girls. However, earlier work suggests that the association between pubertal development and sexual behavior was stronger for white than black girls (Zelnik et al., 1981) and for white boys than for black boys (Morris et al., 1982; Billy and Udry, 1983). Evidence that a sizable minority of black boys report initiation of intercourse prior to puberty (Westney et al., 1983; Clark et al., 1984) suggests a stronger effect of social environment for black boys than for white boys.

As Hofferth concludes (Vol. II:Ch. 1), although there appears to be a strong relationship between pubertal development, hormone levels, and sexual activity, social factors do intervene in determining when and how both boys and girls initiate sexual intercourse, given maturation. For girls especially, biological factors do not appear to operate independently of the individual's social context and concept of sexual readiness. Therefore, how social factors mediate maturational factors remains an important yet not fully explored issue.

Age at Initiation   Available data suggest that more adolescents are becoming sexually active at earlier ages. Nevertheless, the older the teenager, the more likely he or she is to have had intercourse (Zelnik et al., 1981; computations of cumulative sexual activity by single year of age using data from the National Survey of Family Growth in Vol. II). Apparently, only a minority of young people do not become sexually experienced while still in their teens: more than 80 percent of males and 70 percent of females report having had intercourse before their twentieth birthday. The proportion of sexually active teenagers increases with age. Just under 17 percent of boys and 6 percent of girls reported having had intercourse before the age of 15. Nearly 67 percent of boys and 44 percent of girls reported that they were sexually experienced by age 18 (computations of cumulative sexual activity by single year of age using data from the National Longitudinal Survey in Vol. II). Regardless of age, the first time adolescent girls have intercourse, they tend to have partners who are about three years older; boys' initial partners are approximately one year older (Zelnik and Shah, 1983).

Race and Socioeconomic Status Black boys and girls become sexually experienced at earlier ages than their white counterparts (on average about two years earlier) and, at every age, more black than white teenagers are having intercourse (Zelnik et al., 1981; Vol. II; Bauman and Udry, 1981; Newcomer et al., 1980; Newcomer and Udry, 1983). Sexually experienced blacks, however, appear to have intercourse slightly less frequently than whites (Zelnik et al., 1981; Zabin and Clark, 1981). While there is some evidence that young black girls are slightly more likely to be physically mature than whites of comparable ages (Harlan et al., 1980; Devaney and Hubley, 1981), these differences between the races in physical maturity seem too small to explain the large race differences in early premarital sexual activity (Moore et al., 1985).

Disagreement exists over the source of racial differences in the proportion of teenagers who are sexually active and the age of sexual initiation. Some researchers attribute the disparity wholly or in large part to socioeconomic differences among blacks and whites. Others trace it to significant normative differences in the acceptability of early sexual behavior. These explanations are not quite so divergent as they might first appear, since many who believe that there are subcultural differences trace them to economic and social disadvantage. One hypothesis in this regard suggests that neighborhood environments are very important. Because of past histories of residential segregation, most blacks (even middle-class blacks) live in neighborhoods that are substantially poorer than their white counterparts, and their children are subjected to different pressures than are their white peers (St. John and Grasmick, 1982; Hogan and Kitagawa, 1983). Similarly, the length of time an individual or his or her family has lived in poverty may affect sexual attitudes and behavior.

In addition, many who account for racial differences by socioeconomic explanations concede that chronic economic disadvantages may give rise to different outlooks on marriage and family formation, which in turn affect the acceptability of early sexual behavior (Moore et al., 1986; Abrahamse et al., 1985). Blacks report a greater tolerance for sexual activity outside a marital relationship than whites; they rate marriage as less important than do whites; and they perceive a greater tolerance in their neighborhoods for childbearing outside marriage (Moore et al., 1985). Williams (1977, cited in Moore et al., 1986), for example, reports that of the pregnant black teenagers in his Rochester, N.Y., sample, 70 percent expected a favorable reaction from peers and 65 percent anticipated a positive reaction from the baby's father, compared with 40 and 43 percent, respectively, among the pregnant white girls he studied. Similarly, black teenagers interviewed in the 1976 National Survey of Young Women were considerably less likely to perceive condemnation of an unmarried mother in their neighborhood than were white teenagers (Zelnik et al., 1981). In some studies, blacks also indicate a preference for a younger age at first birth than age at first marriage, while whites report just the opposite (Zabin et al., 1984; Peterson as reported in Moore et al., 1986).

Such attitudes do not cause premarital sexual activity and teenage pregnancy, but neither do they discourage it (Moore et al., 1986). It may be that they simply reflect the prevalence of teenage pregnancy in the black community. As Hofferth points out (Vol. II:Ch. 1), it is difficult to understand the role of attitudes because most studies have been unable to sufficiently control for them. The point at which values and attitudes about premarital sexual activity are usually measured is after sexual initiation, and therefore it seems likely that sexual experience may have already influenced the respondent's views.

A recent unpublished analysis of data from the 1981 National Survey of Children attempted to examine the sources of racial differences in levels of sexual activity and age of initiation of sexual activity (Furstenberg et al., 1985b). Using a variety of indicators of socioeconomic status and social disadvantage, it was possible to reduce only a small portion of the racial difference in the incidence of sexual experience before age 16. However, much of the difference between blacks and whites could be explained by taking into account the racial composition of the schools attended by the survey participants. The investigators found high proportions of sexually experienced teenagers among blacks of the same social background who attended racially isolated schools compared with those who attended schools with white students. Among blacks and whites who attended racially diverse schools, there were only modest differences in the probability of sexual intercourse. In addition, there was some evidence that the racial composition of the schools was also associated with differences in the acceptability of premarital childbearing. To some extent school segregation is, undoubtedly, a surrogate measure for low socioeconomic status among many blacks and reflects the pervasive conditions of disadvantage that characterize the neighborhood environments in which they live. However, further research on this difficult issue is needed.

In conclusion, the research on racial differences continues to show strong black-white differences in sexual intercourse at young ages, even controlling for socioeconomic differences. However, questions have been raised as to the adequacy of these controls, given the substantially unequal distribution of socioeconomic status by race, the inequality within categories of socioeconomic status, and the failure to control for the length of time an individual or his or her family has lived in poverty (Hofferth, Vol. II:Ch. 1). Similarly, repeated documentation of differences in attitudes and behaviors does not definitively resolve the source of racial differences. Whether any such race differences represent subgroup values or more transient attitudinal adjustments to external circumstances is not clear. The data do suggest, however, that there are differences in community standards and expectations that affect the acceptability of early sexual behavior in the peer group. If this finding is true, it has important implications for the kinds of strategies that are likely to be successful in lowering the rates of early pregnancy and childbearing among blacks as well as whites. Current efforts by black community organizations to modify adolescent attitudes may further illuminate this issue. Further research on this rather neglected topic is needed.

Religiousness Religiousness appears to be an important factor distinguishing early from later initiators of sexual activity. Devaney and Hubley (1981) found that women ages 15–19 were more likely to be sexually active if they were not regular church attenders and if they reported that religion was not very important to them. These findings are supported by numerous other studies (Inazu and Fox, 1980; Zelnik et al., 1981; Jessor and Jessor, 1975). Most researchers who have addressed this issue have found that the tendency to be devout and observant of religious custom and teaching is more important than any specific religious affiliation. In particular, Catholicism, which was once regarded as a good index of conservatism on moral issues, has more recently been found not to be a very accurate predictor of sexual experience. Devaney and Hubley (1981) found no difference in the likelihood of reporting sexual experience between Catholics and those of other denominations. Protestant fundamentalism, however, which has gained visibility and followers in recent years, has frequently been associated with strong conservative positions on issues of sexual behavior. As Hofferth reports (Vol. II:Ch. 1), teenage adherents to fundamentalist denominations have been found less likely to have had sexual intercourse outside marriage than members of other denominations (Thornton and Camburn, 1983). Religious teenagers may also be those who are more traditional in general than other teenagers and therefore less likely to engage in behaviors that push toward adulthood (e.g., smoking, drinking). They may also have stronger social supports to enforce behavioral norms.

Intelligence, Academic Aspirations, and Achievement   A number of studies suggest a strong association between low intellectual ability, low academic achievement, a lack of educational goals, and early sexual experience among both blacks and whites. Adolescent girls who score low on intelligence tests and place little value on educational attainment are more likely to have intercourse at an early age than those who are educationally ambitious. Conversely, those who score high on intelligence tests, are academically motivated, and are doing well in school are less likely to initiate sexual activity at a young age (Mott, 1983; Devaney and Hubley, 1981; Furstenberg, 1976; Hogan and Kitagawa, 1983; Udry et al., 1975; Moore et al., 1985; Jessor and Jessor, 1975; Jessor et al., 1983). An earlier analysis by Mott (1983) indicated similar results for young men ages 17–20.

The association between ability, educational aspirations, and performance and the lower likelihood of early sexual experience is undoubtedly tied to several interacting social, economic, psychological, and situational variables. For example, parents' level of education and their aspirations for their children can significantly influence teenagers' own attitudes and expectations about academic achievement (Davies and Kandel, 1981; Spenner and Featherman, 1978). Parents with more education are generally more affluent than parents with less education. Children in families with more educated parents tend to be more goal-oriented, to place a higher value on achievement, and to be more oriented to work than play (Conger, 1973). Chilman (1980b) suggests that these characteristics may make a teenager less likely to engage in premarital intercourse during the junior high or high school years. She also suggests that, especially for girls, involvement in educational achievement (thereby pleasing parents and teachers) may inhibit interest in boys or may make girls less interesting to boys.

The Nature of Sexual Behavior   Regardless of age, each adolescent boy and girl who enters a sexual relationship does so at a particular level of socioemotional and cognitive development and with whatever self-perceptions he or she has formed, as well as within a particular social and cultural context. At least until recently, studies showed that adolescents, especially young white women, gradually advanced their level of sexual intimacy through a series of dating and "going steady" experiences (Vener and Stewart, 1974). There was generally a learning period during which a boy and a girl became better acquainted and developed an affectionate relationship. Research on the incidence of these behaviors suggests that this pattern of gradually developing sexual intimacy during adolescence is still common among white youth, although it is beginning earlier and progressing more rapidly. It does not appear to hold true for young blacks, however.

Existing research findings concerning the nature of teenage sexual behavior, as McAnarney and Schreider (1984) suggest, derive from data on middle or older adolescents. Their applicability to the youngest teens is not clear. When young adolescent girls begin having intercourse, it is generally infrequent and unpredictable (Kantner and Zelnik, 1972). They frequently report the need to be "spontaneous," and therefore the event does not really reflect rational and planned behavior. Especially among very young adolescents, their level of logical operational thinking may not be sufficiently developed for them to recognize that having or not having intercourse is a choice and that without contraception it can result in pregnancy (McAnarney, 1982). As they become older, many researchers believe, teenagers become better able to make well-reasoned, conscious decisions about their sexual behavior. It is interesting to note, however, that research from other developed countries shows that even young sexually active teenagers can effectively avoid pregnancy (Alan Guttmacher Institute, in press). Self-esteem appears unrelated to the initiation of sexual activity for both boys and girls (Mott, 1983; Cvetkovich and Grote, 1980). Nevertheless, there is a dearth of well-developed theoretical models to explain and predict sexual decision making by adolescents (Libby and Carlson, 1973).

Research findings also suggest that sexual activity is generally not an isolated behavior. Adolescents who are sexually active at an early age are also frequently involved in other behaviors that push toward independence and adulthood, often in conflict with adult norms for them. Among transition behaviors most often associated with early sexual activity are smoking, drinking, and drug use (Jessor and Jessor, 1975; Jessor et al., 1983). The extent to which there may be a causal link among these behaviors is not fully understood. There is ambivalence in our society about whether these behaviors represent a healthy assertion of independence or deviant (if not delinquent) behavior (Ensminger, Vol. II:Ch. 2). In this regard, Jessor et al. (1983) suggest that the decision by an adolescent to become sexually active may more accurately reflect the conscious or unconscious decision to assume a particular life-style rather than to adopt a single isolated behavior.

Early dating appears to be associated with early sexual experience (Furstenberg, 1976; Spanier, 1975). The more frequently teenagers (especially girls) date, the more likely they are to have intercourse (Simon and Gagnon, 1970; Presser, 1976b). In addition, while survey data show that more teenagers are sexually active and that there has been a relative decrease in the number of their partners (Zelnik, 1983), several studies suggest that the more committed the relationship between young people, the more likely they are to have intercourse (Spanier, 1975; Furstenberg, 1976; Sorenson, 1973; Reiss, 1976).

Family Characteristics

Parental Support and Controls A number of studies have found that the nature of their relationships with parents affects teenagers' sexual behavior. Adolescent girls are more likely to have premarital intercourse if their mothers fail to combine affection with firm, mild discipline and to set clearly defined limits on behavior. However, as Hofferth (Vol. II:Ch. 1) suggests, since adolescence is a time of testing one's independence and gradually growing away from parents, it is also possible that a decline in the closeness of a mother-daughter relationship follows the initiation of sexual activity rather than preceding or causing it. Alternatively, both decline in closeness and initiation of sexual intercourse could be the result of increased independence.

Some studies also show that young people are more likely to be sexually experienced if they perceive themselves to be in poor communication with their parents and feel that they receive little parental support (Simon et al., 1972; Jessor and Jessor, 1975). As Hofferth (Vol. II:Ch. 1) points out, however, parent-child relationships and parent-child communication, although important, seem to have an ambiguous association. As a result, there is no clear implication for program development. There is evidence that close relationships may be associated with less sexual activity among younger teenagers (Inazu and Fox, 1980). Jessor and Jessor (1975) similarly found that the more consistent the values of teenagers and their parents, the greater sense of connectedness and supportiveness between them, and the closer the young people's ties to home, the less likely they were to become sexually active.

Yet communication may be associated with a higher level of sexual activity among teenagers than a lower one, especially among older teenagers. First, in many cases, less parent-child communication takes place than is commonly assumed; second, such communication, whether to provide information or to prescribe behavior, may not be fully heard by the child; and third, communication about sexual behavior frequently does not occur until after initiation of sexual activity (Newcomer and Udry, 1983; Inazu and Fox, 1980). Fox (1981) points out that parents' (especially mothers') roles in sex education are relatively minor, and that the more traditionally oriented mothers are on matters of sexual morality, sex roles, etc., the less likely they are to initiate discussions of these topics with their children. Unfortunately, however, as Hofferth (Vol. II:Ch. 1) points out, there is little research to specify the context of communication or to distinguish the effects of communication before and after initiation of sexual activity.

One recent study that was able to make this distinction found no relationship between the frequency of communication about sexual topics (before initiation) with the mother or father and the sexual activity of the daughter (Kahn et al., 1984). For boys, communication with the mother was associated with less subsequent sexual activity; communication with the father was associated with more sexual activity. Kahn et al. (1984) conclude that perhaps fathers implicitly, if not explicitly, condone sexual activity among sons, without providing the emphasis on responsibility that mothers communicate.

As with parental communication, the research on the relationship between parental supervision or control of adolescent behavior and the initiation of sexual activity also suggests conflicting results. Hogan and Kitagawa (1983) found that more supervision was associated with less sexual activity among a sample of inner-city black girls. In contrast, other researchers have found that more supervision was unrelated to the initiation of sexual activity (Inazu and Fox, 1980; Newcomer and Udry, 1983). As Hofferth (Vol. II:Ch. 1) points out, generalizations about the impact of parental supervision on sexual activity are not possible without further study.

Other Family Characteristics   There is a strong relationship between a mother's sexual and fertility experience as a teenager and that of her daughter (Newcomer and Udry, 1983; Presser, 1976b). The earlier the mother's first sexual experience and first birth, the earlier the daughter's experience.

Other family factors that appear to affect the level and quality of parental supports and controls, and perhaps in turn influence sexual behavior among teenagers, include family intactness, family composition, and mother's age at marriage. Several studies have shown that girls in nonintact or female-headed families are more likely to become sexually experienced at an early age than those in two-parent families (Zelnik et al., 1981; Newcomer and Udry, 1983; Moore et al., 1985; Inazu and Fox, 1980). Similarly, the larger the family (the more siblings present), the more likely that an older sibling will be sexually active and provide a model for younger siblings (Hogan and Kitagawa, 1983).

Although there is strong evidence of these associations, the mechanisms by which they affect adolescent sexual behavior are not fully understood. For example, some researchers hypothesize that the stress resulting from parental separation or divorce and from the presence of several siblings may cause teenage children (especially daughters) to perceive a lack of attention and affection from their mothers and may lead them to seek such attention in sexual relationships. Others suggest that the inevitable stress of such circumstances may make it more difficult for parents to adequately supervise their teenagers. Still others suggest that, particularly in families in which there has been a divorce or the mother became sexually active at an early age, parents (especially mothers) may indirectly communicate an attitude of permissiveness. All of these are plausible explanations, and they warrant further exploration.

Peer Group Influence

Although research on peer influences on early sexual activity is relatively limited, the attitudes and behavior of peers is frequently cited as the single most important factor affecting the initiation of intercourse by adolescents. It appears, however, that peer influence may have been overrated, particularly among blacks and white males. Hofferth (Vol. II:Ch. 1) cites several significant problems with the research, including the facts that (1) the same individual typically reports on his or her own as well as his or her friends' attitudes and behavior without independent validation and (2) data have been gathered at only one point in time, thus preventing researchers from detecting delayed effects.

Several studies suggest that same-sex peers are a major source of information about sex (Libby and Carlson, 1973; Miller, 1976; Thornburg, 1978). In addition, Cvetkovich and Grote (1980) report that the proportion of their same-sex peers that teenagers believe are sexually experienced and how sexually liberal they believe them to be are powerful predictors of sexual experience among adolescent boys and girls. Newcomer et al. (1980), however, conclude that individual behavior and attitudes are more closely related to what teenagers think their friends do and believe than to what is actually going on. It appears that many teenagers act on perceptions of their friends' attitudes and behavior, whether or not their perceptions are correct.

Peer pressure can take several forms (e.g., challenges and dares, coercion, social acceptability), and its influence seems to vary among young people of different ages and genders. There is some evidence that white boys choose their friends on the basis of sexual activity. Blacks, however, appear neither to be influenced by friends' behavior nor to choose friends on that basis (Billy and Udry, 1983). Girls may be swayed to some extent by what they think or know their female friends are doing, but they are more strongly influenced by their best male friends and their sexual partners (Miller and Simon, 1974; Herold, 1980; Cvetkovich and Grote, 1980; Billy and Udry, 1983). Lewis and Lewis (1984) found that among young adolescents (10–14) peer pressure in the form of challenges and dares significantly influences sexual involvement at several levels (e.g., kissing, fondling, and intercourse), especially among girls. Billy and Udry (1983, 1984), however, suggest that among black boys and girls, peer influence is relatively minor. In general, white girls appear to be most susceptible to peer influences in sexual decision making.

Because adolescence in general is a period in which children's orientation shifts away from parents toward peers, it seems likely that peer influence varies according to age. As teens get older, peers become more influential. Although the body of findings is not conclusive, it also seems likely that the relative influence of peers and parents may also vary depending on the issue. Thus, for example, parents may be more important in teenagers' establishing life goals and developing aspirations, while peers and sexual partners may be more important in forming attitudes about sexual activity. As Hofferth (Vol. II:Ch. 1) points out, however, while peer pressure has been consistently pointed to as an important factor in teenage sexual activity, there is only weak evidence that an individual's behavior changes as a result of interaction with a peer.

DETERMINANTS OF CONTRACEPTIVE USE

The existing research suggests that several factors are strongly associated with contraceptive use by unmarried, sexually active teenagers. Among the most important of these are age of initiation, having a stable relationship with a sexual partner, knowledge of reproduction and contraception, acceptance of one's own sexuality, academic aspirations, and parental support and controls.

Age at Initiation

The older the adolescent girl at the time of initiation of sexual activity, the more likely she is to use contraception and to use it regularly and effectively (Kantner and Zelnik, 1972; Zelnik and Kantner, 1977; Zabin and Clark, 1981; Devaney and Hubley, 1981). In addition, the older the girl, the more likely she is to use a medical method, primarily the pill (Zelnik et al., 1981). Younger girls more often report that they have never used contraception, in part because they have had less time to develop patterns of use. Younger girls are also more likely to be sporadic and ineffective contraceptors, and they are more likely to rely on male methods (Kantner and Zelnik, 1972).

Since a higher proportion of blacks are very young when they initiate intercourse, blacks have a higher incidence of sexual activity without contraception. However, controlling for this difference in age at initiation of sexual activity, blacks are as likely as whites to practice contraception. Among boys, regardless of race, age appears to have little effect on contraceptive use at first intercourse.

Nature of the Relationship

Several studies show a strong association between the stability and degree of commitment in male-female relationships (e.g., going steady, engaged to be married) and the use of contraception (Devaney and Hubley, 1981; Herold, 1980; Hornick et al., 1979; Freeman et al., 1980; Luker, 1975). Devaney and Hubley (1981) found this to be especially true among black teens. Adolescents in such relationships generally engage in intercourse more frequently than adolescents without strong romantic ties to one partner. They are also more likely to use oral contraceptives (Kantner and Zelnik, 1972; Luker, 1975). However, other evidence indicates that teenagers who report frequent sexual activity with different partners are also more likely to use contraceptives than those who have intercourse infrequently.

Academic Aspirations and Achievement

Among both blacks and whites, those girls who have clear educational goals and expectations and are performing well in school appear more likely to use contraception than those who lack a strong achievement orientation (Devaney and Hubley, 1981). Similarly, the better educated their parents, the more likely adolescent girls are to use contraceptives consistently (Zelnik et al., 1981). Cvetkovich and Grote (1980) found that the same was true for black boys. Black girls are more likely than whites, net of other factors, to have used a medical method of contraception (e.g., the pill or IUD) at last intercourse, and black girls with better educated parents are even more likely than their peers to have used a medical method (Zelnik et al., 1981). Furstenberg and Brooks-Gunn (1985b), in their follow-up study of teenage mothers in Baltimore, found that many young women in their sample were below grade level at the time they became pregnant, suggesting a potentially significant relationship between school achievement and the likelihood of an unintended pregnancy. Other researchers have also found this relationship (Wertheimer and Moore, 1982).

Knowledge of Reproduction and Contraception

Many adults assume that if adolescents know how their bodies work, the time each month when females are at greatest risk of pregnancy, the methods they can use to protect against unintended pregnancy, and how to obtain contraceptives, they will be more likely to seek out family planning services and to use methods of contraception effectively (McAnarney and Schreider, 1984). Indeed, available research findings confirm the fact that knowledge about sex and contraception are associated with greater frequency of contraceptive use among boys and girls (Cvetkovich and Grote, 1980). In addition, most teenagers, even young ones, have a general understanding of conception, and they know that a girl can become pregnant if she has intercourse (Moore et al., 1986; Jenkins, 1983; Zabin and Clark, 1981). However, researchers who have questioned adolescent girls about their levels of sexual knowledge have found that many teenagers do not know enough of the basic facts to use contraception effectively (Zelnik and Shah, 1983). The level and accuracy of knowledge among teenage girls who are sexually experienced and those who are not differ very little (Kantner and Zelnik, 1972). Similarly, comparisons of adolescent girls seeking contraception, seeking abortion, or carrying a pregnancy to term show little difference in their levels of knowledge about sexuality and birth control (Goldsmith et al., 1972).

As Moore et al. (1986) point out, some types of sexual knowledge are inevitably more crucial than others, and primary in this regard is an understanding of pregnancy risk. Despite what they have learned about timing and the risk of becoming pregnant, many younger adolescents apparently believe they are not at risk because they are so young (Kantner and Zelnik, 1973). Those just entering puberty may be accurate, yet, as they become fully mature, these girls will be as vulnerable to pregnancy as adult women. Many others who successfully avoid pregnancy initially come to believe they are immune and do not need to use contraception (Moore et al., 1986). As previously discussed, many researchers conclude that younger teenagers are handicapped in assessing the personal risk of pregnancy because of their cognitive immaturity (Cvetkovich and Grote, 1975; Cobliner, 1981; McAnarney and Schreider, 1984). Since many are still incapable of thinking abstractly and relating actions to specific consequences—particularly when their early personal experience is contrary to what they have learned—they have a difficult time planning for sexual intercourse and using contraception. This has not been shown in cross-cultural studies of adolescent sexual behavior, however (Alan Guttmacher Institute, in press).

As McAnarney and Schreider (1984) point out, the issue here is not just whether more sex education should be directed at adolescents; they conclude that it should. What seems to be more critical, however, is the need to develop a better understanding of the relationship between what young people know and how they behave. A recent important study of a small sample of model sex education programs found that, while a variety of programs were quite effective at increasing teenagers' level of knowledge about conception and contraception, they had little impact on their behavior: whether they became sexually active and whether they used contraception (Kirby, 1984). The relationship between what adolescents know and how they behave is perhaps the most salient issue.

Acceptance of One's Own Sexuality and Attitude About Contraception

Several studies have found regular and effective contraceptive use among adolescent girls to be strongly associated with acceptance of their own sexual behavior. Girls who acknowledge that they are sexually active are more likely to obtain and use contraceptives (Lindemann, 1974). In addition, the more people who know about a teenager's use of birth control, the more likely she is to be contracepting (Philliber et al., 1983). Inability to acknowledge her own sexuality, on the other hand, may inhibit an adolescent girl from obtaining and using contraceptives. As a consequence, many have difficulty coming to terms with their own sexual behavior and admitting that they are violating internalized norms and taking pregnancy risks. Research has shown that many teenagers, especially younger girls, delay using contraceptives for up to a year after they become sexually active (Zelnik et al., 1981). In part, this may be a consequence of their inability to acknowledge their own sexuality.

Similarly, having a low level of guilt about one's sexual behavior and having a positive attitude about contraception are also strongly associated with effective use (Herold, 1980). In particular, fear that contraception will have negative health effects and will interfere with pleasure has been shown to be related to less frequent use (Cvetkovich and Grote, 1980; Poppen, 1979; Forrest and Henshaw, 1983). Related to this, Polit et al. (1981) found that teenage girls who believe that the female should take responsibility for birth control tend to be more effective contraceptors.

Although very little research has included teenage boys, available studies suggest that knowledge about and attitudes toward birth control are very important to contraceptive use as reported by boys (Cvetkovich and Grote, 1981; Polit et al., 1981). Unfortunately, levels of knowledge appear to be quite low (Finkel and Finkel, 1975).

Developmental Characteristics

Adolescent girls with a high level of self-esteem, who perceive that they have a large measure of control over their lives and that they are competent and capable of choosing and shaping their destinies, are more likely to be effective users of contraceptives than those who have a low sense of competence and believe that events in their lives are largely beyond their control. Similarly, girls who tend to be passive and to hold traditional attitudes about female dependence in male-female relationships are also generally poor contraceptors (Cvetkovich and Grote, 1980; Fox, 1980; Steinhoff, 1976). Related to this, McAnarney and Schreider (1984) report that girls who are impulsive, who find it difficult to plan ahead, and who are risk-takers also tend to have poor records of contraceptive use. Taken together, these traits are related to low levels of ego development and to a lack of ego strength, which in turn are associated with poor contraceptive use (Miller, 1976). Among boys, those who are impulsive, socially irresponsible, and oriented to risk-taking tend to be poor users of contraceptives (Cvetkovich and Grote, 1980).

Parental Support and Controls

Several studies indicate that if a teenage girl has good lines of communication with her mother and her mother is a source of information about birth control, she is likely to be a more frequent user of contraceptives (Furstenberg, 1976; Flaherty and Maracek, 1982). Mothers with positive birth control attitudes are more likely to discuss contraception with their daughters, as do those who have greater knowledge of reproduction and contraceptive methods. These discussions, even if they are isolated or infrequent, appear to positively influence teenage contraceptive use (Fox, 1980, 1981). Similarly, family support (especially from mothers) in seeking family planning services and following a birth control regimen appears to lead to more consistent contraceptive use

(Ktsanes, 1977). Furthermore, there is evidence that the type of maternal discipline employed is associated with frequency of contraceptive use. In particular, daughters who are limited by parental rules and experience punishments for violations, and for whom restrictions of privileges are imposed rather than corporal punishment, are more likely to use contraception (Flaherty and Maracek, 1982). Unfortunately, however, most of these studies have failed to control for other confounding factors, such as socioeconomic status and family structure, which may significantly affect the strength of the reported findings.

As Hofferth (Vol. II:Ch. 3) concludes, most family background variables (e.g., family composition and size, socioeconomic status, etc.) appear to be less directly related to teenage contraceptive use than are mother-daughter communication about contraception and mothers' support of their daughters' use of contraception. Neither religiousness nor religious affiliation, for example, was found to be associated with contraceptive use, net of other factors (Zelnik et al., 1981). Parents' education, both mothers' and fathers', is the one background factor that does seem to affect daughters' use of birth control methods. However, the mechanism by which parental education affects contraceptive use among adolescents is not well understood. Does parents' education influence teenagers' achievement orientation and thereby affect their use of birth control? Or do better educated parents tend to discuss contraception more openly with their adolescent children and to be more supportive of their teenagers' use of birth control? Or both? These questions cannot be answered on the basis of existing knowledge. The role of peers in contraceptive use is also poorly understood.

Why some youth are effective contraceptors and others are not is still a little researched issue (Hofferth, Vol. II:Ch. 3). In particular, we know little about actual contraceptive practice and why contraceptive failure rates vary by age.

DETERMINANTS OF ABORTION

The existing research on this topic suggests that a number of factors are associated with the decision to terminate a pregnancy by abortion. Among the most important of these are whether the pregnancy was intended, contraceptive use, academic aspirations, the influence of family and peers, and access to abortion services.

Unintendedness

Among the most important factors affecting the outcome of a pregnancy is whether it was intended. Girls who report that they wanted the pregnancy are more likely to give birth, while those who report that they did not want the pregnancy are more likely to have an abortion (Zelnik et al., 1981). The issue of intendedness is complicated, however, since reports of whether a pregnancy was wanted are generally collected after the pregnancy has been discovered. In many situations it seems likely that although the conception was unintended, a girl may decide in retrospect (either consciously or unconsciously) that she must have wanted to be pregnant once she learns that she is pregnant and has decided against obtaining an abortion.

Academic Aspirations and Achievement

Girls who are doing well in school before pregnancy and who have a strong future orientation are more likely to choose abortion to resolve an unintended pregnancy than those who are not good students and who lack high educational and vocational goals (Steinhoff, 1976; Evans et al., 1976; Eisen et al., 1983; Leibowitz et al., 1980; Devaney and Hubley, 1981). This holds for both blacks and whites. As with contraception, parental education also appears to be a very significant factor in pregnancy resolution. The higher the parents' level of education, the greater the likelihood that a teenager will have an abortion rather than carry an unintended pregnancy to term (Zelnik et al., 1981).

Contraceptive Use

Concern that abortion may become a substitute for contraception is not supported by the available research. In 1979, teenagers who had terminated an unintended pregnancy by abortion were less likely to have experienced a second pregnancy within two years than those girls who carried their first pregnancy to term (Koenig and Zelnik, 1982). Data from the National Center for Health Statistics suggest that about 12 percent of abortions to 15- to 17-year-olds and 22 percent of abortions to 18- to 19-year-olds are repeat abortions (National Center for Health Statistics, 1984b). Furthermore, clinic studies show that, three weeks following an abortion, less than 10 percent of girls were not using any method of contraception, while more than 80 percent were using the pill or IUD (Alan Guttmacher Institute, 1981). Although such studies using clinic patients undoubtedly reflect the behavior of a self-selected sample, they do suggest that contraceptive behavior following an abortion may be better rather than worse among some teenagers (Forrest and Henshaw, 1983).

Family Characteristics

Several studies of adolescent girls who choose abortion have found that family background factors are significant predictors. In particular, it appears that whites are more likely than blacks to terminate an unintended pregnancy, and that girls from families with higher socioeconomic status are more likely to abort than those from poverty backgrounds, especially from families on welfare (Zelnik et al., 1981). A note of caution in the interpretation of socioeconomic data is important, however, because survey respondents tend to underreport pregnancy and abortion. Girls from less religious families have been found more likely to choose abortion than those from more devout families. Surprisingly, however, rates of abortion were found to be higher for white Catholic girls than for either white non-Catholics or Hispanic Catholics, suggesting that religious affiliation may not be an important determination in the decision to abort (Eisen et al., 1983).

Parents', especially mothers', attitudes about abortion have also been shown to significantly influence the outcome of an unintended pregnancy. Girls whose mothers are more favorably disposed to abortion are less likely to have a birth (Eisen et al., 1983). Among very young teenagers, it appears that parents have a major influence on the decision to terminate a pregnancy (Steinhoff, 1976; Rosen, 1980).

Peer Influences

The attitudes of peers also seem to influence decisions concerning pregnancy resolution. The more positive a girlfriend's or boyfriend's opinion of abortion, the less likely an adolescent girl is to have a birth (Eisen et al., 1983). In contrast, girls who have friends or family members who are teenage single parents are more likely to carry their pregnancies to term (Eisen et al., 1983).

Access to Abortion Services

Teenagers are less likely than women in their twenties to obtain abortions during the safer, earlier weeks of gestation. The younger the teenager, the more likely she is to delay. As the Alan Guttmacher Institute (1981) reports, only 34 percent of abortions to girls age 15 and younger are performed during the first eight weeks of gestation, compared with 41 percent of abortions among girls ages 15–19, and 51 percent of those among women ages 20–24. At the other extreme, 14 percent of abortions to girls 15 and younger are performed at 16 weeks and later (Alan Guttmacher Institute, 1981). Such delays increase the health risks associated with pregnancy termination.

The Alan Guttmacher Institute (1981) cites several likely reasons for the delay. First, many teenagers, particularly the very young, fail to recognize the signs of pregnancy early. Many adolescent girls ordinarily experience menstrual irregularities and therefore do not distinguish them from early signs of pregnancy. Many others simply deny the unpleasant reality of an unintended pregnancy until it becomes unavoidable. In addition, access to abortion services appears to be limited for many teenagers. Though most school-age adolescents, especially very young teenagers, consult their parents in deciding to obtain an abortion, parental consent requirements in many states (or the perception of such requirements) are thought to inhibit some teenagers from seeking and obtaining abortions. Geographical distance from clinics or hospitals that perform abortions, as well as costs, have also been shown to limit teenagers' access to abortion, especially school-age girls and those from poor families (Alan Guttmacher Institute, 1981).

DETERMINANTS OF MARRIAGE BEFORE CHILDBEARING (LEGITIMATION)

Although there are more conceptions to unmarried adolescents now than a generation ago, they are less likely today to resolve a pregnancy by marrying. The proportion of unmarried adolescents conceiving who married before the birth decreased from approximately 31 percent in 1970 to approximately 23 percent in 1981 (O'Connell and Rogers, 1984).

The existing research on determinants of marriage to legitimate a birth is limited. Nevertheless, race, age at initiation, and the availability of financial assistance appear to be significant factors.

Race and Socioeconomic Status

White teenagers and those from families of higher socioeconomic status are more likely, if they are pregnant, to marry before bearing a child (Zelnik et al., 1981; O'Connell and Moore, 1980). In 1980–1981, approximately 28 percent of white unmarried teenagers ages 15–19 who conceived were married before the birth. In contrast, only about 9 percent of all black teenagers married to legitimate a birth (O'Connell and Rogers, 1984). Indeed, in all age groups, black women are now more likely to be unmarried than to be married (Moore et al., 1986). Among teenagers, however, the primary reason is never having married rather than divorce, separation, or the death of a spouse.

Age

Older teenagers are more likely than younger ones to marry to legitimate a birth. In 1981 only 11 percent of 14-year-olds married, while 63 percent of 19-year-olds married before bearing a child (O'Connell and Rogers, 1984). The highest proportion of marriages occurs among older white teenagers.

Availability of Financial Assistance

Two recent studies have found that two factors are strongly associated with decisions to carry a premarital pregnancy to term: (1) the availability of financial aid from the family of origin and (2) the availability of public financial assistance (Eisen et al., 1983; Leibowitz et al., 1980). They found that a major factor distinguishing those who married from those who gave birth without marriage was the source of support. Girls whose families had been receiving financial aid from the state during their pregnancies were less likely to marry than those who had not received such assistance (Eisen et al., 1983). In contrast, Moore and Caldwell (1977) found no significant association between Aid to Families With Dependent Children benefit levels and acceptance rates and whether a pregnant teenager married before the birth.

DETERMINANTS OF ADOPTION

Because there are no systematically collected national data on adoption, it is impossible to derive precise estimates of the number and proportion of teenagers who choose this means of pregnancy resolution.

There is also very limited research comparing teenagers who make adoption plans and those who keep their babies and raise them as single mothers. As Hofferth (Vol. II:Ch. 4) reports, the results suggest that teenagers who make adoption plans are similar to those who have abortions but differ from those who take on parenting responsibilities. They tend to be older and to come from families of higher socioeconomic status. They tend to have stronger academic ambitions and to be performing better in school. They tend to hold more traditional attitudes about abortion and family life. In contrast, parenting teenagers tend to have less schooling, to have dropped out of school, to have less well formulated educational and occupational goals, and to come from single-parent families (Hofferth, Vol. II:Ch. 4).

There is virtually no research on factors affecting the decision of unmarried adolescents to place their children for adoption. However, two studies are now under way that may shed some light on this important topic (Kallen, 1984; Resnick, 1984).

DETERMINANTS OF NONMARITAL CHILDBEARING

The existing research suggests that several factors are strongly associated with nonmarital childbearing: race, attitudes, poverty and unemployment, and the availability of financial assistance.

Race

Although the rate of childbearing has increased dramatically among unmarried white adolescents since 1970, black adolescents have always been more likely to give birth outside marriage. Black teenagers account for 14 percent of the adolescent population and 46 percent of all births to unmarried 15- to 19-year-olds (National Center for Health Statistics, 1984b). In 1982, over 98 percent of births to black teenagers under age 15 occurred outside marriage, and 87 percent of births to black teenagers ages 15–19 occurred outside marriage. The comparable figures for white teenagers in these age groups were 78 and 36 percent, respectively (Vol. II:appendix tables, section on births).

The underlying causes of childbearing among unmarried young black adolescents are complex and difficult to disentangle. Most researchers agree that the rising proportion of births to unmarried black teenagers over the past generation is attributable to the declining rate of marriage to legitimate a birth. In part it is also attributable to changing patterns of sexual activity and contraception among blacks. Black girls are twice as likely as white girls to have premarital intercourse, and they generally become sexually active at younger ages than whites. The higher proportion of blacks who are very young when they first have intercourse is associated with a higher incidence of sexual activity without contraception. As one might expect, blacks are more likely to become pregnant and to become pregnant at younger ages. They are also disproportionately more likely to resort to abortion. However, since the higher abortion rate among blacks does not erase the dramatic race difference in rates of unintended pregnancy, births are much more prevalent among black than white teenagers (Moore et al., 1986).

Attitudes Toward Nonmarital Childbearing

There are many accepted family forms in the black community, including the nuclear family (father, mother, and children), the attenuated family (father or mother and children), the extended, multigenerational family (some combination of grandparents, aunts, uncles, parents, and children), and augmented families (one of the above types that also includes unrelated friends, boarders, or guests) (Billingsley, 1970). As several scholars have commented, this diversity of family forms makes single parenthood less unusual and provides more socially acceptable opportunities for accommodating young black single mothers and their children than are available in the white community (Williams, 1977, cited in Moore et al., 1986; Miller, 1983). Stack (1974) describes a support network among low-income urban blacks that helps cushion individuals from the conditions of life in poverty. She concludes that many young mothers find greater security in this network than in marriage. Black families seem to be more supportive of young mothers, and it may be that this supportiveness ameliorates a teenager's fear of becoming a mother (Moore et al., 1986). Still, many researchers and advocates argue that childbearing by unmarried adolescents is not highly valued in the black community. Although there is a greater tolerance of unmarried parenthood, it is generally viewed as unfortunate (Moore et al., 1986). Furstenberg (1976) found that among a low-income urban clinic population, only 20 percent of teenagers were pleased to learn they were pregnant; another 20 percent had mixed feelings; and the remainder were disappointed or upset. Very few of these teenagers reported that their mothers were pleased; most mothers were reportedly hurt and depressed or angry (Furstenberg, 1976).

As discussed earlier, differences in attitudes about childbearing by very young unmarried teenagers appear to be closely related to community and neighborhood standards of tolerance and acceptability. Most blacks live in poorer neighborhoods than whites. Therefore, as many researchers argue, race differences in adolescent pregnancy and childbearing may be significantly linked to social and economic disadvantage (Hogan and Kitagawa, 1983).

Recent research also suggests that an important factor influencing attitudes about nonmarital childbearing are perceptions of opportunities that are unrelated to reproductive behavior. In short, willingness to bear a child outside marriage is closely related to the implied costs of doing so (Abrahamse et al., 1985). These researchers infer that among low-income girls with low academic and occupational expectations living in single-parent families, the perceived opportunity costs of early, nonmarital childbearing were very low, since their willingness to risk such parenthood was quite high. They infer that young girls whose lives and perceived opportunities are not currently gratifying may be more open to motherhood, which they may perceive as a potential source of gratification. Because blacks are more likely than whites to be poor, to live in nonintact families, and to demonstrate low academic ability and have low expectations, they may also be more willing to bear a child while unmarried (Abrahamse et al., 1985). Nathanson and Becker (1983), however, were unable to find any relationship between perceived opportunities and the contraceptive behavior of adolescents.

Abrahamse et al. (1985) also showed a strong relationship between rebelliousness (i.e., disciplinary problems in school, cutting classes, and absenteeism) among adolescent girls and willingness to become an unmarried mother. Similarly, girls who reported that they rarely talked to their parents about their plans and activities expressed greater willingness to have a child outside marriage than those who reported that they talked to their parents often. And girls who reported that their parents were less likely to monitor and keep track of their activities were also at greater risk of unmarried motherhood, although this pattern was found to be much stronger for whites than for blacks (Abrahamse et al., 1985).

Poverty and Unemployment

As previously discussed, bleak social and economic prospects for many black girls from low-income families may be associated with their early initiation of sexual activity and lack of effective contraceptive practice. Poverty and poor employment opportunities are closely associated with nonmarital childbearing (Presser, 1974; Ross and Sawhill, 1975; Furstenberg, 1976). High rates of youth unemployment and a lack of economic resources, especially among black teenagers, frequently make marriage unmanageable for an adolescent couple, despite the impending birth of a baby.

Availability of Financial Assistance

Concern over the high rates of welfare dependence in the United States have led many critics to question whether the availability of Aid to Families With Dependent Children (AFDC) and other, noncash benefits is an unfortunate incentive for young women to give birth outside marriage. The existing body of research suggests that there is no evidence to support this assumption, although the relationship between welfare and unmarried adolescent childbearing is complex (Ross and Sawhill, 1975; Presser, 1974; Moore and Caldwell, 1977; Ellwood and Bane, 1984). Presser (1974) found that there were no significant differences in fertility attitudes or behaviors among the welfare recipients and nonrecipients in her New York City study. Similarly, Furstenberg (1976) found that unmarried teenage girls do not get pregnant in order to receive public assistance, but that girls from low-income, female-headed families (many of whom are receiving welfare benefits) are more likely to become single mothers themselves. Moore and Caldwell (1977) suggest that because welfare assistance is available, a young woman faced with a premarital pregnancy may be more likely to choose single parenthood over abortion or adoption or marriage, especially if the father is a poor prospect for support. They found little empirical evidence, however, that welfare benefit levels affect decisions to become sexually active, to become pregnant, or to marry or have an abortion, or to relinquish a child for adoption. As they note, the vast majority of adolescent pregnancies are unintended, and welfare is only one of a number of factors that influence teenagers' decisions regarding pregnancy resolution. Finally, Ellwood and Bane (1984) conclude that largely unmeasurable differences in culture, attitudes, and expectations, rather than differences in levels of welfare support, explain differences in birth rates to unmarried teenagers across the country.

CONCLUSION

As this chapter has described, a variety of individual, family, and social factors are associated with sexual behavior and decision making. Some of these factors directly affect decisions to initiate sexual activity, to contracept, to abort, to marry, or to have a child while unmarried. Others affect decisions indirectly by influencing other relevant factors.

Among the most important factors are adolescents' attitudes about sexual behavior, contraception, abortion, marriage, and single parenthood. Attitudes are inevitably tied to the specific social, economic, and cultural circumstances of a person's life, as well as to a person's overall development as a masculine or feminine human being. Attitudes are related in complex ways to the development of aspirations, interests, and abilities, the capability to form intimate interpersonal relationships, and the transition from dependence on families of origin to independence, marriage, and parenthood.

Several studies of social and psychological factors associated with adolescents' sexual behavior conclude that self-perception (not self-esteem)—that is, the sense of what and who one is, can be, and wants to be—is at the heart of teenagers' sexual decision making. The perception (rather than the reality) of peer attitudes and behaviors also appears to be central and, as McAnarney and Schreider (1984) suggest, applies to both boys and girls. It is what governs one's internal response to external influences and events, and it is the basis for assessing the risks and consequences of sexual behavior.

We have seen that an important aspect of self-perception among teenagers is their educational, occupational, and family formation expectations. Expectations, in turn, are significantly influenced by perceptions of opportunities, regardless of whether these perceptions reflect reality. Teenagers, especially girls, with a strong achievement orientation and clear future goals are less likely to become sexually involved at an early age, more likely to be regular and effective contraceptors if they are sexually active, and less likely to bear a child if they experience an unintended pregnancy. In contrast, girls who lack a strong achievement orientation and who have low educational expectations are more likely to become sexually involved at a young age, to be less regular and effective contraceptors, and to carry an unintended pregnancy to term. These findings suggest that for adolescents with clearly formulated expectations and high aspirations, their perceptions of the risks of pregnancy, when measured against their perceptions of future potential, are quite high. Many other teenagers, however, do not perceive the risks as great enough to deter sexual activity without contraception. They are the ones at highest risk of pregnancy and childbearing.

Research underscores the variety of family background characteristics, psychological factors, and environmental conditions that influence teenagers' self-perceptions and, in turn, influence their perceptions of the risks of pregnancy and childbearing. Race, socioeconomic status, family structure, family size, and parents' education are strongly associated with attitudes about sexual and fertility behavior. Yet, as several researchers point out, not all adolescent girls from poor black inner-city backgrounds or rural white poverty and not all girls from single-parent households or from large families are at higher risk of early pregnancy and childbearing (Furstenberg and Brooks-Gunn, 1985b; McAnarney and Schreider, 1984). What makes the difference? It remains for future research to answer this essential question about the factors affecting sexual decision making among adolescents and the mechanisms by which they work.

5

Consequences of Adolescent Childbearing

Scientific knowledge about the risks and consequences of adolescent childbearing has grown in the past 15 years. A substantial body of research now exists indicating that becoming a parent as a teenager leads to lower social and economic attainment for young mothers and their families and that it entails considerable health and developmental risks. As many researchers note, individual differences such as family background, race, and socioeconomic status influence the attainment of young women and their families. Nevertheless, early childbearing appears to have independent negative effects beyond the impact of social, economic, and cultural factors (Moore and Burt, 1982). In some cases the mother's age directly affects outcomes; in other cases the mother's age influences other relevant factors that in turn affect her social, economic, and physical well-being and that of her child.

This chapter discusses the consequences of adolescent pregnancy and childbearing in terms of health risks and outcomes, educational attainment, family structure and size, work status and income, financial dependence and poverty, and socioemotional and cognitive outcomes for the children of teenage mothers.

HEALTH RISKS AND OUTCOMES

Research on the health risks and outcomes of adolescent pregnancy and childbearing shows that pregnant teenagers, especially those under age 15, have higher rates of complications, maternal morbidity and mortality, and premature and/or low birthweight babies (Strobino, Vol. II:Ch. 5).

123

Miscarriages and stillbirths are more frequent among teenagers than among adult women (Menken, 1980; Mednick and Baker, 1980). In addition, children born to teenage mothers are more likely to be injured and to be hospitalized by age five (Taylor et al., 1983). However, despite some evidence that the health risks to teenage mothers and their babies cannot be entirely eliminated, in general the medical problems associated with adolescent pregnancy can be greatly reduced with appropriate health care, especially prenatal care and good nutrition (Strobino, Vol. II:Ch. 5; Institute of Medicine, 1985; Baldwin and Cain, 1980; Griffiths, 1977; Hardy and Flagle, 1980; McAnarney et al., 1978).

Many researchers and health care professionals believe that the greatest difficulty in this regard is the behavior patterns of teenagers themselves. It is not unusual for them to neglect their physical health, regardless of pregnancy (Marino and King, 1980). In addition, poor eating habits are relatively common among this age group. Among low-income teenagers, for whom the financial impediments to good health care and nutrition are greater, poor health and poor health habits are even more prevalent. Often they enter pregnancy with poor health habits; they fail to make the necessary adjustments in their life-style to promote a healthy pregnancy; and they often do not seek regular prenatal care until late in the pregnancy, if at all (Alan Guttmacher Institute, 1981; Children's Defense Fund, 1985). As a consequence, teenage mothers from low-income families are at especially high risk of pregnancy complications, and their babies are at greater risk of long-term health and developmental problems. Recent research in the United States has concluded that many adverse health consequences found to be associated with teenage pregnancy and childbearing in pre-1970 studies may be due to socioeconomic factors that were not adequately controlled rather than to young age per se (Makinson, 1985; Menken, 1980; Hollingsworth et al., 1982).

Despite the fact that many of the health problems associated with early pregnancy and childbearing can be dramatically reduced with early, regular, and risk-appropriate (i.e., appropriate to the defined level of risk) prenatal care, the youngest mothers (those under age 15) and their infants face greater risks than older teenagers and adult women and their children. These very young mothers have high rates of pregnancy complications including toxemia, anemia, prolonged labor, and premature labor (Strobino, Vol. II:Ch. 5; Bonham and Placek, 1978; Menken, 1980). Mothers under age 15, for example, experience a rate of maternal death that is 2.5 times that for mothers ages 20–24 (Alan Guttmacher Institute, 1981).

Similarly, mothers under 15 are twice as likely to have infants that are premature or low birthweight (less than 5.5 pounds) (Alan Guttmacher Institute, 1981; Bonham and Placek, 1978; Jekel et al., 1975; Menken, 1980; Nye, 1976). As Moore and Burt (1982) point out, poor and black teenagers suffer proportionately more of these health difficulties than middle-class and white teenagers, and differences in rates by age (though relatively small) remain after race and income factors have been controlled.

Approximately 40 percent of all adolescent pregnancies are terminated by induced abortion. Complications following induced abortion are generally lower among adolescents than among older women, regardless of the gestation at which the abortion is performed or the method used (Strobino, Vol. II:Ch. 5; Cates et al., 1983). Two exceptions are cervical injury (Tyler, 1983; Hogue et al., 1982) and death-to-case rates from sepsis (Grimes et al., 1981), which are more frequent among teenagers. However, within gestation, teenagers have been shown to have the lowest overall death rates from legally induced abortion among all age groups (Cates et al., 1983). Strobino further concludes from her review of the research (Vol. II:Ch. 5) that if there is an increased risk of unfavorable outcomes (including spontaneous abortion) in pregnancies following an induced abortion, the risk is small and appears to be more significantly associated with differing characteristics of the women—for example, race, poverty status, poor health and health habits—than with abortion history (Hogue et al., 1982; Daling and Emanuel, 1977; Madore et al., 1981; Schoenbaum et al., 1980; Kline et al., 1978). Among adult women the odds of a second-trimester spontaneous abortion increased somewhat as the number of prior induced abortions increased (Levin et al., 1980), which suggests the need for additional research on the delayed effects of induced abortion on teenagers. However, Cates et al. (1983) concluded that, like any surgical procedure, induced abortion is not without risks. In general, though, these risks are not greater for teenagers than for adult women, and, in some cases, they are lower.

EDUCATIONAL ATTAINMENT

Throughout the past two decades, educational attainment has become more significant in determining a young person's life chances. One's education substantially affects one's income and occupational opportunities (Hofferth et al., 1978; McClendon, 1976). It also affects one's chances for employment (Furstenberg, 1976).

Hofferth (Vol. II:Ch. 6) highlights a number of studies that strongly support the conclusion that young women who give birth while they are in junior high school or high school complete on average fewer years of school, are less likely to earn a high school diploma, and are less likely to go on to college and graduate study than those who delay childbearing until their twenties (Mott and Marsiglio, 1985; Card and Wise, 1978; Furstenberg, 1976; Presser, 1976a; Trussell, 1976; Waite and Moore, 1978; Haggstrom et al., 1983). Later research that has controlled for socioeconomic background, academic ability, and motivational factors has also found that early childbearers are more likely to have reduced educational attainment than later childbearers (Card and Wise, 1978; Haggstrom et al., 1983; Moore and Hofferth, 1980; Hofferth and Moore, 1979; Moore et al., 1978; Waite and Moore, 1978). The younger the mother at the time of birth, the greater the educational decrement, although this effect is somewhat less significant for blacks than for whites (Waite and Moore, 1978). Teenage fathers are also negatively affected, but not to the same degree that teenage mothers are (Card and Wise, 1978).

As several researchers have found, the causal relationship between educational completion and age at first birth runs in both directions, particularly among older childbearers. That is, the older a young woman at first birth, the more education she is likely to receive (Rindfuss et al., 1980; Hofferth and Moore, 1979); the more years of schooling that a young woman has completed, the more likely she is to delay childbearing (Hofferth and Moore, 1979; Marini, 1984).

As Hofferth (Vol. II:Ch. 6) reports, recent research on the relationship between educational attainment and early childbearing has focused on the complex effects of dropping out of school. The clear conclusion of these studies is that young women who have a first birth while they are still under 18 are more likely to drop out of school than those who do not (Moore et al., 1978; Marini, 1984). While many young women drop out at the time they give birth, it appears that many others drop out during the year before the birth of their child. Although some are undoubtedly pregnant at the time, it also seems likely that many young women who drop out become pregnant within several months after leaving school (Moore et al., 1978).

Ironically, those who give birth at ages 16, 17, and 18 are at greater risk of not finishing high school than those who give birth at younger ages. Hofferth (Vol. II:Ch. 6) reports that teens who have a first birth at younger ages are more likely to stay in their parental home and therefore to stay in school or return to school (Furstenberg and Crawford, 1978). In contrast, those who give birth at ages 16 to 18 are likely to make other adult transitions at the same time—for example, establishing independent living arrangements, getting a job, or getting married—all of which make it more difficult for a young woman to continue her education. In particular, teenagers who marry are at higher risk of dropping out of school, and those who both marry and bear a child have the highest probability of dropping out of school (Moore et al., 1978).

Do high school dropouts catch up? Hofferth (Vol. II:Ch. 6) suggests that the answer is generally no. Although many make progress, especially in their late twenties, teenage mothers typically do not catch up completely. However, the effects seem less pronounced for young black women than for their white counterparts. In large part, this probably reflects the fact that in black families and the black community in general, the necessary support mechanisms are better developed to help young unmarried women cope with early childbearing (Hill, 1977; Williams, 1977, as cited in Moore et al., 1986; Miller, 1983).

Differences in educational attainment between teenagers who give birth and those who do not are significant in the first several years following the birth of their child, but there is evidence that they diminish somewhat over time. Furstenberg and Brooks-Gunn (1985a) found in their 17-year follow-up of a sample of teenage mothers in Baltimore (mostly black) that of all educational attainment following the birth of a first child, more than half took place six or more years after that birth. More than half of the young women in this study reported at least one year of additional schooling after five years of motherhood, while a significant proportion went on to earn a high school diploma or equivalent, and many went on to postsecondary education. Although the results do not suggest that these adolescent mothers completely caught up with their classmates who did not give birth, they do point out that many teenage mothers who interrupt schooling to have a child do resume their educational careers later in life (Furstenberg and Brooks-Gunn, 1985a). Short-term (1 to 5 years following a first birth) and long-term (6 to 15 years following a first birth) educational outcomes may be very different for some proportion of early childbearers.

In addition, it seems likely that for more recent cohorts of adolescents, the difference in educational attainment between those who give birth while still of school age and those who do not has lessened (Mott and Maxwell, 1981). Until the mid-1970s, young pregnant women were frequently prohibited from staying in school. Title IX of the Education Amendments of 1972 (implemented in 1975) prohibits publicly supported educational programs from discriminating on the basis of pregnancy status. As a result, school systems make a variety of arrangements for helping expectant mothers continue their education, either in regular classes or in alternative programs. However, as McCarthy and Radish (1982) point out, young women who do not give birth early also get more schooling. As a result, it seems unlikely that the gap will be diminished.

FAMILY STRUCTURE AND FAMILY SIZE

Early marriage is strongly associated with early childbearing. One-third of brides age 17 and younger are pregnant at marriage (Bureau of the Census, 1984a). Although the rate of nonmarital childbearing has increased significantly over the past two decades, approximately half of all adolescent mothers are married at the time they give birth (O'Connell and Rogers, 1984). Marriage to legitimate a birth is more common among whites than among blacks, and it is far more common among older teenagers (18- and 19-year-olds) than among younger ones (O'Connell and Rogers, 1984; McCarthy and Menken, 1979). More recent cohorts of teenagers are less likely to marry to legitimate a pregnancy than past cohorts were.

Unfortunately, the majority of adolescent marriages are highly unstable (Bumpass and Sweet, 1972; Card and Wise, 1978; Furstenberg, 1976; Glick and Norton, 1979). Furstenberg (1976) found among his Baltimore sample that more than half the marriages had dissolved by the time of the 5-year follow-up and, among those women who were still married, a substantial proportion reported severe marital problems. Those who were divorced or never married were generally disinclined to enter or reenter marriage (Furstenberg, 1976). At the 17-year follow-up, Furstenberg and Brooks-Gunn (1985a) found that, despite their initial intentions, less than one-quarter of their sample (then in their early thirties) had never married, and less than 10 percent had neither married nor entered a cohabitational arrangement. However, the relationships of the women who married or cohabited were not permanent. Approximately two-thirds of all first marriages were dissolved, as were many second marriages, and the dissolution of cohabitational arrangements was even greater (Furstenberg and Brooks-Gunn, 1985a). Thus, while early childbearing appears to accelerate the pace of marriage for some, it also appears to accelerate the pace of separation and divorce. After 17 years, the early childbearers in the Baltimore study were less likely to be married than peers who delayed childbearing, and they were significantly less likely to have remained in their first marriage (Furstenberg and Brooks-Gunn, 1985a). Other researchers have found that remarriage is generally far less likely following marital disruption among blacks than among whites (Ross and Sawhill, 1975). Adolescent parenthood, especially among low-income blacks, has serious negative implications for long-term marital stability and ultimately for the economic well-being of a young mother and her children. Nevertheless, teenage mothers who marry before the birth of their child rather than afterward appear less likely to separate from their husbands in later years (McLaughlin et al., 1986). Among the small proportion of early childbearers who do enter stable marital relationships, economic outcomes are far more favorable than for those who do not marry and become single heads of household (Furstenberg and Brooks-Gunn, 1985a). In addition, infants born to teenage mothers who are married at the time of birth have more favorable outcomes (i.e., less likely to have low birthweight, more likely to breast-feed) than those of unmarried mothers.

Teenage childbearing is also strongly associated with higher levels of completed fertility, closer spacing of births, more nonmarital births, and higher proportions of unintended births (Trussell and Menken, 1978; Moore and Hofferth, 1978; Card and Wise, 1978). Moore and Hofferth (1978) found that women ages 35–52 who had their first child at age 15 or younger had three more children on average than women who delayed their first birth to age 24, after controlling for race, religion, education, and other fertility determinants. Similarly, Card and Wise (1978) found that, by age 29, women whose first birth occurred at age 18 or younger had 3.1 children on average, compared with 2.2 children for a matched sample of women who began childbearing in their early twenties.

Among recent cohorts, however, these effects seem to have diminished somewhat, particularly among blacks (Trussell and Menken, 1978; Millman and Hendershot, 1980). Furstenberg and Brooks-Gunn's (1985a) 17-year follow-up of their sample of early childbearers revealed that most women had fewer children than they had originally indicated they eventually wanted and fewer than they had indicated that they expected to eventually have when reinterviewed at the 5-year follow-up. Among this group of mainly inner-city black women, approximately 20 percent had one child, 40 percent had two children, 30 percent had three children, and about 8 percent had four or more children. More than 60 percent of all additional births among these women occurred within five years after the first birth. Rather than rely on various methods of contraception, sterilization was the chosen means of fertility control for more than half (57 percent) of the women in the study (Furstenberg and Brooks-Gunn, 1985a). This follows the current U.S. pattern in which sterilization is the contraceptive method of more than half of couples with two or more children. Approximately half of women currently obtaining tubal sterilization are under 30 and 20 percent are under 25 (Centers for Disease Control, 1983).

Although the differences in levels of completed fertility between early and later childbearers is declining, women who have their first child as teenagers still tend to have larger families, by about one child on average. This difference has important implications for their economic well-being and that of their children, as well as for their prospects of welfare dependence.

WORK STATUS AND INCOME

In part because of their educational deficits and larger family size, adolescent mothers are less likely to find stable and remunerative employment than their peers who delay childbearing. Several researchers have found a significant difference in work status and income between early and late childbearers, which appears to be at least in part attributable to the timing of parenthood (Card and Wise, 1978; Hofferth and Moore, 1979; Trussell and Abowd, 1979). While differences in socioeconomic background and ability have some effect, they do not fully explain the differences in patterns of labor force participation and levels of earnings between early and later childbearers.

Hofferth et al. (1978) conclude that, since early childbearing affects educational attainment and family size, it indirectly affects work status and income. Because teenage mothers tend to have more children at closer intervals, they accumulate less work experience and have lower hourly wages, net of other factors. In addition, because they generally complete less schooling and consequently have lower-status occupations, they earn lower wages. Taken together, these facts suggest that an early birth has negative indirect effects on the labor market position of young mothers and contributes to their lack of satisfaction with their jobs (Card and Wise, 1978; Haggstrom and Morrison, 1979). However, these effects appear to be more significant for whites than for blacks, for two reasons. First, young black mothers do accumulate somewhat more work experience than their white counterparts, and, second, the difference in work experience between early and late childbearers is less significant for blacks than for whites (Koo and Bilsborrow, 1979).

The differences in work status between early and later childbearers vary over the family life cycle. Card and Wise (1978) report that although teenage mothers are less likely to be working 1 year and 5 years after high school, 11 years later (when they are in their twenties) they are more likely than later childbearers to be employed. These findings are supported by Furstenberg and Brooks-Gunn's (1985a) study as well. Although the employment disparities between the adolescent mothers in the Baltimore study sample and their classmates who had not given birth were great at the 5-year follow-up, the differences had diminished somewhat by the 17-year follow-up. Five years after birth, less than half the young mothers held jobs and were partially or wholly self-supporting, compared with 70 percent of their peers who delayed childbearing. Moreover, the jobs held by classmates were more skilled and better paid. Twelve years later, however, 67 percent of the teenage mothers were working—a figure that is roughly comparable to that of their peers, many of whom were then taking time out to raise children (Furstenberg and Brooks-Gunn, 1985a). Thus it appears that differences in work status between early and later childbearers decline over time. In fact, because of economic need, early childbearers may be more likely to be employed over the long term; however, there is evidence that differences in the types of jobs they hold are not diminished over time (Hofferth, Vol. II:Ch. 6).

Income differences also decline. In this regard, Trussell and Abowd (1979) found that delay of childbearing raises the "reservation wage," the wage that is sufficient to attract one into the labor force, particularly among white women. Many later childbearers, a greater proportion of whom are married, are likely to leave the labor force when they give birth, unless their jobs provide an income (and presumably a level of job satisfaction) that outweighs the attractions of full-time motherhood, especially if their husbands' employment provides a satisfactory level of economic security. In addition, Koo and Bilsborrow (1979) found that many later childbearers who continue to work or return to work are employed less than full-time. As a result, the differences in income earned by the women themselves, as well as the work status differences between early and later childbearers, are less significant in their late twenties and early thirties than they were in their early twenties, when other socioeconomic, ability, and motivational factors are taken into account.

Overall, the effects of an early birth on work status and income are much greater for whites than for blacks. Hofferth (Vol. II:Ch. 6) offers several possible explanations. First, because teenage childbearing is more common in the black community, social institutions have devised mechanisms to help young women cope with the event. Second, social and economic opportunities for young black women have not developed over the past two decades to the extent that they have for young white women. As a result, the opportunity costs of early childbearing are not as great for blacks as for whites. Third, because the reservation wage is lower for blacks than for whites, they are attracted into paid employment by lower wages than are white mothers. Finally, because blacks tend to begin and end childbearing earlier, they are more likely to devote themselves to employment in their late twenties and thirties than many whites who delay childbearing.

While the popular image of severe and life-long social and economic disadvantage for adolescent mothers is exaggerated, women who begin childbearing as teenagers are nevertheless at greater disadvantage than those who delay childbearing. Because they are likely to complete less schooling and to have more children, their ability to obtain positions with higher wages is reduced, and their earnings usually must support a larger family. In addition, because those who begin childbearing at a younger age have fewer prospects of achieving a stable marital relationship, many more of these women are the only or the major source of economic support for their families. Although research has not addressed whether adolescent mothers are less likely to receive child support from absent fathers, few mothers receive a majority of their income from this source (Bureau of the Census, 1985c). Despite the fact that differences in work status and income between early and later childbearers diminish somewhat over time, women who enter parenthood as teenagers are at greater risk of living in poverty, both in the short and long term.

POVERTY AND FINANCIAL DEPENDENCE

Teenagers who become mothers are disproportionately poor and dependent on public assistance for their economic support (Moore and Burt, 1982; Furstenberg, 1976; Presser, 1975). Estimates of welfare expenditures to adolescent mothers in 1975 suggest that approximately 50–56 percent of the Aid to Families With Dependent Children (AFDC) budget in that year was directed to households in which the mother was

a teenager at the time her first child was born. These households accounted for approximately $5 billion in AFDC expenditures; when food
stamp benefits were also considered, the total approached $6.5 billion
(Moore, 1978; Moore et al., 1981). In addition, because AFDC recipients are also eligible for Medicaid benefits, the total rises by another $2.1
billion ($934 million for Medicaid services to the children of teenage
mothers and $1.2 billion for adolescent mothers themselves) when
health care costs are added. In all, Moore et al. (1981) estimated that
more than $8.6 billion in public assistance through these three programs
was provided to households in which the mother was an adolescent
parent in 1975. A more recent estimate of 1985 outlays suggests that
total welfare-related expenditures attributable to teenage childbearing
has nearly doubled in the past 10 years, to $16.6 billion: $8.3 billion for
AFDC, $3.4 billion for food stamps, and $4.9 billion for Medicaid
(Burt, 1986). As with the earlier estimate, the 1985 figure is conservative, since it includes only sums expended in the three major programs.

Other researchers have found that not only are teenage mothers more
likely than older childbearers to be receiving AFDC, but also the
amounts of their grants are larger, primarily because of their larger
average family size (Block and Dubin, 1981; Scheirer, 1981).

In part, teenage mothers are dependent on welfare because welfare use
is more prevalent among those for whom the difficulties and expenses
associated with arranging child care may seriously affect their ability and
motivation to be self-supporting. Particularly among young mothers,
blacks, unmarried mothers, and high school dropouts, child care con-
straints frequently interfere with employment (Presser, 1980). Women
with little education and low incomes also face greater difficulties in
finding jobs that pay well and that offer fringe benefits important to
workers with children, for example, comprehensive health care coverage
(Moore and Burt, 1982).

Despite the fact that teenage mothers are disproportionately represented in welfare programs, it appears that public assistance is not their
preferred means of support (Furstenberg, 1976). Nor is welfare dependence continuous for the majority of young mothers. Furstenberg and
Brooks-Gunn (1985a) found that among the women in their Baltimore
sample, the probability of becoming a welfare recipient rose rapidly
during the five years following the birth of a first child. After five years,
however, very few teenage mothers went on welfare for the first time,
and the probability of their going off welfare increased sharply. Al-

though some women ultimately received public assistance again during the 17-year study, most who went back on welfare went off again when circumstances permitted. Moreover, during the 5 years preceding the 17-year follow-up, two-thirds of the women in the sample did not receive any welfare assistance. Furstenberg and Brooks-Gunn (1985a) conclude that, although a small minority of women were consistently dependent on public support, chronic or near-chronic welfare dependence was the exception rather than the rule among the teenage mothers they studied.

These findings are supported by other researchers who found that teenagers who bear children enter the welfare system earlier in the family life cycle and leave it sooner than do women from similar socioeconomic backgrounds who delay childbearing until their twenties (Block and Dubin, 1981). In addition, however, early childbearers tend to enter and exit the welfare system earlier in the family life cycle because they rely on public support to complete their education and then enter the job market. McAnarney et al. (1985) conclude that short-term public support for many teenage mothers may be critical to their eventual financial independence and success and that of their children. Nevertheless, this dependence imposes a considerable cost on taxpayers.

OUTCOMES FOR CHILDREN OF TEENAGE MOTHERS

In addition to the numerous health risks that the children of teenage mothers face, they are also at greater risk of lower intellectual and academic achievement, social behavior problems, and problems of self-control (Hofferth, Vol. II:Ch. 8). In addition, data suggest that they may be more likely to become adolescent parents themselves than are the children of older mothers.

Research on the relationship between early parenting and child development is relatively sparse. Yet the limited evidence indicates that the age of the mother at the birth of her child does affect the child's intelligence as measured on standardized tests (Broman, 1981; Maracek, 1979; Furstenberg, 1976; Belmont et al., 1981; Cohen et al., 1980; Levin, 1983; Moore, 1986; Davis and Grossbard-Schechtman, 1980). It also affects academic achievement, retention in grade, and other parental and teacher evaluations of school performance (Kinard and Reinherz, 1984; Moore, 1986; Vincenzi and Brewer, 1982; Maracek, 1979; Furstenberg and Brooks-Gunn, 1985a, 1985b; Card, 1978). Small but consistent differences in cognitive functioning appear in the preschool years and continue into elementary school and beyond. These effects are consistent for both blacks and whites and for both boys and girls (although in some cases the effects on boys are greater) (Hofferth, Vol. II:Ch. 8). As Hofferth points out, however, the direct effects are small, while the indirect effects seem to be larger. The salient question is what factors account for these differences between the children of early and later childbearers.

Teenage mothers, as we have seen, tend to be poor and less well-educated, and their children are likely to grow up in disadvantaged neighborhoods, to attend low-quality schools, and experience high rates of family instability. Indirect effects on the cognitive development and performance of the children of adolescent mothers appear to operate through family structure (i.e., single parenthood), maternal education (i.e., mother's limited schooling), and larger family size. Among these, mother's education has been shown to be most significant. Children of adolescent mothers score consistently lower on IQ tests and on vocabulary and block design tests (Cohen et al., 1980; Levin, 1983; Davis and Grossbard-Schechtman, 1980). According to Davis and Grossbard-Schechtman, children's IQ scores decline by approximately one point for every year of schooling that their mother does not complete. Similarly, Kinard and Reinherz (1984) found that mother's education was the major factor affecting children's achievement scores, with substantial and consistent differences on almost every measure favoring children of more educated mothers. Moore (1986) reports that children born to mothers who had fallen behind or dropped out of school before their first pregnancy had considerably poorer cognitive performance than children born to mothers who were in school or on grade when they became pregnant or who continued school after their first child was born.

Furstenberg (1976) found that the children of the women in the Baltimore sample generally had average scores on an achievement and aptitude test when they were evaluated as four- and five-year-olds, and those who saw their fathers regularly and those living in two-parent families scored somewhat higher. However, by the time these children had reached adolescence (15 to 17 years old), the school achievement of those who were still in school (some had already dropped out) was "dismal." Half had repeated at least one grade, and a quarter had been retained at grade level more than one year (Furstenberg and Brooks-Gunn, 1985a). These findings were supported by Maracek (1979), who also found that among the children of adolescent mothers, every additional year of mother's education reduced the likelihood that the child would be retained in grade by almost 50 percent. Similarly, Moore (1986) reports that the children of adolescent parents are more likely to be behind grade, more likely to be assessed as needing remedial help, and less likely to be doing advanced academic work.

As Hofferth (Vol. II:Ch. 8) points out, however, we know very little about how a mother's level of educational attainment improves the cognitive ability and performance of her child. Is it a reflection of ability, motivation, discipline, encouragement, and support, or all of these factors? Parents with limited education and more children are probably less capable of helping their children to stay in school. They may be less willing or able to reinforce their educational aims, and they may also have less ability to provide emotional and material support to help their children establish and further their educational goals (Furstenberg and Brooks-Gunn, 1985a). Yet the question of how parental education operates remains largely unanswered.

Effects of having a teenage parent on children's socioemotional development are sometimes present but generally less significant than those on cognitive development. Several studies show that the children of young mothers are at greater risk of social impairment (e.g., poor control of anger, feelings of inferiority, fearfulness, etc.) and mild behavior disorders (e.g., rebelliousness, aggressiveness, impulsiveness, etc.) (Maracek, 1979; Mednick and Baker, 1980; Furstenberg and Brooks-Gunn, 1985a). Moore (1986) reports that the sons of teenage mothers are more likely to be rated as impulsive and overactive. Furstenberg and Brooks-Gunn (1985a) found a relatively high incidence of school behavior problems (e.g., school suspension, running away, being stopped by the police, and having inflicted a serious injury on someone else) among the adolescent children of the teenage mothers in their study, although they did not control for relevant background factors such as socioeconomic status and family structure. In addition, they found that substance abuse (e.g., smoking, drinking, and drug use) as well as early sexual experience were prevalent among these children. One-quarter of the adolescent daughters in the sample had already had a pregnancy at the time of the 17-year follow-up. As with cognitive outcomes, Hofferth (Vol. II:Ch. 8) concludes from her review of the available research that most of the effect of having a teenage parent on children's socioemotional development is indirect and operates through unstable family structure. Especially for teenage children, the lack of parental support that often results from marital instability may have some negative effects on socioemotional development. Additional research that controls for relevant background and mediating factors is needed.

Although the study of adolescent mothering styles and skills has been largely neglected until the past five years, recent work supports the conclusion that the effects of maternal age in this area are also largely indirect and operate through a young woman's education, family structure, support system, knowledge of childrearing, and childrearing experience (McAnarney et al., 1984). McAnarney et al. (1985) conclude that the prevailing assumption that teenage mothers are poor parents is too simplistic and is not supported by the research. Few differences have been found between adolescent and older mothers with the exception of vocalization, which may be linked to lower cognitive scores during preschool for the children of younger mothers (Field, 1981; Sandler et al., 1981). Educators and social workers expect a higher incidence of learning disabilities, delinquency, and abuse among the children of teenage mothers, but the existing record is incomplete and unclear. Thus, for example, when socioeconomic factors and family structure are controlled, young mothers do not appear more likely to abuse or neglect their children than other mothers (Sahler, 1980; Kinard and Klerman, 1980). Kinard and Klerman conclude that both adolescent births and reported cases of child abuse are more common among families with low socioeconomic status, and it is possible that poverty strongly affects both early pregnancy and child abuse. These issues require further study.

The available research suggests that having a teenage mother negatively affects a child's development, and the effects do not decrease over time. Also apparently significant is the risk of the children of adolescent parents' becoming adolescent parents themselves. In this regard, Moore (1986) reports that the children of white adolescent mothers are more likely than those of black adolescent mothers to accept early childbearing as a possibility for themselves and somewhat more likely to have started dating at a younger age. Studies show that the effects of having a teenage parent on children's development are mediated through a variety of other factors, including mother's education, family structure, family size, and poverty, the very factors that most strongly predict early sexual activity, ineffective contraceptive use, and early nonmarital childbearing.

However, the assumption that economic dependence and early nonmarital childbearing are perpetuated over generations is not supported by the available research. Indeed, one of the most striking results of the Furstenberg and Brooks-Gunn (1985a) 17-year follow-up of the Baltimore women and their children is the wide diversity of outcomes among both generations. Many of the teenage mothers appear to have found routes to social and economic recovery, and some of their adolescent children appear to be on the track toward productive adult lives. Nevertheless, a substantial proportion of the children of mothers in the study sample were not doing well at the 17-year follow-up. Moore (1986) reports similar heterogeneity among adolescent mothers whose children had reached their teenage years. Yet she also finds that the families of origin of adolescent parents were significantly more likely to have low incomes and to live in neighborhoods that they themselves describe as undesirable for their children. The cycle of school failure, frustration, and disinterest among the children of adolescent mothers is of greatest concern in this context, because we know that it is strongly associated with early sexual activity and pregnancy in girls and with antisocial behavior in boys. For both sexes it bodes ill for future educational attainment, marital stability, employment and income, and later socioeconomic well-being.

CONCLUSION

The conclusion one must draw from the existing research on the consequences of early childbearing is that women who become parents as teenagers are at greater risk of social and economic disadvantage throughout their lives than those who delay childbearing until their twenties. They are less likely to complete their education, to be employed, to earn high wages, and to be happily married; and they are more likely to have larger families and to receive welfare. Despite their poor prospects, though, many young mothers do adapt to their circumstances over the long term and find routes to social and economic recovery. Although adolescent mothers overall do not do as well in later life as women who postpone parenthood, many manage to overcome the handicap of having a child in their teens (Furstenberg and Brooks-Gunn, 1985a). The undifferentiated stereotype of the ignorant teenage mother with hordes of children living on welfare not only underestimates a young woman's chances of recovery, but may also inhibit her opportunities. Researchers have learned a great deal in recent years about which young mothers are at greatest risk of long-term disadvantage and why, and which can be assisted through various types of intervention. While questions remain to be answered, existing knowledge can be used to identify the strategies that are most likely to help young women in different social, economic, and cultural circumstances overcome the detrimental effects of an early first birth and to clarify when in the life span these approaches are most likely to be effective. In this regard, it seems important to keep in mind that not all young mothers follow the same recovery route, nor do they achieve educational, financial, and personal success on the same schedule, if at all.

It is not only teenage mothers who are at risk. Their children are more vulnerable to a number of health risks, including disease, physical disability, and infant death. Children of young mothers also face risks of cognitive deficits and socioemotional problems. Few of these problems are the direct result of their mother's age at first birth, however. Instead, available evidence suggests that they are mediated to some extent by the social, economic, and cultural conditions of the children's lives. Of special importance is their mother's education, family stability, and, perhaps to a lesser extent, family size. Knowledge about how these factors operate is incomplete, yet we do know they are strongly associated with the same circumstances, attitudes, and behaviors that frequently predict school failure, early sexual experience, ineffective contraceptive use, and thus adolescent pregnancy. Available evidence suggests that the children of teenage parents are especially prone to having children early in life themselves. The significant danger signals warrant further investigation and suggest directions for future intervention.

6

Preventive Interventions

In the past 15 years, there has been dramatic growth in the number and variety of interventions aimed at preventing teenage pregnancy and child-bearing. Many programs have been promoted and supported by the federal government, others have been initiated by states and local communities, and still others have developed as a result of investments by private foundations and philanthropic groups. Virtually all represent strong underlying assumptions concerning the nature of the problem and what constitute the most appropriate and effective approaches to solving it.

Preventive interventions are programs aimed at helping young women avoid unintended pregnancy and childbearing. They are of three general types (Dryfoos, 1983):

- those that impart knowledge or influence attitudes,
- those that provide access to contraception,
- those that enhance life options.

The first two categories represent traditional approaches to pregnancy prevention through increased knowledge and access to services; the majority of programs are of these types. They are aimed at enhancing young people's ability to avoid early childbearing, and they are intended to directly influence the process of decision making by adolescent girls (and boys) at the time of choice (e.g., initiation of sexual intercourse, contraceptive use, pregnancy resolution). Preventive interventions in the third category are intended to influence sexual decision making indirectly by developing and strengthening adolescents' "motivation to avoid early childbearing" (Dryfoos, 1984c). They are based on the assumption that broadening opportunities, especially through educational enhancement, will provide meaningful alternatives to childbearing. In addition, efforts to coordinate and strengthen prevention strategies at the community level have been launched by several coalitions and interest groups.

Although many preventive interventions have been developed and implemented, few have been rigorously evaluated. There are several reasons for this lack of systematic information on effects and effectiveness. First, many programs have failed to clearly define objectives as a basis for measuring outcomes; they have also frequently failed to distinguish direct and indirect outcomes. Reducing the number of early unintended pregnancies, for example, is not an explicit objective of many preventive programs other than family planning services, even though it may be an important secondary outcome. Programs designed to increase knowledge and influence attitudes, as well as those intended to enhance life options, are frequently unable to show long-term changes in pregnancy rates. They may, however, significantly affect other factors, such as school achievement and peer influences, which have been shown to be related to adolescent sexual behavior.

Second, unlike a reduction in the number of births to teenagers, a reduction in the number of pregnancies is often difficult to measure. Because many pregnancies are terminated by abortion and some end in miscarriage, conceptions are frequently not reported.

Third, reductions in the number of pregnancies may reflect a variety of factors other than or in addition to program effects, for example, changes in the age and racial characteristics of the local target population; economic changes, such as the opening or closing of a plant that may alter local employment and income opportunities; changes in local school policies and school populations, such as those caused by busing, school closings, and redistricting; and the availability of other community health, social service, and income programs. All these kinds of factors can confound the results of evaluation in ways that are difficult to detect.

Finally, in addition to methodological impediments to accurate evaluation of programs, there are several practical problems. Evaluation research is expensive (often as costly as the program itself), and project grants and contracts have all too often failed to include funds earmarked for outcome measurement. Service providers typically lack the necessary research training and technical skills to mount a sophisticated evaluation, and the time to conduct it appropriately. Moreover, programs are often funded for 3- to 5-year periods, while the measurement of effects and effectiveness should continue over longer periods to generate useful information concerning outcomes.

In short, knowledge about preventive interventions is incomplete, and assessments frequently have not linked direct and indirect results. Yet accumulated program experience, along with a growing body of evaluation data, provides some insight into how various approaches work, for whom, under what circumstances, at what costs, and with what intended and unintended consequences.

The remaining sections of this chapter summarize what is known about various preventive interventions of the three specified types.

PROGRAMS THAT IMPART KNOWLEDGE AND/OR INFLUENCE ATTITUDES

A variety of programs has been developed to impart knowledge about sexual behavior, human relationships, reproduction, and contraception and to influence teenagers' attitudes about sexuality and fertility. These have included sex education and family life education courses, assertiveness and decision-making training, programs to encourage family communication, teenage theatre projects, and popular media approaches. These programs are provided by an array of community institutions, including schools, churches, youth service agencies, and public health agencies. In some cases programs have been developed and implemented as discrete interventions; in other cases they have integrated more than one approach.

Sex Education and Family Life Education

Sex education (i.e., the communication of information concerning human reproduction and family relationships), once regarded as the responsibility of parents and guardians, has to some extent become an accepted part of public education. Despite occasional conflicts that still arise at the local level, a substantial majority of the American public agrees that children should know about the reproductive process in order to develop the capability to make informed decisions about their own sexual behavior. Moreover, public opinion polls indicate that most adults—parents and nonparents alike—favor sex education in schools (Gallup, 1978, 1980; NBC News, 1982; Smith, 1980). Not surprisingly, adolescents also express strong support for sex education programs (Norman and Harris, 1981). This broad public support has become manifest in the political process as well. Over the past decade, state guidelines for sex education have become progressively more supportive. By 1981, only 7 of the 50 states discouraged and only 1 state prohibited instruction on specific topics (Kirby and Scales, 1981). When conflict does arise, in general it is no longer over whether schools should play a role in sex education, but rather over the inclusion of specific controversial topics, such as contraception, abortion, or homosexuality (Hottois and Milner, 1975).

As a result, sex education in schools is burgeoning. A 1982 national survey of 179 school districts in large cities, jointly conducted by the Urban Institute and the National Association of State Boards of Education, found that three-quarters of school districts provided some sex education in their high schools and junior high schools and two-thirds provided it in their elementary schools (Sonnenstein and Pittman, 1982). These reports are consistent with surveys of individual adolescents, three-quarters of whom report having had some sex education before leaving school (Zelnik and Kim, 1982).

While schools across the country demonstrate strong agreement on the goals of sex education, they differ somewhat in the content and comprehensiveness of their programs. One study reports that 94 percent of school districts agree that a major goal is to promote rational and informed decision making about sexuality; 77 percent agree that a goal is to increase a student's knowledge of reproduction; 25 percent report that a goal is to reduce the sexual activity of teenagers; and 21 percent say that a goal is to reduce teenage childbearing (Alan Guttmacher Institute, 1981, as referenced in Hofferth, Vol. II:Ch. 9).

Most schools offer short programs, 10 hours or less, that tend to focus on the basics of anatomy, human reproduction, and physical and psychological changes during puberty; they are often integrated with other courses, such as health or physical education. Very few schools offer comprehensive programs of more than 40 hours, and, even in schools that do offer comprehensive programs, not all students take the courses (Sonnenstein and Pittman, 1982). Kirby (1984) estimates that less than 10 percent of all students take comprehensive sex education courses.

Although to date there has been no systematic review of elementary school curricula, Kirby (1984) reports that very few schools include sex education in the early grades. Those that do generally focus on correct names for body parts, reproduction in animals, family roles and responsibilities, and basic social skills. In the fifth and sixth grades, many schools do provide sessions on the physical and emotional changes that take place during puberty, but few cover social interaction such as dating and intercourse (Kirby, 1984). In junior high schools, many schools cover anatomy, the physical and psychological changes of puberty, reproduction, dating, responsibilities in interpersonal relations, and sexually transmitted diseases. A smaller proportion teach about contraceptive methods. High school programs typically include a wider variety of topics, including teenage sexuality, pregnancy, and childbirth, as well as those taught at the junior high school level (Orr, 1982). About three-quarters of the separate courses at the high school level cover family planning, contraceptive methods, and abortion. About half include masturbation and homosexuality. Very few programs include information on sexual techniques (Kirby, 1984). In general, the more comprehensive the program, the wider the variety of topics covered and the greater the depth of coverage of basic topics.

Instruction in values as a part of sex education has been controversial. Some educators have advocated a value-free approach in order to avoid offending individuals and families with different orientations and to encourage teenagers to make decisions about sexual matters in light of their own values and beliefs. More recently, however, there has been a trend toward teaching what are regarded as basic universal values—for example, "All people should be treated with respect and dignity"; "Individuals should carefully consider the consequences of their actions for themselves, others, and for society" (Kirby, 1984). Comprehensive programs typically devote more time to clarifying values and increasing decision making and communication skills than shorter programs do.

In addition to what is taught in schools, other community organizations have developed and implemented programs: family planning agencies such as Planned Parenthood, churches, and other youth-serving organizations such as the YWCA, Girls' Clubs, Boys' Clubs, Scouts, and the Salvation Army. Both ideologically liberal and conservative organizations now offer programs that reflect their particular values on issues of human sexuality.

Among both school-based and community-based programs there is evidence of increasing efforts to involve parents, on the assumption that improved parent-child communication on issues of sexual behavior, contraception, abortion, marriage, and childbearing may help teenagers make more rational decisions. Similarly, a few programs have begun to use peer counseling approaches—that is, to train selected young people to talk with peers and serve as information resources—on the assumption that teenagers may find it less embarrassing to discuss these matters among themselves and that they are likely to listen to and follow the example of other young people whom they admire and respect. Evidence of the effectiveness of these approaches is limited. Kirby (1984) found that among young children, parent-child programs improved both children's and parents' perceptions of children's comfort in talking about sex and birth control in the short run, although their perceptions were not significantly improved in the long run. Among older children the program had fewer positive effects, but it still appears to have increased somewhat the comfort and frequency of parent-child conversations about sexuality. Peer approaches have not been carefully evaluated; however, Talbot et al. (1982) examined a broad range of peer advocate programs and found that they seemed to have a large effect on peer participants: they appeared to raise consciousness among those trained as peer educators, and these young people benefited from their responsibility to instruct and counsel others. The effect of these programs in actually reaching peers, especially males, however, seems questionable (Talbot et al., 1982; Dryfoos, 1985).

More recently, many schools and community organizations are teaching about sexuality in the broader context of family life education. While family life education varies substantially in its content and focus, typically it includes attention to (1) the roles and responsibilities of families; (2) social problems in families, such as child abuse and sexual abuse, divorce, drug and alcohol use, and teenage pregnancy; (3) social and personal interaction with parents, peers, the opposite sex, and persons who are racially and culturally different; (4) the life course, including important events and transitions from birth to death; (5) family formation, including marriage, childbearing, and career and financial planning; (6) body structure, functioning, hygiene, and disease; and (7) sexuality. In addition, family life education courses tend to emphasize values and attitudes (Muraskin and Jargowsky, 1985).

Several recent studies of sex education and family life education programs have shown them to be effective at increasing students' knowledge and understanding of these subjects (Kirby, 1984; Eisen et al., 1985; Finkel and Finkel, 1984). Kirby (1984) found that younger students showed greater knowledge gains than older students, although this may simply reflect the fact that they had more to learn. This study also found that longer, more comprehensive courses did not appear to have a significantly greater impact on knowledge than did shorter courses.

There is some evidence that sex education may influence attitudes, but as Hofferth (Vol. II:Ch. 9) points out, research to date has documented only limited effects. Although it appears to make students more tolerant of others' attitudes and behavior, it has not been found to alter individuals' attitudes and beliefs about nonmarital sexual activity, birth control, gender roles, sexuality in life, and the importance of family.

Despite the fact that less than one-quarter of school districts cite fertility control as a program goal, there has been substantial public interest in how sex education affects behavior. Many critics have expressed concern that teaching sex education promotes early or more frequent sexual activity among teenagers. Others have worried that it may not be effective enough in promoting responsible contraceptive practice among sexually active young people (Zelnik and Kim, 1982; Kirby, 1984; Cooper, 1983).

Available studies have found no association between the probability of initiating sexual activity and having had sex education (Zelnik and Kim, 1982; Kirby, 1984; Furstenberg et al., 1985a). Zelnik and Kim (1982) found that among teenagers who were already sexually active, those who reported receiving some sex education were somewhat more likely to use contraception and somewhat less likely to become pregnant. As Hofferth (Vol. II:Ch. 9) points out, however, these data are based on survey responses with only a limited number of questions from which to infer the relationship between sex education and sexual decision making. Thus, while the results are useful, they are not definitive. In contrast, in the programs he studied Kirby (1984) found no effects on contraceptive use (frequency of either intercourse without contraception or effective use of contraception) or on pregnancies. Again, however, some caution is required in generalizing from these results. Programs included for assessment in this study were not randomly selected but instead represented the range of variation in approaches and providers. Preference was given to those considered "potentially effective." Opportunities for following participants long enough to detect change in pregnancy rates was seldom possible. Accordingly, as Hofferth (Vol. II:Ch. 9) concludes, although helpful, the existing evaluation research on sex education is not sufficient to judge with absolute certainty the effects and effectiveness of these programs.

Complete and accurate cost data for sex and family life education programs are not available. Yet, as Dryfoos (1984c) reports, they are low relative to the costs of many other prevention programs, and dramatically lower than the costs of programs to support adolescent mothers and their children. A recent study of the costs of prevention services in Illinois reported the average cost per student at $10 per year (Reis, 1984).

Assertiveness and Decision-Making Training

A second intervention intended to impart knowledge and change attitudes about sexual behavior is assertiveness and decision-making training. Several programs of this type have been developed in recent years, usually as an adjunct to sex education, not an alternative. In some cases the approaches embodied in these programs have been included as components of comprehensive sex education programs (Kirby, 1984). Typically, their goal is to teach problem-solving skills, decision-making skills, and interpersonal communication skills in order to help young people employ knowledge about reproduction and contraception in developing and implementing personal approaches to sexual activity. These skills are taught through a variety of techniques that includes modeling, role playing, and rehearsal. Some programs take no explicit value position on sexual behavior; instead they encourage each participant to develop his or her own objectives and carry them out (Schinke and Gilchrist, 1984; Schinke et al., 1981). Others promote sexual abstinence by counseling adolescent girls and boys on how to resist pressures to become sexually active before they are ready for such involvement. Many projects of this type employ peer counselors.

Schinke et al. (1981) provide evaluation data for a small number of subjects who participated in the Life Skills Counseling program in Seattle, Wash. The results show that the young people who took part in the course had better problem-solving and communication skills and more knowledge of reproduction and birth control than those who did not. They also had more favorable attitudes toward contraception, more diligent contraceptive practice, greater likelihood of contraceptive use at last intercourse, and greater reliance on more effective methods than did subjects in the control group. As Hofferth (Vol. II:Ch. 9) notes, unfortunately no information was reported on sexual activity. In addition, while encouraging, these findings are based on a very small and probably self-selected group of participants. The approach would have to be tested on larger and more representative populations before its effectiveness could be projected.

The Postponing Sexual Involvement program in the Atlanta, Ga., public schools is aimed primarily at teenagers under age 16. Its purpose is to help young people delay the initiation of sexual activity until they are ready for such involvement. Originally designed as an optional series of four 90-minute workshops for students and their parents, it is now being implemented as a mandatory six-week course for all eighth graders. Peer counselors are being used in some discussion groups. No evaluation data are currently available. As with the Seattle program, preliminary indications are that this may be a promising approach, especially for girls; however, evidence to support broad claims of effectiveness does not currently exist. No cost data are available for programs of this type.

Family Communication Programs

Several programs are currently under way with support from the federal Office of Adolescent Pregnancy Programs (OAPP) to prevent or delay early sexual activity among young teens by improving parent-child communication. They are intended to develop and test approaches to "enable parents to better communicate their values and attitudes regarding sexual behavior to their children and to help their adolescents develop positive self-concepts and improved decision-making skills to enable them to exercise greater responsibility over their sexual behavior" (Montana State University as quoted in Hofferth, Vol. II:Ch. 9). Many are based on fundamental communications techniques—for example, taking time to establish relationships, recognizing natural communication barriers, focusing on the adolescent's concerns and interests, and getting parents to share their own thoughts and feelings. The majority of these projects have just begun and evaluation results are not yet available. Nevertheless, as Hofferth (Vol. II:Ch. 9) concludes from a review of their evaluation plans, it seems unlikely that they will provide much evidence of effectiveness in preventing unintended pregnancies. Although most of the evaluations will measure effects on parent-child communication and related values and attitudes, few will actually measure impact on sexual activity among adolescent participants.

Another program of this type, the Family Communication Program implemented in San Francisco and Fresno, Calif., during 1981 and 1982, was aimed at increasing the frequency and improving the quality of parent-child communication about sexuality and thereby ultimately reducing unintended pregnancies. Unlike the OAPP projects, this program made no attempt to specify the content of parent-child communications. Instead it mobilized a variety of community groups to work with parents and teenagers and developed a media campaign using radio and television advertisements as well as publicity and printed materials. An evaluation of the program found that it increased the number of parents who reported that they "use every opportunity" to teach their children about sex and that these parents initiated discussions of sexuality more often than their children. The evaluation also showed that television was more effective than other media forms in reaching the public (Public Response Associates, 1982).

In sum, research on the effectiveness of family communication approaches has shown that such programs or program components (e.g., within broader family life education programs) can be effective in the short run at increasing parent-child discussions of sexual topics. But there is no direct evidence of how long-lasting these gains are, nor of the effectiveness of these programs in reducing the incidence of unintended pregnancy. Data on program costs are not available. Moreover, as discussed in Chapter 4, support for the hypothesis that such communication actually discourages early sexual activity is weak, but there is some evidence that mother-daughter communications may encourage contraceptive use (Furstenberg, 1976; Flaherty and Maracek, 1982; Fox, 1980, 1981).

Teenage Theatre

In recent years, numerous community organizations have initiated theatre projects in which brief skits portraying the negative consequences of early childbearing are presented. Generally the projects involve teenagers themselves in preparing the scripts, staging the productions, and acting the parts. Some have involved live stage productions in schools and community organizations; others have involved radio and television spots accompanied by information concerning local family planning, maternal and child health, or other relevant health and social services. Based on the assumption that peers can significantly influence teenagers' attitudes and behavior, teenage theatre projects have sought to raise consciousness about sexual activity, pregnancy, and childbearing among adolescents and to provide outreach for local service agencies and organizations.

One particularly interesting example of this type of project is a 30-episode soap opera produced by the Tacoma-Pierce County, Wash.,

Health Department that was presented in 60-second spots on a local rock radio station. The soap opera, called "General High School," portrayed a typical sequence of circumstances requiring social decision-making skills by teenage boys and girls and then played out the consequences of the characters' decisions concerning their sexual and fertility behavior (Dryfoos, 1984c).

No evaluation data are available to indicate the effectiveness of such projects in increasing teenagers' awareness and understanding of the issues associated with early sexual activity, pregnancy, and childbearing or in changing their attitudes or behavior. Nevertheless, they have increasingly attracted the interest and attention of youth leaders and health and social service providers.

Media Approaches

A growing number of professionals, service providers, and concerned advocacy groups have begun to experiment with media initiatives to raise consciousness about the issues of adolescent pregnancy and childbearing and to provide outreach to teenagers in need of support and services. These have taken the form of public service announcements on radio and television as well as organized efforts to influence programming content on afternoon and evening television.

In this regard, the Center for Population Options (CPO) has initiated a Los Angeles-based media project intended to serve as a factual resource for television programmers and to encourage more responsible presentation of sexual content. In particular, the project has been concerned with the portrayal of male-female relationships and nonmarital sexual activity, as well as the lack of attention to pregnancy prevention and responsible contraceptive use. The project has not been formally evaluated, but CPO staff report that TV executives acknowledge the power of ratings in choosing programming content. While there is no general guide for the treatment of sexuality, network executives consistently avoid subjects, such as contraception and abortion, that are not considered "entertaining" and that seem likely to offend some significant proportion of viewers. The notable exceptions are several investigative news reports, talk shows, and call-in shows that have begun to address these topics in a more candid manner. While this kind of programming has helped create a growing awareness of the issues of early sexuality and fertility, it has focused on problem behavior, for example, sexually transmitted disease (unpublished CPO memorandum, April 23, 1985). In short, although media project staff report that television programmers sometimes call to check the accuracy of some material, they have been slow to change their programming approach to sexuality issues.

Public service announcements represent another avenue for using radio and television to raise consciousness about adolescent pregnancy and childbearing and for reaching out to teenagers in need of health and social services, especially family planning services. Although the panel discovered several projects that had prepared and distributed public service announcements primarily to radio stations, the number was remarkably few. None has been carefully evaluated, although the Center for Population Options initiated one project in 1982–1983 that included an evaluation design: the Adolescent Media Project was intended to determine the relative effectiveness of reaching Washington, D.C., youth with sexuality and family planning information through public service announcements, bus cards, and handout fliers. Each advertised a CPO telephone hot line for teenagers to call for information, counseling, or referrals to area family planning clinics. Three types of public service announcements were prepared and distributed to local youth-oriented radio stations, including (1) tapes featuring prominent rock and athletic stars promoting responsible sexual behavior among young people and citing the hot line telephone number; (2) "live copy," to be read on the air by radio staff, featuring commonly held "myths" about sexuality and fertility and urging listeners to call the hot line for additional information; and (3) live copy that was less explicit in its language about sexuality and contraception and conveyed the message that abstinence is acceptable, urging listeners to call the hot line for additional information.

The Adolescent Media Project did not produce scientific evidence, but it did provide several interesting insights. First, many stations were unwilling to play the tapes, preferring live copy for their disc jockey to read. Second, station public service directors were frequently unwilling to air the messages (live or recorded) during prime listening hours. Third, station public service directors were most receptive to public service announcements that addressed the issues of adolescent sexuality and fertility much less explicitly. Overall, the radio public service messages were more frequently cited as the source of referral to the hot line than either the bus cards or the handouts, suggesting the potential effectiveness of such media campaigns, if they are able to present their content so that it appeals to teenagers but does not offend radio executives.

A third media approach to increasing adolescent awareness of sexual responsibility and the use of contraception is contraceptive advertising. As discussed in Chapter 3, television networks and radio stations in the United States have been reluctant to advertise nonprescription contraceptive methods for fear of offending some of their audience. Yet the experience in Europe offers some interesting points of comparison in this regard. Alan Guttmacher Institute researchers report that in the Netherlands and Sweden, where nonprescription methods are advertised openly on television and in the popular media, teenagers, when questioned, demonstrate a greater awareness of alternative means of birth control. Although there is no scientific evidence that contraceptive advertising has actually increased contraceptive use among teenagers in these countries, the researchers found that adolescents believed these methods were easily accessible to them (Alan Guttmacher Institute, in press).

Media approaches, especially through public service announcements, seem to be relatively undeveloped and potentially effective information and outreach tools. Similarly, contraceptive advertising on television and radio may be a useful means of raising teenagers' awareness of the need for contraception and of making them feel that contraceptive methods are easily accessible. However, evaluation of these types of intervention is problematic, since it is difficult to determine what proportion of the target youth population is actually reached by such messages.

PROGRAMS THAT PROVIDE ACCESS TO CONTRACEPTION

Family planning services include a variety of health, educational, and counseling services related to birth control, including contraceptive services, pregnancy testing and counseling, and information and referral. Family planning services are available to teenagers from organized health service providers, such as public health departments, local hospital outpatient clinics, school-based clinics, and private, freestanding clinic facilities, as well as from private physicians. Some family planning service providers offer a full range of reproductive health services, including testing and treatment for sexually transmitted diseases, obstetrics, abortion, and sterilization. However, most refer obstetrical, abortion, or sterilization patients to specialized hospital and clinic facilities or to private physicians.

Contraceptive Services

Oral contraceptives, diaphragms, and intrauterine devices (IUDs, rarely used by teenagers) must be obtained through a physician in private practice or in family planning or other health care clinics. Condoms and spermicides can be purchased at pharmacies, and, in some areas, other types of stores. In 1982, 73 percent of teenage women using contraceptives relied on the pill, an IUD, or a diaphragm; of these, 90 percent used the pill (Bachrach, 1984). Of those teens who had used any family planning services, 45 percent had last used a private physician, 49 percent a clinic, and 6 percent a counselor. Teenagers' first source of contraceptive services was slightly more likely to have been a clinic (53 percent) than a private physician (41 percent) (Pratt and Hendershot, 1984).

Black teens are more likely to rely on a clinic as their first source of prescription contraception than to visit a private physician (72 versus 28 percent), while white teenagers rely almost equally on both sources (48 versus 52 percent) (Zelnik et al., 1984). In 1983, there were 5,200 family planning clinics in the United States (Table 6-1). All but 5 percent of sexually active adolescents lived in a county with at least one clinic, although 14 percent in nonmetropolitan counties had no clinic nearby (Table 6-2). In 1983, 5 million patients were served in these clinics; about one-third of them (1.6 million) were under age 20. Of these teenage clinic patients, 57 percent were ages 18–19 and 43 percent were under age 18 (Table 6-3).

TABLE 6-1   Number and Percent Distribution of Family Planning Clinic Services in the United States, 1983

	Total	Hospital	Health Department	Planned Parenthood	Other
Agencies	2,462	275	1,419	182	586
	(100)	(11)	(58)	(7)	(24)
Clinic sites	5,174	377	2,928	698	1,171
	(100)	(7)	(57)	(13)	(23)
Patients (thousands)	4,966	551	1,974	1,388	1,053
	(100)	(11)	(40)	(28)	(21)
Average number of patients per site	960	1,462	674	1,989	899

SOURCE: A. Torres and J.D. Forrest, 1985, "Family Planning Clinic Services in the United States, 1983," *Family Planning Perspectives* 17(1):32, January/February. Reprinted by permission.

TABLE 6-2 Teenagers and U.S. Counties Without Family Planning
Clinics, 1983

	Total	Metro	Nonmetro
Number of counties with no provider and as	757	57	700
percentage of all U.S. counties	(24)	(8)	(29)
Women under age 20 at risk of unintended	249	79	171
pregnancy (thousands) and as percentage of all	(5)	(2)	(14)
women under age 20 at risk			

SOURCE: A. Torres and J.D. Forrest, 1985, "Family Planning Clinic Services in the United States, 1983," *Family Planning Perspectives* 17(1):31, January/February. Reprinted by permission.

Public health departments served 40 percent of all patients, Planned Parenthood clinics served 28 percent, and hospital clinics served 11 percent; clinics run by a variety of other community-based organizations served 21 percent (e.g., neighborhood health centers, women's health centers, community action groups, etc.) (Table 6-1).

The core of services provided to teenagers at an initial visit to a family planning clinic includes: information concerning the range of contraceptive methods, their use, effectiveness, and potential risks; counseling in the choice of an appropriate method; medical assessment involving a pelvic exam, breast exam, blood pressure check, blood test, and a Pap smear. About two-thirds of all first visits include a pregnancy test and urinalysis to test for possible contraindications to the use of some contraceptive method. In addition, about two-thirds of all first visits include testing for sexually transmitted disease (Torres and Forrest, 1985). Although many clinics have made attempts to reach and serve young men as well, they have generally had little success. Family planning clinics tend to be female-oriented in their approach and in the primary health and social services they offer, and therefore are rarely visited by young men unless they are accompanying a female partner.

Family planning clinics are generally more willing to provide contraceptive services to unmarried adolescents under age 18 without parental consent or notification than are private physicians. Among organized providers, only 1 percent of Planned Parenthood affiliates have consent or notification requirements, while 10 percent of public health departments and other providers and 19 percent of hospitals require that parents are either informed or give permission for minors to receive services. A somewhat larger proportion of family planning agencies have

TABLE 6-3 Number of Patients Under Age 20 Served by Family Planning Providers, 1969–1983, in thousands

Year[a]	Patients Under Age 20	Patients Ages 18–19	Patients Under Age 18
1969	214	N/A	N/A
	(20)	—	—
1970	300	N/A	N/A
	(21)	—	—
1971	460	N/A	N/A
	(24)	—	—
1972	691	460	231
	(27)	(18)	(9)
1973	855	553	302
	(28)	(18)	(10)
1974	945	581	358
	(29)	(18)	(11)
1975	1,175	725	450
	(30)	(18)	(12)
1976	1,237	734	503
	(30)	(18)	(12)
1977	1,303	747	556
	(31)	(18)	(13)
1978	1,451	804	647
	(32)	(18)	(14)
1979	1,478	810	668
	(33)	(18)	(15)
1980	1,532	850	682
	(33)	(18)	(15)
1981	1,508	823	685
	(33)	(18)	(15)
1982	N/A	N/A	N/A
1983	1,568	895	673
	(32)	(18)	(14)

NOTE: Numbers in parentheses indicate percentage of all patients.

[a]Data provided are for fiscal years through 1974, and for calendar years thereafter.

SOURCE: Alan Guttmacher Institute, 1984, *Organized Family Planning Services in the United States, 1981–1983,* New York, AGI. Reprinted by permission.

parental consent or notification requirements for teenagers under 15 (Torres et al., 1980).

Data from a national sample of private physicians show that 86 percent of obstetrician-gynecologists, general practitioners, and pediatricians are willing to provide contraceptives to adolescent women. However, only

59 percent indicated a willingness to serve unmarried minors without parental consent. Obstetrician-gynecologists are more likely to serve teenagers than the other physician specialists and are likely to have fewer policy restrictions. Pediatricians were found least willing to serve teenage family planning patients and were most likely to refer them to other sources of care (Orr, 1984b; Orr and Forrest, 1985). Physicians' willingness to serve unmarried minors without parental consent is somewhat related to state policies. In 29 states and the District of Columbia, minors are specifically authorized to give their own consent for family planning services.

In the other 21 states, either there are no such laws or the laws are ambiguous. Physicians in states that do not have explicit consent laws for minors were found significantly less likely to serve unmarried teenagers on their own authority (Orr, 1984b). Thus, in practice, young teenagers have less access to contraceptive services through private physicians than through clinics.

Researchers at the Alan Guttmacher Institute estimated that in 1981 more than 5 million young women ages 15–19 were at risk of an unintended pregnancy; 57 percent of them received family planning services during that year—approximately 30 percent from organized programs and 21 percent from private physicians (Torres and Forrest, 1985). Family planning agencies offer a variety of services in addition to contraceptive counseling and service (Table 6-4). Almost all offer pregnancy testing and counseling and testing for sexually transmitted disease. Between 40 and 50 percent provide prenatal care, special training for staff working with teenagers, teen outreach, and programs for parents of teenagers and for teenage mothers. Only 20 percent have programs for boys, however, and only 1 percent of the caseload is male.

Family planning clinic patients are predominately poor, reflecting the intent of these programs, most of which receive Title X funding, to make services available to disadvantaged women. In 1983, 83 percent of patients reported incomes below 150 percent of poverty and 13 percent were receiving public assistance (Torres and Forrest, 1985). The number of adolescents using family planning clinics increased dramatically between the program's beginning in 1969 and 1983—from 214,000 to 1.6 million. The proportion of teenage clinic patients increased quickly from 20 percent in 1969 to 27 percent in 1972, 30 percent in 1975, and 33 percent in 1979; subsequently, it has been stable at 32–33 percent. Patients under age 18 accounted for nearly all of the increase—from 9

TABLE 6-4   Services Provided by Family Planning Agencies, 1983

Service or Program	Percentage
Pregnancy	
Testing	99
Counseling	92
Sexually Transmitted Diseases	
Testing	95
Treatment	71
Infertility	
Counseling	60
Treatment	19
Prenatal care	46
Genetic counseling	32
Community education	79
Special staff training for helping teenagers	47
Teen outreach	44
Programs for parents	50
Programs for adolescent mothers	39
Programs for young men	20

SOURCE: A. Torres, 1984, "The Effects of Federal Funding Cuts on Family Planning Services, 1980–1983," *Family Planning Perspectives* 16(3):137, May/June. Reprinted by permission.

percent in 1972 to 15 percent in 1979. The proportion of 18- to 19-year-old clinic patients remained constant at 18 percent (Torres and Forrest, 1983). Data concerning changes in the number of adolescents obtaining contraceptive services from private physicians are not available. Data from the National Surveys of Young Women show increased use of clinics between 1976 and 1979. In 1976, clinics were the first source of contraceptives for 45 percent of never-married teenagers who had ever used the pill. In 1979, 53 percent of all teenagers who had ever used the pill, diaphragm, or IUD had originally obtained it from a clinic. This change was due primarily to the increased reliance of black teens on clinics (Zelnik et al., 1984).

Among teenagers seeking contraceptive services from organized providers, a majority "are sure" or "think" their parents know they are coming to a clinic—59 percent. A significant minority, however, 41 percent, report that their parents are not aware of their clinic attendance. Among teenagers who report that their parents know of their clinic attendance, the majority indicate that they voluntarily informed their parents; most of the remainder indicate that their parents suggested the visit. Adolescent girls age 15 and younger were most likely to report that their parents suggested the visit. Only a small minority say their parents were informed because the clinic required it (Torres et al., 1980).

Among those who say that their parents don't know, a majority indicate that they would not come to a family planning clinic if parental notification were required. While many of these adolescent girls report that they would use drugstore or other nonprescription methods of contraception under these circumstances, some say that they would use no method. Only a very small proportion suggest that they would abstain from having sex (Torres et al., 1980). Twenty-six percent of teenage clinic patients said they came to a clinic rather than a private physician because they were afraid the doctor would tell their parents (Chamie et al., 1982). Thus it appears that parental consent or notification requirements are one factor affecting whether some teenagers will obtain contraceptive services and where they will go for them.

Another factor is cost. Fees charged by private physicians are significantly higher than those charged by clinics, and fewer private physicians will accept Medicaid payment for services. Orr and Forrest (1985) estimated that in 1983 the average fee charged by private physicians for an initial family planning visit was $42, and only 17 percent would reduce the fee for low-income patients. This fee does not include the cost of the prescribed contraceptive. Birth control pills, the most commonly prescribed method for adolescents by both clinics and private physicians, cost between $8.75 and $15.00 per cycle (Hofferth, Vol. II:Ch. 9). In contrast, in 1984, average clinic fees for an initial visit and three-month supply of pills ranged from zero to $51, depending on the patient's income and age. About half of all family planning agencies charged patients under 18 nothing or less than they would a comparable older woman (Torres, 1984). In 1982, 41 percent of teenage clinic patients received services free or had them paid for by Medicaid. The average fee among patients who paid was about $11 (Chamie et al., 1982). Moreover, women who obtain prescription contraceptives through a clinic often do so at a significantly reduced cost (Hofferth, Vol. II:Ch. 9).

Only 53 percent of physicians who will give teenage patients contraceptives accept Medicaid reimbursement, although most of those who do not accept this form of payment indicated that they will refer eligible adolescents to other sources (Orr, 1984b). In contrast, virtually all organized family planning service providers will accept Medicaid payment. Chamie et al. (1982) found that the primary reason adolescent clinic patients give for choosing a clinic rather than a private physician is cost (65 percent); the second most frequently cited reason is that the physician might tell her parents (26 percent).

Estimates of the unit costs of providing contraceptive services to adolescents in Illinois (including clinic visits and prescriptions) were $75 per patient per year (Reis, 1984). Almost all agencies providing organized family planning services receive federal funding, and half receive funding from their state and/or local government; almost all collect fees from patients, and 4 in 10 have funding from other, private sources (Table 6-5).

On average, federal funding accounts for almost two-thirds of the income of family planning agencies; other government funds represent 17 percent. The largest source of federal funding is Title X of the Public Health Service Act. In fiscal 1983, $117 million was spent by the federal government for contraceptive services under Title X (Gold and Nestor, 1985). Title X funds are used in every state. Most states (39–40 in fiscal 1983) also used funds from the Maternal and Child Health (MCH) block grant for family planning services, $19 million in fiscal 1983, which includes both federal funds and a relatively small amount of state matching funds. Only 28 percent of agencies receive these funds, however, and they account for only 7 percent of average agency income. Funds from

TABLE 6-5   Sources of Funding for Family Planning Agencies, 1983

Source	Percentage Receiving	Mean Percentage of Funds Received
Federal	98	63
Title X	77	33
Title XIX	90	10
MCH block grant	28	7
Social Services block grant	45	13
State and local government	52	17
Patient fees	92	13
Other private	41	7
Total	100	100

NOTE: Percentages may add to more than 100 because most agencies received funds from more than one source.

SOURCE: A. Torres, 1984, "The Effects of Federal Funding Cuts on Family Planning Services, 1980–1983," *Family Planning Perspectives* 16(3):135–136, May/June. Reprinted by permission.

the Social Services block grant were used for family planning services in about half the states in fiscal 1983: 45 percent of agencies received these funds, which amounted to $38 million. Ninety percent of agencies serve Medicaid-eligible patients and receive reimbursement from Title XIX of the Social Security Act (Medicaid). In fiscal 1983, $108 million of Medicaid funds were used to reimburse organizations and private physicians for contraceptive services. Family planning agencies accounted for about half this amount, and Medicaid reimbursements represented an average of 10 percent of their income (Gold and Nestor, 1985).

As discussed in Chapters 2 and 4, sexually active adolescents who practice contraception are less likely to experience an unintended pregnancy than those who do not (Zelnik et al., 1981). Those who use a prescription method (i.e., pills or an IUD) are significantly less likely to become pregnant than those who use nonprescription methods (i.e., condom, foam, rhythm, withdrawal) (Ory et al., 1983; Koenig and Zelnik, 1982). Next to sterilization, the pill is the most effective contraceptive when properly used. Effectiveness of use varies by age of user, socioeconomic status, and experience with a method. Younger women tend to have higher contraceptive failure rates with virtually all methods, and for most methods, women under age 22 are about twice as likely to experience an unintended pregnancy as women age 30 or older. This difference is probably due to a combination of factors: younger women are generally less experienced users; they have less accurate information about side effects; they are more fertile; and they may have more difficulty obtaining contraceptive services. Women under age 22 have approximately a 4.7 percent failure rate with the pill, compared with a 9.1 percent failure rate with the IUD, a 20.6 percent failure rate with the condom, and 32–41 percent failure rates with all other methods, including the diaphragm and rhythm (Ory et al., 1983). (Note: These rate estimates are based on use among married women between 1970 and 1976.)

Although many teenagers express concern about the negative health effects of pill use, for women age 15–19 who do not smoke, oral contraceptives carry the lowest mortality risk of any method except for barrier methods backed up by abortion: an estimated 0.5 deaths per 100,000 nonsterile women. The mortality risk associated with pill use is significantly lower than that associated with pregnancy and childbearing. The risk associated with condom use and other barrier methods is in fact the risk associated with unintended pregnancy and childbirth. However, the mortality risk associated with the use of any method is extremely low for women under age 30 (Ory et al., 1983).

Among pill users, a variety of minor symptoms, including nausea, breast enlargement, weight gain, and dizziness are common complaints not requiring hospitalization. Although these typically disappear with continued use, they are often disturbing enough to cause many women, especially teenagers, to discontinue use out of fear that they may foreshadow more major complications, such as cardiovascular problems, benign liver tumors, and gall bladder disease. Hospitalizations associated with these complications do occur among women who take pills with higher doses of estrogen, among those with histories of impaired liver function, gall bladder disease, hypertension and thromboembolic disorders (e.g., phlebitis), and among those age 35 and older. They are, however, extremely rare among women under age 25: only 4 per 100,000 pill users. In addition, the pill affords protection against several health complications that frequently lead to hospitalization, including benign breast disease, uterine and endometrial cancers, ectopic pregnancy, and ovarian retention cysts. The protection appears to persist long after pill use is discontinued and may provide protection to women in their forties and fifties when the risk of these conditions is relatively high (Ory et al., 1983). Health risks associated with the IUD are significantly greater than those associated with the pill and relate mainly to pelvic inflammatory disease. The major problems requiring hospitalization that are attributable to the use of barrier methods and rhythm are the complications of pregnancy due to method failure (Ory et al., 1983).

Both clinics and private physicians are likely to recommend prescription methods that cannot be obtained without a medical visit. Clinics provide clients with information concerning the variety of contraceptive methods and provide all reversible methods at the clinic. Only 11 percent of private physicians who will prescribe contraceptives for adolescent women prescribe all three methods that must be obtained from a physician or clinic: 90 percent prescribe oral contraceptives, 61 percent will fit a diaphragm, and 23 percent will insert an IUD (Orr, 1984b). Among new family planning clinic patients under age 20, 70 percent were using no method of contraception before their first visit, compared with 12 percent after the visit. Those using no method include girls who were already pregnant, who chose not to use contraception, or who chose not to be sexually active. As Table 6-6 shows, 70 percent of all new patients chose the pill (representing 80 percent of those who left the clinic with a

TABLE 6-6   Contraceptive Methods Used by New Family Planning Clinic
Patients Under Age 20, 1980 (in percent)

Method	Before First Visit	After First Visit
Contraceptive pills	21	70
Diaphragm	1	4
IUD	1	1
Spermicides/condom	3	11
Natural family planning/rhythm	1	*
Other	3	2
None	70	12
Total	100	100

*Less than 0.5 percent.

SOURCE: A. Torres and J.D. Forrest, 1983, "Family Planning Clinic Services in the
United States, 1981," *Family Planning Perspectives* 15:278. Reprinted by permission.

contraceptive method) and 13 percent of those who obtained contraceptives chose spermicides or condoms or both.

Zelnik et al. (1984) found that teenagers who received contraceptive services from a clinic are more likely than those who use private physicians to be poor, black, and to have been younger at first intercourse. They found that clinic patients were more likely to experience an unintended pregnancy than those who obtained a method from a private physician, but after they introduced controls for race and age at first use of contraception, there was no significant difference in subsequent pregnancy rates. The pattern of prior contraceptive use, race, and socioeconomic status are more significant factors than source of contraceptive services in assessing the risk of unintended pregnancy. More research has been done on the impact of using family planning clinics, but no other work has investigated the separate impact of using private physicians for contraceptive services. Clinic attendance for contraceptive services does have a positive effect on contraceptive behavior, a negative effect on birth rates, and presumably a negative effect on the incidence of unintended pregnancy (Forrest et al., 1981). Clinic patients are more likely than their counterparts who are not in family planning programs to use more reliable methods and less likely to use no method at all (Forrest et al., 1981).

Research on clinic attendance shows that several factors are important in attracting adolescents to organized family planning facilities. One indicator of effectiveness in drawing teenagers is mean delay between first intercourse and first clinic visit (Kisker, 1985). On average, teens first visit a clinic or doctor for contraception 11 months after they have first had sexual intercourse (Zelnik et al., 1984). About one in five teenage family planning clinic patients first comes to the clinic for a pregnancy test (Chamie et al., 1982). As Hofferth (Vol. II:Ch. 9) reports, among the most significant determinants of clinic attendance are those related to outreach and community relations, convenience, and the clinic's competition in providing contraceptive services. Thus, clinics that offer a community education program for teenagers in combination with the provision of contraceptive services (physical examination and prescription) have a lower mean delay between first intercourse and first visit. Those that obtain the support of local church groups, develop active relationships with local youth organizations, are open on weekends and in the evenings, accept walk-in clients, are conveniently located, require less counselor time per patient, and provide fewer services have a lower mean delay. Mean delay is also lower in Planned Parenthood clinics, in facilities of medium size (1,000–2,500 clients), and in those located in more prosperous areas where mean levels of schooling are higher. Mean delay is greater if local drugstores make nonprescription contraceptives easily available; however, the number of local private physicians who are willing to serve adolescent family planning patients does not appear to have any significant effect on clinic attendance (Kisker, 1985).

Continued attendance at a clinic is closely related to contraceptive continuation, although it is not synonymous (Shea et al., 1984). Adolescents who return to the clinic at regularly scheduled intervals (usually three months and six months after the initial visit) were found to be more reliable contraceptors. Those who did not keep scheduled followup appointments during the first six months were found more likely to be inconsistent contraceptive users. Adolescents who made more than the regularly scheduled follow-up visits, particularly in the first two months, were frequently found to be having difficulty with their contraceptive method. These patients, despite their repeated visits, were more likely to become discouraged and either switch methods or discontinue contraceptive use altogether. Another study revealed that there may be many reasons why adolescents do not continue as clinic patients, and those who stop coming are not necessarily at greater risk of pregnancy (Coughlin, 1978). A significant proportion of those who were followed up after a six-month absence reported that they were not sexually active; others were pregnant; still others had changed providers or switched to a nonprescription method. Less than 20 percent of the respondents in this study indicated that they were still sexually active but using no method at all (Coughlin, 1978). In sum, continued attendance at a clinic does not necessarily mean that teenagers are contracepting effectively and continuously. Similarly, because an adolescent girl does not continue to attend the same clinic at regularly scheduled intervals does not necessarily mean she is not contracepting. Many of the factors associated with continued attendance are the same as those associated with reasons for first attendance (Kisker, 1985). Satisfaction with the prescribed or recommended contraceptive method also appears to be an important determinant of whether teenagers will return for regularly scheduled follow-up visits (Shea et al., 1984).

Critics of family planning programs suggest that the availability of contraceptive services has caused higher rates of sexual activity, unintended pregnancy, abortion, and births to unmarried teenagers. Indeed, the period of significant increase in teenage sexual activity during the 1970s was paralleled by a significant growth in the availability of contraceptive services for both adult women and adolescents. However, whether there is a causal connection or whether both trends were responses to the same changing social context and mores is unclear. Using data for California, Kasun (1982) concluded that increased spending on contraceptive services led to increased levels of sexual activity and, as a result, increased pregnancies, abortion, and births outside marriage. However, as Hofferth (Vol. II:Ch. 9) points out, associations do not show causation, and Kasun (1982) did not control for initial differences between California and the rest of the United States, did not conduct a rigorous statistical analysis controlling for other factors that might affect levels of sexual activity among different subgroups or at different points in time, and did not measure sexual activity.

In contrast, Moore and Caldwell (1977) found no association between the availability of family planning services and the probability that an adolescent girl would initiate sexual intercourse, net of other factors (age, socioeconomic status, family structure, urban/rural residence, religiousness, birth cohort). However, as Hofferth (Vol. II:Ch. 9) concludes, more research is needed on this issue.

Research on the impact of family planning programs on teen pregnancy is also limited because of the lack of abortion and pregnancy data.

Births, however, are more readily measured. Hofferth (Vol. II:Ch. 9) reports only one study that has addressed this issue. Using data from the 1971 National Survey of Young Women, Moore and Caldwell (1977) found that black teenagers ages 16–18 living in areas with the most subsidized contraceptive services were significantly less likely to become pregnant than their peers. This finding did not apply to other sub-groups. According to these investigators, however, black teenagers are overrepresented among users of subsidized contraceptive services compared with whites and therefore may be more affected by the availability of such services.

Condom Distribution Programs

Programs aimed at condom distribution are more narrowly targeted toward young men than traditional contraceptive services provided by family planning agencies. Although many clinics have initiated efforts to involve young men in their programs, there is little evidence of success. Before oral contraceptives were widely available, condoms were the contraceptive method of choice among many U.S. men and women. However, the advent of the pill caused many to regard birth control as a "women's issue," and the condom fell out of fashion (Scales and Beckstein, 1982). In recent years, many family planning providers and public health officials concerned about pregnancy prevention and the reproductive health of adolescents have once again begun to promote condom use. Two factors are especially relevant to their renewed interest in condom use by teenagers: (1) recognition that the vulnerable period between first intercourse and first use of prescription contraception methods by adolescent girls is frequently as long as a year and (2) concern about the spread of sexually transmitted diseases, especially genital herpes and more recently the acquired immune deficiency virus. Although the international family planning literature describes a number of approaches to condom distribution in developing countries, few domestic program models have emerged (Dryfoos, 1985).

Studies of male attitudes about contraception and, in particular, condom use have shown that a majority of adolescent boys believe that "sexually active teenagers have a harder time" obtaining contraceptive methods than do adults, that "use of birth control makes sex seem preplanned," and that "only females should use birth control" (Finkel and Finkel, 1975). However, a majority of boys in the same survey believed that a male who uses a condom "shows respect for his girlfriend." Similarly, a study of black males who attended an adolescent clinic in Baltimore found that more than 90 percent believed they share responsibility for preventing pregnancy with their partners (although less than 20 percent believed that the full or major responsibility was theirs). Approximately 40 percent believed condoms were very good at preventing pregnancy, and the same number reported use of a condom at last intercourse (Clark et al., 1984). In this regard, Finkel and Finkel (1975) found that over 90 percent of the boys they surveyed who reported use of a condom at last intercourse also reported that they always or sometimes used one, indicating an inclination toward condom use. While acknowledging the general problem of adolescent male attitudes about contraceptive responsibility, Clark et al. (1984) conclude that the substantial level of condom use among the inner-city population they studied suggests a good basis on which to build contraceptive programs targeted at males. However, many boys and girls apparently still believe that condoms will interfere with sexual pleasure. Therefore, programs need to address attitudes toward condom use (Dryfoos, 1985).

Condom distribution programs have been implemented by a variety of organizations, including public health departments, Planned Parenthood affiliates, and university hospitals. Distribution has been managed by organizations ranging from family planning providers and public health organizations to youth organizations, public employment programs, and labor unions. Locations of distribution have included clinics, emergency rooms, pharmacies, recreation centers, union halls, pool halls, barber shops, restaurants, bars, and gas stations. Some programs have employed male outreach workers to counsel adolescent males on condom use and to hand out instructional materials along with free samples; others have relied on less assertive approaches, simply making condoms available in places where young men congregate. In some communities, free-standing storefronts have been established for disseminating literature, counseling on reproductive health and contraceptive use, and condom distribution. The Rubber Tree in Seattle, Wash., is a prototype of such a program (Parke and Neville, Vol. II:Ch. 7). In other places condom advocates have organized a National Condom Week around Valentine's Day to launch a public awareness campaign. Recently, in Oakland, Calif., pharmacies were encouraged to advertise, hand out coupons and free samples, and to sell condoms at reduced prices.

None of these approaches has been rigorously evaluated, although data from a condom distribution program sponsored by the University of North Carolina population program in the late 1960s tracked use over a year (Arnold, 1973). That program operated through an antipoverty summer youth program and used male outreach workers to establish distribution points in pool halls, barber shops, a restaurant, and a grocery store. As reported by Dryfoos (1985), a study of program operations found that consumers used distribution sites near their homes, although the location itself was insignificant, and that more condoms were distributed during the week than on weekends. Users were found to be similar to the general population in the target area. After a year, the majority (69 to 81 percent) of respondents reported use of a condom at last intercourse, and fertility rates among black adolescent girls residing in the target area declined significantly (19 percent) compared with those in similar communities in the county that were outside the target area. Although these findings suggest the potential usefulness of new efforts to implement and test condom distribution programs, they do not provide any conclusive evidence of the effectiveness of such an approach. As Dryfoos (1985) suggests, evaluation of the effectiveness of programs of this type is difficult in most communities today because of the large number of other factors that influence fertility rates.

School-Based Clinics

Family planning clinic attendance has grown among teenagers over the past decade. Nevertheless, concern on the part of advocacy groups and health and education professionals that many teenagers lack sufficient access to health services has generated a growing number of school-based clinics, many of which include family planning services. During the past five years, 43 such programs have been initiated in junior and senior high schools in 24 different communities. The Center for Population Options has identified an additional 50 communities that are now beginning to develop school-based programs (Kirby, 1985). A wide range of organizations has taken responsibility for establishing and operating clinics, including hospitals and medical schools, community clinics, public health departments, and Planned Parenthood affiliates.

In general, the goal of school-based clinics is to improve the overall physical and mental health of teenagers, including the reduction of teenage pregnancy. However, none considers adolescent family planning to be its sole purpose. Most offer a variety of services, including athletic physicals, general health assessments, treatment for minor illnesses and injuries, laboratory and diagnostic screenings (e.g., sickle cell anemia and sexually transmitted diseases), immunizations, first aid and hygiene, Early and Periodic Screening, Diagnosis and Treatment testing, family planning counseling and referral, prenatal and post-partum care, drug and alcohol abuse programs, nutrition and weight reduction programs, family counseling, and information and referral for health and social services not provided. Because of the range of services that most clinics provide, they serve both boys and girls. Some involve boys in family planning, typically when they come in for athletic physicals and are asked to provide information concerning sexual activity as a part of their medical history. Clinics vary in the range of services they offer, in some cases because of the differing needs of their students, in other cases because of the availability of funding or state and local restrictions.

Clinics also vary in the scope of their family planning services. At a minimum they all provide counseling, make referrals to family planning clinics or private physicians, and do follow-up after referrals. Approximately three-quarters of those currently in operation conduct pelvic exams and write prescriptions for contraceptive methods. Several actually distribute contraceptives at the clinic. Kirby (1985) observes that clinic policies concerning birth control are often consistent with their policies about other treatments: if they write prescriptions for other medications, they also generally write prescriptions for contraceptives; if they dispense other medications, they typically dispense contraceptives as well. None of the existing school-based clinics performs abortions. Kirby (1985) reports that while some will present a pregnant student with all the legal options, few, if any, make referrals to abortion providers.

School-based clinics are intended to capitalize on many of the features that existing research has shown are associated with teenagers' attendance at family planning clinics, including convenience, comfort, confidentiality, and cost. Located within the school building or on school grounds, clinics are accessible. Students don't have to take a bus or drive to another part of town or request their parents' assistance in getting them to the services. Most clinics operate during school hours and do not require appointments. Because they are visible entities in the school, clinic staff become familiar to students and vice versa. In addition, because the programs are geared to the needs of adolescents and students are aware that their friends use the services, school-based clinics seem more approachable to many young people than doctors' offices, hospitals, or freestanding adult clinics. Most if not all school-based clinics require written consent from parents before students can receive medical services. Generally parents are asked to sign a blanket permission form at the beginning of the academic year, but they are not informed when students come to the clinic for services. Nor are patient records accessible to teachers or school officials. Moreover, because the clinics provide a wide range of services, the reason for an individual's visit cannot be automatically assumed. In most clinics, services are provided free to registered students, although several charge a nominal annual fee (average $12) to help offset operating costs (Kirby, 1985).

The annual costs of school-based clinics vary dramatically depending on their size, staffing, and range of services. Kirby (1985) reports that they range from about $25,000 to $250,000 per year, averaging about $125 per student. Clinics are supported by a variety of sources, including various federal and state funds, local funds and in-kind support, and private foundation and corporation grants.

An evaluation of the effectiveness of approximately 10 school-based clinics is now under way by the Center for Population Options. Data from the St. Paul, Minn., Maternal and Infant Care Project, which began in 1973, show that the fertility rate in schools with clinics has dropped substantially—from 79 births per 1,000 in 1973 to 26 births per 1,000 in 1983–1984 (Edwards et al., 1980). These figures compare favorably with national statistics that showed a birth rate of 45 per 1,000 for whites in 1977 and in 1982. Unfortunately, as Hofferth (Vol. II:Ch. 9) points out, no information is available from the St. Paul project on the trend in pregnancies and abortions, so we don't know how much of the decline in births is due to a decrease in pregnancies and how much to an increase in abortion. The 12-month and 24-month contraception continuation rates (after the initial visit) were also quite favorable: 93 percent and 82 percent, respectively, by 1976–1977. Moreover, the dropout rate among girls who delivered and kept their babies declined from 45 percent to 10 percent between 1973 and 1976–1977 (Edwards et al., 1980).

These findings are extremely encouraging and to some extent are responsible for the current avid interest in school-based clinics. The Select Committee on Children, Youth and Families (U.S. Congress, House, 1986), in a recent report on adolescent pregnancy, strongly recommended the establishment of school-based clinics. However, the evidence requires further corroboration. As Dryfoos (1984b) reports, while fertility rates are still decreasing in the St. Paul schools with clinics, no comparisons have been made with matched high schools or populations. Study designs for the programs included in the evaluation will vary somewhat from clinic to clinic, but the major strategy is to administer questionnaires in both program and matched nonprogram schools at two points in time as well as to search birth records and academic files. This study is expected to provide valuable understanding of the costs, effects, and effectiveness of these programs.

Although the school-based model seems intuitively sensible and appears to have a number of advantages over other health delivery models for adolescents, it also has some limitations. First, school-based clinics are generally restricted to serving teenagers enrolled in school. Most cannot serve students who have dropped out, many of whom have significant health care needs. Second, many school-based clinics operate only during the academic school year and thus are not open to students over weekends, on holidays, and during vacations. Third, clinics that do not fill prescriptions (e.g., birth control pills) force students to go elsewhere to obtain contraceptives, which may deter some teens from effective contraceptive practice. The evaluation that is now under way will help in assessing the seriousness of these limitations.

A variation on the school-based clinic model aimed at overcoming some of these limitations is suggested by the Self Center in Baltimore, Md. This program, established and directed by the Johns Hopkins School of Medicine, initially focused its services on the students at a predominantly black, inner-city senior high school and junior high school. The program combined sex education with family planning and counseling services. Located in a storefront adjacent to, but clearly separate from, the two schools, the center was not constrained by the school calendar or schedule in its days and hours of operation. Both boys and girls could use the clinic and were eligible for services as long as they remained in one or another of the two schools. All services were free. Center staff, including a nurse practitioner and a social worker, were visible figures in the schools, providing sex education classes, individual counseling, and clinic outreach. During after-school hours, the same staff were available in the clinic to conduct rap sessions and educational groups. Teenagers who attended the clinic for contraceptive services were followed up through the schools. Those who experienced pregnancies were referred to the Johns Hopkins Adolescent Pregnancy Program for comprehensive prenatal health care and social services or to an abortion clinic.

The Self Center was developed as a three-year demonstration project with an evaluation component. Data were collected by self-administered questionnaires at the outset and periodically throughout the period of operation to assess changes in student knowledge, attitudes, and behavior. Students in the program schools were compared with students in two other urban schools; the control sample was carefully matched for race and socioeconomic status. The researchers measured program effects according to clients' length of exposure to the program (Zabin et al., 1986).

Among the significant findings from the first report of the evaluation are improvements in levels of knowledge, especially among younger students. In particular, girls showed a substantial increase in knowledge about the fertile time in their monthly cycle. Both boys and girls showed improvement in their understanding of contraceptive methods. The program had little effect on students' attitudes about teenage pregnancy, the ideal age for childbearing, or the acceptability of sex between two people (Zabin et al., 1986).

Most interesting, however, are the findings concerning effects on behavior. Despite very high baseline levels of sexual activity, the evaluation showed a postponement of first intercourse that averaged seven months for girls who were exposed to the program for the full three years. Those with less exposure showed much shorter delays, suggesting the importance of early intervention before the initiation of intercourse to effect change. If such delays can be replicated in other similar school-based or school-related clinics, they refute the argument that easy access to services encourages early intercourse (Zabin et al., 1986).

The most dramatic behavioral change, however, was in clinic attendance. The proportions of sexually active students having attended a clinic rose for students of both genders and at all grade levels. In addition, the proportion of girls with no sexual experience who attended in preparation for first coitus and those who attended in the early months after initiation of sexual activity increased markedly. Perhaps especially significant for its implications for future interventions is the high level of male attendance among junior high school students. More than half of the junior high program registrants were boys (Zabin et al., 1986).

Changes in contraceptive use were also significant, with upward trends for all groups. However, younger students' use increased more the longer their exposure to the program, suggesting that early risk can be reduced with early access to services. Finally, increased and prompt clinic attendance and increased use of contraception appear to have had a significant impact on pregnancy. While conceptions increased dramatically in the control group schools during this period (from 32 to 51 percent), in the program schools, conceptions dropped by 26 percent (Zabin et al., 1986).

The Self Center model differs somewhat from the typical school-based clinic. Nevertheless, if these results can be replicated in other settings, they give solid support to the school-based clinic movement. This program suggests that the provision of free proximate contraceptive services that are linked to a strong education component may accelerate contraceptive behavior among sexually active teenagers without encouraging sexual intercourse among those who are not personally ready for such involvement. Further efforts to test this model and compare it with the typical school-based clinic model are needed.

Pregnancy Testing and Counseling

Pregnancy testing is available to teenagers in public health centers, hospitals, family planning clinics, and abortion clinics, from private physicians, and even at many drugstores. This service is generally provided at little or no cost to the client. In addition, home pregnancy tests are becoming increasingly popular among teenagers as well as adult women, because they afford an opportunity to detect a suspected pregnancy in privacy, at relatively low cost. Although they are not a substitute for laboratory testing and a pelvic exam, home tests are generally an accurate indicator of pregnancy when properly used. Teenagers frequently delay testing for pregnancy either because they do not recognize the early physical signs of pregnancy or because they are reluctant to inform parents and do not know where to go for testing. As a result, many girls who are pregnant do not get confirmation until they are well into or beyond the first trimester of pregnancy. This delay has serious implications for their receiving adequate prenatal care, which in turn has implications for the health of their children. In addition, it affects their options for pregnancy resolution.

If a pregnancy test is positive, most adolescent girls need non-judgmental counseling to outline the available options for pregnancy resolution as well as necessary referral to prenatal and maternity care, social services, financial support, or abortion services, and subsequent follow-up. If the test is negative, they usually need contraceptive counseling and referral for birth control. Adherence to principles of voluntarism and informed consent require that facilities provide their patients with an account of the possible risks, benefits, and consequences of maternity and abortion, the available alternatives, including adoption, and the resources available for needed care (Alan Guttmacher Institute, 1981). Nevertheless, where a girl goes for pregnancy testing may affect the amount and type of pregnancy counseling she receives. Since nearly 20 percent of family planning clinic patients first come to the facility because of a suspected pregnancy, most clinics have established pregnancy testing and counseling programs (Alan Guttmacher Institute, 1981). Clinics receiving federal support under Title X are required by law to inform patients of their full range of legal options. Private pro-life organizations, such as Birthright, provide pregnancy testing, but generally do not discuss or refer a teenager for contraception if she is not pregnant and do not present pregnancy termination as an option or refer clients to abortion services (Alan Guttmacher Institute, 1981). Most school-based clinics provide pregnancy testing and counseling, but few discuss abortion or refer students to abortion providers (Kirby, 1985). Abortion clinics also perform pregnancy testing and counseling; while there may be some bias in the message provided by counselors in these settings, it also seems likely that most patients at such clinics have already decided how to resolve their pregnancies.

No rigorous study of pregnancy testing and counseling services has been done, nor has any careful assessment of how the auspices of service delivery affect decisions concerning pregnancy outcome for different clients. Available studies of decision making, however, suggest that many teenagers have already made up their minds about whether to abort or carry to term before they seek pregnancy testing and counseling services and therefore choose service providers on this basis (Rosen, 1980).

Hot Lines

Telephone hot lines that teenagers can use anonymously to obtain accurate information about contraception, pregnancy, abortion, sexually transmitted diseases or other reproductive health problems, and adoption alternatives have developed in several cities. Hot line operators can dispel myths about contraceptive methods, symptoms of disease, pregnancy care and complications, etc., and can provide outreach for local clinics and other service providers. Hot lines are typically operated by public health departments, family planning and adolescent health clinics, or local advocacy organizations and youth-serving agencies. Typically they are staffed by trained volunteers who can connect directly with health and mental health professionals when emergency situations arise.

The experience of several hot lines offers interesting insights. The Cleveland Program for Sexual Learning's hot line Sexline was developed in response to the need for general information and referral as expressed by various parent and community groups (Nickel and Delaney, 1985). Over a three-year period the service answered more than 32,000 calls, although there was no tracking system to determine how many resulted in clinic visits or contraceptive use. In New York City, a similar hot line to provide information and referral linked callers directly to clinics by scheduling appointments for those who expressed interest in obtaining contraceptive services.

Hot lines appear to be a potentially effective means of providing teenagers with information and referring them to services. However, evidence of the effectiveness of these programs in increasing contraceptive use and reducing unintended pregnancies and births among adolescents is not currently available.

PROGRAMS THAT ENHANCE LIFE OPTIONS

The availability of information, education programs, and family planning services has increased adolescents' capability to prevent early unintended pregnancy and childbearing. For many highly motivated teenagers these programs have provided the basic tools for making informed decisions about their sexual behavior and receiving the necessary health and social services to control their fertility. Unless young people are motivated to avoid pregnancy, however, these programs may have little positive effect. A variety of initiatives have been established to enhance young people's sense of their future—their sense of self-worth, their understanding of the value of education, and their awareness of work and career options.

Programs to Improve Life Planning

Programs to improve life planning are based on the assumption that the motivation to delay parenthood is closely related to decisions concerning life goals and an understanding of how early childbearing will affect one's ability to achieve one's goals. Most of these interventions have been directed at adolescent girls; very few have been directed at boys. Most have been organized through various youth-serving agencies, for example, Girls' Clubs and Boys' Clubs.

Project Choice is an extracurricular club organized and run by volunteer youth leaders. It is intended to help at-risk young women explore future career options other than motherhood and to understand the necessary steps in achieving alternative career goals. Meetings are held weekly after school, and activities involve information-sharing discussion to help participants establish personal goals. Leaders provide support in the form of encouragement and reinforcement to move teenagers along their chosen paths. Information concerning contraception and access to contraceptive services is provided, but altering contraceptive behavior is neither the only nor the primary goal of the program (Alexander, 1984). An evaluation of Project Choice did not provide convincing evidence of its effectiveness, although as Hofferth (Vol. II:Ch. 9) suggests, the research design was not very rigorous (e.g., poorly selected control groups, abstract outcome measures) and the stated goals of the program were not clearly delineated. In addition, because only a small number of girls participated in the program, there is little evidence of its effectiveness and generalizability.

Similarly, the Teen Outreach Project sponsored by the Junior League in St. Louis, Mo., involved an after-school program in two high schools aimed at improving self-esteem and reducing the incidence of unintended pregnancy and dropping out of school. High-risk students were invited to join discussion groups and to act as volunteers in community service programs. The program was replicated in eight cities and evaluated. Preliminary results suggest that the program was successful in lowering pregnancy rates and reducing course failure; however, it had little effect on the likelihood of being suspended from school (Philliber, 1985).

A second approach to improving life planning skills is represented by the Life Planning Project developed by the Center for Population Options. Its curricular materials link vocational choice with family design and pregnancy prevention. The program, which is currently being tested in three cities, involves the intensive participation of a broad range of youth-serving organizations in each community, whose staff were trained by CPO consultants to use the curricular materials to provide their adolescent members with more accurate information and sensitive guidance related to adolescent reproductive health. The major objective of the project is to help teenagers prevent pregnancy, especially as a part of understanding and planning for their personal and economic futures (Center for Population Options, 1984).

In a related effort, the Girls' Clubs of Santa Barbara, Calif., developed a workbook for adolescent girls entitled *Choices.* The workbook provides teenagers with problem-solving exercises that require sexual decision-making and life-planning skills. The purpose of the exercises is to help girls think about their futures in the areas of family life and work outside the home. The exercises are structured to enhance the development of skills and to present teenagers with an understanding of the social and economic consequences of early childbearing, in particular the likely effects on educational attainment and occupational choice (Quinn, 1985). *Choices* is currently being evaluated. A comparable workbook for boys, entitled *Challenges,* has also been produced.

In addition, the *Choices* workbook is being incorporated into a more comprehensive experimental program that will be implemented by Girls' Clubs at eight sites across the country (four experimental and four control). The program will include four age-related components and will be aimed at girls ages 12–18. The first component will involve mother-daughter workshops to foster communication about sexual behavior and values among young teenagers. The second component, modeled after the Postponing Sexual Involvement program in Atlanta, will encourage young teenagers to delay sexual intercourse, teaching them how to say "no." The third component, to be directed at 15- to 18-year-olds, will apply the *Choices* curriculum to help girls develop educational and career aspirations. And the fourth component, also intended for older girls, will link club members to clinic services. The program will involve both pretest and posttest questionnaires to measure effects on girls' attitudes about education, work, and family formation as well as on their sexual, contraceptive, and fertility behavior. This evaluation is expected to significantly increase knowledge of the effects and effectiveness of life planning approaches.

Role Model and Mentoring Programs

Role model and mentoring programs are organized to provide individual support, counseling, and tutoring for teenagers by trained peer counselors, mentors, and adult community volunteers. Some have pregnancy prevention (or prevention of a repeat pregnancy) as an explicit goal; others are aimed at providing models of desirable social behavior, of which sexual and fertility behavior are only part. Among many youth-serving organizations this has long been an accepted approach, for example, Big Brothers and Big Sisters, and it has been used with both boys and girls. More recently, the National Urban League has initiated a program through Kappa Alpha Psi, the national black fraternity. College-age fraternity brothers serve as role models and mentors to inner-city boys ages 11–15. They spend three evenings a week with the young male participants, one-to-one or one-to-two, in a diverse program of school remediation, recreation, and community service activities. Special attention is given to encouraging responsible sexual behavior. A similar program through Delta Sigma Theta, a national black sorority, has recently been organized. The use of "community women" in Project Redirection is discussed in Chapter 7.

No data are currently available to assess the effectiveness of such role model and mentoring programs in reducing adolescent pregnancies. The Kappa Alpha Psi and Delta Sigma Theta programs will be evaluated as a part of the Too Early Childbearing Network, and this information should provide insights concerning effects on school retention, achievement, decision-making skills, and aspirations and attitudes as well as on sexual and fertility behavior.

Programs to Improve School Performance

Based in part on concern that low achievement and school dropout rates are associated with adolescent fertility and that young women who give birth before graduation are less likely to finish school, many school systems have begun to develop programs to bolster achievement and to keep adolescents enrolled in school.

Over the past 20 years an enormous body of research has developed on issues of effective schooling (Garbarino and Asp, 1981; Averch et al., 1972; Tyack, 1974). Among those factors most often cited as key to secondary school success are (1) a student's perception of the connection between present schooling and prospects for their future life options and (2) mastery of basic cognitive and social skills. An adolescent who regards competent performance in the role of student as a precondition for successful transition to the roles of adulthood has the necessary motivation for school (Garbarino and Asp, 1981; Stinchcombe, 1964).

Unfortunately for many socially and economically disadvantaged youth, these connections are not evident (Greer, 1972). In addition, mastery of basic cognitive and social skills has been shown to significantly affect students' level of motivation (Garbarino and Asp, 1981; Gold, 1969). Doing well reinforces the desire to do well. Conversely, failure frequently diminishes the perception of one's ability to perform and one's identification with the role of student. Academic achievement and school retention are related to socioeconomic status.

Research has shown that the quality of schools (as measured by staff training, the availability of learning resources, teacher/student ratios, etc.) affects achievement and school retention, especially among disadvantaged groups—the poor and racial and ethnic minorities (Rutter, 1983). As a result, some 2,500 alternative schools (special programs to improve school performance) have been established throughout the United States (Dryfoos, 1983). They are located within regular secondary schools, in separate facilities, and even in the workplace. The purpose of the programs is to provide educational opportunities that are responsive to the special needs of at-risk students, particularly those who are behind grade level and are experiencing behavior and attendance problems. Most of these programs stress individualized learning, counseling, social supports, and remedial education, and they often include work-study arrangements. An essential ingredient is strong interpersonal relations between the staff and the students.

Assessments of the outcomes of special programs to improve school performance indicate that they can be effective in keeping young people in school and boosting achievement. There are no data, however, on whether such programs lower fertility rates. Studies that focus on how and to what extent such programs influence adolescent sexual and fertility behavior are needed.

Youth Employment Programs

Concern about high youth unemployment rates, especially among minorities, has led to the development of numerous programs over the past 20 years to enhance the employability of young people by teaching job skills and job search skills, by providing incentives to employers to hire disadvantaged youth, and by actually placing individuals in jobs. Many of these were large-scale programs supported by the U.S. Department of Labor. Most were intended to address the employment problems of young men, not young women. Delaying family formation or preventing repeat childbearing has not been a primary goal of youth employment programs, and few have given any attention at all to the family responsibilities of program participants (Simms, 1985). Despite the vast literature on the effects and effectiveness of such interventions, there is little evidence of their impact on adolescent sexual and fertility behavior. Only the evaluation of the Job Corps program has specifically addressed the issue. Participation in this program appeared to delay family formation and reduce the incidence of nonmarital childbearing. In addition, the positive effects of the program on employment, earnings, educational attainment, and welfare receipt were larger for women without children than for those with children (Mallar et al., 1978).

A study, which is now under way using data from the federally supported Youth Incentive Entitlement Pilot Projects (YIEPP), promises to yield additional information on the impact of youth employment programs on family formation. This program provided jobs to 16- to 19-year-olds enrolled in school if they met specified attendance and performance standards (Simms, 1985). Although preliminary findings suggest that the program had no effect on the high rate of childbearing, the current study will analyze these data in greater detail, looking specifically at the effects on particular subgroups of participants.

Two other demonstrations that are currently under way or recently completed should provide useful information concerning the potential for youth employment programs to help delay childbearing. First, in 1985, Public/Private Ventures initiated the Summer Training and Education Program (STEP), a summer employment and remedial education demonstration program for 14- and 15-year-olds. The short-term goals of the program are to (1) produce learning gains (rather than declines) during the summer months and (2) improve knowledge of birth control and the consequences of teenage pregnancy and childbearing. Longer-term goals include (1) improved school performance and high school graduation, (2) improved labor market performance, and (3) reduced adolescent childbearing. The program has been implemented in five U.S. cities and will involve 3,000 young people randomly assigned to treatment and control groups. The program is planned to continue through the summers of 1986 and 1987 and a longitudinal phase of the study will follow treatments and controls through 1992—six months beyond their scheduled dates of high school graduation (Branch et al., 1986). Preliminary findings from the first summer indicate that the impact of participation in STEP varied by sex, race, and site. Overall, treatment youth outscored their controls in reading and math by approximately one-quarter of a grade equivalent. Girls showed even greater gains, and Hispanic teenagers, whose high school dropout rates are significantly higher than for both blacks and whites, appear to have benefited most. Hispanic boys and girls in the treatment group outscored their controls in both reading and math by half a grade equivalent (Branch et al., 1986).

The other demonstration is the Teen Fathers Collaboration Project, sponsored by Bank Street College between April 1983 and March 1985. The program involved 400 teenage fathers in eight cities across the country. These young men received job training, counseling and referral services, educational counseling, and parenting education. The goal was to improve their educational status, labor market participation, and parenting skills and behavior. Pretest and posttest data were collected, but no results are yet available (Hofferth, Vol. II:Ch. 9).

As with alternative school programs, more research is needed on the effects of youth employment programs on adolescent sexual and fertility behavior. In part that means making the delay of childbearing an explicit goal of such demonstrations. As Moore et al. (1984) report, most young people, even minority members and those from disadvantaged backgrounds, have high occupational aspirations. Many of them, however, fail to understand the implications of early family formation for achieving their goals.

Comprehensive Community-Based Prevention Programs

Several community-based programs have been established in recent years to provide educational, vocational, recreational, legal, health, and social services to disadvantaged young people in an integrated services setting. Pregnancy prevention is usually only one (although an important one) of the goals of these support programs. Most are located in youth centers and offer a variety of services on-site. Typically, for services they are not equipped to provide, staff refer clients to other agencies and resources within the community (e.g., abortion clinics) and provide appropriate follow-up. These programs generally emphasize a coordinated youth-oriented approach, which recognizes that many of the young people they serve come from multiproblem families and require more than one type of support or service.

The two most well-known examples of this type of intervention are

The Bridge Over Troubled Waters, located in the heart of Boston's troubled "Tenderloin" district, and The Door, located in lower Manhattan. Both are multiservice centers that serve young people, boys and girls, ages 12–21. No systematic evaluation of either of these programs has been done; thus there are no data bearing specifically on the question of their short- and long-term effects on sexual and fertility behavior. Nor are there any available cost data. Hofferth (Vol. II:Ch. 9) reports, however, that an evaluation of The Door is now in the planning stages.

COALITIONS AND INTEREST GROUPS

A variety of national, state, and local coalitions has been formed in recent years to address the problems of teenage pregnancy and childbearing. A major objective of these groups and organizations has been the development and implementation of effective prevention strategies. Typically, these coalitions have sought to involve a wide range of relevant public and private agencies, advocacy organizations, and service providers in needs assessment, program planning, implementation, networking, and evaluation activities. The major premise behind such coalitions is that effective solutions must come from collective ownership of the problems and cooperative efforts to identify and mobilize available resources to address them.

Among the most visible national interest groups to have formed adolescent pregnancy coalitions are the Children's Defense Fund and the National Urban League. The Children's Defense Fund has directed its efforts toward (1) consciousness raising among black women's groups and religious constituencies, (2) information sharing about promising outreach and service delivery approaches, (3) gathering and disseminating research information, (4) advocating public policy initiatives, and (5) examining the role of the media and its messages to minority youth. In conjunction with four other major national organizations (i.e., the Association of Junior Leagues, the National Council of Negro Women, the National Coalition of 100 Black Women, and the March of Dimes Birth Defects Foundation), the Children's Defense Fund has launched its Adolescent Pregnancy Childwatch Program to stimulate and support local communities' efforts to address the problems of adolescent pregnancy and childbearing, especially as they pertain to minority youth. A manual presenting a framework for assessing local needs, identifying and mobilizing available service resources, generating local support, and analyzing program outcomes was developed. Teams from 44 communities across the country were trained to implement the program. The Children's Defense Fund staff will continue to provide coordination, technical assistance, and support for these local initiatives as well as to monitor their success.

The National Urban League has similarly established a network of 10 adolescent pregnancy programs, three focused on alternative approaches to prevention, including parent-child communication and mentoring, and seven focused on alternative strategies to help teenagers who are already pregnant. All of these projects participate in the Too Early Childbearing Network, a data gathering and information system.

At the state level, numerous coalitions and task forces have been established to focus attention, energy, and resources on the problems of teenage pregnancy and childbearing. These initiatives vary: some involve the coordination of state-level public agencies; others involve private advocates, interest groups, and service providers. Some are public initiatives; others are voluntary. Some focus on developing policies and programs and coordinating the allocation of state-level and statewide resources; others stress coordination between state-level agencies and local program planning efforts. One of the most important functions of all these efforts is to build networks and promote communication among public- and private-sector groups who share concern about pregnancy prevention. The Reagan administration's effort to diminish federal responsibility for health and human services during the past several years has put the spotlight on the states. State-level commissioners of health and welfare acknowledge that they currently have the opportunity and responsibility to provide policy and program leadership on these issues.

It will be difficult to measure the impact of these types of coalitions and task forces in actually preventing early pregnancy and childbearing. However, their high visibility suggests that they have been successful at raising public and professional consciousness about the issues of adolescent pregnancy and childbearing and the need to address them at the state and local level.

MEASURING THE COSTS AND BENEFITS OF PREVENTION PROGRAMS

Policy makers, program administrators, and advocates frequently call for information on the costs and benefits of alternative programs, especially those aimed at pregnancy prevention. Such information is often unavailable because adequate measures of costs (i.e., the dollar value of a program's "input") and effectiveness (i.e., the amount of "output" that results from each unit of "input") are missing. For this reason, traditional cost-benefit analyses of adolescent pregnancy programs are often problematic.

Burt and Levy (Vol. II:Ch. 10) suggest that one coherent measure of a program's output is the savings in public costs, for example, welfare costs, medical costs, food stamp, social service, and housing costs. They further suggest that these costs should be aggregated and discounted over the first 20 years of life for a child born to an adolescent mother. Discounting future costs in this way recognizes that, because of positive interest rates, predictable future costs can be reduced if they are anticipated and necessary funds are allocated at the time of birth in order to take advantage of investment earning. Thus, for example, with a 7 percent interest rate, a $5.00 cost next year requires setting aside $4.67 today.

Using this framework, an intervention generates positive savings, even if it only postpones a pregnancy for a year. Based on their calculations, Burt and Levy project that the current discounted value of future public costs associated with a first birth to a teenager in 1985 are as follows:

Age of teenager at first birth	20-year discounted public expenditures
15	$18,130
16	17,851
17	17,464
18	12,214
19	10,671

These costs include assumptions about subsequent births, the likelihood of the young mother's receiving Aid to Families With Dependent Children (AFDC), the likelihood of high school completion, employment, and medical risk as discussed in Chapter 5. The costs are reduced with each year that a first birth is postponed because of reduced probabilities of receiving welfare, smaller completed family size, and fewer medical complications for later childbearers. From these estimates it is apparent that there is a potential savings of public costs for every year that a first birth to a teenager can be postponed. However, the greatest savings would be associated with postponing a first birth until age 18 or 19, assuming that a teenage girl continues and completes high school.

While a delay from age 16 to age 17, for example, will save an estimated $1,530 (discounted over one year), a delay by the same girl to age 18 will save $7,182 (discounted over two years)—savings of an additional $5,652 for a second year of delay. The clear implication of this analysis is that program efforts will have the greatest payoff in terms of cost-effectiveness if they are aimed at helping teenagers delay childbearing until they are at least 18 years old and have completed high school (Burt and Levy, Vol. II:Ch. 10).

This type of cost-benefit analysis assumes specific knowledge of a program's effectiveness in postponing pregnancies that would not otherwise have been delayed. If, as is often the case, however, such information is unavailable, a complete estimation of the net benefits (i.e., the dollar value of benefits less program costs) of an intervention is not possible. Burt and Levy (Vol. II:Ch. 10) suggest as an alternative a simpler break-even analysis. Using this latter approach, the benefit of a program is measured by the number or proportion of program participants who must postpone pregnancy (i.e., the amount of output) to offset the costs of the intervention (i.e., the amount of input). In such analysis, the evaluator calculates the value of the output, for example, the savings in public costs, and compares it with the input, for example, the unit costs of providing services. Thus, if a program costs $500 per participant per year, and the value of postponing an unintended pregnancy for one year for a 17-year-old girl is $6,049, then the program must result in postponements for 1 out of every 12 17-year-old participants in order to be cost-effective. Using this type of break-even analysis, one can assess whether anticipated program effects are within the range of feasibility for being cost-effective. In many situations, in which an administrator may not know a program's precise effectiveness in postponing pregnancies that would not otherwise have been delayed, such analysis can be helpful in predicting whether possible likely outcomes will make the intervention worth implementing.

The clear message from such analyses is that the effectiveness of prevention programs need not be assumed to be very high in order to justify investment. Although the costs of operating programs to reduce the incidence of pregnancy cover a wide range—from an estimated $10 per participant per year for sex education courses to an estimated $125 per participant per year for comprehensive school-based adolescent health clinics—in general these costs are significantly less than the costs to taxpayers that result from nonmarital adolescent childbearing. Most prevention programs need only demonstrate the delay of a relatively few adolescent pregnancies that lead to births in order to be cost-effective, assuming that they do not have any unintended or undesirable side effects that would outweigh their benefits.

Measuring the unintended effects of prevention programs is difficult, yet critics of such interventions frequently point to their potentially harmful consequences. In particular, attention has focused on the extent to which such programs reduce the actual or perceived risks (costs) of early nonmarital sexual behavior and therefore lead teenagers to engage in it more freely. Sex education programs and contraceptive services are especially vulnerable to charges that they may induce more sexual activity among adolescents than would otherwise occur. Similarly, some critics have expressed concern that more intercourse with contraception may also lead to more intercourse without contraception, which in turn might lead to more unintended and untimely pregnancies than would otherwise occur. Available data suggest that these types of interventions have not inadvertently increased levels of adolescent sexual risk taking, but the available data are admittedly imperfect. In addition to measuring the monetary costs and savings of prevention programs, more attention should be devoted to measuring the unintended and potentially undesirable effects of such programs as well.

CONCLUSION

Among the three general categories of preventive interventions there are some interesting and innovative program models with the potential for preventing unintended pregnancy. Yet the ability of almost all these programs to demonstrate their impact on teenage fertility is limited. To do this they would need to show the rate of pregnancies prevented as a direct result of intervention; this would require knowledge of the pregnancy rates for adolescent clients before and after intervention or comparative rates for matched control groups. These kinds of outcome measures are difficult to find. With few exceptions, even programs with the specific objective of preventing pregnancy and childbearing cannot directly demonstrate that this goal has been achieved (Dryfoos, 1983). Although several evaluations are currently under way that may yield more information in this regard, there were only three programs among all those the panel examined that actually documented reductions in adolescent pregnancy. First are contraceptive services: greater use of contraception by teenagers has been shown to reduce the incidence of pregnancy. To the extent that the availability of family planning services encourages teenagers who would not otherwise be sexually active to initiate intercourse, the positive effects of such programs on pregnancy prevention could be overwhelmed. However, there is no available evidence to indicate that availability and access to contraceptive services influences adolescents' decisions to become sexually active, while it does significantly affect their capacity to avoid pregnancy if they are engaging in intercourse.

Second, the St. Paul, Minn., school-based clinic had the specific goal of lowering fertility among its clients and succeeded in doing so. So too did the Self Center in Baltimore, Md. As discussed earlier, however, because the St. Paul program did not collect data on pregnancy, we cannot be sure whether lower fertility rates represent a decrease in the incidence of pregnancy or an increase in the use of abortion services to avert childbearing. The Baltimore program, however, provides powerful evidence of reductions in pregnancies as well as some postponement of initiation of sexual activity for those students with longer exposure to the program.

Third, the Teen Outreach Project in St. Louis, Mo., suggests a reduction in pregnancy. Given the small scale of this project, replication is needed to confirm the results.

With the exception of programs that provide family planning services and several of the comprehensive youth service programs, few of the preventive interventions we examined have pregnancy prevention as a primary goal. Most programs to provide knowledge and influence attitudes and to enhance life options have other primary (direct) objectives yet may also have the potential for preventing pregnancy. In most cases, these programs have not collected the kinds of data necessary to demonstrate their effects on pregnancy or fertility. Several, however, have been successful in meeting their primary (direct) program objectives:

- Sex education programs can effectively provide information concerning reproduction and contraception.
- Family communication programs can help increase the number and frequency of discussions about values and sexual behavior between parents and their children.
- Assertiveness and decision-making training can increase teenagers' problem-solving and communication skills and even increase diligent contraceptive practice.

- Contraceptive services can increase birth control use and improve contraceptive continuation among adolescents.
- Programs to improve school performance can prevent dropping out of school and boost academic achievement.
- Youth employment programs can teach job skills and place teenagers in jobs.

Evidence from the available research on the antecedents of early unintended pregnancy and childbearing suggests that success in achieving these primary objectives may indirectly have positive secondary effects on fertility reduction among adolescents.

Unfortunately, there is little information available on the costs of alternative interventions. While there are data on the unit costs of family planning services (e.g., contraceptive services, school-based clinics, etc.) and some scattered data for other programs (e.g., sex education), we know very little about the costs of other types of preventive interventions. Policy makers, program administrators, and advocates frequently call for information on the costs and benefits of alternative programs, especially those aimed at pregnancy prevention. However, in the absence of adequate measures of costs (i.e., the dollar value of a program's "output") and effectiveness (i.e., the amount of "output" that results from each unit of "input"), cost-benefit analyses of adolescent pregnancy programs are problematic.

As an alternative to traditional estimations of the net benefits of prevention programs, break-even analysis (as described above, the estimation of the number or proportion of program participants who must postpone pregnancy to offset the costs of the intervention) offers an alternative for assessing cost-effectiveness. Cost-effectiveness is typically measured in terms of savings of public costs, including welfare, medical costs, food stamps and related social services, and housing. Estimations of the dollar value of postponing a pregnancy suggest that the greatest savings of public costs will result from postponing a first birth until age 18, if the adolescent girl continues and completes high school. Thus, the greatest payoff in terms of cost-effectiveness of prevention programs can be expected from interventions aimed at helping teenagers delay a first pregnancy and birth until they are past their eighteenth birthday and have received a high school diploma.

7

Interventions for Pregnant and Parenting Adolescents

Like the growth in interventions designed to prevent or delay pregnancy among adolescents, there has also been dramatic growth in the number and variety of interventions designed to assist pregnant and parenting teenagers and their children. And since 1973, there has been an increase in services for women who decide against carrying their pregnancies to term. Programs designed to overcome the negative health, social, and economic consequences of early childbearing have been initiated by the federal government, by states and localities, and by private foundations and philanthropic groups.

This chapter describes interventions of five general types:

- those that provide abortion services;
- those that provide prenatal and perinatal health care services;
- those that provide economic support;
- those that improve the social, emotional, and cognitive development of the children of teenage mothers;
- those that enhance the life options of teenage parents.

The first category, abortion services, provides an alternative to childbearing once a pregnancy has occurred. Programs in the next three categories provide services to pregnant and parenting teenagers to meet their immediate health and subsistence needs and to improve the development of their children. They are intended to directly improve the health and well-being of young mothers (and to a limited extent young fathers) and their children. Programs in the last category are aimed at enhancing adolescents' motivation to become mature and economically self-sufficient individuals and sensitive, responsible parents. They are intended to indirectly improve the health and social and economic well-being of young mothers, young fathers, and their children by helping them want to help themselves.

Among the numerous programs that are in operation, many provide specialized services to meet short-term health, financial, and social service needs (e.g., prenatal care, nutrition services, income supports). Others are more comprehensive, providing a mix of needed supports and services. In addition, while some interventions directly affect health and economic well-being, others influence factors such as educational attainment and employability that in turn affect these outcomes.

The short-term and long-term goals of some programs may differ. For example, helping a young mother obtain Aid to Families With Dependent Children (AFDC) support and stay in her parental home during her pregnancy and for a period immediately following the birth of her baby may ultimately enhance her ability to become economically self-sufficient and live independently. The measures of success for such a program are different at different points in time. Some programs have been carefully evaluated and demonstrate clear positive effects; others have shown less encouraging results; still others have not been rigorously assessed, and some have not been evaluated at all. In short, as with preventive interventions, knowledge of the relative effects and effectiveness of alternative approaches is incomplete. Yet accumulated program experience and a growing body of evaluation data provide some insights concerning how and how well various interventions work, for whom, under what circumstances, at what costs, and with what intended and unintended consequences.

The remaining sections of this chapter summarize what is known about programs related to the five categories.

ABORTION SERVICES

Induced abortion became legal nationwide in the United States in 1973. In some states abortions became legal somewhat earlier, however, and illegal abortions have long been obtained by those who knew where to go and could pay for services. Although the availability of legal abortion services does not cause abortion, it has been associated with increased use, as discussed in Chapter 2. Although the legality of abortion and the availability of abortion services remain controversial, a variety of recent public opinion polls suggest that more than two-thirds of U.S. women agree or agree strongly that a pregnant woman should have the right to decide whether she wants to terminate a pregnancy and that she should have access to legal services to do so (Yankelovich, Skelley, and White, 1981, as reported by Henshaw and Martire, 1982; ABC/*Washington Post,* 1982; NBC, 1982; CBS/*New York Times,* 1980; Harris, 1979).

Abortions are performed in hospitals, freestanding clinics (some of them nonprofit, others for-profit), private physicians' offices, and a few family planning clinics. By 1980, freestanding abortion clinics provided more than three-quarters of all legal abortions. Most of the other quarter are performed in hospitals (Henshaw et al., 1984). Ninety-five percent of the nonhospital abortion providers offer contraceptive services as well. A quarter of family planning clinics provide abortion services at the same site or at another site in the same agency (Chamie et al., 1982), but there are strict restrictions against using any federal family planning funds for abortion services. Many short-stay general hospitals do not provide this service, and no Roman Catholic hospital does so. In addition, 58 percent of obstetrician-gynecologists report that they do not perform the procedure for moral or religious reasons or because they lack access to equipped hospital facilities (Orr and Forrest, 1985). Very few nonhospital family planning clinics perform abortions (although they routinely refer patients to other service providers).

Abortion providers vary to some degree in their policies and the specific services they offer: 72 percent will perform an abortion through the tenth week of gestation; 32 percent will perform one at 13 weeks; 21 percent at 15 weeks; and only 5 percent at 21 weeks (Henshaw et al., 1984). While some clinics consider abortions at 13 and 14 weeks to be second-trimester procedures, others do not. When surveyed, however, 82 percent indicate that they do not perform abortions after the first trimester of pregnancy. Larger clinics (with a caseload of 2,500 or more) and those that operate for profit are more likely to perform second-trimester procedures than facilities with caseloads of less than 1,000. Hospitals are more likely than clinics or private physicians to perform abortions at later gestations (Henshaw et al., 1984).

Virtually all abortion clinics provide contraception counseling either on the day of the procedure or at the follow-up visit: 85 percent of clinics give or sell contraceptives to the client on their premises on the day of the procedure. All clinics make abortion counseling available on request; such counseling generally consists of describing the procedure and explaining its risks, obtaining informed consent, and confirming that it was the patient's own decision to have the procedure. Henshaw (1982) reports that 90 percent of clinics routinely counsel all first-abortion patients; 88 percent of clinics provide decision counseling to help a young woman explore the various factors that are involved in making an informed decision about the termination of her pregnancy. Nonprofit clinics appear to place greater emphasis on counseling than for-profit facilities. As a matter of policy, 68 percent of clinics provide a pregnancy test before performing an abortion, even when a test has been provided elsewhere. In addition, 93 percent routinely provide a post-abortion clinic visit.

In recent years, several states have passed legislation requiring parental consent or a judicial bypass of parental consent (i.e., minors can petition courts to allow the procedure without parental consent) for minor adolescents to obtain abortions. Regardless of state laws, however, some providers independently require parental consent for the procedure. A 1981 study reported that parental consent for minors is not required by three-quarters of abortion clinics, but 15 percent report that they always require consent for a minor to obtain services, and an additional 7 percent report that they require it under certain circumstances (e.g., if the client is under age 15) (Henshaw, 1982). An earlier study found a larger proportion of clinics requiring parental consent for all minors, especially for those under age 15 (Torres et al., 1980). Of the 1,170 unmarried abortion patients under age 18 surveyed in the earlier study, 44 percent were 17 years old, 32 percent were 16, 17 percent were 15, and 7 percent were 14 or younger. A majority reported that their parents knew they were obtaining an abortion. The younger the patient, the more likely she was to report that her parents knew and the more likely she was to have been referred to the clinic by her parents. Approximately 25 percent of the teenagers surveyed in this study said their parents did not know and that they would not have come to the clinic if parental consent or notification were required (Torres et al., 1980). A recent study of the impact of the parental notification requirement in Minnesota found that approximately 43 percent of adolescent minors surveyed used the judicial bypass alternative rather than notify *both* parents of their desire to obtain an abortion; about a quarter of them reported having notified one parent (Blum et al., 1985).

In mid-1983, nonhospital facilities charged an average of $227 for an abortion at 10 weeks with local anesthesia and $230 with general anesthesia (Henshaw et al., 1984). (The fees of nonprofit clinics were not significantly different from those of for-profit clinics—Henshaw, 1982.)

By comparison, hospital charges, including the doctor's fee, are higher. They averaged $735 in 1981, including an average of $330 for the doctor's fee. Second-trimester abortions were more expensive, although the increase in charges was greater for clinic procedures than for hospital procedures (Henshaw, 1982). When questioned about how they were paying for an abortion, 30 percent of girls under age 18 reported that their male partner was providing payment; 26 percent reported that their parents were paying; 18 percent said they were sharing the expenses with their male partner or parents; 18 percent said that Medicaid was paying; and 8 percent said they were providing payment alone. Girls 15 or younger were most likely to report receiving financial help from parents. (These data were collected during a period when the federal government was not paying for abortions under Medicaid except when the mother's life was threatened or when the pregnancy occurred as a result of rape or incest, but a number of states were paying for abortions to women eligible under Title XIX of the Social Security Act—Torres et al., 1980).

Alan Guttmacher Institute researchers conclude that many young women do not have access to abortion services, even though services have expanded dramatically in this country since 1973. In 1980, 6 percent of U.S. residents obtaining abortions did so outside their state of residence (Henshaw and O'Reilly, 1983). Teenagers traveled an average of 45 miles from home to obtain services, many outside their county of residence (Torres et al., 1980).

What effects has the nationwide legalization of abortion had on rates of childbearing and on the sexual and fertility behavior of adolescents who have terminated a pregnancy? The available evidence consistently shows that rates of childbearing have decreased since 1973 in states and countries with higher abortion rates (Henshaw, 1983; Field, 1981; Brann, 1979; Moore and Caldwell, 1977). Concern that the availability of abortion services will lead to higher rates of sexual activity and pregnancy and less reliance on contraception is not supported by the available research literature. As discussed in Chapter 4, the availability of abortion does not appear to affect either sexual activity or the probability of becoming pregnant. Koenig and Zelnik (1982) found that an adolescent girl who aborted a first pregnancy was significantly less likely to become pregnant again within 24 months than a comparable girl who carried her first pregnancy to term. Implicit in this finding is the fact that girls who have terminated a pregnancy practice contraception more effectively after the procedure than before. From a public health point of view, the total number of pregnancy-related deaths averted between 1973 and 1983 by the replacement of unwanted and mistimed births and illegal abortions with legal abortions to American women (including teenagers) is estimated to be approximately 1,500, and the number of life-threatening but not fatal complications averted probably reached several tens of thousands (Tietze, 1984).

In 1977, the federal government imposed restrictions on the availability of Medicaid funding for abortions, and since 1981 Medicaid abortions have been funded only if the mother's life would be endangered by carrying the pregnancy to term. This curtailment of public funding appears to have had little impact on rates of abortion or childbearing among adolescents, since about 80 percent of Medicaid-eligible women (including teenagers) living in states that discontinued publicly subsidized abortion paid for the procedure themselves in 1978 (Trussell et al., 1980). In addition, in many states, the number of Medicaid-funded abortions was very limited even when support was available from the federal government. As a result, the imposition of federal restrictions had little effect on abortion rates in these jurisdictions (Cates, 1981). Evidence suggests, however, that the cutoff of federal funding has caused many low-income women, including adolescents, to delay their abortions because of difficulties in obtaining the money needed to pay for services. For those affected, the delay has averaged approximately two to three weeks. For some this has meant that the abortion was postponed until the second trimester of pregnancy (Henshaw and Wallisch, 1984), thus increasing the health risks associated with the procedure.

Parental notification and parental consent statutes enacted in a number of states in recent years similarly appear to increase the likelihood that a pregnant teenager will delay obtaining an abortion, thereby increasing the possible health risks (Donovan, 1983). Although there are no outcome studies available on notice statutes, Melton and Pliner (1986) argue that unless such provisions actually result in parental consultation, they are likely to simply present hurdles that result in delay.

States that require consent by one or both living parents have included provisions for "bypassing" parents and seeking the approval for an abortion from a judge. Typically these statutes require a two-level inquiry. First, if the judge finds the minor to be mature, her privacy must be respected. Second, if the minor is immature, the judge must determine whether an abortion would be in her best interest. As a matter of practice, most proceedings have turned out to be pro forma endorsements of minors' decisions (Melton and Pliner, 1986). Most minors are found to be mature, and abortions are almost always found to be in the best interest of immature minors. In Massachusetts, for example, between April 1981, when the consent statute took effect, and February 1983, about 1,300 minors sought an abortion through the judicial bypass procedure. In 90 percent of the cases the minor was judged to be mature; in the remaining cases, all but five requests for abortions were approved, according to the best interest standard. In three of the cases denied, the trial court's decision was overturned on appeal; in one case the judge invited the minor to seek approval from another judge, who granted the petition; and in the last case the minor decided to go to a neighboring state for an abortion (Mnookin, 1985). Similar findings have been reported in Minnesota (Donovan, 1983).

Because it takes several days to obtain access to the courts and may require travel outside one's resident county, there is a de facto waiting period associated with the judicial bypass procedure. This delay generally necessitates a teenager's missing school and may lead to a postponement of the abortion depending on how formidable the process of obtaining a lawyer and going to court turns out to be (Melton and Pliner, 1986). In both Massachusetts and Minnesota, which have adopted parental consent requirements, there has been a marked drop (approximately one-third) in the number of adolescent abortions, apparently as a result of minors choosing to go to neighboring states and thereby avoid the judicial bypass procedure (Donovan, 1983; Mnookin, 1985). It is unknown whether the parental consent statutes are increasing the numbers of unwanted children born to teenagers (Melton and Pliner, 1986), and no research has systematically examined the psychological effects of these judicial procedures on the minors who go through them.

There are few studies of the psychological effects of abortion among teenagers. Most of the available research deals with adult women or mixed samples that have not separately examined adolescents. Although abortion is a stressful experience, most studies have found that it is not likely to cause severe emotional problems, particularly among women who do not have preexisting psychological problems, and frequently the response is one of relief (Adler and Dolcini, 1986). The same appears to be true for adolescents (Olson, 1980), although several studies found an association between age and psychological after-effects (Adler, 1975;

Bracken et al., 1974; Adler and Dolcini, 1986). Adler and Dolcini (1986) suggest that, while statistically significant, the magnitude of the differences between teenagers and adult women is not generally very great and the negative reactions of adolescents (primarily depression) are still generally mild. Factors that may contribute to the *comparatively* more negative response of adolescents include gestational stage, delay in obtaining an abortion, and social supports. In addition, Kummer (1963) found that primiparous women, including teenagers, who have had a previous induced abortion appear more prone to depression during their next pregnancy than women who have not had an abortion. Severe emotional responses are very rare (Maracek, 1986). Despite these findings, the existing body of evidence on this matter is not conclusive and further study focused specifically on adolescent girls is needed. Similarly, very little is known about the effects of an abortion on young male partners, in part because many abortion clinics exclude them from counseling. The male perspective on abortion seems to be important in itself and also because the attitudes and reactions of male partners are likely to affect the young women undergoing the procedure.

PROGRAMS THAT PROVIDE HEALTH CARE SERVICES

The health care needs of pregnant girls and of young mothers and their babies are numerous. A variety of specialized services to fill those needs exist, including prenatal care and delivery, pediatric care, family planning and reproductive health care, nutritional services, and health education (e.g., first aid, nutrition, sex education, and hygiene). Given current knowledge and technology, it is possible to prevent or ameliorate many of the most burdensome maternal and child health problems. Maternal and child health services and health promotion activities are available in most communities through a variety of public and private providers.

Prenatal Care and Delivery

A substantial literature suggests that timely prenatal care plays an important role in preventing problems such as prematurity and low birthweight, especially among low-income, minority, and adolescent girls, who are regarded as high-risk (Strobino, Vol. II:Ch. 5; Institute of Medicine, 1985; Singh et al., 1985; Shadish and Reis, 1984). Complications of pregnancy are more likely to occur among women who receive no prenatal care until the third trimester of pregnancy or who receive no prenatal care at all (Kessel et al., 1984). In recognition of these facts, national objectives have been formulated to emphasize the importance of making good prenatal care available to all women (Singh et al., 1985): the Surgeon General has called for an increase to 90 percent by 1990 in the proportion of women in age, racial, and ethnic risk groups who receive care in the first trimester (Golden et al., 1984). The standards of maternity care developed by the American College of Obstetricians and Gynecologists, now widely accepted in practice, recommend that every woman have a comprehensive program of prenatal care, beginning as early in the first trimester as possible. For uncomplicated pregnancies the standards recommend regular visits every 4 weeks for the first 28 weeks of pregnancy, one visit every 2 weeks for the next 8 weeks, and weekly visits during the last 4 weeks or until delivery (American College of Obstetricians and Gynecologists, 1982).

Available data on trends in the use of prenatal care services show that use increased among all age and racial groups during the 1970s; use of services is now widespread throughout the United States, although not at the levels prescribed by the Surgeon General (Singh et al., 1985). Data also show that the proportion of minority women and teenagers who received such care remained at lower than average levels during the 1970s, and between 1980 and 1982 there was a decline in the proportion of 15- to 19-year-olds of all races receiving first-trimester care (National Center for Health Statistics, 1983, 1984a). Using "no prenatal visits at all or no visits until the third trimester" as a measure of inadequate prenatal care, Singh et al. (1985) found that women from low-income backgrounds and those who are young, nonwhite, and unmarried and who have completed less than 12 years of school are at substantially greater risk of inadequate care. They conclude that the need for education concerning the importance of adequate health care during pregnancy and publicly funded services to provide such care are especially important for those who are poor, those who are teenagers, and those who are unmarried.

A variety of programs has been initiated to help high-risk adolescents obtain adequate prenatal care. Many are provided through public health departments, university hospitals, freestanding clinics, school-based clinics, and youth-serving agencies as well as by private physicians. Some of these institutions provide prenatal care as a special service; others serve pregnant adolescents in the context of more comprehensive programs.

Cost is one important factor influencing teenagers' use of prenatal care services. Maternity care is expensive. The Health Insurance Association of America estimated that in 1982, total estimated costs for an uncomplicated delivery were more than $2,300, and a cesarean delivery cost nearly $3,600 (Health Insurance Association of America, 1982). In 1985 these costs were likely to total more than $3,200 for a normal delivery and $5,000 for a cesarean delivery (Gold and Kenney, 1985).

Teenagers disproportionately rely on Medicaid and other federal maternal and child health programs to pay for their prenatal health care and labor and delivery. They are therefore more likely to attend clinics than to receive care from private physicians. Because of low levels of reimbursement, about half of physicians offering obstetric services do not participate in Medicaid (Gold and Kenney, 1985). In addition, pregnant girls sometimes have special problems in obtaining Medicaid coverage. Girls under 18 who live in a household receiving AFDC are entitled to Medicaid-subsidized care. However, they usually need to present a parent's Medicaid card at the clinic, and many teenagers delay the initiation of care rather than confront their parents with their pregnancy before it is obvious. For adolescents living in households that do not receive AFDC and who are unwilling or unable to obtain their parents' support for prenatal care, most generally leave home and establish separate households if they want to receive Medicaid-subsidized care (Gold and Kenney, 1985). In addition, in some states the waiting period for a medical assistance card following verification of the pregnancy typically delays early receipt of care. Similarly, in some states cards are issued for two-month periods and renewal may be a difficult and time-consuming process, thus discouraging some teenagers from seeking prenatal services (Maryland Governor's Task Force on Teen Pregnancy, 1985).

Teenagers in some states may be able to avoid some of the gaps in Medicaid coverage by virtue of a requirement that Medicaid-eligible individuals under age 21 receive services through the Early and Periodic Screening, Diagnosis and Treatment Program (EPSDT). Although it is not clear to what extent states use this provision to serve pregnant teenagers, there is some evidence that eligible adolescents covered under this program may receive a more generous package of services than is provided to other Medicaid recipients (Gold and Kenney, 1985). The Maternal and Child Health block grant (MCH) also offers some flexibility in filling gaps in Medicaid coverage. MCH funds are not reimbursements, but rather direct grants to hospitals and clinics to provide services to target populations. Emphasis is on the provision of care to mothers and children in poverty, and institutions are prohibited from charging fees. MCH provisions clearly state that monies may be used for prenatal care; however, the use of funds for hospital deliveries is more ambiguous, especially if the young mother is not "high risk" (Gold and Kenney, 1985). Unfortunately, as Gold and Kenney (1985) conclude, MCH does not require certain minimum services, does not specify eligibility, and does not require accountability in the use of the funds. It is thus difficult to know what proportion of teenagers benefit from these block grants relative to other publicly subsidized services.

Another important factor affecting the timeliness of teenagers' initiating prenatal care is delay in obtaining pregnancy testing and counseling. Because many adolescent girls fail to recognize the early signs of pregnancy or choose to ignore them, they do not initiate prenatal care during the first trimester. Programs that make pregnancy testing easily accessible, confidential, and free or at very low cost to teenagers have been shown to help in getting young expectant mothers into prenatal care earlier (Nickel and Delany, 1985). School-based clinics and other freestanding clinic facilities that are sensitive to the special needs of adolescents may be especially effective in this regard. In addition, many school-based clinics provide prenatal care on site and therefore are easily accessible to pregnant teenagers who remain in school. Most of these programs emphasize frequent contact with clients; when students miss regularly scheduled appointments, the staff are able to contact them at school (Kirby, 1985). The St. Paul, Minn., school-based clinics demonstrated favorable outcomes: in 1982 the proportion of pregnant teenagers at these clinics who began prenatal care in the first trimester was very high, 94 percent, compared with slightly over half among a comparable national sample of white teenage mothers (Hofferth, Vol. II:Ch. 9).

Other hospital-based and community-based programs directed at getting teenagers into prenatal care early and keeping them in care throughout their pregnancy have also been successful. The Improved Pregnancy Outcome Project (IPO), conducted by the University of North Carolina, was intended to improve outcomes among a sample of poor, rural, black young women. The project used nurse-midwives to provide prenatal and postpartum care and provided outreach and transportation services as part of a comprehensive counseling, education, and health care package. The project showed a significant increase in the proportion of teenagers who received adequate prenatal care, although there was no effect on the birthweight of their infants (Hofferth, Vol. II:Ch. 9). The

Young Mothers Program (YMP) for never-married pregnant girls under 18 in New Haven, Conn., also demonstrated success at providing participants with adequate prenatal care; they had significantly healthier babies during the perinatal period (Klerman and Jekel, 1973). Unfortunately, however, these positive effects were not sustained for subsequent children born to mothers who participated in the program. Many of these children had poor health outcomes (Hofferth, Vol. II:Ch. 9). Several of the Too Early Childbearing Network prevention and care programs also show encouraging results in providing adequate prenatal care. As Hofferth (Vol. II:Ch. 9) reports, four of the seven programs showed the incidence of low birthweight babies to be below national comparison figures.

Teenagers, especially poor nonwhite and minority teenagers, are at greater risk of inadequate prenatal care than other groups in the population. As a result, many special programs aimed at educating them about the benefits of care and at getting pregnant girls involved in regular care have been initiated, either as specialized services or as components of comprehensive care programs. In general these approaches have demonstrated positive effects in providing adequate care and producing healthy pregnancy outcomes. However, as the Klerman and Jekel (1973) study suggests, the outcomes of subsequent pregnancies may not be as consistently positive, raising questions about the duration of effectiveness and what happens to young mothers once they leave intensive prenatal care programs.

Nutritional Services

A variety of nutrition-related factors have been shown to affect pregnancy outcomes, especially low birthweight. Teenagers seem to be at especially high risk of nutritional deprivation during pregnancy, as are adult women who are poor, unmarried, and poorly educated (Institute of Medicine, 1985). Research on nutritional deprivation has consistently concluded that nutritional assessment and services should be major components of prenatal care, especially for women in high-risk groups.

The Special Supplemental Food Program for Women, Infants and Children (WIC), supported by the U.S. Department of Agriculture, is aimed at meeting the special nutritional needs of high-risk pregnant and lactating women, infants, and children up to age five who meet specified eligibility standards involving income and nutritional risk. For pregnant women the program provides vouchers to purchase nutritious foods, education about nutrition, and close referral ties to prenatal services (Hayes, 1982). About 500,000 women of all ages receive WIC services annually, involving about 15 percent of total U.S. births (Institute of Medicine, 1985). Once these high-risk women, including teenagers, enter the WIC program, more than 90 percent participate until they give birth (Kotelchuck et al., 1984).

Evaluation studies show that prenatal participation in WIC is associated with improved pregnancy outcomes, especially an improvement in low birthweight status among infants of participating mothers (Kennedy et al., 1982; Kotelchuck et al., 1984; Metcoff et al., 1982). Although a recent report by the U.S. General Accounting Office (GAO) notes that the quality of the evidence regarding WIC programs is uneven, the report also states that the evidence is strongest with regard to increases in mean birthweight and decreases in the percentage of low birthweight infants (U.S. General Accounting Office, 1984). Evaluation studies also show that early and consistent program participation is related to the magnitude of benefit and that WIC nutritional supplements following the birth of the child can lead to improved outcomes in subsequent pregnancies. In addition, there is some evidence that WIC participation may serve as a means of recruiting many high-risk women, including pregnant teenagers, into prenatal care (Institute of Medicine, 1985).

Estimates of the costs of the WIC program vary from state to state. In Illinois, Reis (1984) estimates the unit costs to be $310 per pregnant adolescent per year.

WIC is not the only prenatal and perinatal nutrition intervention. Many comprehensive care programs for pregnant and parenting teenagers have also included nutrition education and services as components of their service package. Others have linked their program participants to local WIC services.

Pediatric Care

Well-baby care, as well as emergency care for the children of young mothers, are also important health needs. As with prenatal care, many pediatric care programs and well-baby clinics have been developed by public health departments, hospitals, freestanding clinics, and school-based clinics. In some of these institutional settings, pediatric care is provided as a specialized service; in others it is provided as a component of more comprehensive programs. Services are also available, of course, from private physicians. However, because many teenage parents rely on publicly subsidized services and because private physicians are less likely to accept Medicaid reimbursement, teenagers are more likely to seek pediatric care for their children from clinic facilities if they seek it at all. There is evidence in some states that Medicaid eligibility standards and application procedures may discourage some young mothers from seeking well-baby care for their children (Maryland Governor's Task Force on Teen Pregnancy, 1985).

Several program models are of interest in this regard. The Prenatal/ Early Infancy Project tested a visiting nurse and transportation service designed to improve pregnancy outcomes and child health and development in a group of families at risk of pregnancy and perinatal dysfunction (Olds et al., 1983). The nurse visitation program was initiated during pregnancy and followed the families through the second year of the child's life. Although the program included mothers of all ages, special analyses focused on adolescents and other special risk groups. In one of the better research studies of services to pregnant and parenting teenagers, families were randomly assigned to one of four treatment groups: (1) no service other than regular prenatal health care; (2) transportation to prenatal care and well-child visits; (3) home visits by a nurse during pregnancy in addition to transportation and screening; and (4) home visits until the child was age two in addition to other transportation and screening services. Pregnancy outcomes for mothers and children and perinatal health were better in the third and fourth groups. Treatment effects were strongest for the highest risk groups—adolescents and unmarried mothers (Olds et al., 1983).

Similarly, the Johns Hopkins Adolescent Pregnancy Program (HAC), which began in 1974 as a special obstetrical clinic for high risk-teenagers, developed the Teenage Clinic (TAC) to provide extended primary health care for adolescent parents and their infants identified as being at highest risk of perinatal dysfunction. The program provides a comprehensive package of services, including well-baby care, general adolescent health care, family planning services, nutrition and health education, counseling, and linkage to a variety of needed services. Using several measures of child health (number of sick visits, hospitalizations, emergency room visits, etc.), the babies of teenage mothers in the TAC program showed better outcomes than the babies of teenage mothers who had been in the HAC program only (Hardy, 1983).

No cost data are available from these types of programs; however, Illinois estimates of the costs of pediatric care during the first year of life ranged from $150 per year for normal newborns, to $2,000 for normal newborns who experience some health problems, to $35,000 for very low birthweight babies. These estimates do not include costs for the care of infants born with serious congenital problems (e.g., cerebral palsy, birth defects) that require long-term special medical care (Reis, 1984).

Family Planning and Reproductive Health Services

A major concern among health, education, and social service professionals dealing with pregnant and parenting teenagers is their high rate of repeat pregnancies. Among teenagers interviewed in 1979, 17.5 percent of those who experienced a premarital pregnancy conceived again within a year. Within two years, more than 31 percent had a repeat pregnancy. Among those adolescent girls whose first pregnancy ended in a live birth, 30 percent had a subsequent pregnancy within two years, compared with 25 percent of those whose first pregnancy was terminated by abortion (Mott and Maxwell, 1981; Koenig and Zelnik, 1982).

Contraceptive services, as described in Chapter 6, are available to adolescent girls through a variety of programs and organizations regardless of whether they have already had a birth. In addition, most comprehensive care programs for pregnant and parenting teenagers have made reducing the number of repeat pregnancies a major goal. They typically provide contraceptive counseling and services on site, or refer clients to family planning clinics soon after delivery, and provide follow-up.

A review of the outcomes of several comprehensive care programs provides little encouraging news. Only the St. Paul school-based clinics have demonstrated any significant reduction in the number of repeat pregnancies. Of the teenage mothers who stayed in school and received contraceptive services from the St. Paul school clinics between 1974 and 1980, only 1.3 percent experienced a repeat pregnancy one year after birth compared with 18.2 percent of white teenagers nationally (Hofferth, Vol. II:Ch. 9). It is important to note, however, that the data relate only to those who stayed in school (since clinic eligibility is related to school enrollment). Since dropouts are more likely to have births, estimates of program success in this regard may be somewhat inflated (Hofferth, Vol. II:Ch. 9).

In addition, data concerning repeat pregnancies within two years of the first birth may provide a more relevant indicator, since national survey data show that many second pregnancies occur in this period. Project Redirection, for example, showed a lower repeat pregnancy rate among the experimental group than the control group at 12 months, 14 percent compared with 20 percent. By 24 months, however, the group difference had disappeared: nearly half the teenagers in both groups had a subsequent pregnancy (Polit-O'Hara et al., 1984).

Other comprehensive care programs have demonstrated repeat pregnancy rates similar to those found in national survey data (Klerman and Jekel, 1971; Burt et al., 1984; Hardy, 1983; JRB Associates, 1981; McAnarney and Bayer, 1981). While several projects within the Too Early Childbearing Network (Mitchell and Walker, 1984) showed the incidence of repeat pregnancy to be lower than a selected sample of local women and than national incidence data, Hofferth (Vol. II:Ch. 9) points out difficulties in the comparability of the control subjects represented in these data sets.

The Young Mothers Program (YMP), evaluated by Klerman and Jekel (1973), and the Project Redirection programs, evaluated by the Manpower Demonstration Research Corporation, raise an interesting issue concerning the duration of effects from comprehensive care programs. Both programs demonstrated positive pregnancy outcomes for mothers and babies and lower subsequent fertility at the end of the first year of participation. However, at 24 months, participants in both the YMP project and Project Redirection had increased rates of repeat pregnancy, suggesting that the positive effects of these programs on fertility were not very long-lasting. A major unanswered question is whether these types of interventions can positively affect adolescent behavior beyond the period of initial program participation.

A related question has to do with the unintended incentive effects of comprehensive care programs. The Teen Clinic Program at Johns Hopkins University Hospital found high rates of repeat pregnancy among teenage mothers as their children approached age two and their period of program participation was ending. Program staff have expressed concern that many young mothers become so dependent on the program that it perhaps creates an unintended incentive for repeat pregnancies.

Because young women who experience repeat pregnancies are especially at risk of social and economic disadvantage, providing contraceptive services and identifying ways to effectively motivate them to avoid pregnancy remain high priorities. The existing evaluation research and program experience are not very helpful in this regard.

PROGRAMS THAT PROVIDE ECONOMIC SUPPORT

Economic disadvantage is prevalent among teenagers who give birth and raise their children. While some teenage mothers receive economic support from their male partners, the teenage couple's families of origin, or the young mother's own earnings, researchers have found that teenage parents resort disproportionately to public sources of economic support (Furstenberg, 1976; Haggstrom and Morrison, 1979; Moore, 1978; Presser, 1975; Moore and Burt, 1982). Teenage mothers who do not marry or whose husbands are absent and unwilling or unable to provide financial support are generally eligible to receive AFDC and with it food stamps and Medicaid benefits.

Aid to Families With Dependent Children

Several studies indicate that the single largest source of public support for teenage mothers and their children is through the federally funded and state-administered AFDC program. It provides cash assistance to needy women who are eligible by virtue of being a female family head with children under age 18 and who meet specific eligibility requirements regarding income. Female subfamily heads (i.e., teenage mothers living in the same household with their mothers or other unrelated primary householder) are also eligible for themselves and their children or for their children only. Some states have established programs to support families in which the father is present but unemployed and who also fall below specified income levels. Food stamp vouchers and Medicaid health insurance are available to AFDC recipients (Hofferth, Vol. II:Ch. 9).

Based on the 1975 AFDC survey, Moore (1981) estimated that 56 percent of mothers receiving AFDC were teenagers at the time of first birth. Total welfare and health costs of teenage childbearing were estimated at $8.5 billion in 1975 for AFDC, food stamps, and Medicaid expenditures for prenatal care and delivery (Moore et al., 1981). More recently, Burt and Levy (Vol. II:Ch. 10) estimated that approximately 53 percent of mothers receiving support from these sources began their childbearing as teenagers and that the total single-year cost for AFDC, food stamps, and Medicaid benefits attributable to teenage childbearing was $16.65 billion in 1985. The cost for a first birth to an unmarried teenager in that year was estimated to be $13,902 (Burt and Levy, Vol. II:Ch. 10).

Many factors are associated with welfare status, as we discussed in Chapters 4 and 5: marital status, race, educational attainment, employment history, age at first birth, and subsequent fertility (Burden and Klerman, 1984). As Rivera-Casale et al. (1984) point out, in general the probability of being on welfare after the birth of a first child is greatest among black families in which the child was born outside marriage and the mother has limited education and labor market experience. While the presence of one child presents significant obstacles to social and economic opportunities for adolescent parents, having several children further lowers their chances of becoming economically self-sufficient (Rivera-Casale et al., 1984). Nevertheless, it is important to keep in mind that not all teenage mothers go on welfare, and many of those who must do not remain dependent indefinitely.

There has been considerable debate over the extent to which the availability of AFDC benefits creates an incentive to early childbearing. As Hofferth (Vol. II:Ch. 9) notes, several recent studies have tested the association between welfare and adolescent fertility, and none has found any impact of either level of AFDC benefits or acceptance rates on birth rates among unmarried teenagers (Field, 1981; Moore and Caldwell, 1977; Moore, 1980). There is, however, some evidence that the level of AFDC benefits may affect family and household structure. In particular, one recent study shows that the availability of welfare support slightly increases the probability that a young mother will live independently of her family of origin (Ellwood and Bane, 1984). As Hofferth (Vol. II:Ch. 9) concludes, these issues need further investigation, especially the extent to which state AFDC and Medicaid policies encourage or discourage pregnant girls and young mothers from remaining in their parents' households for some period following birth rather than establishing their own independent living arrangements.

Child Support Enforcement

By law in most states the biological father of a child is liable for financial support regardless of whether he and the mother are married. Unfortunately, however, the partners of adolescent mothers frequently come from low-income families, and many, although not all, are teenagers themselves. If they are teenagers, they are often in school, perhaps working part-time, usually at a low wage, or they are unemployed. Among minority teenagers in urban areas, unemployment is especially widespread. As a result, many teenage fathers are unable to make a substantial contribution to the mother's or the child's financial support during the first several years of the child's life. Not all fathers of children born to teenage mothers are teenagers themselves; yet even among fathers in their twenties, many are unable or unwilling to provide financial support. For these reasons, child support payments from male partners are likely to be small and erratic, and enforcement of child support obligations, among young fathers especially, has been limited (Rivera-Casale et al., 1984).

Under the provisions of Title IV-D of the Social Security Act, Congress established the Child Support Enforcement Program (CSEP) in 1974. The program is aimed at helping states locate absent fathers, establish their paternity, and enforce their child support obligations. Typically a woman applies for AFDC benefits in her second trimester of pregnancy. As a part of the application procedure, she assigns her right to support to the state and agrees to cooperate in locating the father. The state Child Support Enforcement Unit (CSEU) typically takes jurisdiction immediately or shortly following the birth, although in some states the CSEU may delay until the mother is 18 years of age. The state usually attempts to establish paternity and obtain support from the father. If support payments are not sufficient to eliminate AFDC eligibility, full AFDC benefits are paid to the mother and child, and the state collects support from the father to offset welfare costs. Because there is no attention in the statutes to teenagers, the treatment of teenage mothers and fathers differs from state to state. In some jurisdictions fathers are not pursued until they are 18 years of age. In others the AFDC eligibility of the adolescent mother is determined by her parents' ability to support her and her baby. In one state, Wisconsin, recent legislation requires grandparents (maternal and paternal) to provide support for the children of their teenage children under age 18. The extent to which such provisions help counter the adverse consequences of births to young teenagers by providing measures that strengthen family financial responsibility is not known.

As Rivera-Casale et al. (1984) found, most adolescent fathers do not earn enough to support their offspring, and for this reason have not been seriously pursued by child support enforcement authorities. In many states adolescents are protected by laws that hamper enforcement (e.g., statutes that protect the identity of minors). In addition, a variety of factors may inhibit a teenage mother from identifying the father of her child (e.g., off-the-record payments from the father or his family). However, it appears that the threat of enforcement may negatively affect a young mother's receipt of AFDC, medical care, and other necessary benefits if she does not want to reveal the father's identity (Rivera-Casale et al., 1984).

Many advocates of aggressive child support enforcement have argued that not only will it benefit the involved mothers and children and reduce welfare outlays, but it will also serve as an inducement to young men to be more sexually responsible. In this regard, Hartley (1975) reports that in Norway between 1916 and 1956 a strong effort was made to enforce fathers' child financial support obligations by attaching wages, and as a result illegitimacy rates declined. In Sweden fathers are held financially responsible for their children, and this statute is enforced by the state. Such support is not required of fathers in the Netherlands, unless the mother sues; however, men can obtain custody rights to children only through marriage or adoption. Researchers who conducted a cross-national study of adolescent pregnancy and childbearing conclude that such policies probably play a role in the general picture of low teenage birth rates in these countries (Alan Guttmacher Institute, in press). The deterrent effect of child support enforcement is unproven in the United States. However, one recent study in Minnesota found that most boys of high school age were unaware of the existence of child support enforcement statutes, thus suggesting that these provisions currently have little deterrent value (Wattenberg, 1984). Further study of the effects of child support enforcement among both the fathers of children born to adolescent mothers and the grandparents is needed.

PROGRAMS THAT ENHANCE THE DEVELOPMENT OF THE CHILDREN OF ADOLESCENT MOTHERS

Beyond the numerous health risks that children of adolescent parents face, they are also at risk of social, emotional, and cognitive deficits. Teenage mothers, as we have seen, tend to be poor, unmarried, and less well-educated than later childbearers. Their children disproportionately grow up in economically disadvantaged neighborhoods, attend low-quality schools, and experience high rates of family instability (Hofferth, Vol. II:Ch. 9). In response to these conditions, several types of interventions have been initiated to enhance the development of the children of adolescent parents, including child care programs, parenting education programs, special programs for fathers, and emergency services.

Child Care Programs

Among those services that have consistently been shown to be essential to a young mother's completion of school, job training, and employment status is child care (Burt et al., 1984; Furstenberg, 1980; Presser, 1980). For adolescent parents who remain in their family of origin, child care is often provided by grandmothers and extended family members. However, in households in which grandmothers themselves are employed outside the home and for adolescent parents living independently, infant and preschool child care that is convenient and available at low cost may be the only solution if they are to complete their education and enter the job market.

Unfortunately, reasonably priced child care, especially infant care, is in short supply in many areas. A recent survey of services provided by agencies serving pregnant and parenting teenagers revealed that child care was one of the services least often provided (JRB Associates, 1981), despite the fact that many other studies have indicated that both agencies and young mothers assign it a high priority (American Institutes for Research, 1979; Goldstein and Wallace, 1978; Klerman, 1983).

In addition to the general shortage of organized child care services, many of the programs that do exist are not well adapted to the special needs of teenagers. For example, to accommodate the schedule of a young mother-student, facilities must open early and be accessible by school bus or public transportation. In addition, because many adolescents are inexperienced in their parenting roles, they require special attention in explaining observed problems, coordinating child care routines with home care routines, and in obtaining special services (e.g., health care, social and developmental services) when those are required (Klerman, 1983; McGee, 1982).

Child care services to meet the needs of young mothers can be provided in several different organizational contexts, including high schools and alternative schools, youth-serving agencies and neighborhood social service centers, local churches, free-standing for-profit and nonprofit child care facilities, and family day care homes. Although there have been no rigorous studies of child care services for adolescent parents, many project directors and child care providers highlight the need to assist teenage mothers in using child care appropriately (McGee, 1982). Several recent projects have attempted to do that. The Alliance for Young Families in Boston has organized a Teen Parent Family Support Project to provide neighborhood-based family child care for teenage parents and their families. Similarly, several of the school-based clinic programs and alternative school programs have included on-site child care or child care referral as a component of their service package. Many of the on-site child care programs require that adolescent parents spend a portion of their time each day or each week in the child care center to gain experience in caring for their own children as well as other children at different ages and different developmental stages. Child care providers in these settings typically counsel and instruct young parent volunteers on basic care and feeding, infant and toddler stimulation, parent-child interactions, and recognition of health and developmental difficulties. Some of these facilities also offer the services of a trained mental health worker to observe the children and parent-child interactions. This person, in addition to the professional child care worker, serves as a resource for young parents and can spot potential problems early and intervene to help improve parent-child relationships (Nickel and Delaney, 1985).

School-based child care remains controversial in many communities, especially among school board members and school administrators. Despite the fact that most school-based child care is funded through Title XX of the Social Security Act, many school officials regard it as a costly service outside the primary mission of their institutions. Other barriers to school-based child care have also emerged around more logistical issues, such as restrictions that prohibit young mothers from taking their babies on school buses. Similarly, employment programs that have concentrated on job training and job placement have generally regarded child care as beyond their jurisdiction, despite the fact that the availability of convenient, low-cost child care services may be essential for many adolescent mothers' participation in paid employment.

Child care costs vary dramatically depending on the type of care and the setting and whether services are totally or partially subsidized. Estimates of public costs for child care for the children of adolescent mothers in Illinois are $2,840 per child per year for those who do not have physical or emotional problems requiring special services (Reis, 1984).

Unfortunately, existing research and program evaluation provide little basis for specifying the special child care requirements of adolescent parents or for documenting the costs, effects, and effectiveness of such programs. Nevertheless, agency officials, researchers, and young parents themselves continually point to the acute need for such services.

Parenting Education

Current research stresses the importance of physical contact, verbalization, visual stimulation, play, and many other aspects of parent-infant interaction for children's social, emotional, and cognitive development (Belsky, 1982). As a result, many professionals dealing with pregnant and parenting adolescents have highlighted the need for interventions to teach both mothers and fathers about crucial aspects of infant and child development and child care and to help them develop good parenting skills. In particular, professionals frequently point to the need to help young parents learn to talk to their babies in order to stimulate the infant's verbal development. Teenagers themselves acknowledge their need for information, training, and support to become effective parents.

Parenting programs for high-risk parents often begin during pregnancy and continue after birth. Some have a specialized focus on pregnancy and childbirth preparation or on infant care, development, and parenting skills; others have a more comprehensive approach. Parenting programs are provided by hospitals and family clinics, general social service and youth-serving agencies, and privately organized parent education and support organizations. In addition, most comprehensive care programs for pregnant and parenting teenagers devote significant attention to parenting education, whether school-based, hospital-based, or community agency-based (Burt et al., 1984; Nickel and Delaney 1985; McAnarney, 1977; Badger et al., 1976).

There has been little rigorous research on the costs, effects, and effectiveness of parent education programs. However, several studies are of interest. Research on adolescent parents as a part of the High/Scope Project in Ypsilanti, Mich., showed that expectant adolescent parents and those with young infants consistently underestimated the mental activity of their infants and therefore did not talk to them or adequately stimulate infant learning. One of the major goals of this program was to alter the talking style of child care that is often characteristic of younger teen mothers (Epstein, 1980). Similarly, a program to work with young mothers immediately following birth during their stay in the hospital found that young new parents can learn to understand their infants' communication needs and capabilities if someone acting as a role model shows them how to recognize and respond to the signals (Helfer and Wilson, 1982).

The Cincinnati-based Infant Stimulation/Mother Training Project (IS/MT) was conceived as an attempt to intervene in the lives of the local population of teenage welfare mothers and their newborn infants. The project model included weekly mother-infant classes and was intended to reinforce the mother's role as primary caretaker. It was also intended to test the possibility of providing parenting education within the setting of a pediatric care facility (Badger, 1977). The pilot project provided evidence that the infants of socially and economically disadvantaged teenagers who attended classes performed well on Bayley Infant Scales and Uzgiris-Hunt Infant Ordinal Scales at 12 months. Young inner-city mothers in the project expressed strong interest in learning good mothering techniques and demonstrated a high rate of attendance. In addition, researchers found that including parenting education with comprehensive pediatric services had other benefits for physical health, nutrition, and crisis intervention (Badger, 1977, 1981). The IS/MT Project has now been expanded to an ongoing service program at Cincinnati General Hospital. Also, recognizing the dearth of longitudinal data on teenage mothers and their children, 3-year and 5-year follow-ups were conducted on those from the pilot project who could be located. The follow-ups suggest that the parenting education program positively affected the young mothers' ability to realize educational and employment goals and to plan and limit family size (Badger, 1981).

Similarly, the Rochester Adolescent Maternity Project (RAMP) in Rochester, N.Y., was originally designed to prevent developmental delays in infants by teaching adolescent parents how to stimulate their infants. The project achieved positive outcomes for the infants and also had an unanticipated positive effect on school retention and job placement among the mothers who were participants. Staff and evaluators have suggested the possibility that these young mothers' development of feelings of competence in the area of parenting may have contributed to their motivation and sense of competence in other areas (McAnarney, 1977).

All of these projects and others that have not been described in detail are small in scale. While some, for example RAMP and IS/MT, did involve experimental and control groups, most did not have rigorous evaluation designs. In short, the existing body of research and program evaluation on parent education is not sufficient to generalize the long-term effects for either the adolescent parents or their children. Nevertheless, the body of program experience suggests that such interventions can have promising effects on children's social, emotional, and cognitive development. Program models should be further developed and tested.

Parenthood Programs for Young Men

Concern that parenting education has all too often focused on the adolescent mother has led to several new small-scale programs that focus particular attention on nurturing the role of the adolescent father. As Parke and Neville (Vol. II:Ch. 7) suggest, there is considerable diversity in the ways in which teenage fathers organize their relationships with mother and child. Some marry and live with the mother in a nuclear family unit; others cohabit with the mother but remain unmarried; still others remain unmarried and live separately. The range in quantity and quality of father-child contact varies substantially, and therefore interventions to encourage father involvement must be responsive to this diversity.

Much of the research on father-child interactions has shown that positive results can be obtained by early intervention, for example, involving fathers in childbirth education, labor and delivery, and infant care training, immediately prior to the baby's birth, at the time of birth, and in the early days and weeks thereafter (Klaus and Kennell, 1982; Lamb, 1977; Parke et al., 1980). For some adolescent fathers who feel committed to the mother and exhibit a strong interest in an active parenting role, these approaches may yield positive results. However, as Parke and Neville (Vol. II:Ch. 7) suggest, not all adolescent fathers are ready for or receptive to parenting in the prenatal and early postpartum period. Indeed, many assume an active paternal role only when the child is beyond infancy, suggesting the need for programs that are also aimed at increasing positive father-child relationships later in the child's development (Zelazo and Kearsley, 1980).

In addition, programs aimed at enhancing father-child involvement may address only one aspect of the kind of support many adolescent males need in assuming parenthood roles. Academic education, job training, and life skills education, which are discussed in the next section, are also important. As a result, several interventions to encourage adolescent fathering have introduced more comprehensive approaches that combine parent education with regular school activities, employment programs, and life planning courses. In particular, Parke and Neville (Vol. II:Ch. 7) point to the potential benefit of school-based programs that include child care centers that encourage or require young fathers, as well as mothers, to become involved in caretaking. As with young mothers, these programs offer opportunities to provide young fathers with instruction on infant care and development.

Another example of a multifaceted approach to adolescent fatherhood is the Teen Father Collaboration Project, a two-year national demonstration under the direction of Bank Street College (Klinman et al., 1985). The eight-site program serves approximately 400 adolescent fathers each year, and projects differ depending on the special characteristics and needs of their racially and ethnically diverse populations. Most include only fathers who are under age 20, although a couple of sites do serve older partners of adolescent mothers as well. In general, the projects provide individual and group counseling, job training and placement services, family planning workshops, prenatal and parenting education, and couples counseling. Some provide these services on-site; others link clients to existing agency programs within their communities. The project does involve an evaluation component, but as Parke and Neville (Vol. II:Ch. 7) conclude, design shortcomings may preclude its generating any conclusive evidence of the effects and effectiveness of this intervention model for adolescent fathers. At the very least, however, the project will provide indications of promising directions for future demonstration and evaluation in this area.

Emergency Services

Among many socially and economically disadvantaged populations, including pregnant and parenting teenagers, emergency services represent an important aspect of necessary support and assistance. These services may include crisis intervention, emergency shelter, and legal assistance. Typically these services are available through public agencies that serve teenagers as a part of a larger at-risk target population. However, many comprehensive care programs for pregnant and parenting adolescents provide necessary referral and follow-up to get teenagers to those public agencies that can offer emergency help and ensure that they receive the services they need. There are no evaluation studies that have focused on the effects and effectiveness of various emergency services in meeting the specific needs of pregnant and parenting adolescents. To the extent that these programs have been studied, adolescent parents have not been distinguished from other clients or patients. Because most comprehensive care programs handle emergency services by referral, their evaluations do not address questions concerning the outcomes, quality, or responsiveness of the outside agencies to which program participants were referred (Quint and Riccio, 1985). In sum, we know very little about these services as they are used by pregnant and parenting teenagers.

PROGRAMS THAT ENHANCE LIFE OPTIONS FOR ADOLESCENT PARENTS

The availability of health care, income supports, and programs to enhance their children's development has increased adolescents' capability to overcome many of the negative social, economic, and health outcomes that threaten early childbearers. For many highly motivated teenagers, these interventions provide the necessary tools to ensure healthy pregnancy outcomes for the mother and child, to meet short-term financial and social service needs, and to enhance child development and parenting skills. As with prevention programs, however, unless young people are motivated to make effective use of available supports and services, these programs can have little positive effect. Accordingly, a variety of interventions has been initiated to help teenagers develop a sense of future and the motivation to overcome the difficulties that early childbearing presents.

Several of these programs were discussed in Chapter 6 with regard to preventive interventions; here they are described as they apply specifically to pregnant and parenting teenagers. Others were not previously discussed.

Programs to Improve Life Planning

Programs designed to improve life planning are intended to help pregnant and parenting teenagers make decisions concerning life goals that include, but go beyond, the birth of their babies. Many preventive programs to improve life planning emphasize goal setting and making teenagers aware of the consequences of an unintended birth on achieving their goals. Life-planning programs address the same issues (e.g., the consequences of subsequent childbearing for educational and occupational attainment) and include many of the same techniques (e.g., presenting educational career options and helping teenagers identify the necessary steps to achieve these goals) used in preventive programs. In contrast, however, they generally encourage young parents to recognize their children as special responsibilities that should be incorporated into their long-term plans and objectives. Most life-planning programs and curricula for pregnant and parenting teenagers are components of comprehensive care programs. Life planning has received special attention in the Community of Caring programs, the Project Redirection programs, in several of the Too Early Childbearing programs, and the Family Focus drop-in centers as well as several of the Teen Father Collaboration Projects (Joseph P. Kennedy, Jr., Foundation, 1982; Polit-O'Hara et al., 1984; Mitchell and Walker, 1985; Nickel and Delaney, 1985; Bank Street College, no date).

There are no evaluation data to suggest either the short-term or long-term effectiveness of life-planning programs in helping teenage parents complete their education, achieve economic self-sufficiency, or develop stable families.

Life Skills Training

Courses that instruct teenagers on basic aspects of daily life have been incorporated into several alternative school programs for adolescent parents and into some regular secondary school course offerings. They are also included in many comprehensive care programs. Typically these courses include consumer education, budgeting and household financial management, homemaking skills, and information concerning available community supports and services and how to gain access to them. Their primary goal is to give teenagers adequate instruction and training to manage their lives in independent living arrangements.

None of these training courses has been rigorously evaluated. Thus there is little available information concerning their impact on teenagers' level of knowledge about the topics covered or on their subsequent behavior. However, many professionals working with pregnant and parenting teenagers as well as other teenagers acknowledge the importance of such instruction. In addition, the Sarasota, Fla., school system has included life skills training as a course requirement for graduation for all high school students. The systemwide curriculum was originally developed in the local alternative school for pregnant and parenting teenagers. Further efforts to develop and test such life skills training approaches are needed.

Alternative Schools

Studies show that only 50 to 60 percent of all adolescent girls who become mothers ever finish high school (Mott and Marsiglio, 1985; Card and Wise, 1978). Educational status is one of the most accurate predictors of eventual employment and economic self-sufficiency. It is also associated with the development of effective parenting skills and child outcomes (Baldwin and Cain, 1980). Therefore, special attention to the educational needs of pregnant and parenting teenagers has become a high priority in many communities and among most professionals working with early childbearers.

Passage of Title IX of the Education Amendments (1972) prohibits discrimination in education because of pregnancy, childbearing, or marital status. As a result, all school systems receiving federal funds must allow students to remain in school throughout pregnancy and to return following the birth of their child. Despite their legal rights to continue their education, however, many teenagers find it difficult to do so (Mott and Marsiglio, 1985). School routines, regulations, and facilities are frequently not well adapted to the special needs of pregnant girls. And most schools do not provide the kinds of special supports and services (e.g., child care) that many mothers need to maintain school attendance.

As a result, school systems across the country have established alternative school programs for pregnant and parenting teens either within regular secondary schools or in separate facilities. Typically these programs are intended to help students maintain their academic standing, but learning is individually paced and instruction is responsive to individual differences in students' past performance, abilities, and attitudes. In addition, many alternative school programs provide special instruction in sex education, health and hygiene, life planning, life skills training, parenting education, and job training, all of which are geared to the special needs of these students. Most programs include on-site child care, and these facilities serve as parenting education laboratories for new and expectant mothers, as well as providing services that make it possible for young mothers to continue their education. Many alternative school programs also link students to other services and supports within the community (e.g., family planning, nutrition supplements, prenatal care, income supports, housing, etc.) by providing referral and follow-up. Typically students are enrolled in these programs during their pregnancy and for several months following delivery, after which time they are expected to return to their regular school.

In evaluating alternative school programs, Zellman (1982) found that programs vary significantly in the intensiveness of their academic components and the comprehensiveness of their social service and support components. These variations in turn affect the success of the programs. Furstenberg and Brooks-Gunn (1985b) found that there were positive lasting effects (i.e., high school graduation) for girls in their sample who were enrolled in an alternative school program in Baltimore. Evaluation of the CYESIS program in Sarasota, Fla., as a part of the Too Early Childbearing Network, sheds some light on other factors that influence program success. That program, which represents a comprehensive model, has received considerable financial and moral support from the local school board, secondary school principals, and guidance counselors, as well as the community at large. As a result, participation in the program does not carry any special stigma. Students are routinely referred to the program, and their transition back to their regular schools at the appropriate time is encouraged and facilitated.

Zellman (1982) found that passive attitudes or resistance to alternative programs on the part of school officials can significantly hamper the effectiveness of these types of interventions. She also questions the extent to which alternative school programs in some communities have provided a vehicle to exclude adolescent mothers and mothers-to-be from regular school programs.

In light of the importance of educational attainment for the future prospects of teenage parents and their children, greater attention should be given to developing and testing alternative school models in order to improve knowledge of how and for whom they can be effective interventions. Research should also compare the outcomes of teenagers in these special programs with those who stay in regular high school settings.

Employment Programs

There is general agreement that pregnant and parenting teenagers, especially 18- and 19-year-olds and those who are approaching high school graduation, are in greater need of career counseling, job training, and job placement services than younger girls. Nevertheless, programs that encourage younger teenagers to begin to explore career options and that provide part-time and summer employment opportunities have also been established in many communities. Early work experience and job training are recognized as critical to the future employability and self-sufficiency of young mothers (Polit-O'Hara et al., 1984).

Few of the large federally supported youth employment programs have been sensitive to the special needs and family responsibilities of pregnant and parenting teenagers (e.g., child care). They have not demonstrated strong positive effects on employment and earnings of young women with children (Simms, 1985; Mallar et al., 1978), nor have they shown much effect on fertility behavior (Simms, 1985).

Among comprehensive care programs for pregnant and parenting teenagers, employment versus employability goals have been controversial. Many critics have expressed concern that emphasizing employment by providing job skills training and job placement may negatively affect the educational attainment of young teenagers who have not completed high school. Accordingly, Project Redirection did not include employment per se as one of its objectives. The program's emphasis was on development of employability—i.e., the acquisition of job skills and the motivation to work. Thus, while the program did not promote immediate employment, the development of job skills through part-time or temporary employment was considered a positive step toward eventual regular employment and self-sufficiency (Polit-O'Hara et al., 1984). The evaluation of Project Redirection showed that the program did not result in higher rates of actual employment at the end of the study. However, on average, participants had accumulated significantly more work experience than those in the control group. They also scored higher on employability knowledge tests and career maturity scales, indicating increased knowledge of the work world (e.g., how to complete a job application, how to perform during an interview, what skills various jobs require, etc.) and greater motivation to work. These effects were stronger for participants with longer program enrollments and for those living in AFDC households (Polit-O'Hara et al., 1984).

Other smaller-scale programs across the country have also been aimed at enhancing employability among pregnant and parenting teens, although they have generally not been as rigorously evaluated as Project Redirection. Within local communities, many of these programs have developed strong ties to the business community and have depended on local employers as advisers and future employment resources for their participants (Nickel and Delaney, 1985).

Family Care Programs

For the adolescent mother who chooses single parenthood, several alternative living arrangements are theoretically available. She and her child may establish an independent household, alone or with other unrelated individuals. She may continue to live with her parents in their home or with other relatives. Or she may establish residence in a foster home or group facility. Her decision is usually influenced by her own preferences, her parents' feelings, available financial resources, and her needs for a variety of types of assistance (Klerman, 1983).

Research suggests that while the young mother and child in an independent household may have food, shelter, and medical care provided, the absence of other individuals, especially supportive adults, may have negative consequences for her and her child. Young mothers living on their own are more likely to drop out of school because of problems in locating adequate child care and the lack of parental encouragement, which is likely to have negative effects on her employability and her child's cognitive development. The absence of parental supervision may make sexual activity and contraceptive neglect easier, thus leading to rapid subsequent childbearing. In addition, bearing the full burden of childrearing may cause frustration that leads to inadequate childrearing (Klerman, 1983; Baldwin and Cain, 1980; Kinard and Klerman, 1980). These findings support the notion that family-based care—in the adolescent's family of origin, with relatives, or with a supportive foster family—may be beneficial to the young single mother and her child (Klerman, 1983; Furstenberg and Crawford, 1978; Zitner and Miller, 1980).

The potential benefit of family support for pregnant and parenting teenagers has stimulated numerous efforts to encourage and strengthen family care. Most of these have involved the inclusion of grandparents or other family members in existing agency programs for adolescent mothers through home visits, interviews and follow-up, and special group activities for families. In addition, some agencies have initiated special counseling and support activities for the families of pregnant and parenting teenagers. As Klerman (1983) points out, many families need assistance in dealing with the trauma surrounding the pregnancy itself, as well as the conflicts that inevitably arise when a new family unit is incorporated into the existing one. New grandparents may also require help in managing their new two-generation childrearing roles (Stokes and Greenstone, 1981).

Advocates of such programs suggest that major social and economic benefits are likely outcomes—for example, school completion, delays in subsequent childbearing, employment, reduced need for welfare for young mothers, and enhanced physical, psychological, and cognitive development for their children (Klerman, 1983; Ooms, 1981). However, careful analysis of the short-term and long-term effects of these programs has not been done. It remains for future research and program evaluation to confirm or disprove these claims.

Role Models and Mentoring Programs

Recognition that many teenagers, including those who are parents, are frequently reluctant to seek assistance until a problem becomes a crisis, several programs have been initiated to help them take advantage of the services that are available. Among these approaches are mentoring programs that use trained adult community volunteers as role models to help them overcome the variety of personal and social difficulties that their pregnancy and impending parenthood create.

The most visible of these interventions has been the community women component of Project Redirection, in which volunteers who were not professional caseworkers were drawn from the community, trained, and assigned to participants when they enrolled in the program. The community women helped to communicate with teenagers and reinforce the messages of the program: the need to obtain adequate medical care during and after pregnancy; the need to stay in school and graduate; the need to delay subsequent childbearing; the need to be a responsible and caring parent; the importance of work as the key to independence; and the importance of clarifying personal priorities for male-female relationships (Quint and Riccio, 1985). Community women helped their teenagers get to needed services, offered advice and practical assistance, and served as a listening ear. They also played a critical role in program operations, extending the capacity of the regular staff and helping to develop effective strategies for dealing with the individual problems of the girls (Quint and Riccio, 1985).

The community women component of Project Redirection was not separately evaluated for its effects on schooling, employability, or subsequent fertility; however, reports of the program highlight some of the special strengths and weaknesses of this aspect of the overall program. Predictably, the quality of the relationship between individual teenagers and their community women varied with personalities and circumstances. Observers report that the relationships were often particularly close when the young women became estranged from their own families. For such a participant the community woman sometimes served as a surrogate mother. By the same token, many teenagers who were dissatisfied with the program attributed their dissatisfaction to alienation from their community women. In addition, high rates of turnover, common among many volunteer programs, also affected the community women component. Only 22 percent of the volunteers enrolled at the outset in 1980 were still active in 1982. Staff learned that the volunteers required support, nurturing, and reinforcement if they were to be effective and that charismatic individuals who are strongly committed can make a difference (Quint and Riccio, 1985).

Unfortunately, the Project Redirection evaluation does not provide definitive evidence of the effectiveness of mentoring programs in attaining the education, work, parenting, and fertility outcomes that were the goals of the program. It does, however, suggest the need to further examine role models as a potentially useful approach to reaching pregnant and parenting teenagers.

Comprehensive Care Programs

During the late 1970s, there was growing public and professional awareness that most pregnant and parenting teenagers have multiple needs and that many of the services they required were "fragmented, inefficient, and inadequate" (Forbush, 1978). In response, comprehensive care programs became the preferred approach for assisting the target population, many of whom come from severely economically disadvantaged backgrounds. The 1978 Adolescent Health Services and Pregnancy Prevention Act endorsed this intervention model, and since the late 1970s comprehensive care programs have been developed in several communities across the country. Typically, their goals have been (1) continuation of education, (2) delay of subsequent pregnancies, (3) acquisition of employability and job skills, (4) improved maternal and infant health, and (5) acquisition of life management skills. Their general approach has been to provide a comprehensive mix of health care, education, and social services on-site and in coordination with other local agencies. Core services have included parental, postpartum, and pediatric health care, remedial education, employment training and counseling, family planning services, life planning assistance and life skills training, and parenting education. In addition, many comprehensive care programs have featured a case management approach, whereby individualized service plans are developed on the basis of individual needs assessments.

Hofferth (Vol. II:Ch. 9) describes and critiques the findings of several of the most visible comprehensive care programs:

- Project Redirection, supported jointly by the Ford Foundation and the U.S. Department of Labor and evaluated by the American Institute for Research and the Manpower Demonstration Research Corporation;
- The Too Early Childbearing Network, supported by the Charles Stewart Mott Foundation, evaluated by Deborah Walker of Harvard University and Anita Mitchell of the Southwest Regional Laboratory;
- The Adolescent Family Life Comprehensive Care Projects supported by the federal Office of Adolescent Pregnancy Programs and evaluated by the Urban Institute;
- The Adolescent Pregnancy Projects, also supported by the OAPP and evaluated by JRB Associates;
- The Young Mothers Program, operated by the Yale-New Haven Hospital and evaluated by Lorraine Klerman, then at Brandeis University, and James Jekel, then at Yale University;
- The Prenatal/Early Infancy Project, operated by the University of Rochester School of Medicine and evaluated by the program staff;
- The Johns Hopkins Adolescent Pregnancy Program, operated by the Johns Hopkins University Hospital and evaluated by the program staff;
- The St. Paul Maternal-Infant Care Program, operated by St. Paul Ramsey Hospital and evaluated by the program staff; and
- The Rochester Adolescent Maternity Project, operated by the University of Rochester School of Medicine and evaluated by the program staff.

The outcomes of specific aspects of these programs have been discussed throughout this chapter in the context of separate intervention components. Several more general findings are of special interest. First, among the programs reviewed, there was strong evidence of positive, short-term effects in their particular areas of concentration. That is, programs tended to improve outcomes for those areas on which they were specifically focused, for example, reducing the number of repeat pregnancies or keeping pregnant teenagers in school. Substantial long-term effects, however, especially on delay in subsequent fertility, have yet to be demonstrated. While clients have been shown to do well while they are in the comprehensive care programs, their later health, education, and employment outcomes are less positive. Those who remain in the programs longer appear to do better than those with shorter tenures (Polit-O'Hara et al., 1984; Klerman and Jekel, 1973), but it is not clear whether these apparent benefits are due to the program or to the self-selection of committed participants.

Second, two of the programs had their most positive effects on their most disadvantaged participants, suggesting that those in greatest need may derive the greatest benefit from comprehensive care programs (Olds et al., 1983; Polit-O'Hara et al., 1984). Other programs, however, had difficulty reaching the youngest teenagers, regarded by many as the population in greatest need (McAnarney and Bayer, 1981).

Third, among programs that rely on a brokerage model, the quantity and quality of services depends on what is available in local communities. While this model may be sensible from the standpoints of administration and cost control, it may hamper the programs from responding adequately and appropriately to the needs of enrollees, especially younger ones (Quint and Riccio, 1985; Burt et al., 1984). Moreover, when services are brokered rather than delivered directly, monitoring the quality of these services and teenagers' participation in them is more difficult.

Fourth, there is some evidence from the several evaluation studies that pregnant and parenting teenagers may require a somewhat different mix of services depending on their age; organizations that serve the youngest adolescents may not be well suited to serve older ones. While adolescent parents and parents-to-be in all age groups require the same health services, school-age teenagers need more supports and services to help them complete their education. Many younger teenagers remain in their families of origin during and after their pregnancies, suggesting the need for more supports for their families as well. Older teenagers are more work-oriented and therefore typically require services to enhance their employability. Because many 18- and 19-year-olds are living independently, they may need more life management support (Walker and Mitchell, 1985; Quint and Riccio, 1985).

Fifth, comprehensive care programs are costly. Data on costs were not available for all of these programs, and they vary depending on the mix of services and the locality. For example, Project Redirection's operating costs averaged approximately $3,900 per participant per year; these costs are only partial, however, in that they reflect costs borne by the sponsoring agency but not those of outside agencies providing the brokered services (Quint and Riccio, 1985). The operating costs of the projects sponsored by OAPP averaged $2,650 per participant per year for 7 of the 26 projects. Costs were higher for young mothers who entered the program after delivery than for those who entered during their pregnancies (Burt et al., 1984).

All of the comprehensive care programs that were reviewed included an evaluation component, and among them Hofferth (Vol. II:Ch. 9) observes a trend toward more rigorous research designs, including randomly assigned treatment and comparison groups, planned variations in treatment, and sophisticated controls for a variety of intervening factors. She also highlights several significant limitations of these studies. Unfortunately, none of these evaluations, even the most sophisticated, separately analyzed the impact of various components of the program. In the evaluation of Project Redirection, for example, it is impossible to assess the relative effects of the individual participant plan, the community women, and peer group sessions on participants' educational, employability, life management, and health outcomes.

The selection of control groups also poses problems in interpreting the findings of several studies. The OAPP projects lacked a control group altogether. The Too Early Childbearing Network has sought to develop controls for its projects using existing national and/or local comparison data. However, Hofferth (Vol. II:Ch. 9) suggests that while this is a useful approach, in some cases it has resulted in an overstatement of program effects because the matched data are not comparable in terms of race, socioeconomic status, age, marital status, etc. The Project Redirection control group was the most carefully matched among the program evaluations that were reviewed. However, researchers conducting the evaluation expressed concern about the difficulty in finding "pure" controls in the communities in which the programs were operating, as a basis for assessing the benefit of the services offered in the programs.

Because of the wide variety and growing number of programs and services for pregnant and parenting teenagers, they had difficulty identifying a totally unserved control group.

The comprehensive services model is based on an assumption that certain essential resources exist at the local level, including (1) basic health, educational, and social services and funds to operate them, (2) political and popular support, (3) clients, and (4) effective interventive technology (i.e., proven theory for program design). However, a recent study (Weatherly et al., 1985) found many of these basic resources lacking. Adequately funded services with well-trained service providers were often unavailable or inaccessible; local support was frequently limited; and interventive approaches were frequently "overlaid with ideology and pragmatic concerns for organizational maintenance" (Weatherly et al., 1985). In addition, these researchers confirmed a finding from several of the evaluation studies, that pregnant and parenting teenagers are an inherently difficult group to serve in conventional bureaucratic settings. Because they are a diverse population (e.g., age, developmental maturity, race, socioeconomic status, family status, aspirations and expectations), they require individualized assistance. Weatherly et al. (1985) found that a programmatic choice to serve any part of this diverse population often entailed an implicit decision to exclude others. In short, these researchers found that few "comprehensive care" programs for pregnant and parenting teenagers actually meet their goals. They are limited in geographical coverage and the numbers served relative to need. Moreover, and perhaps most important, while some programs do show positive short-term effects, for example, on reducing the number of repeat pregnancies, there is little evidence that these programs are able to remedy many of the other conditions that are associated with early unintended childbearing.

Weatherly et al. (1985) were able to specify necessary conditions for program success: well-developed local health, education, and social services, local civic cultures supportive of services, flexible local funding sources, traditions of interagency collaboration, mechanisms for local coordination, and supportive state policies. However, they conclude that few localities possess these resources, and effective comprehensive care programs can be developed and maintained only under exceptional circumstances.

In sum, the existing research and evaluation literature on comprehensive care programs provides little evidence that these interventions constitute a solution to the problems associated with early unintended pregnancy and childbearing. While they can provide short-term support and services to young women in crisis, they do not address many of the more fundamental conditions that lead to adolescent pregnancy and that undermine successful adjustment, including poverty and unemployment.

Adoption Services

Among those adolescents who carry their pregnancies to term, some are unwilling or unable to care for their children. For these young women, adoption services—which facilitate the termination of their parental rights and permanently place their children in unrelated adoptive families—provide an alternative.

There are strong indications from agency data that the number of young women interested in relinquishing their children is declining. In Minnesota, for example, there were 6,107 births to teenage mothers in 1982 and only 45 newborn adoptions in 1983 and in 1984 (data presented by Jane Bose, Children's Home Society of Minnesota). However, the actual numbers nationwide and the magnitude of the trend are not clear. It seems that more young unmarried mothers who give birth are keeping and raising their children than one or two decades ago, although there appears to have been little change in the propensity of teenage mothers to place their babies for adoption since the mid-1970s (Bachrach, 1986). In addition, there has been a substantial decline in the rate at which children born outside marriage are adopted by unrelated persons (Muraskin, 1983). However, agency data alone do not provide a reliable source on this matter, since private adoptions (arranged between individuals rather than through an agency) have become more prevalent during the past several years in some states. Despite the apparent decline in the number of women choosing adoption over parenting, there has been renewed interest in programs to enhance the adoption alternative in the early 1980s. The Adolescent Family Life Program passed by Congress in 1981 as Title XX of the Public Health Service Act places high priority on finding ways to make adoption an attractive option to unmarried teenagers who become pregnant.

Adoption services generally include education and counseling for the birth mother during her pregnancy (and sometimes afterward), prenatal care, nutrition services if they are needed, obstetrical care for labor and delivery, identification and selection of adoptive families, and legal services to carry out the relinquishment by the birth mother and adoption by the new family. As Muraskin (1983) points out, in some cases these services are provided as a comprehensive package in a residential facility. Residential programs, however, seem to be the exception. More often, more than one agency or service provider is involved in the process. Teenagers rarely go to an adoption agency for pregnancy testing; therefore, if they are seriously considering relinquishment, they must be referred to a public or private adoption agency by a family planning clinic or other facility that provides pregnancy testing and counseling. Most adoption agencies arrange and refer clients to the necessary health and social services they require during pregnancy, labor, and delivery but do not usually provide these services on-site. Although they typically screen and select adoptive families and handle the legal aspects of the relinquishment and adoption proceedings, they generally do not provide counseling and support for the birth mother after she has relinquished the child (Muraskin, 1983). This fragmentation of needed services may serve as a disincentive for some pregnant teenagers to make adoption plans.

Research on adoption decision making and adoption services is sparse. The Office of Adolescent Pregnancy Programs as a part of its mandate under the provisions of the Adolescent Family Life Act has commissioned two studies to address these issues (Kallen, 1984; Resnick, 1984). As Muraskin (1983) suggests, however, much more extensive research on the effectiveness of adoption services, for both the young birth mother and for adoptive families, is needed.

CONCLUSION

Over the past three decades a variety of programs to reduce the individual and societal costs of early childbearing have been developed and implemented in communities across the country. Policy makers and service providers have approached problems of teenage parenthood from a variety of professional and philosophical perspectives. As McGee (1982:6) observes:

Doctors and health workers have been concerned about the health consequences [for mothers and children]. Schools have been concerned about drop-out rates among pregnant [and parenting] teenagers. Social workers have been concerned about illegitimacy and the problems of young-parent families. Family planning professionals have been concerned about the inconsistent use of contraception, the rapid repeat pregnancy rate among young mothers, and the increased reliance on abortion. Policy analysts have been concerned about the increasing use of public assistance by teen mothers.

Several researchers have concluded that the result of this plethora of service providers and interventions is not, as one might expect, an oversupply of services to pregnant and parenting teenagers (Moore and Burt, 1982; McGee, 1982; Klerman, 1983; Alan Guttmacher Institute, 1981; Weatherly et al., 1985). Instead, they believe that many necessary supports and services are unavailable, and those that are available are often inaccessible, inappropriate, or do not cover the population in need. Moreover, although many of the interventions described in this chapter represent interesting and innovative program models with the potential to help overcome the negative social, economic, and health consequences of early childbearing, we know frustratingly little about their costs, effects, and effectiveness.

Only a few programs have been rigorously evaluated; many have not even collected basic pretest and posttest data to indicate outcomes along specified dimensions. Among those for which outcome information is available, there is some evidence of positive short-term effects on targeted goals:

- The availability of abortion services effectively prevents childbearing;
- Prenatal care can produce healthy outcomes for the young mother and her baby;
- Nutrition services can help reduce the incidence of low birthweight;
- Regular preventive pediatric care can improve the health of infants and young children;
- Contraceptive services can increase birth control use and continuation;
- Income support can improve the economic well-being of disadvantaged adolescent families, both those living independently and those living in someone else's household;
- Child care services can facilitate young mothers' return to school or entry into the job market;
- Parenting education can improve teenage parents' knowledge of infant and child development and child care and can prevent early developmental delays in their children;

- Alternative school programs can help pregnant and parenting teenagers stay in school and can boost their academic achievement;
- Employment programs can teach job skills and place teenagers in jobs.

There is little information on the longer-term effects of these interventions, although evidence from the available research suggests that success in achieving the short-term goals may assist adolescents to become mature and economically self-sufficient individuals and sensitive, responsible parents.

Evaluations of comprehensive care programs have not analyzed the impact of separate service components on teenagers' capability and motivation to overcome the problems associated with early childbearing. Thus, there is little basis for judging which aspects of these programs, either singly or in combination, have the greatest promise for producing positive outcomes. Moreover, although the available evaluations suggest that many programs have the potential to effectively help teenagers through the crisis of pregnancy, birth, and the early months of parenthood, there is no evidence of sustained, positive effects over time. In part this may be because such interventions cannot address the fundamental problems in many young people's lives that preceded the immediate circumstances of their pregnancy. In part, however, it may be because the time frames for evaluating these programs have not been long enough. Outcomes at 12 months and 24 months after delivery have been shown to be quite different along several dimensions. It may well be that at 5-year, 10-year, and 15-year follow-ups, the outcomes would look quite different. Certainly Furstenberg and Brooks-Gunn's (1985b) Baltimore research suggests that, over time, many early childbearers, even those from the most disadvantaged backgrounds, do find pathways to success. Despite the complexity and expense of longitudinal research, long-term follow-ups of samples of clients from selected programs may yield valuable understanding of the strength and duration of program effects.

8

Priorities for Data Collection and Research

The panel has reviewed a broad array of data sets, research studies, and program evaluations for their contribution to the understanding of adolescent sexual and fertility behavior. In previous chapters we summarized the trends in teenage sexual activity, pregnancy, abortion, and childbearing as well as knowledge about the antecedents and consequences of these behaviors. We have also presented conclusions about the effectiveness of existing interventions to prevent or delay these behaviors and to ameliorate their negative consequences. We have found that, over the past several years, researchers have made significant advances in knowledge about teenage sexuality, pregnancy, and parenting, yet, as we have repeatedly indicated, many questions remain unanswered, and they suggest priorities for future data collection and research.

Essential to framing an agenda for research is an underlying concept of the applications of increased knowledge. What do concerned policy makers, program administrators, advocates, parents, and adolescents need to know? How would such information make a difference for public and private, collective and individual efforts to develop solutions to the problems of early unintended pregnancy and childbearing? The relationship between empirical study, theory building, and policy formulation is interactive and continuously evolving. Advances in one domain inevitably influence new initiatives in others. Implicit in the research questions that have been highlighted in previous chapters is the need to link data collection, analyses of attitudes and behavior, and the design of interventions to underlying theoretical constructs, for example, theories of adolescent development, theories of social structure, or theories of human ecology.

What is the meaning of sexual behavior in the context of psychosocial, cognitive, and physical development? What does it mean in relation to race, family structure, and socioeconomic status? What does it mean in different cultural communities and neighborhood environments? Within such frameworks, data needs can be specified, measures can be derived, hypotheses concerning the relationships among relevant variables can be tested, and programmatic approaches can be developed with some logical connection between these often separate activities.

The remaining sections of this chapter present the panel's recommendations for data collection, research on adolescent sexual and fertility behavior, program evaluation, and experimentation.

PRIORITIES FOR DATA COLLECTION

The panel recommends that data systems that monitor fertility and fertility-related behaviors be maintained and strengthened. Such data are essential for understanding trends and correlates of adolescent sexual activity, contraceptive use, pregnancy, abortion, and childbearing and as a basis for policy and program development. Fiscal cutbacks that affect ongoing data collection programs could seriously damage the quality and availability of these data systems.

Data concerning levels and variations in teenage sexual activity, contraceptive use, pregnancy, abortion, childbearing, and other fertility-related behaviors are the basis for the panel's deliberations. Such data will continue to be essential for future research and analysis on these difficult issues. Relevant information is available from several sources, including large-scale surveys, federal and state administrative reporting systems, and service providers. As described in Chapter 2, data from each of these sources has particular strengths and weaknesses. Individual data systems vary in their underlying purposes and special emphases as well as their specific characteristics (for example, definitions, sample size, data collection intervals). For these reasons, and because information on sensitive issues requires validation from more than one source, a multidimensional strategy for data collection is essential.

We note here several general issues regarding the collection of information in large-scale data systems that affect their usefulness in studies of adolescent sexual and fertility behavior. First, in many cases the definitions of key concepts (for example, pregnancy risk) are not uniform across data sets, thus making it difficult for researchers studying particular phenomena or relationships to merge or compare information from different sources. In addition, within individual data sets, standardized information is often unavailable in sufficient detail to support the desired analyses (for example, data on single years of age and data on race and ethnicity). At a minimum, national data sets should include the categories recommended by the Office of Management and Budget (OMB) regarding race (black, white, Asian/Pacific Islander, Native American) and ethnicity (Hispanic/non-Hispanic) as separate items. More detailed race and ethnicity data in large-scale data sources would significantly enhance their value. Second, several large-scale data systems contain information on other behaviors (for example, health, education, and drug and alcohol use) that relate to adolescent behavior or fertility. These information sources constitute opportunities for monitoring the concurrence of various behaviors and for conducting analyses of the relationships between them. Unfortunately, several factors prevent their full use for these purposes: in some surveys the data are not collected on a regular basis; in others there are serious gaps in coverage; in still others the data are not collected at the individual level, or the linkages among relevant topics are not made. Data sets collected primarily to study drug use and alcohol use, for example, would be enhanced by including even minimal data on fertility. This would facilitate interdisciplinary studies of the health consequences of common sources of variation in behavior and studies of patterns of substance abuse as they relate to sexual behavior, contraception, and pregnancy. Similarly, data sets focused primarily on education have not typically collected detailed information on sexual and fertility behavior, even though such behavior has been shown to be linked to dropping out of school.

The discussion of priorities for data collection is organized according to the types of relevant data sources: large-scale surveys, national and state-level reporting systems, and data collected by service providers.

Large-Scale Surveys

Major large-scale surveys that provide cross-sectional information on aspects of adolescent sexual and fertility behavior include general population surveys, health and fertility surveys, and youth surveys. Many of these data sources have had long-standing federal support, yet recent fiscal pressures have threatened to compromise the quality of several of the surveys and to diminish their value to fertility researchers. The panel endorses the protection and maintenance of these data sets and highlights several specific ways in which their usefulness in studies of adolescent pregnancy and childbearing might be enhanced.

General Population Surveys   General population surveys contain a broad array of descriptive information on characteristics of the U.S. population. Because they provide lengthy time series, they permit analyses of population trends (including fertility) over time. Because of their very large sample sizes, they support analyses of small population subgroups that are difficult to study using other data sources. Two general population surveys are especially relevant: the decennial census and the Current Population Survey.

The decennial census provides the largest sample and most complete information on general characteristics of the U.S. population of any available data system. In addition to identifying patterns of change in household and family composition, racial and ethnic composition, age composition, geographic distribution, and personal income, it is invaluable as a benchmark in the development of population estimates at state and local levels. Especially useful to fertility researchers is the information collected on children ever born and marital history, particularly given the available geographic detail for states, cities, and towns. Data on children ever born are critical to analyses of fertility among small populations, such as small ethnic groups and recent immigrants. In similar fashion, data on marital history permit researchers to trace patterns of marriage and family structure among diverse population subgroups. In addition, because of its broad coverage of the population, the decennial census frequently provides the basis for the sampling designs of other data collection activites.

Unfortunately, however, census data are not detailed in many areas of interest to researchers studying adolescent sexual and fertility behavior. For example, they do not contain information on sexual activity, contraception, pregnancy, and abortion. Although there is significant pressure against expanding the census, the usefulness of these data to fertility researchers could be further enhanced by inclusion of information on rare events, such as adoption. In addition, providing published data on special population groups that do not generally receive attention in other surveys, such as native Americans, would also be helpful. This detail, available from the 1970 census, was deleted from the 1980 tabulation program for reasons of economy, although the detail is available on the tape record. Given the current pressures to further cut the costs of data collection, it is important to ensure that, at a minimum, the fertility data included in the 1980 survey will also be included in 1990.

The Current Population Survey (CPS) is the source of monthly estimates of employment and unemployment, including extensive detail on population characteristics. Through the regular addition of supplemental questions, the survey also provides both annual and one-time information on a broad spectrum of subjects, such as family and personal income, poverty, receipt of noncash transfers, annual work experience, school enrollment, and migration. Among the many supplements that have generally been included annually on the CPS are questions on fertility and expectations for future births. These data permit analyses of fertility as they relate to other social characteristics, e.g., age, marital status, occupation, and living arrangements. Most important, however, data are not currently collected on births to unmarried women under age 18. Should such data be included in the CPS, it would greatly facilitate analyses of public income transfers and child support to teenage mothers as well as their patterns of labor force participation.

Health and Fertility Surveys   Ongoing data collection activities related to health and fertility behavior either are or can be made extremely useful for research on adolescents. These surveys include information on sexual activity, contraception, pregnancy, abortion, and childbearing, and they permit analyses of fertility patterns, infertility, reproductive health, contraception, and fertility intentions. Three data sets are especially relevant: the National Survey of Family Growth, the National Natality Survey, and the Health and Nutrition Examination Survey.

The National Survey of Family Growth (NSFG) is a basic source of data on the sexual and fertility behavior of U.S. women as well as on pregnancy outcomes, maternal and child health care, and family formation. Because the NSFG represents the continuation of a line of fertility surveys extending back to 1955, it is possible to use these data for analyses of changes over time in patterns of sexual activity, contraception, pregnancy, and family formation and composition. In the 1982 survey and planned for the 1987 survey are data on women ages 15–44 without regard for marital status or childbearing history (although parental consent is required for minors who are interviewed). Blacks are overrepresented in the sample in order to provide more reliable data for this subgroup. As a result, these data are especially useful for national estimates of adolescent pregnancy and childbearing. The NSFG also includes information on abortion and adoption, although these data are less reliably reported. The National Center for Health Statistics and other federal agencies supporting the NSFG should be encouraged to explore ways of improving the collection of data on abortion and adoption as a part of this survey. In addition, to the extent that the survey could be expanded to include community-level data, such as community and local population characteristics (e.g., racial and ethnic composition, unemployment rates, median income), or if it is possible to merge such data with the survey's respondent data, its usefulness would be enhanced.

The National Natality Survey (NNS), conducted in 1980, was intended to extend data available from the nation's vital statistics system: it provides detailed information on births, late fetal losses, and infant mortality in that year. This follow-back survey sampled one of every 350 birth certificates (oversampling low birthweight infants) and collected information from the mothers, the attending physicians, and the health care facilities. The data set includes valuable information on the health and health care of the mother as well as other relevant family background characteristics. Because of its large sample size, it offers special advantages to researchers. Unfortunately, however, only married mothers were asked to complete the mother's questionnaire in 1980, thus creating a significant gap in information concerning birth outcomes to unmarried mothers, a large proportion of whom are adolescents and/or black. The practice of not contacting unmarried mothers also severely limited information that could be obtained on adoption, since presumably very few married mothers relinquish their infants.

The Health and Nutrition Examination Survey (HANES) is a general source of information on the health status and health behavior of the U.S. population. Two cycles of the survey, each conducted over a three- to four-year period, were initiated in 1971 and 1976. A third cycle is planned to begin in 1988. HANES combines interviews of survey subjects with direct physical examinations, thus enabling researchers to match and compare respondent attitudes and perceptions of health status to objective measures of their physical condition. Successive cycles of the survey have been targeted to different segments of the population (e.g., Hispanics) and different sets of health conditions (e.g., sensory defects). HANES contains general information on fertility among adult and adolescent women. Questions concerning the sexual and fertility behavior of adult and adolescent males, however, were not included in previous cycles. Should such items be added in the next cycle, they would significantly expand available knowledge of male attitudes and behavior. Similarly, the child health component of the survey also offers opportunities to improve available data on adolescent health and health-related behavior associated with sexuality and fertility. In particular, increased emphasis on physical and psychological maturity and mental health conditions (e.g., depression, anxiety) would greatly enhance knowledge concerning the relationship between biological, developmental, and environmental factors influencing adolescent sexual and fertility behavior.

Youth Surveys   Other ongoing surveys have less direct focus on adolescent fertility-related behavior but are valuable sources of data on young adults. These include the National Longitudinal Survey-Youth Cohort and the High School and Beyond Survey, among others. The data on social, educational, occupational, and other aspects of adolescent life make them amenable to analyses directed at the effects and antecedents of early sexual activity and family formation. Many youth surveys include males and thereby facilitate the analysis of male adolescent sexual activity, parenting, and family formation in conjunction with education and labor market experiences. The usefulness of these surveys to fertility researchers could be enhanced with greater emphasis on measuring adolescent aspirations and expectations for educational and career attainment jointly with measures of marriage and family formation.

National and State-Level Reporting Systems

Several national and state-level administrative reporting systems contain information on specific demographic, public health, education, and social service topics. Typically these reporting systems rely on data collection by state-level agencies; information from the states is then compiled by designated federal agencies.

Of special importance to fertility researchers is the vital statistics system, which provides continuing information on births, deaths, marriages, and divorces. Limited demographic and health information is collected from the 50 states, which is summarized and tabulated at the federal level and can be analyzed to highlight health problems among infants and to measure progress made by national health programs. These data serve three major purposes: first, they provide the national monitoring of year-by-year changes in fertility and provide race and age-specific data for subnational areas. Second, they provide data to address research questions of importance regarding correlates of adolescent fertility behavior. Third, they are essential in the preparation of population projections. Vital statistics, like census data, offer wide coverage for descriptive studies but limited information for causal analysis.

The usefulness of vital statistics data to researchers concerned with adolescent sexual and fertility behavior could be improved in several specific ways. First, only 41 states and the District of Columbia currently report mother's marital status on birth certificates. This information is essential to analyses of nonmarital childbearing as it is related to birth outcomes. Because there are so many births to unmarried teenagers, especially black teenagers, information concerning marital status is significant in studying this population group. Second, the possibility of linking birth and death records would greatly enhance our understanding of the relationship of factors associated with a pregnancy and its outcome. Adolescents, for example, are at elevated risk of bearing low birthweight infants and of having an infant die. A linked birth and death system would enable researchers to relate mother's characteristics (education, marital status, use of prenatal care, etc.) to birth outcomes. Third, better identification of racial and ethnic groups could also expand research linking special population subgroups to birth outcomes. In this regard, states could be encouraged to modify their birth and death certificates to employ the OMB categories previously discussed. Fourth, the addition of certain new items of information could be extremely beneficial for research linking health conditions and health care to birth outcomes: data on smoking, weight and height prior to pregnancy, and insurance coverage of both the mother and the newborn. Moreover, although significantly more controversial, inclusion of the mother's social security number would greatly facilitate research that would link successive births to the same woman in order to examine repeat patterns of adverse pregnancy outcome. Many of these suggestions have already been implemented in several states and have proven to be both feasible and valuable.

Data From Service Providers

Information concerning the supply, use, and costs of specific health and fertility-related services, such as family planning and abortion services, are collected by service providers and compiled by government and private organizations concerned with monitoring these services. Because these data are typically collected for management purposes, they are frequently inadequate for research purposes. For example, relevant background information on service clients is frequently neglected, and clients' use of services across time is not tracked.

For three fertility-related services, data are inadequate and therefore limit researchers' capability to study them in relation to adolescent sexual and fertility behavior: family planning services, adoption, and abortion.

Data on family planning services are important to understand how the contraceptive clinic system serves adolescents. Since 1981, the federal government has not provided funds for monitoring family planning clinic performance, which includes the characteristics of services providers, service components, and patients and the costs of care. The latest available data are for 1983, and these were collected by the Alan Guttmacher Institute with private support. The federal government should resume monitoring the availability of contraceptive services and their use by all patients, including adolescents.

Adoption is a potentially important type of pregnancy resolution about which very little is known. As we discussed in Chapters 2, 4, and 7, this is in part a result of the discontinuation of the national reporting system in 1975. Currently the only national system that gathers annual information on adoption is the Voluntary Cooperative Information System managed by the American Public Welfare Association. This system collects data only on children placed for adoption by public child welfare agencies. Therefore its enumeration of adoptions nationwide is incomplete and unreliable in assessing trends. While it contains some information on the characteristics of adopted children and adoptive families, it contains little or no information on the characteristics of the birth parents, the adoption process, and the subsequent fertility of the birth mother. The development of a nationwide adoption information system to account for all types of adoptions (public agency, private agency, independent) on an annual basis would be extremely useful in tracing trends in adoption and the effects of recent federal policies to encourage adoption as an alternative to abortion for unmarried teenagers.

Weaknesses in data on abortion hinder analysis of both pregnancy and abortion among adolescents. In particular, information from surveys undercounts the number of women having unintended pregnancies and abortions. Information on abortion is collected by several public and private organizations, and each source has some important shortcomings. State health agencies collect data that are compiled by the Centers for Disease Control: included is information on the distribution of abortions by age, race, parity (number of children ever born to a particular woman), and other characteristics, but the incidence of abortion is underestimated because not all providers are covered. The National Center for Health Statistics collects data from selected state vital registration offices: they are valuable for their content but are limited in coverage to a small number of states. The Alan Guttmacher Institute collects data directly from service providers and compiles them: they provide a more complete enumeration but are limited in background characteristics. Taken together, these data sources provide a relatively complete count of abortions and information on relevant background characteristics of women obtaining abortions at the national and state levels. It is important that these data collection efforts continue with special attention to improving coverage and the timeliness of reports.

In surveys of women, such as the National Survey of Family Growth and the National Longitudinal Survey, unintended pregnancies ending in abortion are greatly underreported. Since it is difficult to assess which respondents are most likely not to report such pregnancies, analyses of determinants of pregnancy and abortion are hampered. Efforts should be made to correct for such underreporting and to find ways to reduce it in future surveys.

PRIORITIES FOR RESEARCH ON ADOLESCENT SEXUAL AND FERTILITY BEHAVIOR

The panel recommends the continued support of a broad-based research program on adolescent sexuality and fertility to enhance understanding of the causes and consequences of these behaviors and to inform policy and program development.

Over the past decade, research has added significantly to the knowledge of trends, correlates, antecedents, and consequences of adolescent sexual and fertility behavior. These research findings have provided an essential basis for the panel's deliberations. Numerous studies have examined the short- and long-term effects of early pregnancy and childbearing on young women's health, education, fertility, marital experiences, employment, and economic well-being. Others have explored the effects on the children of teenage mothers and, to a much lesser extent, on young fathers. Still others have examined the social, developmental, cultural, and economic antecedents of early sexual activity, contraceptive use, pregnancy, abortion, and childbearing to identify factors affecting sexual decision making. In short, knowledge of adolescent sexuality and fertility has increased substantially, yet many questions remain unanswered. In some cases, the gaps reflect issues that have not been adequately studied because of methodological problems; in other cases, new issues have emerged from the accumulation of findings.

Throughout this report, we have highlighted a variety of salient questions; many of these have focused on special population subgroups (e.g., small ethnic groups) and rare demographic events (e.g., adoption). In framing an agenda for future research, however, it would be useful to fit these questions into a broader framework for understanding factors that influence adolescents' sexual decision making at each stage in the sequence of choices, from the initiation of intercourse to parenthood, and the consequences. As we have emphasized, each choice is complex. Each is affected by the circumstances under which it is made and the range of available options. The historical time, the ecological setting, and the developmental characteristics and accumulated life experiences of individual adolescents are all potentially important factors influencing the process of choice and its outcomes. Accordingly, the panel's recommendations for future research on adolescent sexual and fertility behavior are organized under four domains of antecedents and outcomes: individuals, families, communities, and society.

Individuals

Much of the existing research on adolescent sexual decision making and its consequences has focused on teenage girls between the ages of 15 and 19. We know a great deal about the characteristics of young women in this age group who become sexually active, who experience pregnancy, and who bear children. We know much less about the sexual and fertility behavior of teenagers under age 15 or about adolescent males of all ages. Similarly, although much of the research has focused on black-white race differences in attitudes and behavior, less attention has been given to small racial and ethnic groups, such as native Americans and Hispanic subgroups.

Efforts to preserve and improve large-scale national data sets should be supplemented by efforts to initiate more intensive small-scale studies of selected communities and population subgroups. More detailed data are needed on the relation between biological, social, emotional, cultural, and economic factors influencing sexual decision making and its consequences. In particular, ethnographic studies are needed to develop detailed profiles of the characteristics, attitudes, and behavior of individuals and families living in different circumstances and environments. And more longitudinal studies are needed to examine changes in attitudes and behavior over time.

Very Young Teenagers Very young teenagers represent an important but understudied group. To a large extent, research on the causes and consequences of sexuality, pregnancy, and parenting in this age group has been impeded by the lack of available data and the difficulties of collecting it. In order to gather information from minors on these sensitive issues, parental permission is usually required, and parents frequently deny requests to interview very young adolescents. In addition, since sexual activity among those age 14 and younger is relatively rare in the population as a whole, researchers must develop innovative sampling approaches and research designs in order to generate adequate cases for analysis. These problems have hampered understanding of the early antecedents of sexual activity, including the possibility of incest and sexual abuse. Since race differences in sexual activity are greatest at very young ages, the difficulties in obtaining data have also hampered studies of the significance of race relative to other biological, social, economic, and cultural factors in the initiation of intercourse.

The numbers of very young teens who are sexually experienced, who become pregnant, and who bear children is quite small compared with the numbers of older teenagers. Yet the growth in fertility among girls under age 15 has been significant over the past two decades, and the health, social, educational, and economic consequences of initiating childbearing in early adolescence have been shown to be extensive and far-reaching. The children of very young mothers also appear to be at high risk of health and cognitive problems. Yet relatively little research emphasis has been placed on age-specific differences, and few studies have focused on very young teenagers. Most of those that have are based on small samples and are concentrated predominantly on obstetrical issues, such as gestation, birthweight, etc. More research is needed on the factors influencing sexual decision making and the developmental effects of choices concerning the initiation of sexual activity, contraceptive use, and pregnancy resolution among very young teenagers. Knowledge gained from such studies would help identify potentially effective means of intervening to prevent unplanned pregnancies and to promote desirable outcomes among young unmarried teenagers who choose abortion, adoption, or childbearing.

Adolescent Males Adolescent males of all ages have also been inadequately studied. In part, this lack of research attention results from the dearth of available data on male sexual behavior and fertility. Males are not included in most large-scale fertility surveys; surveys that do include such information have significant shortcomings. In particular, it has been difficult to obtain data from boys: they are less likely than girls to agree to be interviewed on sensitive issues of pregnancy and childbearing, and they are less likely to provide accurate information. It appears that in some cases boys overreport sexual activity and underreport pregnancy and childbearing. Beyond the difficulties of obtaining data, however, the lack of research on males reflects the fact that policy makers, service providers, parents, and teenagers themselves have traditionally regarded adolescent pregnancy and childbearing as a female problem. More recently, public and professional attention has begun to focus on the role and responsibility of males in sexual decision making. Education and contraceptive services targeted at young men have begun to develop, as have programs to support and assist teenage fathers. Such initiatives would be greatly enhanced by more and better research on male attitudes, motivations, and experiences, and such studies need to be informed by careful attention to methodological issues.

Related Behaviors　Adolescent sexual, contraceptive, and fertility behavior may share attributes with other transition behaviors, for example, dropping out of school, drug use, smoking, political activity, and delinquency. Recent research suggests that, for many young people, sexual permissiveness is not an isolated phenomenon but rather one component of a complex pattern of interrelated behaviors. Teenagers engaging in one type of behavior may be at greater risk of adopting others. For some young people, these behaviors may not constitute problems; for others, they may have serious negative effects. Such findings suggest the need to examine sexuality in the broader context of normal and abnormal adolescent development. They also suggest the possibility of identifying effective intervention approaches in one domain (e.g., smoking) that may have applicability in others (e.g., pregnancy prevention).

Of special importance in this regard are studies of the relationship between education experiences and fertility. While pregnancy and childbearing are often the cause of dropping out of school, a significant proportion of teenage girls leave school before they conceive. These young women constitute a special risk group. Less is known about the relationship between academic achievement, educational attainment, and male fertility. Research to explore these issues could be helpful in identifying common approaches to improving school performance and preventing early unintended pregnancy.

Psychosocial Antecedents and Consequences of Sexual Decision Making
Research on the antecedents and consequences of teenage sexual and fertility behavior has largely focused on the health outcomes for young mothers and their infants, as well as the social, educational, and economic influences and outcomes for young women who become pregnant, give birth, and raise their children. Studies of the antecedents and consequences of adolescent sexual activity have focused almost exclusively on social, educational, and economic factors influencing the initiation of sexual intercourse, contraceptive use, pregnancy, and sexually transmitted diseases. Few studies have examined the psychosocial antecedents and consequences of sexual activity among teenagers. We know very little about the meaning of sexual behavior among different cultural subgroups and its influence on adolescents' conscious and unconscious motives. Similarly, we know very little about the short- and long-term psychological and social effects of sexual intercourse on adolescents of different genders, ages, and stages of development, and on those from different families, cultural subgroups, and community environments. Are there any independent negative effects of early sexual activity other than pregnancy? If so, what, for whom, and under what circumstances? Answers to these questions would be useful to parents, professionals, and teenagers themselves in developing attitudes toward sexual intercourse and approaches to pregnancy prevention.

Similarly, few studies have measured the psychosocial effects of alternative choices for pregnancy resolution, such as abortion and adoption, on young women and young men. Most studies examining the psychological effects of abortion, for example, have failed to distinguish adolescents from adult women in clinic samples. And none has examined the effects on male partners. While a very few studies have found some measurable differences in the short-term emotional well-being of teenage girls and older women, with teenagers being slightly more negatively affected, these analyses have generally not controlled for important mediating variables, such as the timing of the procedure. Moreover, they have not measured longer-term effects on psychological development, self-esteem, patterns of sexual behavior, the formation of stable male-female relationships, and subsequent fertility. Such research is badly needed, both as a guide for policy and as a guide for those who counsel teenagers concerning pregnancy resolution and help them cope with their choices.

Similarly, while there is some existing research on social and developmental outcomes among adopted children, there has been virtually no research on the effects of the decision to relinquish the child, as well as factors affecting the decision, on birth parents. The lack of national adoption data and efforts to protect the confidentiality of young mothers who place their children for adoption have significantly impeded studies in this area. Despite the methodological problems, however, research is needed to follow up young birth mothers (and birth fathers) and to explore the effects of relinquishment on their psychological well-being, later satisfaction with the decision, self-esteem, personal relationships, and subsequent fertility. As with abortion, policy debates on this controversial issue have not been informed by sound research. Finally, research on the determinants and consequences of adolescent marriages, which is also limited, is urgently needed to understand this important alternative for pregnancy resolution.

Families

An assumption implicit in much of the existing research is that individual teenage girls are solely responsible for creating the problems of adolescent pregnancy and for coping with the consequences. Research examining the role of families and individual family members in adolescent sexual decision making is limited. Most studies in this area have focused on mother-daughter relationships. The role of fathers and the relationship of parents to sons and of siblings to each other have been largely ignored.

Nevertheless, several recent studies have begun to shed some light on the kinds of family variables that influence teenagers' decisions on whether to initiate sexual activity, whether to use contraception, and how to resolve an unintended pregnancy. Among the most salient factors associated with early sexual experience is living in a female-headed household, yet the processes by which growing up in a fatherless family influences the initiation of sexual activity among both boys and girls are not clearly understood. Similarly, research on the effects of parent-child communication (both directly, through discussions about sexuality and contraception, and indirectly, through the sexual attitudes and sex roles that are prevalent in the home) has produced conflicting and inconclusive results. Although numerous programs have been initiated to enhance parent-child communication on sexual topics, there is little scientific basis for understanding how these approaches are likely to affect teenagers' decisions to delay initiation of sexual activity or to be more diligent contraceptors. More research is also needed on the role of family members—mothers, fathers, siblings, and extended family—on adolescent sexual decision making among both boys and girls at all stages in the sequence of choices.

For an adolescent girl who becomes a mother, it appears that the attitudes and actions of her family of origin can significantly affect decisions concerning the management of her life and that of her child—where she will live before and after pregnancy, her continued schooling, labor force participation, child care, and her relationship with the baby's father. Yet studies that have specifically examined the role of the family in helping adolescent mothers adjust to their new parenting roles and responsibilities are scarce. Studies of the families of teenage fathers are missing altogether. Available research suggests that teenage mothers who remain in their families of origin during pregnancy and for a defined period thereafter are likely to receive substantial financial and child care support, and that this support has definite short-term positive effects for the mother and her child. Those young women who remain unmarried, who continue their education, and who themselves come from two-parent households are likely to receive greater family assistance. Yet knowledge concerning how different families manage this support, how issues concerning dependence and authority arise and are handled, and the effects of this support on other family members, especially siblings, is weak. More research is needed, especially longitudinal studies that can illuminate the support and coping process and can identify the long-term consequences for various family members of providing family assistance to a teenage mother. Studies of the role of the families of young fathers, regardless of whether they marry and live with the mothers of their children, are also needed.

A growing body of research has addressed the health and developmental consequences for children of having an adolescent mother. Accumulated findings suggest that these youngsters face increased risks for their own life outcomes, including cognitive development, health status and health behavior, educational attainment, and sexual and fertility behavior. Despite mounting evidence of seriously negative effects, we know very little about the direct and indirect processes by which such outcomes occur. For example, is mother's age a key variable, or is it significant only insofar as it is associated with lower levels of educational attainment, lower socioeconomic status, and single-parenthood? Similarly, researchers have not given much attention to the ways in which such negative outcomes can be ameliorated and with what short- and long-term effects. For example, to what extent can various forms of family support, parenting education, public income transfers, pediatric health care, and child care and child development assistance mediate likely negative outcomes? What kinds of teenage families cope most successfully and which are at highest risk of dysfunction? Knowledge of this type would have significant implications for the formulation of policies (e.g., Aid to Families With Dependent Children and child support enforcement) and the development and design of interventions (e.g., parenting and child development programs).

Communities

Community factors also undoubtedly affect emerging patterns of adolescent sexual and fertility behavior, yet knowledge of how neighborhood environments and community institutions (for example schools and churches) influence attitudes about sexuality, contraception, pregnancy, abortion, and childbearing and patterns of behavior is just beginning to emerge. Race differences in patterns of early sexual activity and fertility are dramatic, yet disagreement exists over the source of these differences: some attribute the disparity wholly or in large part to socioeconomic differences among blacks and whites; others maintain that differences in the acceptability of early nonmarital sexual activity, pregnancy, and parenthood account for the difference. Research has yet to resolve the debate, for in many cases it has failed to ask the right questions.

Blacks are significantly more likely than whites to live in low-income communities in which rates of unemployment are high and intergenerational, mother-headed families are prevalent. They are also more likely to attend racially isolated schools. When asked, blacks in these communities report a greater tolerance for sexual activity outside marriage, they rate marriage as less important, and they perceive a greater tolerance for nonmarital childbearing. What is the relationship between chronic economic disadvantage and outlooks on sexuality, marriage, and family formation? To what extent do perceptions of limited social and economic opportunities affect male and female attitudes about the meaning of pregnancy and childbearing or the benefits of postponement? Do race differences in patterns of sexual and fertility behavior reflect deep-seated subgroup values or more transient attitudinal adjustments to external circumstances? Research to address these neglected issues is urgently needed. As a first step, efforts must be made to develop more adequate measures of socioeconomic status among adolescents given the limitations of the information on income and economic well-being in many existing data sets and the substantially unequal racial distribution within socioeconomic categories.

Society

At the macro level, society—through its government agencies, the courts, and the social, economic, and cultural milieu—also influences the process of adolescent sexual decision making and its outcomes. Changes in American society over the past two decades, including changing patterns of marriage and family structure, shifts in employment and unemployment, the evolving role and status of women, the changing youth culture, and the growing dominance of the media have altered the context of adolescent pregnancy and childbearing. The development of specific government policies and programs, including the legalization of abortion, Title IX of the Education Amendments, Title X of the Public Health Services Act, and the Adolescent Family Life Act, has paralleled important changes in the societal context. Contraceptive use among teenagers has increased, for example, as has the incidence of abortion. Yet we know very little about the intended and unintended, direct and indirect effects of societal and public policy changes on decisions, such as the decision to initiate sexual activity, and on the outcomes of such choices for individuals, families, communities, and society.

Public Policies As we have discussed, several federal and state-level policies are potentially influential. Although some research has examined the relationship between the availability of welfare support on young women's decisions concerning sexual and fertility behavior, this topic has not been adequately studied. The effects of such policies on the attitudes and behavior of young men have hardly been addressed at all. Important questions still remain unanswered about the extent to which sources of income support for women and children have influenced the motivation of young men, especially low-income, inner-city blacks, to form stable marital relationships and to become economically responsible for their families.

Similarly, the effects of parental consent requirements for obtaining contraceptive and abortion services, child support enforcement programs, and grandparent liability provisions have not been adequately studied as they affect male and female sexual decision making, family relationships and assistance, or the well-being of teenage mothers and their children. Such studies are needed as a guide to policy and program development. To the extent that it is possible, research on these issues should include males as well as females and should permit comparisons among different racial, ethnic, socioeconomic, and age subgroups of the adolescent population.

Media Among the most conspicuous changes in U.S. society over the past two decades has been the content and visibility of the media (print, radio, television, movies, etc.). The extensive exposure of the American public to the media and the greater liberality of programming and advertising since the 1960s have been documented elsewhere. Less well-documented, however, are whether and to what extent these changes in media exposure and content have affected changing patterns of adolescent sexual and fertility behavior, whether they simply reflect more pervasive changes in values, attitudes, and behavior that have become accepted throughout society, or both. This issue is difficult to study empirically, and very little relevant research has been done. Several investigators have conducted content analyses of TV programming and have documented the amount of time children and adolescents spend viewing, yet none has convincingly linked program content and exposure to adolescent sexual attitudes and behavior. Such research is needed to understand how the choices of adolescents of different ages, genders, races, and other background characteristics concerning sexual activity, contraception, pregnancy, and pregnancy resolution are influenced by what they see and hear in the media. It is also needed to begin to identify strategies for using the media to promote more responsible sexual, contraceptive, and fertility behavior among teenagers. Such research poses significant methodological problems, especially in developing appropriate control groups and outcome measures.

PRIORITIES FOR PROGRAM EVALUATION RESEARCH

The panel recommends that evaluation to measure the costs, effects, and effectiveness of service programs be an essential component of intervention strategies. Federal and state-level funding agencies should be urged to set aside adequate support for evaluation research, and the research community should be urged to take a more active role in designing and implementing these studies.

Although evaluation research methods have become quite sophisticated over the past two decades, they are frequently not used in studying the effects of adolescent pregnancy programs. As we discussed in Chapters 6 and 7, there are several reasons for the general scarcity of program evaluation research and the poor quality of findings. These include problems of design: many programs have failed to clearly define goals and to distinguish direct and indirect outcomes, thus making it difficult to specify appropriate hypotheses for study. Measurement problems are also common. Specific types of demographic change (for example, reductions in the number of pregnancies) are often difficult to accurately measure because of underreporting of miscarriages and abortions. In addition, a variety of other factors, including local social, demographic, and economic characteristics, can confound program effects or make them difficult to isolate and measure. There are also ethical problems: the human dimensions of adolescent pregnancy and childbearing make it difficult to deny a young woman (and perhaps her child) essential supports and services in order to assign her to a nontreatment control group. Finally, several practical problems have also frequently impeded program evaluation research, affecting the quality of the results. Evaluation research is expensive and project grants and contracts for services often fail to include specially earmarked funds for assessment. Service providers typically lack the training and skills to design sophisticated evaluations and the time to carry them out. Moreover, the time frames for measuring program effects and effectiveness are often too short, thus inaccurately characterizing a program's success or failure in meeting specified objectives.

Outcome Versus Process Evaluation

Program evaluation can have multiple purposes that are valid but often conflicting. One of these is outcome evaluation: to assess the effectiveness of an intervention strategy in achieving its specified objectives. Often research of this type is undertaken to judge the validity of an approach and to determine whether a program should be continued, modified, or expanded. Typically, outcome evaluation involves establishing "before" and "after" measures of program activity and comparing these to a control group that was not exposed to the program. If the treatment remains constant throughout the study period, then the results may in fact represent a valid assessment of the program's success.

Another purpose is process evaluation: to monitor how a particular program works and to document program models. Service providers are often less interested in evaluation for its capability to measure outcomes than for its capability to provide information for program improvement. They are interested in knowing how high-risk teenagers get into the service network, how they respond to alternative approaches, and how long they stay in programs. As data are collected, providers frequently see opportunities to modify the program to improve its efficiency and responsiveness to the needs of clients. While such uses of evaluation data are valid, mid-program modifications hinder the usefulness of the findings to researchers interested in outcome measurement, since the same treatment is not being analyzed throughout the study period.

Their purposes are different, and both types of evaluation should be pursued, yet it is important for program planners to recognize the circumstances under which one or the other type of evaluation is appropriate and is likely to yield useful information. Not every program can or should be the object of a rigorous outcome evaluation. The problems and expense of collecting and analyzing data, identifying appropriate control or comparison groups, and following clients over time frequently make good evaluation infeasible. Poor-quality research, which can often be costly in personnel and fiscal resources, is of little use in assessing the effects of an intervention or predicting its effectiveness in other settings. Outcome evaluation should be pursued on a limited basis when the availability of resources (i.e., time, financial support, technical assistance) and the circumstances of the program (i.e., the size and composition of the client population, appropriate control or comparison groups, low rates of attrition among treatment and control populations, uniform and consistent services or treatments) will support good research. Process evaluation, on the other hand, should be more broadly pursued. All programs should be encouraged and assisted to collect data on their services and their client populations as a basis for assessing whether they are in fact providing the services they were established to provide, in the way they were planned, to the target population that was planned, and within the cost boundaries that were envisioned. Such information can provide a valuable basis for monitoring progress, identifying problems, and making important management decisions about the operations of the program. It can also provide the basis for demonstrating to sponsors and others that a program is in fact doing what it was intended to do and justifying its existence and continuation after an initial trial period.

Several issues are important in the design and conduct of evaluations.

Outcome Measures

Evaluation design should be conducted in tandem with the planning and design of the service program itself. Too often an evaluation component is superimposed after a program has been in operation for some period of time, thus precluding the possibility of obtaining pretest measures as a baseline.

In addition, outcome measures should assess the capability of an intervention to achieve its stated objectives. To the extent that such objectives are not clearly specified in the design of the program, it is difficult to define appropriate outcome measures. In particular, many programs fail to distinguish direct and indirect outcomes. The reduction of pregnancy, for example, is frequently not an explicit goal of many preventive programs other than family planning services, even if it is an important indirect outcome. Interventions to increase knowledge and change attitudes, as well as those intended to enhance life options, are often unable to show long-term reductions in client pregnancy rates. They may, however, significantly affect other outcomes. For example, they may enhance school achievement, which may delay initiation of sexual activity or improve contraceptive use among adolescents. Thus, if evaluation is to be meaningful, both direct and indirect program objectives need to be clearly specified, and the research design must include appropriate measures of the behaviors that the program is aimed at influencing. For example, interventions to encourage delay in sexual initiation must measure changes in sexual behavior among their client populations; programs to improve school performance need to measure not only changes in academic achievement and school retention, but also changes in sexual and fertility behavior.

Several other issues concerning outcome measures are also important. First, many evaluations of adolescent pregnancy programs, both preventive and ameliorative, rely on self-administered questionnaires to collect data from clients. Often, however, researchers have not been sensitive to the reading levels of their study populations, large proportions of which can be expected to have significant reading difficulties. If self-administered questionnaires are used as a means of data collection, they should be appropriately adjusted to the reading level of the study population.

Second, few evaluations have used the same measures of knowledge, attitude, and behavior outcomes, thus impeding the comparison of results from study to study and among alternative interventions. Where reliable and valid established measures are applicable, investigators should be encouraged to use them. Where adequate measures do not exist, new instruments should be developed for use by evaluators in a variety of settings, involving adolescents of different genders, ages, races, and other relevant background characteristics.

Third, with regard to several specific issues, new measures are needed: (1) developmental age—the wide developmental differences between adolescents (boys and girls) of the same age make chronological age or grade in school inadequate measures of maturity in many cases; (2) "wantedness" and "intendedness"—in the context of pregnancy and childbearing, these terms represent complicated concepts that have not been clearly defined and distinguished; (3) program exposure—pretest, interim, and posttest data collection over the time period of an intervention may not adequately take account of uneven exposure by some participants. Clinic and school populations frequently shift, as some clients enter the program after its start, some leave before completion, and still others move in and out more than once during the treatment period.

Sampling and Control Groups

The representativeness of both study sample and control group significantly affects the quality and generalizability of evaluation findings. The size and background characteristics of these groups are important. Many of the evaluations we reviewed involved study populations that were so small that meaningful conclusions about the applicability of the program's approach to other client groups in other settings were impossible. The size of the sample should be large enough to permit generalization. Similarly, the background characteristics of the sample should be carefully screened, since various cultural, demographic, religious, and economic factors can influence the variables under study.

In addition, too often the program population is chosen as a matter of convenience (i.e., individuals who voluntarily seek services) rather than because it is best suited to answer the relevant questions concerning program effects and effectiveness. Although random samples chosen against clearly specified preselection criteria are not always feasible (e.g., too expensive, too few potential study subjects from which to choose), evaluators must take account of the issues of self-selection in study populations that are drawn from clinic samples and voluntary participants in various school-, church-, and community-based organizations. To the extent that randomization can be incorporated in sample selection, it should be. When it cannot, evaluators should be encouraged to develop innovative research designs and sampling techniques to enhance representativeness.

An issue of particular concern in studying program effects on very young adolescents is the need to obtain parental consent for their participation. As previously discussed, getting consent is not always easy or possible, yet eliminating young teenagers whose parents will not sanction their participation can significantly bias the study findings.

Ideally, when measuring the effects of a program on a target population, researchers should compare those exposed to the treatment with a comparable group who are not exposed. However, identifying and then matching "pure" controls to study populations has frequently proved difficult. Because of the broad array of preventive and ameliorative supports and services that has been implemented nationwide, it is difficult in many communities to find individuals and groups who are receiving no services at all as a basis for comparison. To overcome this difficulty, researchers need to explore innovative ways of identifying appropriate comparison groups when pure controls are impossible, for example, by using data from national surveys or from other communities that can be matched along relevant dimensions.

Finally, researchers need to be able to minimize attrition among both treatment and control or comparison groups in order to achieve valid results from their studies. When clients leave a program before they have received all the services or treatment that was intended or when they are not followed up after their scheduled departure, findings concerning those who stay in and are tracked may be skewed in ways that are difficult to detect. The reasons for a client's leaving prematurely may affect conclusions concerning a program's effectiveness if, for example, only highly motivated clients or those with strong family support systems or those who can travel easily to the service center remain. The same is true for control or comparison groups: attrition can significantly affect findings concerning the outcomes of the program. To avoid these problems, researchers need to have large enough samples so that attrition will not adversely affect the quality of the findings. In addition, they need to develop aggressive and innovative approaches to follow up and track clients after they leave a program.

Intervening Variables

As a part of the research design for a program evaluation, independent, dependent, and intervening variables and their potential relationship should be clearly specified. A variety of intervening factors can confound the study results unless they are identified and carefully controlled. For example, as we have previously noted, demographic changes (e.g., reductions in the number of adolescent pregnancies) may reflect a variety of factors other than or in addition to program effects. Changes in the composition of the local population or other changes in the social, economic, or cultural context of the intervention can affect program outcomes. Similarly, the presence, absence, or change in other local health, education, social service, and income programs can influence study results in ways that are sometimes difficult to detect. Researchers need to take account of the possible influence of such intervening variables in their research designs.

Units of Analysis

Studying the effects of specific program components may be as important, if not more important, than examining the overall outcomes of various interventions. This is especially true for assessments of comprehensive programs that integrate and coordinate an array of necessary supports and services and may employ several sequential or simultaneous approaches to serving high-risk teenagers. Many evaluations of comprehensive programs have failed to separate program components for purposes of analysis, and as a result we know very little about which aspects of these programs are most effective and how they individually, or in combination, contribute to overall program outcomes.

Cost Data

Cost-benefit analyses of alternative programs have been hampered by the lack of available data on cost. Very few evaluation studies have collected information on the unit costs of service provision (i.e., the costs per program participant per year) as well as more complex measures or the costs per birth or the potential savings from births that are postponed as a result of the program. Such analyses are needed in order to compare the relative benefits of different types of programs with their costs. As a first step, attention should be given to the development of appropriate measures of "input" and "output" that can be reasonably applied to different intervention models in different settings.

Time Frames

The time frames for evaluation are also important. Outcomes may look different at six months, one year, two years, and five years. Drawing conclusions about a program's success or failure on the basis of a short-term follow-up may inaccurately characterize it. For example, to conclude that a program was successful in preventing or delaying subsequent births on the basis of measurement at one year after a first birth probably overstates its effectiveness, since we know that a high proportion of repeat pregnancies and births occur in the second year. Longitudinal research is admittedly expensive and complex, yet follow-ups of selected samples of program participants over time may yield valuable information concerning the duration of program effects for particular subgroups of the target population.

Financial and Technical Assistance

Many of the programs we examined lack the necessary capability to rigorously measure their effects and effectiveness. In addition, retrospective record searches and client follow-up studies are expensive and time-consuming and cannot typically be conducted by program administrators whose primary responsibility is service provision. Research design, data collection, and analysis require a level of technical expertise not typically found among project directors and clinical staff. Without a university affiliation or other strong evaluation support—both financial and technical—most programs are unable to design and carry out the kinds of sophisticated evaluations that are necessary to document their processes and outcomes.

In this regard, it is important to train young researchers to bridge the gap between their disciplinary domains and the provider community in order to build a strong evaluation ability. Too few scholars of adolescent development are also sophisticated in program evaluation methods. Because academic incentives discourage program research, too few are able and willing to assist service providers in the design and implementation of evaluation components for adolescent pregnancy programs. Federal and local funds should be committed to developing such a capability at the regional and local level.

PRIORITIES FOR EXPERIMENTATION

The panel recommends that federal funding agencies, private foundations, and researchers cooperate in designing, implementing, and evaluating experimental approaches for pregnancy prevention among high-risk adolescents and for improving the well-being of teenage parents and their children.

The problems of adolescent pregnancy and childbearing are many and complex. From our comprehensive review of research and interventions, we have found only limited documentation of successful program models for pregnancy prevention and for the support and care of pregnant and parenting teenagers and their children. Given the diversity of personal circumstances among adolescents in this country and the uncertainty and controversy surrounding these issues, a multiplicity of approaches will continue to be needed.

To successfully avoid early unintended pregnancy, young people need both the ability and the motivation to do so. They need information concerning reproduction and contraception, they need effective means of birth control, and they need access to services. They also need to perceive that there are positive benefits associated with postponing family formation, and that education and job training can significantly improve their social and economic well-being. Many specialized and comprehensive programs have been developed to provide education, to deliver contraceptive services, and to enhance teenagers' perceptions of life options. We need to continue to monitor these existing program development efforts and expand them to include experimentation with innovative models and novel approaches.

In the course of our study, several areas for new program development surfaced. First, delaying the initiation of sexual intercourse is one means of pregnancy prevention, yet little is known about effective approaches to encourage teenagers to delay sexual initiation. Several kinds of programs are under way that aim to discourage early sexual activity among unmarried teenagers, including family life education programs, assertiveness programs, and programs to provide role models for high-risk youth. These initiatives should continue to be monitored. In addition, new approaches to encourage delay of sexual intercourse should be designed, implemented, and evaluated. Moreover, further effort is needed to explore ways of providing birth control information to young teenagers, including information on contraception, without making it difficult for those who choose not to initiate intercourse to maintain more traditional attitudes and behavior.

Second, the contraceptive pill and, to a somewhat lesser extent, the condom represent effective means of birth control when they are used appropriately. Yet research suggests that many adolescents find these methods difficult to use and therefore are frequently inconsistent or ineffective contraceptors. While additional efforts are needed to encourage sexually active teenagers to diligently use existing methods, especially the pill and the condom, special attention should be given to developing and testing new contraceptive technologies that are more appropriate to the needs of adolescents.

Third, efforts should be devoted to creating positive economic incentives for adolescents to stay in school and avoid pregnancy. For too many high-risk young people, there are too few disincentives to childbearing. Several interesting proposals have surfaced recently to develop pilot programs to reward high-risk teenagers who complete high school without having a baby by providing annual or lump-sum cash payments. Other possibilities along these lines include the provision of special secondary and postsecondary scholarships or job opportunities. For example, it appears that many teenage mothers use their AFDC payments to make it possible to finish high school. Experimental programs should be developed to examine alternative financial assistance mechanisms for secondary education that do not foster welfare dependence. Funds should be made available for carefully designed and evaluated demonstration programs of this type.

Similarly, teenage parents need both the ability and the motivation to manage their lives, care for their children, and delay repeat pregnancies. Experimentation with bold approaches to encourage young mothers to become economically self-sufficient and to encourage young fathers to become financially responsible and actively involved in their children's lives is also warranted. Again, efforts should be devoted to creating positive incentives for these behaviors. Economic rewards are a powerful motivating force and could be an effective tool for encouraging positive life choices among high-risk teenage parents. Demonstrations to test innovative models should be initiated and carefully evaluated.

Finally, parents are responsible for the financial support of their children, yet many fathers of children born to adolescent mothers, especially teenagers, have not assumed economic responsibility for their families. Further efforts are needed to develop effective means of child support enforcement. In particular, new initiatives are needed to link child support to education and work requirements in the form of registration with the state employment service and participation in job training and job search activities, as well as the provision of work opportunities. For school-age fathers who are still enrolled in school, part-time and summer employment requirements should be tested. For those who are out of school and are not participating in other job training programs, special pilot programs to require job training and employment should be developed, implemented, and evaluated as a means of improving the provision of child support.

9

Priorities for Policies and Programs

Like many others who have addressed the issues of adolescent pregnancy and childbearing in recent years, the Panel on Adolescent Pregnancy and Childbearing has recognized that the problems are complex and controversial. Solutions will not be easily or rapidly attained. Although the age of initiation and rates of sexual activity are comparable, the United States leads most other developed countries in the rate of early pregnancies, abortions, and births to adolescent mothers. Fertility varies by age, race, and socioeconomic status, but early pregnancy and childbearing are not limited to any single subgroup. They are not confined by urban or rural boundaries, nor is their impact limited to a single gender or generation. Everyone is affected, directly or indirectly. Adolescent pregnancy and childbearing are issues of broad national concern, and they are issues that require urgent attention.

Regardless of one's political philosophy or moral perspective, the basic facts are disturbing: more than 1 million adolescents become pregnant each year. Just over 400,000 teenagers obtain abortions, and nearly 470,000 give birth. The majority of these births are to unmarried mothers, nearly half of whom have not yet reached their eighteenth birthday.

For teenage parents and their children, prospects for a healthy and independent life are significantly reduced. Young mothers, in the absence of adequate nutrition and appropriate prenatal health care, are at a heightened risk of pregnancy complications and poor birth outcomes; they are also more likely to experience a subsequent pregnancy while still in their teens. The infants of teenage mothers also face greater health risks, including low birthweight, accidents, illness, and infant mortality. Teenage marriages, when they occur, are characterized by a high degree of instability. In addition, teenage parents, both female and male, suffer the negative impact that untimely parenting has on their educational attainment and the related limitation of career opportunities. Teenage parents are more likely than those who delay childbearing to experience serious unemployment and inadequate income. Because these young people often fare poorly in the workplace, they and their children are highly likely to become dependent on public assistance and to remain dependent longer. Society's economic burden in sustaining these families is substantial.

Why do young people who are hardly more than children themselves become parents? Is it due to a lack of individual responsibility, maturity, knowledge, and values? Or does it result from the pervasive problems associated with poverty, including limited education and employment opportunities, and among many high-risk youth, growing up in a fatherless family? The answer to both of these questions seems to be yes. The causes of teenage pregnancy are varied and complex, and to a large extent the issues of individual responsibility and social environment are interrelated. For this reason, the panel has studied and addressed the problems with both individual and societal perspectives in mind.

On the basis of two years of review, analysis, and debate, the panel has reached six general conclusions, which underlie all of its specific conclusions and recommendations for policies and programs:

1. Prevention of adolescent pregnancy should have the highest priority. In both human and monetary terms, it is less costly to prevent pregnancy than to cope with its consequences; and it is less expensive to prevent a repeat pregnancy than to treat the compounded problems.

2. Sexually active teenagers, both boys and girls, need the ability to avoid pregnancy and the motivation to do so. Early, regular, and effective contraceptive use results in fewer unintended pregnancies. Delaying the initiation of sexual activity will also reduce the incidence of pregnancy, but we currently know very little about how to effectively discourage unmarried teenagers from initiating intercourse. Most young people do become sexually active during their teenage years. Therefore, making contraceptive methods available and accessible to those who are sexually active and encouraging them to diligently use these methods is the surest strategy for pregnancy prevention.

3. Society must avoid treating adolescent pregnancy as a problem peculiar to teenage girls. Our concept of the high-risk population must

include boys. Their attitudes, motivations, and behavior are as central to the problems as those of their female partners, and they must also be central to the solutions.

4. There is no single approach or quick fix to solving all the problems of early unintended pregnancy and childbearing. We will continue to need a comprehensive array of policies and programs targeted to the special characteristics of communities and to the circumstances of teenagers from different social, cultural, and economic backgrounds and of different ages. Because adolescents are not a monolithic group, they do not all experience sexual activity, pregnancy, and childbearing in the same way. Our broad goal is the same for all young people: that they develop the necessary capabilities to make and carry out responsible decisions about their sexual and fertility behavior. The strategies for achieving these goals and the specific interventions to carry them out, however, should be sensitive to differences in values, attitudes, and experiences among individuals and groups.

5. If trade-offs are to be made in addressing the special needs of one group over another, priority should be given to those for whom the consequences of an early unintended pregnancy and birth are likely to be most severe: young adolescents and those from the most socially and economically disadvantaged backgrounds. In many ways those at highest risk are hardest to serve, yet they are also the groups that have been shown to benefit most.

6. Responsibility for addressing the problems of adolescent pregnancy and childbearing should be shared among individuals, families, voluntary organizations, communities, and governments. In the United States, we place a high priority on ensuring the rights of individuals to hold different values and the rights of families to raise their children according to their own beliefs. Therefore, public policies should affirm the role and responsibility of families to teach human values. Federal and state governments and community institutions should supplement rather than detract from that role.

The prevalence of adolescent pregnancy and childbearing is well documented. Knowledge about the causes and consequences of these behaviors has greatly expanded over the past decade and a half. Knowledge from the growing body of evaluation literature and accumulated intervention experience, though incomplete in many respects, suggests opportunities and directions for policies and programs aimed at solving these problems. In the remainder of this chapter we present specific conclusions and recom-

mendations within a basic framework for establishing policy goals, identifying alternative strategies to achieve these goals, and selecting specific
programmatic approaches to carry out these strategies.

PRIORITIES FOR POLICIES AND PROGRAMS

The panel's conclusions and recommendations cover a range of activities that includes research, planning, policy development, service delivery,
and monitoring. Some of the specific actions we propose would involve
steps by federal, state, and local policy makers to enact new legislation or
direct the agencies under their jurisdiction to undertake new initiatives.
Others would require the continuation or intensification of public and
private efforts already under way. When existing knowledge supports
new or revised policies and programs or highlights the effectiveness of
ongoing initiatives, we propose specific new or continued programs or
specific agenda for research and development. When existing knowledge
provides insights but is incomplete, we advise further demonstration and
evaluation to enhance understanding of the relative costs, effects, and
effectiveness of promising approaches. When innovative policies have
been initiated but there are as yet no scientifically measurable outcomes,
we urge careful observation and monitoring. Many of our recommendations build on policies, programs, and research that are already under way.
Many reinforce the priorities of other individuals and groups that are
addressing these complex and controversial issues of adolescent pregnancy.

The panel has identified three overarching policy goals, presented in
order of priority, that provide a framework for our specific conclusions and
recommendations:

1. Reduce the rate and incidence of unintended pregnancy among
adolescents, especially among school-age teenagers.
2. Provide alternatives to adolescent childbearing and parenting.
3. Promote positive social, economic, health, and developmental outcomes for adolescent parents and their children.

For most young people in the United States, realizing fulfilling adult
work and family roles depends on completing an education and entering
the labor force before becoming a parent. Many do delay the initiation of
sexual activity until after they have graduated from high school, pursued
postsecondary education or gained work experience or both, and perhaps
married. Many others become sexually active before they have passed these

milestones in the transition from adolescence to adulthood. Regardless of the timing they choose for initiation of sexual activity, however, all adolescents need the ability and the motivation to avoid becoming parents before they are socially, emotionally, and economically prepared. As a society, our approach to pregnancy prevention must be targeted to the complex social, emotional, and physical needs of all adolescents. Pregnancy prevention strategies must provide teenagers the necessary support and encouragement to strive for fulfilling, productive adult roles in addition to parenthood.

Despite the amount of energy and resources that are devoted to prevention strategies, however, some teenagers will experience unintended and untimely pregnancies. Given the potentially adverse consequences of early parenting for the life chances of these young people, there should be alternatives to childbearing and childrearing. Abortion is a legal option for all women, including adolescents. We acknowledge that voluntary termination of pregnancy is controversial, and for many in our society it is morally reprehensible. Although we strongly prefer prevention of pregnancy to avoid parenthood, abortion is an alternative for teenagers for whom prevention fails. Adoption is also available to those teenagers who choose not to voluntarily terminate their pregnancies yet are unable or unwilling to assume the full responsibilities of parenting.

Finally, for teenagers who choose to bear and to raise their children themselves, supports and services to promote healthy development, responsible parenting, educational attainment, and economic self-sufficiency should be available. Indeed, investing in the quality of life of teenage parents, their families, and their children may be the first step toward preventing early unintended pregnancies in the next generation.

Inherent in this policy framework for addressing the problems of adolescent pregnancy and childbearing is a significant dilemma. In placing the highest priority on prevention, we do not mean to diminish the significant need for supports and services for pregnant and parenting teenagers. Yet, remedial responses, however effective, do not address the basic needs of young people who have not become sexually active and who have not experienced pregnancy. And some have raised concerns that policies and programs that offer support and assistance only after a pregnancy has occurred may even have created the wrong incentives, especially for those from severely disadvantaged backgrounds. *All* young people, regardless of whether they are teenage parents, need to be encouraged to develop positive perceptions of what their lives can be. They need opportunities to achieve their goals, and they need support and assistance from their families and their communities to become healthy, productive adult members of society.

Goal 1: Reduce the Rate and Incidence of Unintended Pregnancy Among Adolescents, Especially Among School-Age Teenagers

The panel is unequivocal in its conviction that the primary goal of policy makers, professionals, parents, and teenagers should be a reduction in the rate and incidence of unintended pregnancy among adolescents, especially among school-age teenagers. Pregnancy prevention would result not only in fewer births but also in fewer abortions to teenagers. Although an unplanned pregnancy can have seriously negative consequences at age 18 or 19 among those who have completed high school, it is likely to present even greater hurdles for younger teenagers. When pregnancy results in childbearing, it increases the probability that adolescent parents will drop out of school and reduces the probability that they will complete high school or pursue postsecondary education. Early childbearing is also associated with larger family size. For these reasons, younger teenage parents are often vulnerable to an array of adverse social and economic consequences, which we have discussed in detail in this report. In addition, the younger the teenage mother at the time of birth, the higher the average estimated public costs of her childbearing and the higher the estimated potential savings of her postponing that birth.

The panel has identified three general strategies that can lead to a reduction in the rate of early pregnancy: enhance the life options of disadvantaged teenagers, delay the initiation of sexual activity, and encourage contraceptive use by sexually active teenagers. Central to all of them is the need for teenagers themselves to embrace values that lead to responsible, healthy, and productive lives, including the avoidance of unplanned and untimely parenting, and to be steadfast in their belief that they can achieve their goals. Parents and family members can and should play a key role in helping young people, both male and female, acquire and retain these values. But individual and family values are influenced by community and societal norms: therefore, the community as a whole must reinforce and support individual and family efforts to discourage early pregnancy and encourage adult self-sufficiency.

Enhance Life Options Poverty and hopelessness, which exacerbate many social problems, play an especially important role in the problems associated with adolescent pregnancy. Sexual activity and pregnancy among teenagers are not confined by race and income, yet the correlation between poverty and adolescent fertility is well documented. Nationally, more than half of Aid to Families With Dependent Children (AFDC) benefits support families in which the mother gave birth as a teenager. The median income of families headed by women under the age of 25 is below the poverty level, and approximately three-quarters of all such families live in poverty.

Research has shown the deleterious effects of poverty on those caught in its cycle: attitudes of fatalism, powerlessness, alienation, and helplessness that are perpetuated from one generation to the next. For too many high-risk teenagers, there are too few disincentives to early childbearing. Inadequate basic skills, poor employment prospects, and few successful role models for overcoming the overwhelmingly negative odds of intergenerational poverty have stifled the motivation of many to delay immediate gratification and avoid pregnancy.

Teenagers need a reason to believe that parenthood is inappropriate at this point in their lives. Accordingly, one important strategy for reducing early unplanned pregnancy is to enhance their life options, by encouraging them to establish career goals in addition to parenthood and by helping them understand the value of educational attainment and employability skills. This strategy is aimed at reducing adolescent fertility by nurturing the motivation to prevent untimely and unplanned parenthood.

We lack program research that clearly demonstrates the effectiveness of this strategy for reducing early pregnancy. Nevertheless, we outline below several interventions that seem promising and merit further development and evaluation.

Life-planning courses   Helping teenagers to understand the seriously negative consequences of an unplanned birth for their present and future lives may be an important component of developing motivation. Life-planning courses are aimed at helping high-risk teenagers identify education, career, and family options, develop life plans and goals, and understand how early childbearing might affect their ability to achieve those goals. Programs of this type have been small-scale, and there is little definitive evidence of their success. Early returns, however, suggest that this may be a promising approach. Intervention models of this type need further development and evaluation. In particular, attention is needed on the related supports and services that are necessary to help teenagers effectively use the information, planning, and decision-making skills they can gain in life-planning courses.

Programs to improve school performance   Boosting school achievement and preventing school dropout may also be a promising approach to reduce early unintended childbearing among school-age teenagers. Teenage pregnancy rates have been shown to be higher among poor achievers. Poor school performance negatively affects self-concept and motivation. It also has adverse effects on later employment opportunities.

As many researchers, service providers, and advocates have observed, educational opportunity and achievement are key to helping high-risk teenagers develop elevated expectations, a sense of can-do, and the basic skills necessary to achieve their goals. Although developing a full agenda of educational reform was not within the mandate or expertise of the panel, we highlight the need for educational interventions—whether alternative schools or special programs in regular schools—to overcome the educational problems and deficiencies of many young people. In particular, such programs need to identify high-risk students early in their educational careers and provide the remediation required to ensure that they develop essential basic skills and achieve smooth education-to-work transitions. Although research has not specifically linked programs to improve school performance with reductions in adolescent pregnancy, such programs merit further development and evaluation to assess their potential effects on fertility.

Employment programs   Chronic unemployment and poor job prospects among some subgroups of the population have had serious adverse effects on many young people's perceptions of opportunity. The lack of meaningful employment options may diminish the motivation to delay parenthood. As with educational reform, the development of a comprehensive plan for youth employment is beyond the mandate and expertise of the panel, yet we emphasize the need to enhance the employability of high-risk youth by providing them with information concerning career alternatives, by teaching job skills and job search skills, and by helping them gain work experience while completing their educations. Again, although research has not specifically linked youth employment programs to reductions in adolescent pregnancy, such programs merit further development and evaluation to assess their potential effects on fertility.

Role models   All young people adopt role models—whether in their families, among their peers, or in their communities—that significantly influence their developing values, attitudes, and behavior. Providing high-risk teenagers with positive examples on which to model their behavior may help them form aspirations, expectations, and activity patterns that match desired norms. Role model and mentoring programs are intended to help teenagers see in others what they can become themselves. Most emphasize the importance of educational attainment, employability, and responsible sexual and fertility behavior. These interventions are relatively new and to date most have been small in scale. As a result, there is no definitive evidence of their success in reducing early unintended pregnancy, yet they merit further examination and trial.

Delay Sexual Initiation   A second strategy for reducing the rate of teenage pregnancy is to help teenagers, both male and female, develop ways to postpone sexual initiation until they are capable of making wise and responsible decisions concerning their personal lives and family formation. For young teenagers especially, pregnancy and parenthood are often distant, intangible abstractions. Relating sexual decisions to lifelong consequences is difficult. Adolescents who cannot conceptually link current behavior to future contingencies are often unreliable users of contraceptive methods. For them, efforts directed at discouraging the initiation of sexual activity may be an appropriate means of reducing unintended pregnancy. Essential to the success of this strategy are the acquisition of problem-solving and communication skills, understanding of the personal and societal consequences of unprotected sexual activity, and knowledge of how to act responsibly. Enhancing life options, which has been discussed above, may also encourage teenagers to delay the initiation of sexual activity.

Several interventions have the potential for helping young people delay the initiation of sexual activity, although there is little available evidence at this time to document their effectiveness.

Sex education and family life education   Courses that provide information about sexuality and family roles and interactions have been shown to increase students' knowledge of reproduction and the probable consequences of sexual activity without contraception. Although these courses are widely available in school systems nationwide, they vary substantially in their content, their comprehensiveness, and the quality of instruction. They also vary in the extent of parent and community involvement in their planning and implementation. In addition, few school districts have programs that are directed at children of elementary school age. While knowledge alone cannot be expected to alter adolescent behavior, education programs that are combined with other approaches, such as assertiveness and decision-making training and role modeling, may help reinforce family values, responsible behavior, and self-control with regard to sexual activity. Similarly, age-appropriate education programs that provide young children with information concerning sexuality and sex abuse, as well as training to deal with potentially abusive encounters, may help reduce their anxieties and fears about personal sexual development and improve their ability to avoid sexual exploitation. Unfortunately, program research to date has not provided conclusive evidence of the impact of sex and family life education on the timing of sexual initiation.

Assertiveness and decision-making training   Programs that teach adolescents problem-solving, decision-making, and interpersonal communication skills are sometimes aimed at promoting sexual abstinence by counseling younger adolescent boys and girls on how to resist pressures to become sexually active before they are ready. An evaluation of one program using this approach is now under way. If the results of that study are positive, replications and adaptations of this program model may be warranted.

Role models   Many adolescents learn by example; they are attracted to real and fictional characters who seem powerful and successful. Society's response to the behavior of those models helps young people to develop expectations for their own behavior and the behavior of others and to clarify their personal values. When role models exemplify societal ideals, the process can potentially have positive effects on adolescents' attitudes, motivations, and behaviors, including sexual behavior. Several interventions using peer counselors, mentors, and adult community volunteers to work on a one-to-one basis with high-risk teenagers are now being tested. Among the tasks of the role models is to help teenagers find activities other than sexual ones that can fulfill their needs for emotional gratification, for example, sports and community service. If the results of these efforts show positive effects on delay of sexual initiation, replications and adaptations of this approach may be warranted.

Media treatment of sexuality   Among the most pervasive influences on adolescents are the personalities and heroes of television, movies, and rock music. The exploitation of sex, aggression, and violence in media programming and advertising has become a central issue for many individuals and groups concerned about adolescent pregnancy and childbearing (e.g., the Children's Defense Fund, the National Urban League, the Center for Population Options, and several state and local coalitions and task forces). Some of these groups are exploring ways to encourage the media to present more realistic and responsible portrayals of personal and sexual relationships among adult heroes and to discourage sexual activity and parenting among young adolescents. Because most of these efforts are in preliminary stages, it is too early to assess their effects on programming content and advertising approaches. Indeed, the incentives for network executives to alter their current messages and models are weak. Nevertheless, multiple coordinated efforts at the community level and at the national level to exert pressure may have greater potential for effecting change than isolated appeals.

Encourage Contraception   The panel's research has established that the most effective intervention for reducing early unintended pregnancy in sexually active teenagers is diligent contraceptive use. Male contraception, as well as male support for female contraception, is essential. Adolescents who practice contraception are less likely to experience an unplanned pregnancy than those who do not; those who rely on the contraceptive pill are less likely to conceive than those who use nonprescription methods. Although modern contraceptive technology, especially the pill, may have contributed to the liberalization of societal sexual attitudes and practices, which in turn have influenced adolescent behavior, there is no evidence that the availability of contraceptive services per se has caused increased sexual activity among teenagers, male or female. In fact, studies show that many adolescent girls are sexually active a year or more before they obtain contraceptives. This pattern must be changed in order to reduce the incidence of early unintended pregnancy and ultimately the more painful, hazardous, and disruptive alternatives of abortion or untimely childbearing. The panel recognizes that contraception alone cannot control adolescent fertility, but it is a necessary step.

Given current contraceptive technology, the pill and the condom are the most promising methods for adolescents, whose menstrual cycles may be irregular and whose patterns of sexual activity may be sporadic. For women under age 25 who do not smoke, pill use carries a lower risk of health complications and death than any method except for barrier methods. When used appropriately, the pill has the lowest rate of contraceptive failure next to sterilization. For adolescent girls who smoke, the health risks associated with pill use are somewhat greater but still less than the risks of an unintended pregnancy and childbirth. For girls who smoke and for those who have intercourse infrequently, the condom is the best alternative. The primary health risks associated with condom use are those that result from method failure. Condom failure rates are greater than those associated with pill use, but significantly less than other barrier methods or periodic abstinence.

Despite these facts, adolescents are frequently deterred from use of the contraceptive pill and the condom by misunderstandings about their unintended consequences, including exaggerations of the health risks and unpleasant side effects associated with the pill and of the diminution of pleasure from condom use. Efforts should be made by parents, professionals, and the media to correct these misunderstandings. In addition, contraceptive programs should include or be linked to appropriate health and sex education aimed at teaching adolescents about the risks (including the risks of contraceptive failure) associated with alternative contraceptive methods and how to obtain and appropriately use these methods. Apprehensiveness about the health care system and the diagnostic procedures (e.g., the pelvic examination and invasive laboratory tests) associated with contraceptive services may be a barrier preventing some teenagers from coming to a clinic. Although such procedures have become standard practice, it would be useful to explore nonmedical models for the distribution of contraceptive methods, including the pill.

The panel concludes that use of the contraceptive pill is the safest and most effective means of birth control for sexually active adolescents. Aggressive public education is needed to dispel myths about the health risks of pill use by girls in this age group, and contraceptive service programs should explore nonmedical models for distribution of the pill.

The availability of contraceptive services to adolescents depends heavily on public support, in particular funding through Title X of the Public Health Services Act, Medicaid, and other federal and state maternal and child health programs. In light of the demonstrated effectiveness of contraceptive use in reducing early unintended pregnancy, continued support of these programs is essential. To the extent that it is possible, these programs should minimize bureaucratic, geographic, and financial barriers that may deter sexually active adolescents from seeking contraceptive services.

The panel concludes that, to make this strategy effective, there must be continued public support for contraceptive services to adolescents, such as has been supplied primarily through Title X of the Family Planning Services and Population Research Act, Medicaid, and other federal and state maternal and child health programs. Such programs should minimize potential barriers of cost, convenience, and confidentiality.

Several interventions have been shown to encourage diligent contraceptive use among sexually active teenagers.

Sex education   Sex education courses vary in their attention to and treatment of contraception. In several European countries, however, sex education that provides information concerning contraceptive methods, including how to obtain them and how to use them, is associated with earlier and more diligent contraceptive use by adolescents, especially use of the pill.

The panel urges that sex education programs include information on methods of contraception, how to use them, and how to obtain them.

Contraceptive services   There are numerous models for delivering contraceptive services to teenagers, both boys and girls, and services are available from a variety of providers; including public health departments; hospital-, community-, and school-based clinics; private providers; and drugstores. For reasons of cost and confidentiality, teenagers are more likely to seek services from clinic facilities than from private physicians. Several components of the approaches that clinics take to deal with adolescent clients appear to affect the patterns of attendance of sexually active teenagers: (1) aggressive outreach and follow-up, to reach sexually active teenagers who may not have sought contraceptive services, through public information programs, sex education programs, and close links to community youth service organizations that can refer young clients; through assistance in getting them to the clinic; and through monitoring their success in using their chosen contraceptive method; (2) instruction about various contraceptive methods, including their risks and benefits, and the consequences of ineffective or inappropriate use; (3) counseling to help teenagers make responsible decisions about contraception and to help them feel they have some commitment to their chosen method; and (4) sensitivity to the special concerns and apprehensions of teenagers in coming to family planning clinics.

In order to encourage contraceptive use among sexually active teenagers with differing needs and predispositions to use contraceptive services, numerous models and approaches should continue to be available and accessible to teenagers from a variety of service providers. Cost should not be a barrier to receiving contraceptive services.

The panel urges continued support for a variety of contraceptive service models—including private physicians—to reach adolescents. Contraceptive services should be available to all teenagers at low or no cost. Clinic service providers, whether based in hospitals, public health departments, private clinics, or community service organizations, should make efforts to improve the effectiveness of their programs by (1) enhancing their outreach efforts to encourage earlier use of contraceptive methods; (2) exploring more effective counseling approaches to encourage compliance; and (3) enhancing their follow-up of clinic patients to track their contraceptive use.

Two program models for providing contraceptive services to adolescents are of special interest in this regard. First, school-based clinics that provide teenagers with contraceptive services in the context of comprehensive adolescent health care have the potential to reach a large number of boys and girls under age 18. Most school-age adolescents are enrolled in school, and reproductive health services in this setting may be more accessible to them than those provided by more traditional family planning clinics. Because boys attend school-based clinics for other health care needs, such as athletic physicals, these programs may also hold greater potential for encouraging male involvement in contraception than more traditional female-oriented family planning facilities. In these settings, teenagers are also more accessible to clinic staff for purposes of outreach and follow-up. School-based clinics do have some limitations, most important that they generally operate on school schedules and that they are typically not open to students who have dropped out or graduated from high school. Nevertheless, they represent a promising intervention for reducing early unintended pregnancy among enrolled students, especially those in junior and senior high schools with large, high-risk populations. Because school-based clinics are still relatively new and experimental interventions, they require careful evaluation to determine their effects and effectiveness, including possible undesirable side effects (e.g., community resistance and increased rates of early sexual activity). Decisions concerning the establishment of school-based clinics should rest with local communities and their school systems.

The panel concludes that school systems, in cooperation with various health care and youth-serving agencies, should further develop and refine comprehensive school-based clinic models for implementation and evaluation in schools with large, high-risk populations.

Second, condom distribution programs aimed specifically at young men represent another potentially promising means of encouraging male involvement in pregnancy prevention. As previously discussed, efforts to distribute condoms to sexually active adolescent males and instruct them on proper use can be sponsored by a variety of health and social service organizations. Because they do not require special clinic facilities, these programs can more easily reach out to their target population by establishing distribution centers in the places where teenage boys congregate (e.g., youth centers, gyms, video arcades). In addition, data show that many sexually active adolescent girls, who delay obtaining prescription contraceptive methods after initiating intercourse, frequently rely on male methods in the interim. Consequently, promoting condom use among young men may result in greater use of contraception by teenagers at first intercourse or soon thereafter. Condom use has the added benefit of providing protection against sexually transmitted diseases. There is little program research that has explored the effects and effectiveness of different models for condom distribution among young men in the United States. In light of what is known about patterns of contraceptive use by adolescent boys and girls, however, efforts should be launched to develop and evaluate distribution programs.

The panel recommends the development, implementation, and evaluation of condom distribution programs.

Contraceptive advertising   Historically, television networks and radio stations have been resistant to advertising contraceptive methods. Yet studies of factors affecting attitudes and contraceptive behavior in European countries suggest that contraceptive advertising may be one means of increasing teenagers' awareness of contraceptive methods and making them feel that these methods are accessible. There is no evidence to suggest that advertising alone will directly alter behavior; however, the potential of the media through programming and advertising to influence teenagers' attitudes about desirable models for behavior, including sexuality, is significant.

The panel concludes that efforts should be undertaken to develop and test the effects on contraceptive use and unintended pregnancy of paid promotional messages for contraceptives that are directed at sexually active adolescents.

Goal 2: Provide Alternatives to Adolescent Childbearing and Parenting

The panel believes prevention of pregnancy through abstinence or contraception is far preferable to unintended pregnancy among teenagers. Yet there is little evidence that available prevention strategies significantly influence the timing of sexual initiation, and, although improved use of contraception would definitely reduce the incidence, it would not eliminate teenage pregnancy altogether. It would thus be disingenuous to shrink from consideration of the difficult choices facing the nearly 1 million teenagers who become pregnant each year. The options confronting the unmarried pregnant child or woman are (1) terminating the pregnancy, (2) bearing the child and raising it, and (3) relinquishing the child for adoption. In round numbers, 400,000 girls per year choose abortion, 458,000 keep their babies, and 12,000 choose adoption. The panel has therefore examined each of these alternatives.

Abortion   In 1973 the Supreme Court made abortion a legal option for all women in the United States. Despite this fact, abortion remains controversial. Its use by adolescents is especially charged, because it raises significant unresolved issues about the appropriate relationship between the rights and interests of an individual adolescent, her family, and the state. Several states in recent years have restricted minors' access to abortion services without parental consent or judicial bypass of parental consent.

Although abortion for very young teenagers remains a special issue, there is no empirical evidence concerning the cognitive capacity of adolescents to make such decisions or the psychological consequences of abortion that would either support or refute such age restrictions. On the basis of existing research, therefore, the contention that adolescents are unlikely or unable to make well-reasoned decisions or that they are especially vulnerable to serious psychological harm as a result of an abortion is not supported. On the contrary, research has shown that for most abortion patients, including adolescents, relief is a frequent reaction.

Nor has research documented that legally required parental involvement helps teenage girls cope better with their choice to terminate the pregnancy. There is no evidence that it reduces the probability of subsequent unwanted pregnancies or serves any other purpose than to ensure that parents are aware of what their adolescent daughters are doing. There is, however, growing evidence that parental consent statutes cause teenagers to delay their abortions, if for no other reason than that they must undergo the de facto waiting period associated with finding a lawyer and gaining access to the courts. These delays may increase the health risks involved if they result in postponements until the second trimester of pregnancy. There is also growing evidence that many adolescents in states with these statutes are traveling to nearby states to obtain services rather than go through the judicial bypass procedure. It is not currently known, however, whether such statutes are causing an increase in unwanted births to teenagers. Research is needed to address these difficult issues.

In addition, no research has been conducted to determine whether "maturity" (the legal standard for granting a judicial bypass to a minor adolescent seeking an abortion without parental consent) can be reliably and validly assessed. In the absence of clear legal standards for maturity, such assessments run the risk of being inconsistently interpreted and applied, as well as being inaccurate. Along with other legal scholars and professional psychologists who have considered this issue, the panel questions whether a "mature minor" standard can be effectively implemented.

The question has been raised of whether the availability of abortion has undermined delay or contraception. While it is true that adolescent girls in the early phase of sexual activity often do not use contraception regularly, we have found no evidence that abortion is used preferentially to abstinence or contraception as a means of avoiding unwanted child-bearing. Repeat abortions do occur among teenagers as well as among adult women. However, concern that the availability of abortion services will lead to higher rates of teenage sexual activity and pregnancy and less reliance on contraception is not supported by the available research. Adolescents who have had abortions are in fact less likely to experience a repeat pregnancy within two years than those who have given birth.

Most abortions occur during the first trimester of pregnancy and therefore carry little risk of medical complications when they are performed by qualified professionals in appropriately equipped settings. Although the health risks are somewhat greater for second trimester abortions, when performed under appropriate conditions these risks are minimized. In general, the health risks associated with an early, legal abortion are no greater for adolescents than for adult women, and they are also less significant than the risks associated with pregnancy and childbirth. Public health experts estimate that the replacement of unintended births and illegal abortions with legal abortions has averted as many as 1,500 pregnancy-related deaths among American women (including teenagers) since 1973 and life-threatening complications in the tens of thousands.

The role of abortion in society's approach to teenage pregnancy is probably the most contentious issue of all. It is impossible to isolate the decision concerning whether to terminate a pregnancy from innumerable political, religious, ethical, and personal considerations, but these are not subject to the kind of scientific inquiry we have made. The panel believes, however, that certain statements about abortion are fully justified by a combination of scientific evidence and general medical principles, and that to avoid the *facts* (as distinct from a *position*) is intellectually unsound.

The panel urges that at each step along the path from sexual initiation to parenting—regardless of whether one might wish that that step had not been reached—the girl or woman should be treated with the same dignity, confidentiality, kindness, and excellence of health care that are due any patient.

The panel concludes that there is at present no scientific basis for restricting the availability of abortion to adolescents. Evidence shows that to require minor teenagers to seek parental consent often causes them to delay abortions, with attendant health risks. On this basis, the panel concludes that minor adolescents should be encouraged, but not required, to involve their parents and partners in the decision-making process.

The panel believes there should be no compromise in the medical and personal supportive care of the 400,000 adolescents who have an abortion each year. For those adolescents who choose to terminate their pregnancy, abortion services should include both decision counseling and contraceptive counseling.

Several interventions can enhance the availability and accessibility of abortion to adolescents.

Pregnancy testing and counseling   Early confirmation of pregnancy is essential to preserve a young woman's options for its resolution and to minimize the health risks associated with abortion if she decides to terminate her pregnancy. Cost and confidentiality are important factors affecting where and when teenagers go for pregnancy testing. Because many adolescent girls' first visit to a family planning clinic is for pregnancy testing, outreach to encourage them to seek help early may affect the timing of their visit. Pregnancy counseling to outline the available options for pregnancy resolution should also be provided as early as possible. In this regard, adherence to principles of voluntarism and informed consent require that facilities provide their clients, including adolescents, with a full account of the possible risks, benefits, and consequences of maternity, abortion, and adoption as well as the appropriate referral. Teens should be encouraged whenever possible to involve their parents and partners in the decision-making process.

Abortion services   Abortions are available in hospitals, freestanding abortion clinics (nonprofit and for-profit), and in private physicians' offices. Factors of cost and confidentiality lead most teenagers to clinics for services. Although some clinics refer second-trimester patients to a hospital or private physician, and some have adopted parental consent requirements for minor adolescents, most will serve teenagers on their own authority. Abortion counseling, including helping a young woman explore the factors relevant to an informed decision about the termination of her pregnancy, is important for abortion patients, especially young adolescents. Such counseling is likely to enhance the decision-making process and to minimize the emotional strain. Clinics should also encourage minors to involve their partners and parents in their decisions. Counseling for the parents (or other adult family members) of adolescent patients is not typically provided by abortion clinics but may be a useful way of enhancing the family's capability to provide emotional support. Contraceptive counseling is also an important component of abortion services to advise patients how soon after the procedure they will be at risk of pregnancy, to provide information on contraceptive methods, and to help patients obtain those methods.

Adoption   For some teenagers, becoming a parent is not a viable option for pregnancy resolution. For those who lack the resources and motivation to undertake the significant responsibility of raising a child at that point in their lives, alternatives to parenthood are needed. Although adoption seems to have declined in popularity over the past two decades, especially since the nationwide legalization of abortion, the panel recognizes that the development or strengthening of adoption services is needed for those who choose to relinquish their children. As we have noted elsewhere in this report, research on the adoption decision-making process, as well as on the characteristics and special needs of pregnant adolescents who make adoption plans, is missing. Obviously, such research is a first necessary step to improving the quality of relevant services or developing new ones.

The panel recommends that relevant public agencies, in cooperation with the private sector, explore ways of strengthening adoption services, including (1) improved decision counseling for pregnant teenagers and (2) development of effective models for providing comprehensive care to pregnant girls who choose adoption as an alternative to parenthood.

Two existing interventions are especially relevant as components of strategies to support adoption as a viable option to parenthood.

Pregnancy counseling and referral   Teenagers who experience an unintended pregnancy should receive objective, nonjudgmental counseling to inform them of all their options for pregnancy resolution and the associated risks and benefits of each—abortion, parenthood, and adoption. Such counseling should also include decision counseling to help pregnant girls explore their reasons for choosing one course of action over another. Pregnancy counseling can play an important role in teenagers' decisions concerning pregnancy resolution and their later satisfaction with those decisions. Pregnant teenagers should be encouraged to involve their partners and parents in the decision-making process.

Adoption services   For those who elect to carry their pregnancies to term and relinquish their infants for adoption, services should meet the range of physical health care needs and psychological and social supports that these young women need during their pregnancy, during labor and delivery, and after their infants are born and have been placed with adoptive families. Although research on adoption is limited, it does suggest that these services are often fragmented and poorly coordinated and that they frequently focus on the prenatal period but overlook the young woman's need for support and assistance following delivery.

Goal 3: Promote Positive Social, Economic, Health, and Developmental Outcomes for Adolescent Parents and Their Children

Childbearing among school-age adolescents will never be entirely eliminated. The birth rate for teenagers and the number of children born to young mothers have declined over the past decade and a half, and they are projected to continue to decline into the 1990s. Aggressive and committed prevention approaches may further reduce adolescent childbearing. Even so, some teenagers experience unplanned pregnancies and become parents. Many of those who do are at serious risk of health and nutritional deficiencies, single parenthood, unemployment, poverty, and long-term economic dependence. Their children will have a higher probability of physical, social, and cognitive problems and deficiencies. Although parenting teenagers represent a small proportion of the overall adolescent population, their problems and needs entail high public costs.

Accordingly, a third important goal is to promote positive outcomes for adolescent parents and their children. Several strategies can potentially contribute to the achievement of this goal. Central to all of them is the recognition that teenage parents are not just young mothers: teenage fathers must also be a target for policies and programs, as must the families of pregnant and parenting adolescents.

Promote Healthy Birth Outcomes and Support the Physical Health of Young Mothers and Their Babies   Expectant mothers who receive early and regular prenatal care that is appropriate to their level of risk are significantly more likely to have healthy birth outcomes than those who do not. Those who obtain regular preventive health care for themselves and their children are likely to develop more positive health behaviors and their children are more likely to avoid or overcome many of the most difficult child health problems. Although it is possible, given current knowledge and technology, to prevent or ameliorate many maternal and child health problems, many teenagers and their children do not receive essential health care services. In some cases these services are not accessible to them; in many cases they are available but underutilized. Information, outreach, and follow-up are essential aspects of maternal and child health services for adolescents.

The panel recommends continued support for the provision of appropriate health and nutrition services, including prenatal, labor, and delivery care for pregnant adolescents and regular and emergency pediatric care for the children of teenage mothers, through Medicaid; the Early and Periodic Screening, Diagnosis and Treatment Program; and other federal and state maternal and child health programs. Bureaucratic barriers that prevent teenagers from receiving early, regular, and appropriate care for themselves and their children should be minimized.

Several interventions can promote healthy birth outcomes and can help support the physical health of young mothers and their babies.

Prenatal, labor, and delivery care   Early and regular prenatal care significantly reduces the likelihood of pregnancy complications, labor and delivery complications, and maternal morbidity. It also reduces the likelihood that young mothers will deliver premature and low birthweight babies. Although prenatal care services are widely available from public health departments, hospitals, freestanding clinics, school-based clinics, youth service agencies, and private physicians, adolescents are less likely than older mothers to obtain early—or any—prenatal care.

Because of their long-term health benefits, prenatal care services must be available and accessible to all pregnant adolescents. They should begin as early as possible in pregnancy, and they should continue through labor and delivery and during the immediate postpartum period. There should be appropriate linkage between prenatal and delivery care providers so that relevant information about a patient's health status and health history are available at the time of delivery.

Pregnant teenagers rely heavily on federal programs to pay for their prenatal, labor, and delivery care, including support from Medicaid, the

Early and Periodic Screening, Diagnosis and Treatment Program, and other maternal and child health programs. Bureaucratic problems involved in adolescents' applying for subsidized services and establishing their eligibility, especially Medicaid eligibility, have been shown to affect the timing of prenatal care for many pregnant teenagers and may even deter some from seeking any care at all. Such barriers should be minimized.

Program research suggests that two components of service delivery are essential to help pregnant teenagers receive adequate prenatal care beginning in the first trimester of pregnancy. These include pregnancy testing and counseling services as soon as pregnancy is suspected, and information and health education to inform teenagers of the importance of preventive health care and avoidance of health hazards (e.g., smoking) during pregnancy. In addition, the provision of health care services at or in proximity to the school has been shown to enhance school-age teenagers' access to and use of prenatal care. The introduction of comprehensive health clinics in many schools represents a positive step toward strengthening prenatal care services for pregnant students. In the limited evaluation studies that are available, these facilities have demonstrated their effectiveness in increasing the likelihood that pregnant teenagers will initiate care in the first trimester and will be monitored regularly throughout their pregnancy, in accordance with standards set forth by the American College of Obstetricians and Gynecologists. Nevertheless, prenatal care, labor, and delivery services should continue to be available to teenagers in a variety of settings, since many high-risk expectant mothers are not enrolled in school.

Nutrition services   The dietary habits of many adolescents and low-income individuals are poor. During pregnancy and when breast-feeding, nutrition needs are especially critical, and many young mothers suffer from anemia and vitamin deficiencies. The problems of malnourishment include complications in pregnancy and childbirth and low birthweight. In young children, nutritional deficits can delay physical development, increase susceptibility to disease, and negatively affect learning. The Supplemental Food Program for Women, Infants and Children (WIC) provides iron-rich and protein-rich food supplements to low-income pregnant women and mothers and children under age five. It has been shown to reduce the incidence of problems associated with malnourishment. It has also been shown to serve as a means of recruiting high-risk pregnant women into prenatal care.

Pediatric care   Well-baby care, as well as emergency care, has been shown to improve the physical health of all children, especially those at serious risk of perinatal dysfunction. As with prenatal care, information and health education can help young mothers and fathers understand the importance of well-baby care and positive health behaviors for their children's long-term development and well-being.

Pediatric care programs and well-baby clinics are available to teenage parents through public health departments, hospitals, freestanding community clinics, and school-based clinics. These programs involve a variety of service delivery models, including clinic services, home visits, and the integration of other necessary services, such as nutrition services, contraceptive services, and education and career counseling. Most teenage parents who seek publicly subsidized services rely on federal programs to pay for those services, among them Medicaid, the Early and Periodic Screening, Diagnosis and Treatment Program, and to some extent other maternal and child health programs. There is some evidence that eligibility standards and application procedures in some states may discourage needy parents from seeking well-baby and emergency care for their children. These bureaucratic barriers should be minimized.

Prevent Subsequent Untimely and Unintended Births   An untimely and unintended birth tends to have seriously negative social and economic consequences for young mothers, young fathers, and their children. A second untimely and unintended birth is likely to compound the already complex and overwhelming problems. Many adolescents who give birth experience repeat pregnancies within two years. Although most adolescent parents report that they did not intend to become pregnant again so quickly, most did not take effective steps to prevent conception. Contraceptive diligence requires a significant degree of commitment. Many teenage girls are easily dissuaded from regular contraceptive use by boyfriends, by problems in using their chosen method, or by information (often inaccurate) about possible negative side effects. Adolescents who have experienced childbearing are no different. Helping them to prevent subsequent untimely and unintended births requires that their family planning needs receive special attention and emphasis.

Several interventions have the potential for preventing subsequent untimely and unintended births to adolescent parents.

Contraceptive services   The use of contraception reduces the probability of pregnancy. Getting adolescent mothers and fathers to practice contraception regularly can substantially lower the likelihood of a repeat pregnancy and birth. Several aspects of service delivery to this target population are important: aggressive outreach and follow-up to reach parenting teenagers as soon as possible after delivery, assistance in getting them to clinics, and close monitoring of their success or difficulty in using their chosen method; directive advice on contraceptive practice; easy access to convenient, low-cost (or no cost) contraceptive services; and intensive individualized care. Low-key approaches to contraceptive use in several comprehensive pregnancy care programs have been shown to be insufficient. Learning to contracept successfully is difficult for many adult women. For teenagers who lack experience, confidence in their social relationships, and the ability to plan ahead, it is even more difficult. For many parenting teenagers who cannot foresee other viable life options than motherhood, a forceful and consistent message about the risks of subsequent pregnancy and the importance of contraception are essential. While contraceptive services alone cannot control subsequent fertility among teenage parents, they are a necessary first step.

The panel concludes that contraceptive services should be available and accessible to adolescent parents at low or no cost. Because of the special needs of this high-risk population, service providers should strengthen their programs by (1) enhancing their outreach efforts to encourage early use of contraceptive methods; (2) developing intensive individualized counseling and care techniques to encourage compliance; and (3) enhancing their follow-up procedures to track contraceptive use.

Abortion services   For those who experience repeat pregnancies and feel unable to cope with the compounded difficulties of raising more than one child, abortion is an option for pregnancy resolution.

Ensure the Economic Well-being of the Teenage Family   For teenage parents, especially those under age 18 and those without a high school diploma, who have not yet developed the ability to support themselves, economic well-being is a major concern. Adequate income support is a necessary precondition to school completion and to promoting the health and well-being of young mothers and their children. Severe poverty increases the likelihood of poor health, inadequate nutrition, personal frustration, and early economic dependence.

Ensuring the economic security of teenage families until they are able to become self-sufficient is an essential strategy to achieving the larger goal of promoting positive outcomes for these young parents and their children and should involve partners, families, and the community. Two interventions are especially relevant.

Child support enforcement   Fathers should be involved in the financial support of their children. Teenage fathers, who may not have completed school and who are employed only part-time or who are unemployed, are unlikely to be able to make a significant contribution to the support of their children while they are still in their teens. For this reason, young fathers have not typically been actively pursued by the state for child support. However, there has been renewed interest in enforcing child support by fathers of children born to teenage mothers, both to provide additional financial assistance to young mothers and as a means to increase young men's sense of parental responsibility. Indeed, parents are obligated to provide support until their children reach age 18, and even if the father's current level of financial assistance is low, his contribution may increase over time and have long-term positive effects on his children.

There is little existing research or program experience to guide new policies in this area. However, further efforts should be made to explore the effects and effectiveness (short-term and long-term) of child support enforcement among teenage fathers. As a first step, young men should be educated about their child support obligations. In addition, efforts should be made to link child support to education and work requirements in the form of (1) registration with the state employment service and (2) participation in job training and job search activities as well as work opportunities. At a time when an increasing number of states are adopting "workfare" programs for welfare mothers (including the mothers of very young children), it is appropriate to consider similar public jobs programs for the fathers of young children who cannot otherwise find work and provide support for their families.

The families of adolescent parents should also be encouraged to assume responsibility for the support and obligations of their minor children, including the children of teenagers under 18. Research suggests that adolescent mothers, especially school-age girls, who remain in their parents' home and receive support and assistance from their families, fare better in the short term than those who establish independent households. In turn, the children of young mothers benefit from this support and assistance. Program experience in this area is extremely limited, although several states, most notably Wisconsin, have recently enacted statutes requiring grandparent support for the children of adolescent mothers. While it can be assumed that enforcing grandparents' liability will increase the financial resources to teenage parents and their children, there are no data to show whether such provisions will serve the larger purpose of strengthening family bonds and stimulating emotionally supportive parental involvement, or will have less desirable effects.

Aid to Families With Dependent Children   Public assistance for adolescent mothers and their children represents an important source of economic security when husbands or partners and families are unable to meet the necessary level of financial support. The availability of AFDC and related food stamp and Medicaid benefits has raised controversy over the extent to which it encourages young women to become parents before they are able to become economically self-sufficient. Although there is no evidence that AFDC benefits encourage young women to become sexually active or to become pregnant, there is some evidence that they may influence decisions concerning living arrangements of pregnant and parenting teenagers. The 1984 Deficit Reduction Act amendments to the Social Security Act established that teenage parents eligible for AFDC and living with their parents must be included in a household grant. Minor mothers living apart from their families, however, are eligible to receive benefits on their own. This regulation may constitute an incentive for a teenage mother to establish independent living arrangements, thereby undermining her family's obligation and ability to provide financial and emotional support. To the extent that 1984 legislative changes governing AFDC eligibility deny income and Medicaid benefits to young mothers and their children if they remain in the parental home, these provisions should be carefully reviewed. Irrespective of federal action governing AFDC eligibility, the states should explore policy options to allow adolescent parents under age 18 to remain in their families of origin whenever possible until they have completed high school (or the equivalent), until they are able to become economically self-sufficient, or both. There is little research evidence to support policies in this area. One possibility, however, is to link the receipt of AFDC benefits by teenage mothers to remaining in their parents' home, except under conditions that pose a physical or emotional hazard to the adolescent or her baby.

Enhance Life Options for Adolescent Parents　Efforts to improve maternal and child health outcomes, to improve developmental outcomes among the children of adolescent parents, and to prevent subsequent pregnancy may have little positive effect until teenagers can be persuaded to "invest in their own futures." Both the motivation and the means are essential to overcoming the likely negative consequences of early childbearing. Although many teenage mothers (and fathers) report aspirations that are very similar to those of their peers who delay childbearing—a nice home, a good job, and a loving spouse—they frequently have difficulty envisioning in concrete terms how to make their dreams attainable. Therefore, a fourth important strategy for improving social, economic, and health outcomes for adolescent parents and their children is to enhance their life opportunities.

Several approaches appear to be especially promising:

<u>Life management training</u>　Life planning assistance is important to help teenage parents, both male and female, establish education, career, and family formation goals for themselves and to identify pathways to achieving these goals that take account of their parenting responsibilities. Similarly, life skills training to help them learn how to manage their everyday lives independently are important to success in pursuing their chosen work and family goals. Teenage parents need to have realistic dreams of what they can be, in addition to being a parent, and an understanding of how to fulfill those dreams, one step at a time. Research conclusively demonstrating the impact of life management training on the economic self-sufficiency, marital stability, and parenting skills of teenage parents is not available, and efforts to develop and test model programs of this type are needed.

<u>Educational support and remediation</u>　The detrimental effect of early childbearing on educational attainment has been clearly demonstrated. Most teenagers who become mothers before they graduate do not finish high school. Similarly, many adolescent fathers who assume parenting

responsibilities often find it difficult to complete their education. The relationship between school performance, school attendance, and adolescent childbearing is complex. Many teenagers who become parents are at risk of dropping out of high school or have left school before they became pregnant. Parenthood for these young people may represent a more positive immediate experience than education. For those who have consistently failed in the classroom, there is understandably little incentive to return. Yet adolescent parents must be made to recognize that finishing school is essential to fulfilling their other aspirations for home, family, and work. In some cases, regular classrooms and mainstream educational programs may not be appropriate. Many of these young people need intensive remedial education and self-paced instruction to be successful. Alternative school programs, including high school equivalency courses, represent one option; others may include home instruction or TV instruction to meet the special needs of these high-risk students.

Accordingly, the panel urges that a broad array of special education programs and services for pregnant and parenting teenagers be developed and implemented to assist these young people in completing their education.

Employment programs   Regardless of the availability of child support, older pregnant and parenting teenagers (18- and 19-year-olds) need employment services that provide job training and assist in job placement. Those under age 18 need services that emphasize the importance of completing high school, while enhancing their later employability and transition from school to work. Younger teenagers may benefit from information concerning career alternatives and job requirements, job readiness and job search skills, and temporary or part-time work experience. As with employment programs that are aimed at prevention, those serving pregnant and parenting teenagers need to take into account the related service needs of these young people, including child care, transportation, counseling, etc., which can significantly affect their participation and outcomes. Many existing youth employment programs have excluded teenage parents because of their special needs.

In this regard, the problems of adolescent fathers require special attention. Employment opportunities are so inadequate and earnings are so low for many young men, especially minorities, who have been reared in poverty and who lack education, job training, and work experience, that they are not able to participate in their children's support. To encourage teenage fathers to become economically responsible for their offspring and to form self-sufficient two-parent families requires that opportunities be available to them to enhance their employability and earnings.

The panel concludes that efforts should be continued to strengthen and expand age-appropriate employment programs for pregnant girls and teenage parents, both male and female.

Child care services   Research confirms that young parents who have access to and use child care in their families or in their community are more likely to finish high school and to enter the job market. Studies also suggest that some child care services can positively affect the parent-child relationship—for both mothers and fathers. In general, there is a shortage of organized child care services, especially infant care, and services that are geared to the special needs of adolescent parents are few. For many teenage parents who have working parents themselves, family care is unavailable. For teenagers to appropriately use child care, these services must be conveniently located; they must have hours of operation that are compatible with school schedules; they must be affordable; and they must provide emotional support and guidance to young parents who may not fully understand their roles and responsibilities. Some schools and employment training programs are experimenting with on-site child care. Such facilities have the potential for responding to the special needs of adolescents. Neighborhood-based family care and center care can similarly provide the necessary services to help teenagers remain in school or enter the job market and enhance their parenting behavior.

The panel recommends that support be provided for the development, implementation, and evaluation of model child care programs that are targeted to the needs of teenage parents. Schools and other community organizations should place high priority on establishing and maintaining these services for the children of adolescents.

Comprehensive care programs   The experience of comprehensive care programs for pregnant and parenting teenagers has been mixed. While these programs have frequently produced positive short-term outcomes in a number of areas—education, work, parenting, health behavior, and so on—there is no evidence of their having significant long-term positive effects. Indeed, the special needs of teenage parents are many, and coordination of supports and services to respond to those needs is difficult without a centralized case management capability. In addition, because most teenage parents have experienced frustration and failure, they often require intensive, individualized attention, encouragement, and assistance to overcome the complex problems they face. Comprehensive care programs have sought to do this by providing or brokering a mix of services appropriate to the special needs and circumstances of individual teenagers. These programs are expensive, and evaluations have not yielded much insight concerning the value or benefit of the various program components, either singly or in combination. In the absence of more complete understanding of how particular aspects and components of comprehensive care programs work and the extent of their potential benefit to clients beyond the period of participation, large new expenditures for interventions of this type are not warranted.

Nevertheless, we recognize that many teenage parents need a variety of supports and services that are not available within their families. Simply putting these services in place in the community will not ensure that teenagers will benefit from them. Many high-risk adolescent parents require intensive individualized attention and care in order to have their basic needs met, to help them locate and take advantage of available public and private services, and to help them fulfill their aspirations.

The panel urges that public and voluntary community agencies explore ways of developing and evaluating case management capabilities to help adolescent parents obtain necessary supports and services.

Promote the Social, Emotional, and Intellectual Development of the Children of Adolescent Parents   The children of adolescent parents are especially vulnerable to behavior disorders, problems in school adjustment, lower intelligence and achievement scores, and retention in grade. These difficulties are only partly the direct result of their mothers' young age and lack of schooling. They are also affected by poverty, poor nutrition, low birthweight, and living in a single-parent household, many of which are closely associated with adolescent childbearing. Special supports and services are needed by many adolescent parents to prevent or overcome these difficulties and to promote their children's healthy social, emotional, and cognitive development.

One intervention in particular has the potential for furthering this strategy.

Parenting education   Parenting education has been shown to improve young parents' knowledge of children's patterns of growth and development and appropriate child care, as well as to help them learn techniques for stimulating infant response and development. Such programs should be available to teenage parents, both male and female, and should be sensitive, not only to the developmental requirements of infants and toddlers, but to the developmental maturity and capabilities of the young parents. Teenagers who have not grown up in supportive, enriching families may have little positive basis for modeling their own parenting behavior.

The panel urges that parenting education for teenage parents, especially those from severely disadvantaged backgrounds, receive special attention and emphasis. Schools and other community organizations should place high priority on the development, implementation, and evaluation of these programs.

CONCLUSION

As we stated at the beginning of this chapter, the panel's framework for policy and program development is organized around three fundamental goals: the first is reduction of adolescent pregnancy; the second is provision of alternatives to adolescent childbearing and parenting; the third is promotion of positive outcomes for adolescent parents and their children. For each of these goals, several strategies and specific intervention approaches have been presented. It is important to recognize that none of these interventions alone can solve the complex problems of adolescent pregnancy and childbearing; nor can any single strategy address the special needs and characteristics of all youth at risk of untimely and unintended pregnancy and birth. In presenting several strategies for achieving each of these goals, we have tried to take account of the diversity of the adolescent population—of their different values, different social, economic, and cultural backgrounds, different ages and stages of development, different communities and support systems, and different dreams for the future. The strategies toward each goal are interdependent. They are not mutually exclusive. Providing young people with the ability to avoid pregnancy and childbearing or to cope with early unplanned parenthood and helping them develop the will and the willingness to do so are both important. Neither alone is sufficient.

As we have stressed throughout this report, there are no easy answers or quick fixes. Those seeking simple new solutions will find there is really very little that is new or simple. Any efforts to alleviate the problems of adolescent pregnancy and childbearing will ultimately require a sustained, coordinated commitment by policy makers, service providers, parents, and teenagers themselves. Everyone can be touched by the problems; everyone can—indeed, must—contribute to the solution.

The problems of adolescent pregnancy and childbearing are solidly rooted in many of the forces and principles that shape our society—individualism, family autonomy, and free enterprise. As a nation, we have no coherent policy in this area because we have no unitary view of these issues or approach to addressing them, and because we have been unable to define an appropriate public role in decisions regarding the initiation of sexual activity, contraception, pregnancy resolution, and parenting. This ambiguity and disagreement will not be easily resolved. Nor should it. We are a diverse society of individuals, families, and communities with differing values, traditions, and cultures. In short, the panel believes that a number of actions should continue to be taken simultaneously. They must involve government at all levels as well as the private sector, including business and labor, religious groups, special interests, and the media. Some represent immediate steps that can yield short-term results; others will require a longer-term investment of time and resources.

This report represents one step in a continuing, incremental process. As a scientific group, we have strived to clarify the issues, sharpen awareness of crucial decision points, and bring knowledge to bear on the trade-offs and complementarities among different political and ideological positions. Perhaps our most important contribution is to inform the continuing debate concerning this salient and often divisive issue of the limits of scientific understanding.

References

ABC/Washington Post
 1982   Roper Center Poll. Storrs: University of Connecticut.
Abrahamse, A.F., P.A. Morrison, and L.J. Waite
 1985   How Family Characteristics Deter Early Unwed Parenthood. Paper presented
        at the annual meeting of the Population Association of America, Boston.
Adler, N.E.
 1975   "Sample attrition in studies of psycho-social sequelae of abortion: How great a
        problem?" Journal of Applied Social Psychology 6:240–257.
Adler, N.E., and P. Dolcini
 1986   Psychological issues in abortion for adolescents. In G.B. Melton (ed.), Adoles-
        cent Abortion: Psychological and Legal Issues. Lincoln: University of Nebraska
        Press.
Alan Guttmacher Institute
 1981   Teenage Pregnancy: The Problem That Hasn't Gone Away. New York: Alan
        Guttmacher Institute.
 1984   Organized Family Planning Services in the United States, 1981–1983. New
        York: Alan Guttmacher Institute.
 in   Teenage Pregnancy in Developed Countries. New Haven, Conn.: Yale Univer-
 press sity Press.
Alexander, G.
 1984   Project Choice, Interim Report: Year III. San Diego, Calif.: Center for Wom-
        en's Studies and Services.
American College of Obstetricians and Gynecologists
 1982   Standards for Obstetrical-Gynecological Services. Fifth ed. Washington, D.C.:
        American College of Obstetricians and Gynecologists.
American Institutes for Research
 1979   The Ecology of Help-Seeking Behavior Among Adolescent Parents. Cam-
        bridge, Mass.: American Institutes for Research.

Anderson, E.
    1978   A Place on the Corner. Chicago: University of Chicago Press.
Arnold, C.B.
    1973   "A condom distribution program for adolescent males." Pp. 138–145 in D.V. McCalister, V. Thiessen, and H. McDermott (eds.), Readings in Family Planning: A Challenge to the Health Professions. St. Louis, Mo.: Mosby.
Auletta, K.
    1982   The Underclass. New York: Random House.
Averch, H.A., S.J. Carroll, T.S. Donaldson, H.J. Kiesling, and J. Pincus
    1972   How Effective Is Schooling? A Critical Review and Synthesis of Research Findings. Santa Monica, Calif.: The Rand Corporation.
Bachman, J.G., S. Green, and I.D. Wirtanen
    1971   Youth in Transition, Vol. III: Dropping Out—Problem or Symptom? Ann Arbor, Mich.: Institute for Social Research.
Bachrach, C.A.
    1984   "Contraceptive practice among American women, 1973–1982." Family Planning Perspectives 16(1):253–259.
    1986   "Adoption plans, adopted children, and adoptive mothers." Journal of Marriage and the Family 48:243–253, May.
Bachrach, C.A., and W. Mosher
    1984   "Use of contraception in the United States, 1982." Advance Data from Vital and Health Statistics 102(4).
Badger, E.
    1977   "The infant stimulation/mother training project." Pp. 45–62 in B. Caldwell and D. Stedman (eds.), Infant Education. New York: Walker Publishing.
    1981   "Effects of parent education program on teenage mothers and their offspring." Pp. 283–309 in K.G. Scott, T. Field, and E.G. Robertson (eds.), Teenage Parents and Their Offspring. New York: Grune & Stratton.
Badger, E., D. Burns, and B. Rhoads
    1976   Education for adolescent mothers in a hospital setting. American Journal of Public Health 66:469–472.
Baldwin, W., and V. Cain
    1980   "The children of teenage parents." Family Planning Perspectives 12(1):34–43.
Bank Street College
    no   Teen Fathers: Partners in Parenting. New York: Bank Street College of Educa-
    date   tion.
Bauman, K., and J.R. Udry
    1981   "Subjective expected utility and adolescent sexual behavior." Adolescence 14:527–538.
Belmont, L., P. Cohen, J. Dryfoos, Z. Stein, and S. Zayac
    1981   "Maternal age and children's intelligence." Pp. 177–194 in K. Scott, T. Field, and E.G. Robertson (eds.), Teenage Parents and Their Offspring. New York: Grune & Stratton.

Belsky, J., ed.
1982   In the Beginning: Readings on Infancy. New York: Columbia University Press.
Betsey, C.L., R.G. Holister, Jr., and M.R. Papageorgiou, eds.
1985   Youth Employment and Training Programs: The YEDPA Years. Committee on Youth Employment Programs, National Research Council. Washington, D.C.: National Academy Press.
Billingsly, A.
1970   "Illegitimacy and the black community." Pp. 70–85 in Illegitimacy: Changing Services for Changing Times. New York: National Council on Illegitimacy.
Billy, J.O.G., and J.R. Udry
1983   The Effects of Age and Pubertal Development on Adolescent Sexual Behavior. Unpublished manuscript. University of North Carolina.
1984   "Adolescent sexual behavior and friendship choice." Social Forces 62(3):653–678.
Block, A.H., and S. Dubin
1981   Research on the Societal Consequences of Adolescent Childbearing: Welfare Costs at the Local Level. Final Report, NO1-HD–92838, Social and Behavioral Sciences Branch, Center for Population Research, National Institute of Child Health and Human Development, Bethesda, Md.
Blum, W.R., M.D. Resnick, and T.A. Stark
1985   The Impact of a Parental Notification Law on Adolescent Abortion Decision-Making. Unpublished manuscript. University of Minnesota.
Bonham, G.S., and P.J. Placek
1978   "The relationship of maternal health, infant health, and sociodemographic factors to fertility." Public Health Reports 93(3):283–292.
Bracken, M., M. Hachamovitch, and A. Grossman
1974   "The decision to abort and psychological sequelae." Journal of Nervous and Mental Disorders 15:155–161.
Branch, A.Y., J. Milliner, and J. Bumbaugh
1986   Summer Training and Education Program (STEP): Report on the 1985 Summer Experience. Philadelphia: Public/Private Ventures.
Brann, E.
1979   "A multivariate analysis of interstate variation in fertility of teenage girls." American Journal of Public Health 69:661–666.
Broman, S.H.
1981   "Long-term development of children born to teenagers." Pp. 195–224 in K. Scott, T. Field, and E.G. Robertson (eds.), Teenage Parents and Their Offspring. New York: Grune & Stratton.
Bumpass, L., and J.A. Sweet
1972   "Differentials in marital instability: 1970." American Sociological Review 37(6):754–766.

Burden, D.S., and L.V. Klerman
  1984 "Teenage parenthood: factors that lessen economic dependence." Social Work
        29(January/February):11–16.
Bureau of the Census
  1980 "Population Estimates and Projections." Current Population Reports, Series
        P-25, No. 965, 917. Washington, D.C.: U.S. Department of Commerce.
  1984a "Childspacing among birth cohorts of American women: 1905–1959." Cur-
        rent Population Reports. Series P-20, No. 385.
  1984b "Marital status and living arrangements." Current Population Reports. Series
        P-20, No. 389. March 1983.
  1985a "Marital status and living arrangements: March 1984." Current Population
        Reports. Series P-20, No. 399. July 1985.
  1985b "Money income and poverty status of families and persons in the United States:
        1984." Current Population Reports. Series P-60, No. 149.
  1985c Statistical Abstract of the United States. 105th ed. Washington, D.C.: U.S.
        Department of Commerce.
  1985d Statistical Abstract of the United States. 106th ed. Washington, D.C.: U.S.
        Department of Commerce.
Burt, M.
  1986 Estimates of Public Costs for Teenage Childbearing. Unpublished paper pre-
        pared for the Center for Population Options, Washington, D.C.
Burt, M., M.H. Kimmich, J. Goldmuntz, and F.L. Sonnenstein
  1984 Helping Pregnant Adolescents: Outcomes and Costs of Service Delivery. Final
        report on the evaluation of adolescent pregnancy programs. Washington,
        D.C.: Urban Institute.
Card, J.J.
  1978 Long-Term Consequences for Children Born to Adolescent Parents. Final
        report to the National Institute of Child Health and Human Development.
        Palo Alto, Calif.: American Institutes of Research.
Card, J.J., and L.L. Wise
  1978 "Teenage mothers and teenage fathers: The impact of early childbearing on
        the parents' personal and professional lives." Family Planning Perspectives
        10(4):199–205.
Cates, W., Jr.
  1981 "The Hyde Amendment in action." Journal of the American Medical Associ-
        ation 246.
Cates, W., Jr., et al.
  1983 "The risks associated with teenage abortion." New England Journal of
        Medicine 309:621–624.
CBS/New York Times
  1980 CBS News—The New York Times Poll. New York: CBS News.

Center for Population Options
  1984 Life Planning Project: Interim Report June 1, 1983–January 31, 1984. Unpublished report. Center for Population Options, Washington, D.C.

Centers for Disease Control
  1983 Surgical Sterilization Surveillance: Tubal Sterilization and Hysterectomy in Women Aged 15–44. Atlanta, Ga.: U.S. Department of Health and Human Services.

Chamie, M., S. Eisman, J.D. Forrest, M. Orr, and A. Torres
  1982 Factors affecting adolescents' use of family planning clinics. Family Planning Perspectives 14(May/June):126–139.

Children's Defense Fund
  1985 Preventing Children Having Children. Clearinghouse paper no. 1. Washington, D.C.: Children's Defense Fund.

Chilman, C.
  1980a Adolescent Sexuality in a Changing Society. U.S. Government Printing Office Publication No. 10-1426: January. Washington, D.C.: U.S. Department of Health, Education, and Welfare.
  1980b "Toward a reconceptualization of adolescent sexuality." Pp. 101–127 in C. Chilman (ed.), Adolescent Pregnancy and Childbearing: Findings From Research. Washington, D.C.: U.S. Department of Health and Human Services.

Clark, S.D, Jr., L.S. Zabin, and J.B. Hardy
  1984 "Sex, contraception, and parenthood: Experience and attitudes among urban black young men." Family Planning Perspectives 16(March/April):77–82.

Cobliner, W.G.
  1981 "Prevention of adolescent pregnancy: A developmental perspective." In E.R. McAnarney and G. Stickle (eds.), Pregnancy and Childbearing During Adolescence: Research Priorities for the 1980s. New York: Alan R. Liss.

Cohen, P., L. Belmont, J. Dryfoos, Z. Stein, and S. Zayac
  1980 "The effects of teenage motherhood and maternal offspring intelligence." Social Biology 27(2):138–154.

Coleman, J.S.
  1961 The Adolescent Society. New York: Free Press.

Coleman, J.S., et al.
  1966 Equality of Educational Opportunity. Washington, D.C.: U.S. Government Printing Office.

Conger, J.
  1973 Adolescence and Youth. New York: Harper and Row.

Cooper, L.
  1983 The Effectiveness of Family Life Education in Twelve Secondary School Districts. Santa Cruz, Calif.: Network Publications.

Coughlin, D.
   1978   Family Planning and the Teenager: A Service Delivery Assessment. Washing-
          ton, D.C.: U.S. Department of Health, Education and Welfare.
Cvetkovich, G., and B. Grote
   1975   Antecedents of Responsible Family Formation. Progress report paper pre-
          sented at a conference sponsored by the Population Division, National Insti-
          tute of Child Health and Human Development, Bethesda, Md.
   1980   "Psychological development and the social problem of teenage illegitimacy."
          Pp. 15–41 in C. Chilman (ed.), Adolescent Pregnancy and Childbearing:
          Findings From Research. Washington, D.C.: U.S. Department of Health
          and Human Services.
   1981   Male Teenagers' Sexual Debut, Psychosocial Development and Contracep-
          tive Use. Unpublished manuscript. Western Washington University.
Daling, J.R., and I. Emanuel
   1977   "Induced abortion and subsequent outcome of pregnancy in a series of Ameri-
          can women." New England Journal of Medicine 297:1241–1245.
Davies, M., and D. Kandel
   1981   "Parental and peer influences on adolescents' educational plans: some further
          evidence." American Journal of Sociology 84(2):363–387.
Davis, K., and A. Grossbard-Schechtman
   1980   Study on How Mother's Age and Circumstances Affect Children. Final
          report to National Institute for Child Health and Human Development. Los
          Angeles: University of Southern California.
Devaney, B.L., and K.S. Hubley
   1981   The Determinants of Adolescent Pregnancy and Childbearing. Final report to
          the National Institute of Child Health and Human Development. Washing-
          ton, D.C.: Mathematica Policy Research.
Donovan, P.
   1983   "Judging teenagers: How minors fare when they seek court-authorized
          abortions." Family Planning Perspectives 15:259–267.
Douvan, E., and J. Adelson
   1966   The Adolescent Experience. New York: John Wiley.
Dryfoos, J.G.
   1983   Review of Interventions in the Field of Prevention of Adolescent Pregnancy.
          Preliminary report to the Rockefeller Foundation, New York.
   1984a "A new strategy for preventing unintended teenage childbearing." Family
          Planning Perspectives 16:193–195.
   1984b Prevention Strategies: A Progress Report. Report to the Rockefeller Founda-
          tion. New York: Rockefeller Foundation.
   1984c "A time for new thinking about teenage pregnancy." American Journal of
          Public Health 75(1):13–14.

1985 Review of Programs and Services to Foster Responsible Sexual Behavior on the Part of Adolescent Boys. Report to the Carnegie Corporation of New York.

Edwards, L., M. Steinman, K. Arnold, and E. Hakanson
1980 "Adolescent pregnancy prevention services in high school clinics." Family Planning Perspectives 12:6–14.

Eisen, M., G.L. Zellman, A. Leibowitz, W.K. Chow, and J.R. Evans
1983 "Factors discriminating pregnancy resolution decisions of unmarried adolescents." Genetic Psychology Monographs 108:69–95.

Eisen, M., G.L. Zellman, and A. McAlister
1985 A Health Brief Model Approach to Adolescents' Fertility Control: Some Pilot Program Findings. Working paper No.7-002. University of Texas Population Center.

Eisenstadt, S.N.
1977 "Cultural settings and adolescence and youth around the year 2000." In J.P. Hill and F.J. Monks (eds.), Adolescence and Youth in Prospect. Guildford, Surrey, England: IPC Science and Technology Press, Ltd.

Elder, G.H., Jr.
1968 Adolescent Socialization and Personality Development. Chicago: Rand McNally.
1975 "Adolescence in the life cycle." In S. Dragaslin and G.H. Elder, Jr. (eds.), Adolescence in the Life Cycle. Washington, D.C: Hemisphere.
1980 "Adolescence in historical perspective." In J. Adelson (ed.), Handbook of Adolescent Psychology. New York: Wiley.

Ellwood, D., and M.J. Bane
1984 The Impact of AFDC on Family Structure and Living Arrangements. Cambridge, Mass.: Harvard University Press.

Epstein, A.
1980 Assessing the Child Development Information Needed by Adolescent Parents With Very Young Children. A report to the Department of Health, Education, and Welfare. Ypsilanti, Mich.: High/Scope Educational Research Foundation.

Evans, J., G. Selstad, and W. Welcher
1976 "Teenagers: Fertility control behavior and attitudes before and after abortion, childbearing or negative pregnancy test." Family Planning Perspectives 8(4):192–200.

Ezzard, N.V., W. Cates, Jr., D.G. Kramer, and C. Tietze
1982 "Race-specific patterns of abortion use by American teenagers." American Journal of Public Health 72:809.

Field, B.
1981 "A socio-economic analysis of out-of-wedlock birth among teenagers." In

K. Scott, T. Field, and E.G. Robertson (eds.), Teenage Parents and Their Offspring. New York: Grune & Stratton.

Finkel, M.L., and D.J. Finkel

1975   "Sexual and contraceptive knowledge, attitudes and behavior of male adolescents." Family Planning Perspectives 9:356–360.

1984   Sex Education in the High Schools: It Can Make a Difference. An Evaluation of the New York City Family Life Curriculum, Including Sex Education. Revised curriculum. Unpublished manuscript. Cornell University Medical Center.

Flacks, R.

1970   "Social and cultural meanings of student revolt: Some informal comparative observations." Social Problems 17:340–357.

1971   Youth and Social Change. Chicago: Markham.

Flaherty, E., and J. Maracek

1982   Psychological Factors Associated With Fertility Regulation Among Adolescents. Final report to National Institute of Child Health and Human Development. Philadelphia: Philadelphia Health Management Corporation.

Forbush, J.B.

1978   Statement at the hearing before the Subcommittee on Select Education of the Committee on Education and Labor, House of Representatives, on H.R. 12146, July 24, 1978.

Forrest, J.D.

1986   Proportion of U.S. Women Ever Pregnant Before Age 20: A Research Note. Unpublished paper. Alan Guttmacher Institute, New York.

Forrest, J.D., and S.K. Henshaw

1983   "What U.S. women think and do about contraception." Family Planning Perspectives 15(4):157–166.

Forrest, J.D., A. Hermalin, and S. Henshaw

1981   "The impact of family planning clinic programs on adolescent pregnancy." Family Planning Perspectives 13:109–116.

Fox, G.L.

1980   Mother-Daughter Communications re Sexuality. Final report to the National Institute of Child Health and Human Development. Detroit: Merrill-Palmer Institute.

1981   "The family's role in adolescent sexual behavior." Pp. 73–130 in T. Ooms (ed.), Teenage Pregnancy in a Family Context. Philadelphia: Temple University Press.

Freeman, E.W., K. Rickels, G. Huggins, et al.

1980   "Adolescent contraceptive use: Comparisons of male and female attitudes and information." American Journal of Public Health 70:790–797.

Freeman, R.B., and H.J. Holzer
  1985 "Young blacks and jobs—What we now know." The Public Interest 78
         (Winter):18–31.
Furstenberg, F.F., Jr.
  1976 Unplanned Parenthood: The Social Consequences of Teenage Childbearing.
         New York: Free Press.
  1980 "The social consequences of teenage parenthood." In C. Chilman (ed.),
         Adolescent Pregnancy and Childbearing: Findings From Research. NIH
         Publication No. 81-2077 267–308. Washington, D.C.: U.S. Department of
         Health and Human Services.
Furstenberg, F.F., Jr., and J. Brooks-Gunn
  1985a "Adolescent fertility: Causes, consequences and remedies." In L. Aiken and
          D. Mechanic (eds.), Applications of Social Science to Clinical Medicine and
          Health Policy. New Brunswick, N.J.: Rutgers University Press.
  1985b Adolescent Mothers in Later Life. New York: The Commonwealth Fund.
Furstenberg, F.F., Jr., and A.G. Crawford
  1978 "Family support: Helping teenage mothers to cope." Family Planning Per-
         spectives 10(November/December):322–333.
Furstenberg, F.F., Jr., K.A. Moore, and J.L. Peterson
  1985a "Sex education and sexual experience among adolescents." American Journal
          of Public Health 75(11):1331–1332.
Furstenberg, F.F., Jr., S.P. Morgan, K.A. Moore, and J. Peterson
  1985b Exploring Race Differences in the Timing of Intercourse. Unpublished man-
          uscript. University of Pennsylvania.
Gallup, G.
  1978 Reflects Epidemic of Teenage Pregnancies: Growing Number of Americans
         Favor Discussions of Sex in Classrooms. News release. Princeton, N.J.: The
         Gallup Poll.
  1980 Dissatisfaction Motivated Voters. Report No. 183. Princeton, N.J.: Gallup
         Opinion Index.
Garbarino, J., and C.E. Asp
  1981 Successful Schools and Competent Students. Lexington, Mass.: Lexington
         Books.
Glazer, N.
  1985 "Interests and passions." Public Interest 81:17–30.
Glick, P.
  1975 "A demographer looks at American families." Journal of Marriage and the
         Family 37:15–26.
Gold, M.
  1969 "Juvenile delinquency as a symptom of alienation." Journal of Social Issues
         25:121–135.

Gold, R.B., and A.M. Kenney
1985 "Paying for maternity care." Family Planning Perspectives 17(May/June):103–111.

Gold, R.B., and B. Nestor
1985 "Public funding of contraceptive, sterilization and abortion services, 1983." Family Planning Perspectives 17(1):25–29.

Golden, P.M, R.W. Wilson, and J. Kanet
1984 "Prevention profile." Health: United States, 1983. Hyattsville, Md.: National Center for Health Statistics.

Goldsmith, S., M. Gabrielson, and I. Gabrielson
1972 "Teenagers, sex and contraception." Family Planning Perspectives 4(1), January.

Goldstein, H., and H.M. Wallace
1978 "Services and needs of pregnant teenagers in large cities of the United States, 1976." Public Health Reports 93:46–54.

Greenberg, B., R. Abelman, and K. Neuendorf
1981 "Sex on the soap operas: Afternoon delight." Journal of Communication (Summer).

Greer, C.
1972 The Great School Legend: A Revisionist Interpretation of American Public Education. New York: Basic Books.

Griffiths, J.
1977 "Reducing the medical risk of teenage pregnancy." Sexual Medicine Today (October).

Grimes, D.A., et al.
1981 "Fatal septic abortion in the United States, 1975–1977." Obstetrics and Gynecology 57:739–744.

Haggstrom, G.W., and P.A. Morrison
1979 Consequences of Parenthood in Late Adolescence: Findings From the National Longitudinal Study of High School Seniors. Santa Monica, Calif.: The Rand Corporation.

Haggstrom, G.W., D.E. Kanouse, and P.A. Morrison
1983 Accounting for the Educational Shortfalls of Young Mothers. Unpublished manuscript. The Rand Corporation.

Hardy, J.B.
1983 Determinants of Repeated Adolescent Pregnancy. Final report to National Institute of Child Health and Human Development. Baltimore, Md.: Johns Hopkins University Press.

Hardy, J.B., and C.D. Flagle
1980 Results, Costs and Assessment of the Investment Opportunity. Unpublished paper prepared for the Office of Adolescent Pregnancy Programs, U.S. Department of Health and Human Services.

Harlan, W., G. Grillo, J. Carononi-Huntley, and P. Leaverton
  1980 "Secondary sex characteristics of boys 12 to 17 years of age: The U.S. Health Examination Survey." The Journal of Pediatrics 95(2):293–297.

Harris, L.
  1979 Majority Favors Abortion, but Foes Have Political Strength. ABC News-Harris Survey, March 7, 1979.

Hartley, S.F.
  1975 Illegitimacy. Berkeley: University of California Press.

Hayes, C.D. (ed.)
  1982 Making Policies for Children: A Study of the Federal Process. Committee on Child Development Research and Public Policy, National Research Council. Washington, D.C.: National Academy Press.

Health Insurance Association of America
  1982 The Cost of Having a Baby. Washington, D.C.: Health Insurance Association of America.

Helfer, R., and A. Wilson
  1982 "The parent-infant relationship: Promoting a positive beginning through perinatal coaching." Pediatric Clinics of North America 29:(2).

Henshaw, S.K.
  1982 "Freestanding abortion clinics: Services, structure, fees." Family Planning Perspectives 14:248–256.

Henshaw, S.K. (ed.)
  1983 Abortion Services in the United States, Each State and Metropolitan Area, 1979–1980. New York: Alan Guttmacher Institute.

Henshaw, S.K., J.D. Forrest, and E. Blaine
  1984 "Abortion services in the United States, 1981 and 1982." Family Planning Perspectives 16:119–127.

Henshaw, S.K., and G. Martire
  1982 "Mortality and legality." Family Planning Perspectives 14:53–60.

Henshaw, S.K., and K. O'Reilly
  1983 "Characteristics of abortion patients in the United States, 1979 and 1980." Family Planning Perspectives 15(1):5–16.

Henshaw, S.K., and L.S. Wallisch
  1984 "The Medicaid cutoff and abortion services for the poor." Family Planning Perspectives 16:170–180.

Herold, E.
  1980 Contraceptive Attitudes and Behavior of Single Adolescent Females. Final Report, Contract HO1-HD-92809. National Institute of Child Health and Human Development, Bethesda, Md.

Hill, J.P., and F.J. Monks
  1977 "Some perspectives on adolescence in modern societies." In J.P. Hill and F.J.

Monks (eds.), Adolescence and Youth in Prospect. Guildford, Surrey, England: IPC Science and Technology Press, Ltd.

Hill, R.
1977 Informal Adoption Among Black Families. Washington, D.C.: National Urban League.

Hofferth, S.L.
1981 Effects of Number and Timing of Births on Family Well-Being Over the Life Cycle. Final Report to National Institute of Child Health and Human Development Contract #NO1-HD-82850. Washington, D.C.: Urban Institute.

Hofferth, S.L., and K.A. Moore
1979 "Early childbearing and later economic well-being." American Sociological Review 44(5):784–815.

Hofferth, S., K.A. Moore, and S.B. Caldwell
1978 The Consequences of Age at First Childbirth: Labor Force Participation and Earnings. Working Paper 1146-04. Final Report to National Institute of Child Health and Human Development. Washington, D.C.: Urban Institute.

Hogan, D.P., and E.M. Kitagawa
1983 Family Factors in the Fertility of Black Adolescents. Paper presented at the annual meeting of the Population Association of America.

Hogue, C.J., et al.
1982 "The effects of induced abortion on subsequent reproduction." Epidemiological Reviews 4:66–94.

Hollingsworth, D.R., J.M. Kotchen, and M.E. Felice
1982 "Impact of gynecological age on outcome of adolescent pregnancy." In E.R. McAnarney (ed.), Premature Adolescent Pregnancy and Parenthood. New York: Grune & Stratton.

Hornick, J.P., L. Doran, and S.H. Crawford
1979 "Premarital contraceptive usage among male and female adolescents." The Family Coordinator 28:181–190.

Hottois, J., and N.A. Milner
1975 The Sex Education Controversy. Lexington, Mass.: Lexington Books.

Inazu, J.K., and G.L. Fox
1980 "Maternal influence on the sexual behavior of teenage daughters." Journal of Family Issues 1:81–102.

Institute of Medicine
1985 Preventing Low Birthweight. Committee to Study the Prevention of Low Birthweight, Division of Health Promotion and Disease Prevention. Washington, D.C.: National Academy Press.

Jekel, J.F., et al.
1975 "A comparison of the health of index and subsequent babies born to school age mothers." American Journal of Public Health 65(4):370–374.

Jencks, C.
  1972 Inequality: A Reassessment of the Effect of Family and Schooling in America. New York: Basic Books.
Jenkins, R.
  1983 Final Report to the National Institute of Child Health and Human Development. Washington, D.C.: Howard University Hospital.
Jessor, S.L., and R. Jessor
  1975 "Transition from virginity to nonvirginity among youth: A social-psychological study over time." Developmental Psychology 11(4):473–484.
Jessor, R., F. Costa, S.L. Jessor, and J.E. Donovan
  1983 "The time of first intercourse: A prospective study." Journal of Personality and Social Psychology 44:608–626.
Joseph P. Kennedy, Jr., Foundation
  1982 A Community of Caring. New York: Walker.
JRB Associates
  1981 Final Report on the Survey of Services Provided by Adolescent Pregnancy Projects. Final report to the Office of Adolescent Pregnancy Programs, U.S. Department of Health and Human Services. McLean, Va.: JRB Associates.
Kahn, J., K. Smith, and E. Roberts
  1984 Familial Communication and Adolescent Sexual Behavior. Final report to the Office of Adolescent Pregnancy Programs. Cambridge, Mass.: American Institutes for Reseach.
Kallen, D.J.
  1984 Adoption Decisions: Personal and Social Context. Unpublished proposal for a research study funded by the Office of Adolescent Pregnancy Programs, U.S. Department of Health and Human Services.
Kamerman, S.B., and C.D. Hayes (eds.)
  1982 Families That Work: Children in a Changing World. Committee on Child Development Research and Public Policy, National Research Council. Washington, D.C.: National Academy Press.
Kantner, J.F., and M. Zelnik
  1972 "Sexual experience of young unmarried women in the United States." Family Planning Perspectives 4:9–18.
  1973 "Contraception and pregnancy: experience of young unmarried women in the United States." Family Planning Perspectives 5(1):11–25.
Kasun, J.
  1982 "Family planning expenditures in California." Heartbeat (Winter).
Keniston, K.
  1968 Young Radicals. New York: Harcourt, Brace.
  1971 Youth and Dissent. New York: Harcourt, Brace.
Kenkel, W.F.
  1986 "Change and stability in the occupational plans of females." In Sarah M.

Shoffner and William F. Kenkel (eds.), On the Road to Adulthood. Greensboro: University of North Carolina.

Kennedy, E.T., S. Gershoff, R. Reed, and J.E. Austin
1982 "Evaluation of the effect of WIC supplemental feeding on birthweight." Journal of the American Dietetic Association 80:220–227.

Kessel, S., V. Hutchins, P. Placek, and T. Liss
1984 Trends in Underlying Medical Conditions, Complications of Pregnancy, and Complications of Labor to Mothers of In-Wedlock Live Hospital Births: United States, 1972 and 1980. Paper presented at the annual meeting of the Southern Regional Demographic Group, Orlando, Fla.

Kimmich, M.H.
1985 Children's Services in the Reagan Era. Washington, D.C.: Urban Institute.

Kinard, E.M., and L.V. Klerman
1980 "Teenage parenting and child abuse: Are they related?" American Journal of Orthopsychiatry 59(3).

Kinard, E.M., and H. Reinherz
1984 School Achievement and Aptitude in Children of Adolescent Mothers. Paper presented at the annual meeting of the American Public Health Association, Montreal.

Kirby, D.
1984 Sexuality Education: An Evaluation of Programs and Their Effect. Santa Cruz, Calif.: Network Publications.
1985 School-Based Health Clinics: An Emerging Approach to Improving Adolescent Health and Addressing Teenage Pregnancy. Washington, D.C.: Center for Population Options.

Kirby, D., and P. Scales
1981 "An analysis of state guidelines for sex education instruction in public schools." Family Relations 30(2):229–237.

Kisker, E.
1985 "Clinic effectiveness in serving adolescents." Family Planning Perspectives 17(2):83–90.

Klaus, M.H., and J.B. Kennell
1982 "Parent-to-infant attachment." In J. Belsky (ed.), In the Beginning: Readings on Infancy. New York: Columbia University Press.

Klerman, L.V.
1983 Family Home Care: Critical Issues for Services and Policies. New York: Haworth Press.

Klerman, L.V., and J.F. Jekel
1973 School-Age Mothers: Problems, Programs and Policy. Hamden, Conn.: Shoe String Press (Linnet).

Kline, J., et al.
1978 "Induced abortion and spontaneous abortion: No connection?" American Journal of Epidemology 107:290–298.

Klinman, D.G., J.H. Sander, J.L. Rosen, and K.R. Longo
1985 "The teen father collaboration: A demonstration and research model." In M.E. Lamb and A.B. Elster (eds.), Adolescent Fatherhood. New York: Wiley.

Koenig, M.A., and M. Zelnik
1982 "Repeat pregnancies among metropolitan-area teenagers: 1971–1979." Family Planning Perspectives 14(November/December):341–344.
1982 "The risk of premarital first pregnancy among metropolitan-area teenagers: 1976 and 1979." Family Planning Perspectives 14:239–248.

Koo, H.P., and R.E. Bilsborrow
1979 Multivariate Analyses of Effects of Age at First Birth: Results from the 1973 National Survey of Family Growth and 1975 Current Population Survey. Research Triangle, N.C.: Research Triangle Institute.

Kotelchuck, M., J. Schwartz, M. Anderka, and K. Finison
1984 "WIC participation and pregnancy outcomes: Massachusetts statewide evaluation project." American Journal of Public Health 74(October):1086–1092.

Ktsanes, V.
1977 Assessment of Contraception by Teenagers. Final report to the National Institute of Child Health and Human Development, Bethesda, Md.

Kummer, J.
1963 "Post-abortion psychiatric illness—a myth? American Journal of Psychiatry 119:980–983.

Ladner, J.
1972 Tomorrow's Tomorrow: The Black Woman. Garden City, N.J.: Doubleday.

Lamb, M.E.
1977 "Father-infant and mother-infant interaction in the first year of life." Child Development 48:167–181.

Leibowitz, A., M. Eisen, and W. Chow
1980 Decisionmaking in Teenage Pregnancy: An Analysis of Choice. Santa Monica, Calif.: The Rand Corporation.

Lerman, R.I.
1985 Who are the Young Absent Fathers? Unpublished paper. Brandeis University.

Levin, A.A., et al.
1980 "Association of induced abortion with subsequent pregnancy loss." Journal of the American Medical Association 243:2495–2499.

Levin, M.
1983 Consequences of Being Born to an Adolescent Mother. Final Report to National Institute for Child Health and Human Development. Atlanta, Ga.: Emory University.

Levine, M.D., and G.C. Adams
1985 Trends in Adolescent Pregnancy and Parenthood. Paper prepared for the

Conference on Adolescent Pregnancy: State Policies and Programs, sponsored by the American Welfare Association, the Charles Stewart Mott Foundation, and the Johnson Foundation.

Levy, F., and R. Michel
  1985 The Economic Future of the Baby Boom. Paper issued by the Joint Economic Committee of the U.S. Congress. December.

Lewis, C.E., and M.A. Lewis
  1984 "Peer pressure and risk-taking behaviors in children." American Journal of Public Health 74(June):580–584.

Libby, R.W., and J.E. Carlson
  1973 "A theoretical framework for premarital sexual decisions in the dyad." Archives of Sexual Behavior 2:365–378.

Lindemann, C.
  1974 Birth Control and Unmarried Young Women. New York: Springer.

Lowry, D., G. Love, and M. Kirby
  1981 "Sex on the soap operas: Patterns of intimacy." Journal of Communication 31(3):90–96.

Luker, K.
  1975 Taking Chances: Abortion and Decision Not to Contracept. Berkeley: University of California.

Madore, C., et al.
  1981 "A study of the effects of induced abortion on subsequent pregnancy outcome." American Journal of Obstetrics and Gynecology 139:516–521.

Mahler, F.
  1977 "Adolescents' ethics and morals in the year 2000." In J.P. Hill and F.J. Monks (eds.), Adolescence and Youth in Prospect. Guildford, Surrey, England: IPC Science and Technology Press, Ltd.

Makinson, C.
  1985 "The health consequences of teenage fertility." Family Planning Perspectives 17(3):132–139.

Mallar, C., et al.
  1978 Evaluation of the Economic Impact of the Job Corps Program. Washington, D.C.: U.S. Department of Labor.

Maracek, J.
  1979 Economic, Social and Psychological Consequences of Adolescent Childbearing: An Analysis of Data from the Philadelphia Collaborative Perinatal Project. Final report to National Institute for Child Health and Human Development. Swarthmore, Pa.: Swarthmore College.

  1986 "Consequences of adolescent childbearing and abortion." In G.B. Melton (ed.), Adolescent Abortion: Psychological and Legal Issues. Lincoln: University of Nebraska Press.

Marini, M.
  1984 "Women's educational attainment and the timing of entry into parent-
         hood." American Sociological Review 49:491.
Marino, D.D., and J.C. King
  1980 "Nutrition concerns during adolescence." Pediatric Clinics of North Amer-
         ica 27(1):125–139.
Maryland Governor's Task Force on Teen Pregnancy
  1985 A Call to Action. Final report. September. Annapolis: State of Maryland.
Masnick, G., and M.J. Bane
  1980 The Nation's Families: 1960–1980. Boston: Auburn House.
McAnarney, E.R.
  1977 "Development of an adolescent maternity project in Rochester, New York."
         Public Health Reports 92(2), March/April.
  1982 Adolescent Pregnancy: Psychological and Social Antecedents and Prevention.
         Rochester, N.Y.: University of Rochester Medical Center.
McAnarney, E.R., and C.A. Bayer
  1981 Project START—A Report to the New York State Department of Social
         Services. Unpublished report. University of Rochester.
McAnarney, E.R., et al.
  1978 "Obstetric, neonatal, and psychosocial outcome of pregnant adolescents."
         Pediatrics 61(2):199–205.
  1985 "Adolescent pregnancy and childbearing: New data, new challenges." Pedi-
         atrics 75:973–975.
McAnarney, E.R., R.A. Lawrence, M.J. Aten, et al.
  1984 "Adolescent mothers and their infants." Pediatrics 73:358–362.
McAnarney, E.R., and C. Schreider
  1984 Identifying Social and Psychological Antecedents of Adolescent Pregnancy:
         The Contribution of Research to Concepts of Prevention. New York: Wil-
         liam T. Grant Foundation.
McCarthy, J., and J. Menken
  1979 "Marriage, remarriage, marital disruption and age at first birth." Family
         Planning Perspectives 11(1):21–30.
McCarthy, J., and E. Radish
  1982 "Education and childbearing among teenagers." In E.R. McAnarney (ed.),
         Premature Adolescent Pregnancy and Parenthood. New York: Grune &
         Stratton.
McClendon, M.J.
  1976 "The occupational status attainment processes of males and females." Ameri-
         can Sociological Review 4(February):52–64.
McGee, E.A.
  1982 Too Little, Too Late: Services for Teenage Parents. A report to the Ford
         Foundation, New York.

McLaughlin, S.D., W.R. Grady, J.O.G. Billy, N.S. Landale, and L.D. Winges
  1986 "The effects of the sequencing of marriage and first birth during adolescence." Family Planning Perspectives 18(January/February):12–18.
Mednick, B., and R. Baker
  1980 Social & Medical Predictors of Infant Health. Final report to National Institute for Child Health and Human Development. Los Angeles: University of Southern California.
Menken, J.
  1980 "The health and demographic consequences of adolescent pregnancy and childbearing." In C. Chilman (ed.), Adolescent Pregnancy and Childbearing: Findings From Research. Washington, D.C.: U.S. Department of Health and Human Services.
Metcoff, J., P. Costiloe, W. Crosby, H. Sandstead, C.E. Bodwell, and E. Kennedy
  1982 Nutrition in Pregnancy. Final report submitted to the Food and Nutrition Service, U.S. Department of Agriculture, Washington, D.C.
Melton, G.B., and A.J. Pliner
  1986 "Adolescent abortion: A psychological analysis." In G.B. Melton (ed.), Adolescent Abortion: Psychological and Legal Issues. Lincoln: University of Nebraska Press.
Miller, P., and W. Simon
  1974 "Adolescent sexual behavior: Context and change." Social Problems 22(October):58–76.
Miller, S.
  1983 Children and Parents: A Final Report. New York: Child Welfare League of America.
  1976 "Sexual and contraceptive behavior in young unmarried women." Primary Care 3:427–453.
Millman, S.R., and G.E. Hendershot
  1980 "Early fertility and lifetime fertility." Family Planning Perspectives 12(May/June):139–149.
Mitchell, A.M., and D.K. Walker
  1985 Impact Evaluation of Too-Early Childbearing Programs. Final Report to the Charles Stewart Mott Foundation. Los Alamitos, Calif.: Southwest Regional Laboratory.
  1984 Guidelines for Too-Early Childbearing Programs Sponsored by the Charles Stewart Mott Foundation. Los Alamitos, Calif.: Southwest Regional Laboratory.
Mnookin, R.H.
  1985 "Belotti v. Baird: A hard case." Pp. 149–264 in R.H. Mnookin (ed.), In the Interest of Children: Advocacy, Law Reform and Public Policy. New York: W.H. Freeman.

Modell, J., F.F. Furstenberg, Jr., and T. Hershberg
  1976   "Social change and the transition to adulthood in historical perspective."
          Journal of Family History 1:7–32.
Moore, K.A.
  1978   "Teenage childbirth and welfare dependency." Family Planning Perspectives
          10:233–235.
  1980   Policy Determinants of Teenage Childbearing. Final report to National Insti-
          tute of Child Health and Human Development. Washington, D.C.: Urban
          Institute.
  1981   "Government policies related to teenage family formation and functioning:
          An inventory." In T. Ooms (ed.), Teenage Pregnancy in a Family Context.
          Philadelphia: Temple University.
  1986   Children of Teen Parents: Heterogeneity of Outcomes. Final report to the
          National Institute of Child Health and Human Development. Washington,
          D.C.: Child Trends, Inc.
Moore, K.A., and M.R. Burt
  1982   Private Crisis, Public Cost: Policy Perspectives on Teenage Childbearing.
          Washington, D.C.: Urban Institute.
Moore, K.A., and S. Caldwell
  1977   "The effect of government policies on out-of-wedlock sex and pregnancy."
          Family Planning Perspectives 9(July/August):164–169.
Moore, K.A., and S.L. Hofferth
  1978   The Consequences of Age at First Childbirth: Family Size. Working Paper
          1146-02. Washington, D.C.: Urban Institute.
  1980   "Factors affecting early family formation: A path model." Population and
          Environment 3:73–98.
Moore, K.A., J.L. Peterson, and F.F. Furstenberg, Jr.
  1985   Starting Early: The Antecedents of Early, Premarital Intercourse. Revised
          draft of a paper presented at the annual meeting of the Population Association
          of America, Minneapolis.
Moore, K.A., M.C. Simms, and C.L. Betsey
  1984   Information, Services, and Aspirations: Race Differences in Adolescent Fer-
          tility. Washington, D.C.: Urban Institute.
  1986   Choice and Circumstance: Racial Differences in Adolescent Sexuality and
          Fertility. New Brunswick, N.J.: Transaction Books.
Moore, K.A., L.J. Waite, S.B. Caldwell, and S.L. Hofferth
  1978   The Consequences of Age at First Childbirth: Educational Attainment.
          Working paper 1146-01. Washington, D.C.: Urban Institute.
Moore, K.A., R. Wertheimer, and R. Holden
  1981   Teenage Childbearing: Public Sector Costs. Third six-month report submit-
          ted to the Center for Population Research, National Institutes of Health.

Morris, N.M., K. Mallin, and J.R. Udry
  1982 Pubertal Development and Current Sexual Intercourse Among Teenagers.
        Paper presented at the annual meeting of the American Public Health Associa-
        tion.
Mott, F.L.
  1983 Early Fertility Behavior Among American Youth: Evidence From the 1982
        National Longitudinal Surveys of Labor Force Behavior of Youth. Paper
        presented at the annual meeting of the American Public Health Association.
Mott, F.L., and W. Marsiglio
  1985 "Early childbearing and completion of high school." Family Planning Per-
        spectives 17(September/October):234–237.
Mott, F.L., and N.L. Maxwell
  1981 "School-age mothers: 1968 and 1979." Family Planning Perspectives 13(No-
        vember/December):287–292.
Moynihan, P.
  1965 The Negro Family: The Case for National Action. Washington, D.C.:
        Office of Policy Planning and Research, U.S. Department of Labor.
Muraskin, L.
  1983 Adolescent Pregnancy and the Adoption Alternative. Report to the Office of
        Adolescent Pregnancy Programs, U.S. Department of Health and Human
        Services.
Muraskin, L., and P. Jargowsky
  1985 Creating and Implementing Family Life Education in New Jersey. Unpub-
        lished report. National Association of State Boards of Education.
Namerow, P., and S. Philliber
  1982 "The effectiveness of contraceptive programs for teenagers." Journal of
        Adolescent Health Care 2:189–192.
Nathanson, C.A., and M.H. Becker
  1983 Aspirations, Opportunity Structures, and Reproductive Roles as Determi-
        nants of Contraceptive Behavior Among Adolescent Girls. Paper presented at
        the annual meeting of the Population Association of America.
National Center for Health Statistics
  1983 "Advance report of final natality statistics." Monthly Vital Statistics Report
        32(9). Hyattsville, Md.: U.S. Department of Health and Human Services.
  1984a "Advance report of final natality statistics, 1982." Monthly Vital Statistics
        Report, 33(6). Hyattsville, Md.: U.S. Department of Health and Human
        Services.
  1984b Trends in Teenage Childbearing: United States 1970–81. Series 21, No. 41.
        Hyattsville, Md.: U.S. Department of Health and Human Services.
  1986 "Advance report of final natality statistics, 1984." Monthly Vital Statistics
        Report 35(4). Hyattsville, Md.: U.S. Department of Health and Human
        Services.

National Institute of Mental Health
  1982 Television and Behavior: Ten Years of Scientific Progress and Implications for the Eighties. Vol. I: Summary Report. Washington, D.C.: U.S. Department of Health and Human Services.

NBC News
  1982 Poll Results, No. 74. NBC News. February 5, 1982.

Newcomer, S.F., M. Gilbert, and J.R. Udry
  1980 Perceived and Actual Same Sex Behavior as Determinants of Adolescent Sexual Behavior. Paper presented at the annual meeting of the American Psychological Association.

Newcomer, S.F., and J.R. Udry
  1983 Adolescent sexual behavior and popularity. Adolescence 18:515–522.

Nickel, P.S., and H. Delaney
  1985 Working With Teen Parents: A Survey of Promising Approaches. Chicago: Family Resource Coalition.

Nisbett, R.
  1985 "The conservative renaissance in perspective." Public Interest 81:128–141.

Norman, J., and M. Harris
  1981 The Private Life of the American Teenager. New York: Rawson Wade.

Nye, F.I.
  1976 "School age parenthood." Extension Bulletin 667. Cooperative Extension Service, Washington State University.

O'Connell, M., and M.J. Moore
  1980 "The legitimacy status of first births to U.S. women aged 15–24, 1939–1978." Family Planning Perspectives 16(July/August):157–167.

O'Connell, M., and C.C. Rogers
  1984 "Out-of-wedlock births, premarital pregnancies, and their effects on family formation and dissolution." Family Planning Perspectives 16:157–162.

Olds, D., et al.
  1983 Prenatal/Early Infancy Project. Final report to Health Resource Service Administration. Rochester, N.Y.: University of Rochester, Department of Pediatrics.

Olson, L.
  1980 "Social and psychological correlates of pregnancy resolution among women: A review." American Journal of Orthopsychiatry 42:48–60.

O'Neill, J.
  1980 "Trends in the labor force participation of women." Pp. 28–38 in C. Hayes (ed.), Work, Family and Community: Summary Proceedings of an Ad Hoc Meeting. Committee on Child Development Research and Public Policy, National Research Council. Washington, D.C.: National Academy Press.

Ooms, T. (ed.)
  1981 Teenage Pregnancy in a Family Context. Philadelphia: Temple University.

Orr, M.

1982 "Sex education and contraceptive education in U.S. public high schools." Family Planning Perspectives 14:304–313.

1984a The Media and Sex Education: A Review of the Literature. Unpublished paper. New York: Alan Guttmacher Institute.

1984b "Private physicians and the provision of contraceptives to adolescents." Family Planning Perspectives 16(March/April):83–86.

Orr, M., and J.D. Forrest

1985 "The availability of reproductive health services from U.S. private physicians." Family Planning Perspectives 17(March/April):63–69.

Ory, H., J.D. Forrest, and R. Lincoln

1983 Making Choices: Evaluating the Health Risks and Benefits of Birth Control Methods. New York: Alan Guttmacher Institute.

Panel on Youth of the President's Science Advisory Committee

1974 Youth: Transition to Adulthood. Chicago: University of Chicago.

Parke, R.D., T.G. Power, and T. Fisher

1980 "The adolescent father's impact on the mother and child." Journal of Social Issues 36.

Philliber, S.

1985 Teen Outreach: Results of the First Year of a National Replication. Unpublished report. The Charles Stewart Mott Foundation.

Philliber, S., P. Namerow, J. Kaye, and C. Kunkes

1983 Pregnancy Risktaking Among Adolescents. Final report to the National Institute of Child Health and Human Development. New York: Columbia University.

Polit, D.F., J.R. Kahn, and G.M. Enman

1981 Contraceptive Decisionmaking in Adolescent Couples. Final report to National Institute of Child Health and Human Development. American Institutes of Research, Washington, D.C.

Polit-O'Hara, D., J. Kahn, and D. Stevens

1984 Project Redirection Impact Analysis. Draft final report. Jefferson City, Mo.: Humanalysis.

Poppen, P.J.

1979 Psychological Determinants of Adolescent Contraceptive Use. Final report to National Institute of Child Health and Human Development. Washington, D.C.: George Washington University.

Pratt, W.F.

1984 National Center for Health Statistics National Survey of Family Growth, 1982, Cycle III.

Pratt, W.F., and G.E. Hendershot

1984 The Use of Family Planning Services by Sexually Active Teenage Women. Paper presented at the annual meeting of the Population Association of America, Minneapolis.

Pratt, W.F., W.D. Mosher, C.A. Bachrach, and M.C. Horn
1984 Understanding U.S. fertility. Findings from the National Survey of Family Growth, Cycle III. Population Bulletin 39(5):1–42.

Presser, H.B.
1974 "Early motherhood: Ignorance or bliss?" Family Planning Perspectives 6:8–14.
1975 Social Consequences of Teenage Childbearing. Paper presented at the Conference on Research on Consequences of Adolescent Pregnancy and Childbearing, sponsored by the Center for Population Research, National Institute of Child Health and Human Development, and the Alan Guttmacher Institute. Washington, D.C., October 29–30, 1975.
1976a "Social consequences of teenage childbearing." In W. Peterson and L. Day (eds.), Social Demography: The State of the Art. Cambridge, Mass.: Harvard University.
1976b Some Consequences of Adolescent Pregnancies. Paper presented at National Institute of Child Health and Human Development Conference, Bethesda, Md.
1980 Working Women and Child Care. Paper presented at the Research Conference on Women: A Developmental Perspective, sponsored by National Institute of Child Health and Human Development, Bethesda, Md.

Public Response Associates, Inc.
1982 Family Communication Program Survey Conducted for Solem and Associates. San Francisco: Public Response Associates, Inc.

Quinn, J.
1985 Preventing Adolescent Pregnancy: A Proposed Research and Service Program Developed by Girls' Clubs of America, Inc. New York: Girls' Clubs.

Quint, J.C., and J.A. Riccio
1985 The Challenge of Serving Pregnant and Parenting Teens. New York: Manpower Demonstration Research Corporation.

Reis, J.
1984 Teenage Pregnancy and Teenage Parenthood in Illinois: 1979–1983 Costs. Unpublished report. Center for Health Services and Policy Research, Northwestern University.

Reiss, I.L.
1973 Heterosexual Relationships Inside and Outside Marriage. Morristown, N.J.: General Learning Press.
1976 Family Systems in America. Hinsdale, Ill.: Dryden Press.

Resnick, M.
1984 Adoption Decision-Making Project. Research study funded by the Office of Adolescent Pregnancy Programs, U.S. Department of Health and Human Services.

Reuben, D.
  1970 Everything You Always Wanted to Know About Sex But Were Afraid to Ask. New York: David McKay.

Rindfuss, R.R., L. Bumpass, and C. St. John
  1980 "Education and fertility . . . roles women occupy." American Sociological Review 45:431–447.

Rivera-Casale, C., L.V. Klerman, and R. Manela
  1984 "The relevance of child-support enforcement to school-age parents." Child Welfare 58(6):521–531.

Rosen, R.H.
  1980 "Adolescent pregnancy decision-making: Are parents important?" Adolescence 15:43–54.

Ross, H., and I. Sawhill
  1975 Time of Transition: The Growth of Families Headed by Women. Washington, D.C.: Urban Institute.

Rubin, L.B.
  1976 Worlds of Pain. New York: Basic Books.

Rutter, M.
  1983 School effects on pupil progress: research findings and policy implications. Child Development 54(1):1–29.

Sahler, O.J.Z.
  1980 "Adolescent parenting: Potential for child abuse and neglect?" Pediatric Annals 9:67–75.

Sandler, H.M., P. Vietze, and S. O'Coralor
  1981 Obstetric and neonatal outcomes following intervention with pregnant teenagers. Pp. 249–263 in K. Scott, T. Field, and E.G. Robertson (eds.), Teenage Parents and Their Offspring. New York: Grune & Stratton.

Scales, P., and D. Beckstein
  1982 "From macho to mutuality: Helping young men to make effective decisions about sex, contraception and pregnancy." In I. Stuart and C. Wells (eds.), Pregnancy in Adolescence: Needs, Problems and Management. New York: Van Nostrand.

Scheirer, M.A.
  1981 The Indirect Effects of Mother's Age at First Birth on Welfare Payments: Empirical Model Specification, Estimation and Results. Working Paper No. 4. Annandale, Va.: JWK International Corporation.

Schinke, S.P., B. Blythe, and L. Gilchrist
  1981 "Cognitive behavioral prevention of adolescent pregnancy." Journal of Counseling Psychology 28(5):451–454.

Schinke, S.P., and L. Gilchrist
  1984 Life Skills Counseling With Adolescents. Baltimore, Md.: University Park Press.

Schoenbaum, S.C., et al.
 1980 "Outcome of the delivery following an induced or spontaneous abortion."
  American Journal of Obstetrics and Gynecology 136:19–23.

Shadish, W.R., Jr., and J. Reis
 1984 "A review of studies of the effectiveness of programs to improve pregnancy
  outcomes." Evaluation Review 8:747–757.

Shea, J., R. Herceg-Baron, and F.F. Furstenberg, Jr.
 1984 "Factors associated with adolescent use of family planning clinics." American Journal of Public Health 74(November):1227–1230.

Simms, M.
 1985 "The participation of young women in employment and training programs." Pp. 462–485 in C.L. Betsey, R.G. Hollister, Jr., and M.R. Papageorgiou (eds.), Youth Employment and Training Programs: The YEDPA
  Years. Committee on Youth Employment Programs, National Research
  Council. Washington, D.C.: National Academy Press.

Simon, W., and J.H. Gagnon
 1970 The Sexual Scene. Chicago: Aldine.

Simon, W., A.S. Berger, and J.H. Gagnon
 1972 "Beyond anxiety and fantasy: The coital experiences of college youth."
  Journal of Youth and Adolescence 1:203–222.

Singh, S., A. Torres, and J.D. Forrest
 1985 "The need for prenatal care in the United States: Evidence from the 1980
  National Natality Survey." Family Planning Perspectives 17(May/
  June):118–124.

Smith, T.
 1980 A Compendium of Trends on General Social Survey Questions. Chicago:
  National Opinion Research Center.

Sonnenstein, F., and K. Pittman
 1982 Sex Education in Public Schools: A Look at the Big U.S. Cities. Paper
  presented to the annual meeting of the National Council on Family Relations, Washington, D.C.

Sorenson, R.
 1973 Adolescent Sexuality in Contemporary America. New York: World.

Spanier, G.
 1975 "Sexualization and premarital sexual behavior." Family Coordinator 24
  (1 January):33–41.

Spenner, K.I., and D.L. Featherman
 1978 "Achievement ambitions." Annual Review of Sociology 4:373–420. Palo
  Alto, Calif.: Annual Reviews.

Stack, C.
 1974 All Our Kin: Strategies for Survival in the Black Community. New York:
  Harper and Row.

Steinhoff, P.

1976   Premarital Pregnancy and the First Birth. Paper presented at the Conference on the Birth of the First Child and Family Formation, Pacific Grove, Calif., March 1976. Report on part of a larger study, Hawaii Pregnancy, Birth Control and Abortion Study. University of Hawaii.

St. John, C., and H.G. Grasmick

1982   Racial Differences in the Fertility Process: An Elaboration of the Minority-Group Status Hypothesis. Unpublished manuscript. University of Oklahoma.

Stinchcombe, A.

1964   Rebellion in a High School. Chicago: Quadrangle Books.

Stokes, J., and J. Greenstone

1981   "Helping black grandparents and older parents cope with child rearing: A group method." Child Welfare 60:691–701.

Sweet, J.A., and L. Bumpass

1984   Progress Report on Census Monograph on Families and Households—With Special Attention to the Increase in Cohabiting. Working paper 84-12. Center for Demography and Ecology, University of Wisconsin.

Talbot, J.M., L. Rohzbach, C. Coan, and S. Kar

1982   The Status of Teen Peer Advocate Programs in the U.S. Unpublished paper. Los Angeles Regional Family Planning Council.

Taylor, I.B., J. Wadsworth, and N.R. Butler

1983   "Teenage mothering, admission to hospital, and accidents during the first five years." Archives of Disease in Childhood 58(6).

Thornburg, H.D.

1978   "Adolescent sources of initial sex information." Psychiatric Annals 8:419–423.

Thornton, A., and D. Camburn

1983   The Influence of the Family on Premarital Sexual Attitudes and Behavior. Paper presented at the annual meeting of the American Sociological Association.

Tietze, C.

1984   "The public health effects of legal abortion in the United States." Family Planning Perspectives 16:26–28.

Torres, A.

1984   "The effects of federal funding cuts on family planning services, 1980–1983." Family Planning Perspectives 16(3).

Torres, A., and J.D. Forrest

1983   "Family planning clinic services in the United States, 1981." Family Planning Perspectives 15:278.

1985   "Family planning clinic services in the United States, 1983." Family Planning Perspectives 17(January/February):30–35.

Torres, A., J.D. Forrest, and S. Eisman

1980   "Telling parents: Clinic policies and adolescents' use of family planning and abortion services." Family Planning Perspectives 12(November/December):284–292.

Trussell, T.J.
1976 "Economic consequences of teenage childbearing." Family Planning Perspectives 8:184–191.

Trussell, T.J., and J. Abowd
1979 Teenage Mothers, Labor Force Participation and Wage Rates. Paper presented at the annual meeting of the Population Association of America, Philadelphia, April.

Trussell, T.J., and J. Menken
1978 "Early childbearing and subsequent fertility." Family Planning Perspectives 10(4):209–218.

Trussell, T.J., J. Menken, B. Lindheim, and B. Vaughan
1980 "The impact of restricting Medicaid financing for abortion." Family Planning Perspectives 12:120–130.

Tyack, D.B.
1974 The One Best System: A History of American Urban Education. Cambridge, Mass.: Harvard University.

Tyler, C.W., Jr.
1983 "The public health implications of abortion." Annual Review of Public Health 4:223–258.

Udry, J.R.
1979 "Age at menarche, at first intercourse and at first pregnancy." Journal of Biosocial Science 11:433–441.

Udry, J.R., K.E. Bauman, and N.M. Morris
1975 "Changes in premarital coital experience of recent decade-of-birth cohorts of urban American women." Journal of Marriage and the Family 37:783–787.

Udry, J.R., J.O.G. Billy, N.M. Morris, T.R. Groff, and M.H. Raj
1985a "Serum androgenic hormones motivate sexual behavior in adolescent boys." Fertility and Sterility 43(January):90–94.

Udry, J.R., L. Talbert, and N.M. Morris
1985b Biosocial Foundations for Adolescent Female Sexuality. Paper presented at the annual meeting of the American Sociological Association, Washington, D.C.

U.S. Congress, House
1985 Children in Poverty. Committee on Ways and Means. 99th Congress, 1st Session. Washington, D.C.: U.S. Government Printing Office.

1986 Teen Pregnancy: What is Being Done? A State-by-State Look. A report of the Select Committee on Children, Youth and Families, House of Representatives, 99th Congress. December. Washington, D.C.: U.S. Government Printing Office.

U.S. General Accounting Office
1984 WIC Evaluations Provide Some Favorable But No Conclusive Evidence on the Effects Expected for the Special Supplemental Program for Women,

Infants and Children. Report to the Committee on Agriculture, Nutrition, and Forestry, U.S. Senate, Washington, D.C.

Vener, A.M., and C.S. Stewart
  1974 "Adolescent sexual behavior in Middle America revisited: 1970–1973." Journal of Marriage and the Family 36:728–735.

Vincenzi, H., and J. Brewer
  1982 The Educational Performance of Children of Teenage Mothers. Paper presented at the annual meeting of the American Educational Research Association, New York.

Waite, L.J., and K.A. Moore
  1978 "The impact of an early first birth on young women's educational attainment." Social Forces 56:845–865.

Walker, D., and A. Mitchell
  1985 Final Report: Impact Evaluation of Too-Early Childbearing Programs. Unpublished report to the Charles Stewart Mott Foundation, Contract #83-311. Los Alamitos, Calif.: Southwest Regional Laboratory.

Wattenberg, E.
  1984 Protecting the Rights of the Minor Child of Unmarried Minor Parents: Toward a Rational Policy. Paper presented to the Child Support Enforcement Research Workshop, U.S. Department of Health and Human Services.

Weatherly, R., S.B. Perlman, M. Levine, and L.V. Klerman
  1985 Patchwork Programs: Comprehensive Services for Pregnant and Parenting Adolescents. Executive summary from a report prepared for the U.S. Public Health Service, Office of Population Affairs, Grant No. APR 000908-02-0. Washington, D.C.: U.S. Department of Health and Human Services.

Wertheimer, R., and K.A. Moore
  1982 Teenage Childbearing: Public Sector Costs. Final report to National Institute of Child Health and Human Development. Washington, D.C.: Urban Institute.

Westby, D.L., and G.R. Braungart
  1970 "Activists in the history of the future." In Foster and Long (eds.), Protest! Student Activism in America. New York: Morrow.

Westney, O.E., R.R. Jenkins, and C.M. Benjamin
  1983 "Sociosexual development of pre-adolescents." Pp. 273–300 in J. Brooks-Gunn and J. Peterson (eds.), Girls at Puberty. New York: Plenum.

Wilson, W.J.
  1981 "The black community in the 1980s: questions of race, class, and public policy." Annals of the American Academy of Political and Social Sciences 454(March):26–41.

Wilson, W.J., and K.M. Neckerman
  1985 Poverty and Family Structure: The Widening Gap Between Evidence and Public Policy Issues. Unpublished conference paper. Institute for Research on Poverty, University of Wisconsin.

Yankelovich, D.
1974   The New Morality: A Profile of American Youth in the 1970s. New York: McGraw-Hill.

Zabin, L.S., and S.D. Clark, Jr.
1981   "Why they delay: A study of teenage family planning clinic patients." Family Planning Perspectives 13(September/October):205–217.

Zabin, L.S., M.B. Hirsch, E.A. Smith, and J.B. Hardy
1984   "Adolescent sexual attitudes: Are they consistent?" Family Planning Perspectives 16:181–185.

Zabin, L.S., M.B. Hirsch, E.A. Smith, R. Streett, and J.B. Hardy
1986   "Evaluation of a pregnancy prevention program for urban teenagers." Family Planning Perspectives 18:119–126.

Zelazo, P.R., and R.B. Kearsley
1980   "The emergence of functional play in infants: Evidence of a major cognitive transition." Journal of Applied Developmental Psychology 1(2):95–117.

Zellman, G.L.
1982   "Public school programs for adolescent pregnancy and parenthood: An assessment." Family Planning Perspectives 14(January/February):15–21.

Zelnik, M.
1983   "Sexual activity among adolescents: Perspective of a decade." In E.R. McAnarney (ed.), Premature Adolescent Pregnancy and Parenthood. New York: Grune & Stratton.

Zelnik, M., and J.F. Kantner
1977   "Sexual and contraceptive experience of young unmarried women in the United States, 1976 and 1971." Family Planning Perspectives 9:55–71.

1980   "Sexual activity, contraceptive use, and pregnancy among metropolitan-area teenagers." Family Planning Perspectives 12(5), September/October.

Zelnik, M., J. Kantner, and K. Ford
1981   Sex and Pregnancy in Adolescence. Beverly Hills, Calif.: Sage Publications.

Zelnik, M., and Y.J. Kim
1982   "Sex education and its association with teenage sexual activity, pregnancy and contraceptive use." Family Planning Perspectives 14(May/June):117–126.

Zelnik, M., M.A. Koenig, and Y.J. Kim
1984   "Source of prescription contraceptives and subsequent pregnancy among women." Family Planning Perspectives 16(January/February):6–13.

Zelnik, M., and F.K. Shah
1983   "First intercourse among young Americans." Family Planning Perspectives 15:64–72.

Zitner, R., and S. Miller
1980   Our Youngest Parents: A Study of the Use of Support Services by Adolescent Mothers. New York: Child Welfare League of America.

Index